Writing Mothers and Daughters

WRITING MOTHERS AND DAUGHTERS

Renegotiating the Mother
in Western European Narratives
by Women

EDITED BY
ADALGISA GIORGIO

Berghahn Books
New York • Oxford

First published in 2002 by
Berghahn Books
www.berghahnbooks.com

Editorial offices:
604 West 115th Street, New York NY 10025, USA
3 NewTec Place, Magdalen Road, Oxford OX4 1RE, UK

© 2002 Adalgisa Giorgio

All rights reserved.
No part of this publication may be reproduced in any form
or by any means without the written permission
of Berghahn Books.

Library of Congress Cataloging-in-Publication Data
Writing mothers and daughters : renegotiating the mother in Western European narratives by women / edited by Adalgisa Giorgio.
  p. cm.
  Includes bibliographical references and index.
  ISBN 1-57181-953-3 (alk. paper)--ISBN 1-57181-341-1- (pbk: alk. paper)
  1. Mothers in literature. 2. Mothers and daughters in literature. 3. European fiction--20th century--History and criticism. 4. European fiction--Women authors--History and criticism. I. Giorgio, Adalgisa.

PN56.5.M67 W75 2002
809'933520431--dc21

2001025791

British Library Cataloguing in Publication Data
A catalogue record for this book is available
from the British Library.

Printed in the United States on acid-free paper.

ISBN 1-57181-953-3 (hardback)
ISBN 1-57181-341-1 (paperback)

Alla memoria di mia madre Maria Vittoria Maiorino
e di mio padre Santolo Giorgio

L'ultima volta che la vide non sapeva che era
   l'ultima volta che la vedeva.
Perché?
Perché queste cose non si sanno mai.
Allora non fu gentile quell'ultima volta?
Sì, ma non a sufficienza per l'eternità.

(Vivian Lamarque, *Il signore d'oro*, 1986)

CONTENTS

Preface   ix

Acknowledgments   xi

Notes on Contributors   xii

Introduction   Mothers and Daughters in Western Europe: Mapping the Territory
Adalgisa Giorgio   1

Chapter One   Writing the Mother–Daughter Relationship: Psychoanalysis, Culture, and Literary Criticism
Adalgisa Giorgio   11

Chapter Two   Towards a Female Symbolic: Re-Presenting Mothers and Daughters in Contemporary Spanish Narrative by Women
Christine Arkinstall   47

Chapter Three   'The Horror of the Unlived Life': Mother–Daughter Relationships in Contemporary Irish Women's Fiction
Anne Fogarty   85

Chapter Four   The Passion for the Mother: Conflicts and Idealisations in Contemporary Italian Narrative by Women
Adalgisa Giorgio   119

Chapter Five   Writing Mother–Daughter Relationality in the French Context
Alex Hughes   155

Chapter Six	Bad Daughters and Unmotherly Mothers: The New Family Plot in the Contemporary English Novel	
	Paola Splendore	185
Chapter Seven	Power and Powerlessness: Mothers and Daughters in Postwar German and Austrian Literature	
	Chris Weedon	215
Index		251

PREFACE

This book has been long in the making. My interest in the literary representation of the mother–daughter relationship was stimulated by the publication of a number of Italian novels in the 1980s, at a time in my life when I was striving to make sense of my position in the world after leaving my family and country. I discovered that the inner sense of displacement that I felt following the exciting period of adjustment to a different culture, and the ensuing reflection upon who I was, took me back again and again to my mother. When I chanced upon these Italian narratives by women, after completing my doctorate on an English (male) novelist, I realised that my reading was driven by a hunger for understanding what my mother meant in my life. The decision to turn to Italian studies, a decision which I had delayed for a long time, was thus made under the auspices of the Mother. My first publication in Italian in 1991 was devoted to the mother–daughter relationship and ever since I have worked around this theme, sustained by the intellectual as well as the emotional stimulus to understand this highly ambiguous bond within the Italian context.

This book was going to be dedicated to my mother. My parents were both alive and well while I wrote it. My father died suddenly when I was close to completing it. This event made me appreciate his legacy in my life, an aspect disregarded during years of 'maternal' perspective. As I entered the final stages of editing, my mother also died, just as suddenly and unexpectedly, only a couple of months later. Looking through her things after her death, I discovered by her bedside a passage from Saint Augustine on being reunited with one's dead. Can people will themselves to die? I had seen my father's death as an opening up of new possibilities in my relationship with her. During our adolescence, she had made my sister and I a bulwark against her vulnerability, turning us into the mother she had lost when she was only a few months old. With her husband gone, did she want to release us from our duties towards her? Did she think that she would be a burden for us? Or was it the case that, with him gone, she had no more use for us or indeed for herself, on whom he depended physically and emotionally? Her death has enmeshed me even more in the subject-matter of this book and has put me in the position from which most characters of the narratives examined look back on their mothers. I have resisted the temptation of rewriting my chapter on Italian mothers and daughters from the perspective of a motherless daughter. I have, however, rewritten my dedication.

I dedicate this book to the memory of my father, Santolo Giorgio, who taught me to love knowledge, and to the memory of my mother, Maria Vittoria Maiorino, who gave me the strength I needed to pursue this love. They both revered my writing, even though writing kept me away from them, but of the two, my mother was the one who eagerly read my work when it was in Italian. She understood, even though we never talked about it, where this book came from and what it was about.

Adalgisa Giorgio

Acknowledgments

I acknowledge the financial support of the British Academy, which sponsored a study visit to Rome in November 1994 during which I collected the material for the Italian chapter. I thank the Department of European Studies and Modern Languages of the University of Bath for granting an extended period of leave, which enabled me to work on this project. I am also grateful to the novelists Amanda Knering, Fabrizia Ramondino, and Francesca Sanvitale, who discussed their work with me. I would also like to thank the contributors to this volume for their patience and encouragement through the various stages of this project. I owe a special debt to Christine Arkinstall, whose long phone calls and electronic messages from New Zealand have kept me on course in the last few months. I also thank her for commenting on my contributions to this volume. Paola Splendore, who was my teacher at university in Italy, deserves a special mention for her generosity in providing advice, books, and hospitality over the years. Finally, I am grateful to my husband Bill Jackson for reading my work and, most of all, for listening.

Notes on Contributors

CHRISTINE ARKINSTALL is Senior Lecturer in Spanish at the University of Auckland, New Zealand. A specialist in twentieth-century Spanish literature and culture, with a particular interest in the Spanish Civil War and dissident writing under the Franco dictatorship, she is the author of *El sujeto en el exilio: un estudio de la obra poética de Francisco Brines, José Angel Valente y José Manuel Caballero Bonald* (Rodopi 1993) and the editor of *Literature and Quest* (Rodopi 1993). She has published widely on issues of gender, genre, and nation in contemporary Hispanic women writers, and is currently completing two books on the same.

ANNE FOGARTY is a Lecturer in the Department of English, University College Dublin, and is the Director of the James Joyce Summer School. She has published several articles on aspects of contemporary Irish women's writing (Lady Gregory, Kate O'Brien, Eavan Boland, Maria Edgeworth) and on Renaissance literature. She was guest editor of the June 2000 special issue of the *Colby Quarterly*, Irish Women Novelists 1800–1940, and is currently working on a study of Edmund Spenser and English writings about Ireland, 1534–1634.

ADALGISA GIORGIO is Senior Lecturer in Italian in the Department of European Studies and Modern Languages, University of Bath. She has published on twentieth-century women's writing, Italian feminist theory, and Neapolitan narrative. She is joint editor of *Culture and Society in Southern Italy: Past and Present* (University of Reading, 1994) and has contributed to *A History of Women's Writing in Italy* (CUP 2000) with the chapter on the contemporary novel. She is currently coediting a book on Italy in the 1970s and working on a book project on postwar Neapolitan novelists.

ALEX HUGHES is Professor of Twentieth-Century French Literature, University of Birmingham. She is the author of *Violette Leduc: Mothers, Lovers and Language* (MHRA 1994) and joint editor of *French Erotic Fiction. 1880–1990* (Berg 1995). She has recently edited an *Encyclopedia of Contemporary French Culture*, and has just completed *Heterographies: Sexual Difference in French Autobiography*. She is currently working on two edited book projects on gender and French film (with James S. Williams) and the intersections of photography and narrative (with Andrea Noble).

PAOLA SPLENDORE is Professor of English Literature at the University of Roma Tre, Italy. She has written extensively on contemporary English, Indian, and South African authors (B.S. Johnson, V. Woolf, D. Lessing, A. Desai, J.M. Coetzee). She is the author of *Il ritorno del narratore: Voci e strategie del romanzo inglese contemporaneo* (Pratiche 1991) on postmodern English fiction, and has contributed to a new *History of English Literature* (Einaudi 2000).

CHRIS WEEDON is Professor of Critical and Cultural Theory at the University of Wales, College of Cardiff. Her publications include *Feminist Practice and Poststructuralist Theory* (Blackwell 1987 & 1996), the edited volumes *Die Frau in der DDR* (Blackwell 1988) and *Post-War Women's Writing in German* (Berghahn 1997), (with Glenn Jordan) *Cultural Politics: Class, Gender, Race and the Postmodern World* (Blackwell 1995), and *Feminism and the Politics of Difference* (Blackwell 1999). She is currently working on a study of German Women's writing since 1840 and a book on postcolonial British culture.

INTRODUCTION

MOTHERS AND DAUGHTERS IN WESTERN EUROPE

MAPPING THE TERRITORY

Adalgisa Giorgio

The idea for a book on mothers and daughters in a number of contemporary Western European literatures was generated by a variety of factors. It appeared that narratives focusing on the mother–daughter bond were being produced around the world at about the same time, and that there was a growing interest in this subject-matter among theorists and literary critics. First of all, there was the need to understand what is specific to this relationship that makes it a very similar experience for many women beyond geographical, ethnic, and cultural particularities. Secondly, there was the 'literary' need to find out whether these cultural particularities produce representational modes specific to a national literary tradition.

Marianne Hirsch's book *The Mother/Daughter Plot: Narrative, Psychoanalysis, Feminism* (1989) has played a major role in focusing interest on the need for a theory and method to approach mother–daughter narratives encompassing psychoanalytic, linguistic-narratological and cultural paradigms. Hirsch proposes an attractive 'literary history' of the mother–daughter relationship which covers women writers from different periods and countries, starting with Jane Austen and including English, white and black American, French, and German examples. By employing a discursive approach based on contemporary feminist critiques of Freudian and Lacanian psychoanalysis, she moves through the last three centuries to see how this repressed relationship gradually gains visibility in women's writing and to analyse the modes of its representation. While Hirsch's analysis is useful to understand the similarities between texts produced in different cultures during the past thirty years, it also opens the way to the complex and vast enterprise of assessing how cultural difference impinges upon the configurations of the mother–daughter relationship. At the end of her chapter on contemporary narratives by Afro-American writers as texts which begin to articulate maternal subjectivity, she charts the territory of future research, calling for new theories which cease to rely exclusively on psychoanalysis and integrate the latter with historical, social, and economic perspectives (Hirsch 1989: 198–99).

The present volume has been inspired by Hirsch's in two ways: first, it focuses on the theme of the daughter's quest for the mother in contemporary European women's narratives to which her study has alerted us; secondly, it attempts to take her work further, in adopting as much as possible a cultural approach to narratives on mothers and daughters which starts to account for differences in mother–daughter relationships and their representations. The format this volume has taken of being organised in chapters devoted to national literatures, is the result of both methodological and political considerations.

There is no doubt that concepts of nation, national identity, and citizenship have been thrown into question by recent political and ideological transformations in Europe. Nations no longer appear as monolithic, cohesive, and stable entities, owing to movements of people between countries brought about by a variety of factors: increasing globalisation of markets; decolonisation; the fall of the Berlin wall and the end of the Cold War; the internecine conflicts and wars in the Balkans and some Eastern European countries, and the intensification of the divide in resources between North and South and between developed and developing countries. Moreover, current analyses have drawn attention to the constructed nature of national identities, focusing on the rhetorical and political strategies deployed in the nineteenth century to build a national identity (transcending local identities) after territorial unity was achieved and the modern European democratic nations came into being. These also highlight the strategies currently employed to preserve this identity in the face of recent challenges. The nation is, thus, 'a delicate and complex social construction, made of common cultures and histories, of a manifest and mutual consensus ... a tie of citizenship, motivated by shared loyalties and memories' (Rusconi 1993: 7). Inherent in this definition is the possibility that a nation will stop being one, when the close-knit web of motivations and ties on which political relationships and institutions are built collapse.[1]

---

1. On the current debate on nation, nationalism, national identity, cultural identity, and ethnicity, see Anderson 1983, Breuilly 1985, Gellner 1983 and 1987, Hobsbawm 1990, Rutherford 1990, Smith 1991, Balakrishnan 1996, Hall 1997.

It is only an apparent paradox, therefore, that regional, ethnic, and religious identities within nations on the one hand, and national identities on the other, are being fiercely, and often violently, defended just as the boundaries between European nations are being undone by economic and political union. While such countries as France and Germany are witnessing a revival of nationalisms aimed at defending the 'true' core of the nation (by consolidating the ethnic group which has become dominant), others are experiencing the resurgence of ethnic and pseudo-ethnic nationalisms aiming for separation and disintegration of the nation (see, for example, the Basques in Spain or the Northern League in Italy). At the same time, economic globalisation is paralleled by a movement towards cultural globalisation. Increased mobility across national borders and the rapid developments in electronic communications threaten both ethnic and national cultures. The ongoing and fast expansion of the 'infosphere', with the proliferation of messages and virtual meeting sites on the internet, is redefining the concepts of space and time, and this in turn requires a redefinition of our position in the world. This 'deterritorialisation' and dissolution of identity can be perceived as liberating or can lead to disorientation, anxiety, and even panic. A response to the latter is the search for 'forms of reterritorialisation which appeal to belonging, identity and the memory of origin' (Camaiti Hostert 1996: 139).

In such a set-up, does it still make sense to talk of Austrian, French, English, German, Irish, Italian, or Spanish literatures? While European monetary, political, and legal homogenisation is being pursued (even though with circumspection on the part of some member states), we are increasingly asking ourselves if there exists a European culture and how we can promote it.[2] The notions of exile (political, linguistic, cultural, and psychological – voluntary or enforced), displacement, and nomadism have become an important focus of contemporary theoretical and critical debate, and useful interpretive paradigms for past and present literature. That the themes of journey, flight, and travel have become widespread in European national literatures in the last decades of the twentieth century, attests to the fact that both the writers and their characters conceive of themselves as existing within wider cultural referents than just the ones of their culture of origin. The interest of these narratives lies precisely in the tension between the various components of their authors' and characters' cultural make-up and aspirations.[3]

These considerations problematise the project of a book on women's narratives on the mother–daughter relationship in a number of European national literatures. One could have opted for an anthological collection of

---

2. A number of workshops and conferences on the subject are being organised at the moment in Europe.
3. For recent theoretical treatments, see Braidotti 1994 and Kaplan 1996. On exile in literature and culture, see Tucker 1991, Coulson 1997, and Gorrara and Meyer 1998.

essays on selected texts from different literatures or languages, but any selection – no matter what criterion guided it: religious and/or ethnic community, psychological typologies, chronology of publication – would have obscured differences in historical, cultural, and literary traditions, which preliminary work on the subject-matter suggested were important to its understanding. Despite the fact that all European nations are suffering, in varying degrees, from an identity crisis, a straightforward structure of chapters dealing with individual national literatures seemed to best serve the aim of offering an outlook on similarities and differences in literary representations of mother–daughter relationships in Western Europe, as well as reflecting the current situation of a Europe still separated, culturally, along national lines. This 'common sense' solution is also based on the fact that the contributors to this volume are specialists in national literatures and work within university departments where the study and teaching of foreign literatures are still organised around nations, even from within departments of European Studies in which a European interdisciplinary perspective already informs many courses. Paradoxically, this traditional format has the advantage of opening the way to a European comparative perspective.

The aim of this book is threefold: to provide a hitherto lacking systematisation of a substantial body of narratives on the mother–daughter relationship in each country or language; to identify the specificities of each individual body of texts with reference to internal cultural diversities as well as to a specific national literary tradition, and to chart new territory for further investigation of texts both within and across the national boundaries. Criticism on the mother–daughter theme was pioneered by American academics working within departments of English, and, consequently, it has been concerned mainly with English and American literatures (see Davidson and Broner 1980; Garner et al. 1985; Pearlman 1989).[4] Many journal articles on the mother–daughter relationship in the work of contemporary European authors appeared in the 1990s in the wake of Hirsch's study,

---

4. Two French authors, Colette and Simone de Beauvoir, found some space in Davidson and Broner 1980, a pioneering study of the mother–daughter relationship in literature, which, starting with Near Eastern literature and Greek myths, then concentrates on English and American authors (with chapters on English Canadian writers and South-western native American literature). Similarly, Garner et al. 1985 devotes a chapter to George Sand and another to Violette Leduc. Phillips 1996 (orig. 1991) devotes half of her study of the mother–daughter relationship to English literature (with the exception of a chapter on Colette), on which she draws for insights into the history, psychology, and practice of this bond: the aim of her book is to suggest ways of repairing conflicts and build better relationships. Ingman 1998 looks at mother–daughter narratives by English women novelists between the wars, whereas Ingman 1999 is an anthology of extracts from twentieth-century narrative, poetry, and autobiography by anglophone women writers from different geographical and ethnic backgrounds.

whereas book-length studies on individual writers or groups of writers are less numerous (these will be referred to in the chapters of this volume). This volume is the first in offering an overview of an important theme in contemporary women's writing in the various countries considered.

It is necessary to pause at this point to consider the choice of countries/literatures included in this book. I am aware that the phrase 'Western European' is far from being neutral and transparent. The growth of the European Union and the dissolution of the traditional cleavages between Eastern, Western, and Southern Europe have turned the entity 'Europe' into a highly disputed category which requires redefinition (see Goddard et al. 1994). In this volume, 'Western European' is used as a convenient term to cover a number of European literatures that share an investment in certain women's issues. Existing criticism indicated that the mother–daughter relationship had become an important theme in the literatures of the seven countries selected at about the same time. In all of them, it is possible to identify a broad shift from rejection of or indifference to the maternal to a desire on the daughter's part to examine her bond with her mother. This investigation is sometimes undertaken with the aim of understanding the mother's position, and leads in some cases to a reappraisal of the maternal figure as a source of positive female values. Far from romanticising the neglected bond between mother and daughter, the narratives produced in England, France, Germany and Austria, Ireland, Italy, and Spain in the past thirty years portray daughters who attempt to unravel their feelings towards their mothers and to make sense of a highly conflictual relationship in which, however, their identity is grounded. It is still to be ascertained whether the shift from 'matrophobia' – hatred of the mother and fear of becoming her/like her, leading to rejection and, in literature, to textual matricide (see Rich 1976: 235–36) – to 'mother-quest' – the daughter's search for her Self through a recuperation of her maternal heritage – is a feature of the literatures of all seven countries. It is significant, however, that these narratives have appeared simultaneously with a corpus of feminist theory in Europe and in the USA, which emerged in the wake of 1970s feminism. All seven countries have had Western-style women's movements which have shaped women's concerns and have promoted dialogue among women across national boundaries. Feminist analyses of women's cultural and social subordination published in the 1970s put the mother on trial for her complicity with patriarchal norms and for being the agent of their perpetuation, for holding back the daughter's process of individuation, for acting as regulator of her sexuality, and generally for hindering her emancipation and autonomy. Nevertheless, they also contained the germs of the reappraisal of the maternal figure that characterised the 1980s and 1990s. This shared legacy accounts perhaps for the emergence of the mother–daughter theme in the European countries in question. The forms this theme has taken in the different countries depend on their historical, political, and generally cultural heritages. The aim of this volume is to offer an interpretation of these literary and cultural scenarios, and to stimulate similar enterprises, which would test and develop the paradigms evinced in our analyses, for other literatures where the mother–daughter theme is equally important.

Taking as a starting point the belief that psychic structures are bound up with historical, economic, political, social, and cultural processes specific to a certain community or group, and that a text or group of texts cannot be interpreted without reference to the forms of a specific literary tradition, each contributor has adopted an eclectic and widely defined 'cultural' approach. Each chapter draws on a common, though varied body of feminist knowledge and scholarship which denounces the invisibility and suppression of the mother–daughter relationship in Western culture. We have, thus, identified the discursive strategies deployed by the texts to break through this silence and looked at the interplay between texts and contexts. This contextualisation serves to avoid essentialising the mother–daughter relationship. At the same time we have striven not to displace essentialism on to the national/cultural level by avoiding making the claim that there exists a specific, for example, Spanish or French mother–daughter configuration. The narratives analysed in this volume show that each mother–daughter relationship is unique, with the familial and experiential circumstances in which their protagonists are enmeshed impinging upon – and being impinged upon by – the psychic substratum as well as social and cultural structures. Thus, the insights of psychoanalysis into the transgenerational and transcultural aspects of the mother–daughter bond have been integrated with an analysis of the personal and cultural particularities of each mother–daughter relationship.

Although the texts examined have been selected with the aim of showing either a line of development or a typology, each contributor has been careful not to impose an a priori structure upon them, and not to let the theory – psychological or otherwise – overwhelm them. We have also attempted, as far as possible, to provide a choice of texts which reflects the increasingly multicultural composition of each country. However, while attention has been paid to the regional and local cultures within the larger national boundaries, we have not always been able to find texts on mothers and daughters by immigrant writers (for example, those of Turkish origin living in Germany). This may be the result of a combination of factors: the exclusion of immigrant women from the educational and literary institutions; the possibility that the mother–daughter relationship has not begun to be symbolised within their culture of provenance; the possibility that our (the contributors') mental structures and the theoretical tools we employ blind us to the existence of these writers and their narratives, and finally, the possibility that the mother–daughter dyad is irrelevant in some cultures. There is evidence that there exist different kinship structures in Europe which present models of development, mothering, and socialisation not based on the mother–daughter dyad, as, for example, among the immigrant Creole, Malinese Dogon, and Surinamese communities in the Netherlands (see Groen 1993; Leira and Krips 1993: 90). The answer to recent appeals for theorists to deconstruct the maternal fantasies inherent in feminist discourse itself, to steer away from their obsession with the mother and to search for other determinants of gender identity (see Flax 1993) might lie in these alternative models.

Nevertheless, it appears that the mother–daughter dyad is still the dominant structuring principle of female identity in Western cultures. Psychotherapeutical practice in the London Women's Therapy Centre and the Stone Centre in the USA shows that white daughters are still enmeshed with mothers as far as subjectivity and sexuality are concerned (see Flax 1993; Orbach and Eichenbaum 1993; Sayers 1993). Studies with adolescent daughters in America and Europe show that the mother still constitutes the most powerful influence on the daughter's acquisition of femininity and sexuality (see Apter 1990; Gilligan and Rogers 1993; Surrey 1993; de Waal 1993). This can be variously read as a consequence of the universality of the mother–daughter bond, of current familial and societal arrangements in Western culture, and of the inability of therapists, psychologists, and sociologists to find alternative interpretative tools. A volume on the literary representation of the mother–daughter relationship is necessarily biased towards its own subject-matter: it finds its justification in the hard fact that there exists a body of literature which focuses on the relationship and places it at the centre of the daughter's search for self-definition. Unfortunately, it has not been possible, for reasons of space, to extend our investigation to popular literature and our engagement with science fiction, the genre with the highest potential to imagine alternative worlds and possibly alternative mother–daughter plots, has been, by necessity, limited, as the field has been dominated by American authors. Systematic research is needed before even a hypothesis can be made about the concern of women's science fiction with the theme in European countries.

Chapter One provides an overview of the shared – explicit and implicit – theoretical apparatus underpinning the various chapters, and attempts to develop a 'cultural' approach to the mother–daughter relationship in literature. However, it makes no claim to being a comprehensive account either of the vast research on the socio-psychodynamics of the mother–daughter relationship or of the work of the theorists on whom the volume draws. This account deals only with those theories which are concerned specifically with the mother–daughter relationship or are seen as being able to contribute to its understanding and to its interpretation in literature. For reasons of space, it has not been possible to engage with the wider issues called forth by these theories (for instance, theories of femininity and sexual difference, or the trap of essentialism, to name three interrelated ones). As with Chapter One, the subsequent chapters could not have been comprehensive: while analysing a number of texts we have also striven to provide suggestions for analyses of others. No single theory, literary text, or book of literary criticism could pronounce the definitive word on such a complex and compelling relationship. This book confirms that the mother–daughter relationship is a minefield, but that women's scholarship and literary imagination have succeeded in identifying some safe paths through the mines. There is agreement that healthy mother–daughter relations are based on negotiation of tension and on exchange. Yet tension there must be: when no more mines are to be found, it is likely that the mother–daughter relationship has become irrelevant.

Bibliography

Anderson, Benedict (1983) *Imagined Communities: Reflections on the Origin and Spread of Nationalism*. London: Verso. Revised edition: Verso, 1991.
Apter, Terry (1990) *Altered Loves: Mothers and Daughters during Adolescence*. New York: St Martin's Press.
Balakrishnan, Gopal (ed.) (1996) *Mapping the Nation*. London and New York: Verso.
Braidotti, Rosi (1994) *Nomadic Subjects: Embodiment and Sexual Difference in Contemporary Feminist Theory*. New York: Columbia University Press.
Breuilly, John (1985) *Nationalism and the State*. Manchester: University of Manchester Press (orig. 1982).
Camaiti Hostert, Anna (1996) *Passing. Dissolvere le identità, superare le differenze*. Rome: Castelvecchi.
Coulson, Anthony (ed.) (1997) *Exiles and Migrants: Thresholds in European Culture and Society*. Sussex Academic Press: Brighton.
Davidson, Cathy N. and E.M. Broner (eds) (1980) *The Lost Tradition: Mothers and Daughters in Literature*. New York: Frederick Ungar.
Flax, Jane (1993) 'Mothers and Daughters Revisited' in Mens-Verhulst, Schreurs, and Woertman (eds) 1993, 145–56.
Garner, Shirley Nelson, Claire Kahane, and Madelon Sprengnether (eds) (1985) *The (M)other Tongue: Essays in Feminist Psychoanalytic Interpretation*. Ithaca and London: Cornell University Press.
Gellner, Ernest (1983) *Nations and Nationalism*. Oxford: Blackwell.
——— (1987) *Culture, Identity and Politics*. Cambridge: Cambridge University Press.
Gilligan, Carol and Annie Rogers (1993) 'Reframing Daughtering and Mothering: A Paradigm Shift in Psychology' in Mens-Verhulst, Schreurs, and Woertman (eds) 1993, 125–34.
Goddard, Victoria, Josep R. Llobera, and Chris Shore (1994) *The Anthropology of Europe: Identities and Boundaries in Conflict*. Oxford and Providence, USA: Berg.

Gorrara, Claire and Franziska Meyer (eds) (1998) *New Readings*, vol. 4. Department of European Studies, University of Wales, Cardiff.

Groen, Martine (1993) 'Mother–Daughter, the "Black Continent": Is a Multi-Cultural Future Possible?' in Mens-Verhulst, Schreurs, and Woertman (eds) 1993, 97–105.

Hall, Stuart (ed.) (1997) *Representation: Cultural Representations and Signifying Practices*. London: Sage and The Open University.

Hirsch, Marianne (1989) *The Mother/Daughter Plot: Narrative, Psychoanalysis, Feminism*. Bloomington and Indianapolis: Indiana University Press.

Hobsbawm, Eric J. (1990) *Nations and Nationalism since 1780: Programme, Myth, Reality*. Cambridge: Cambridge University Press.

Ingman, Heather (1998) *Women's Fiction between the Wars: Mothers, Daughters and Writing*. Edinburgh: Edinburgh University Press.

Ingman, Heather (ed.) (1999) *Mothers and Daughters in the Twentieth Century: A Literary Anthology*, intro. Ingman. Edinburgh: Edinburgh University Press.

Kaplan, Caren (1996) *Questions of Travel: Postmodern Discourses of Displacement*. Durham and London: Duke University Press.

Leira, Halldis and Madelien Krips (1993) 'Revealing Cultural Myths on Motherhood' in Mens-Verhulst, Schreurs, and Woertman (eds) 1993, 83–96.

Mens-Verhulst, Janneke van, Karlein Schreurs, and Liesbeth Woertman (eds) (1993) *Daughtering and Mothering: Female Subjectivity Reanalysed*. London and New York: Routledge.

Orbach, Susie and Luise Eichenbaum (1993) 'Feminine Subjectivity, Countertransference and the Mother–Daughter Relationship' in Mens-Verhulst, Schreurs, and Woertman (eds) 1993, 70–82.

Pearlman, Mickey (ed.) (1989) *Mother Puzzles: Daughters and Mothers in Contemporary American Literature*. New York, Westport, and London: Greenwood Press.

Phillips, Shelley (1996) *Beyond the Myths: Mother–Daughter Relationships in Psychology, History, Literature and Everyday Life*. Harmondsworth: Penguin (orig. 1991).

Rich, Adrienne (1976) *Of Woman Born: Motherhood as Experience and Institution*. New York: Norton (London: Virago, 1977).

Rusconi, Gian Enrico (1993) *Se cessiamo di essere una nazione*. Bologna: Il Mulino.

Rutherford, Jonathan (ed.) (1990) *Identity: Community, Culture, Difference*. London: Lawrence and Wishart.

Sayers, Janet (1993) 'Maternal and Phallic Power: Fantasy and Symbol' in Mens-Verhulst, Schreurs, and Woertman (eds) 1993, 61–69.

Smith, Anthony (1991) *National Identity*. London: Penguin.

Surrey, Janet (1993) 'The Mother–Daughter Relationship: Themes in Psychotherapy' in Mens-Verhulst, Schreurs, and Woertman (eds) 1993, 114–24.

Tucker, Martin (ed.) (1991) *Literary Exile in the Twentieth Century: An Analysis and Biographical Dictionary*. New York and London: Greenwood Press.

Waal, Mieke de (1993) 'Teenage Daughters on their Mothers' in Mens-Verhulst, Schreurs, and Woertman (eds) 1993, 35–43.

CHAPTER ONE

WRITING THE MOTHER–DAUGHTER RELATIONSHIP

PSYCHOANALYSIS, CULTURE, AND LITERARY CRITICISM

Adalgisa Giorgio

The Critique: Unveiling the Absence

Contemporary discourse on mothers and daughters has been dominated by American and French theorists. Adrienne Rich's book *Of Woman Born: Motherhood as Experience and Institution* (1976) and Alice Walker's essay 'In Search of Our Mothers' Gardens' (1984, written 1974) are regarded as turning points in women's perception and examination of motherhood and of the maternal figure in both the United States and Europe.[1] If Simone de Beauvoir's *Le Deuxième sexe* (1949, *The Second Sex*, 1952) had located women's oppression in their biological difference and their liberation in transcending femininity by means of rejecting motherhood, Rich reclaims this specifically female experience by showing how patriarchy has regulated it and turned it into an oppressive institution. Rich's analysis of the 'institution' of motherhood takes us on a fascinating journey through myth, religion, anthropology and psychoanalysis to uncover the patriarchal repression of the primacy of the mother in the psycho-social development of the female individual. This primacy was being widely recognised by feminists

---

1. Rich's text appeared in French in 1980, in German in 1979, in Italian in 1977, and in Spanish in 1978.

working in various disciplines during the 1970s, leading to an examination of the maternal figure as the vehicle of patriarchal law, which often turned into mother-hating and mother-blaming. Failing to challenge classic psychoanalytic assumptions, books such as Nancy Friday's *My Mother/Myself* (1977) perpetuated the belief that severance from the maternal influence is the condition of the daughter's autonomy and freedom.[2] Rich was the first white feminist to assert the need for women to gain knowledge of their suppressed bond with the mother if they want to gain strength in the world: 'Before sisterhood, there was the knowledge – transitory, fragmented, perhaps, but original and crucial – of mother-and-daughterhood' (1976: 225). Writing the great unwritten mother–daughter story constitutes the first step towards fulfilling women's 'desire to create a world in which strong mothers and strong daughters will be a matter of course' (Rich 1976: 225).

Alice Walker's autobiographical–lyrical essay concentrated, instead, on the need for women to find the source of their creativity in their mothers' repressed one. Contrary to the patriarchal belief and injunction, internalised by women and upheld even by feminists during the 1970s, that femininity and motherhood are antithetical to intellectual and artistic pursuit and that women must inscribe themselves in the realm of the father and occupy a masculine position if they want to access creativity,[3] the Afro-American writer urged black women to search for their mothers' rich spirituality in the unconventional art forms they have left behind – stories, quilts, gardens, recipes – and to connect themselves to them through their own art. Her point of departure is a mother who has left her daughter a legacy of love for beauty and respect for strength: 'in search of my mother's garden, I found my own' (Walker 1984: 243). While Walker was linking herself to a maternal heritage of strong women who had resisted oppression and abuse, white daughters were still unable to move beyond a view of mothers as powerless individuals enmeshed in patriarchy. The starting point of the analyses of white (middle-class) feminists was a maternal figure lacking in social value and authority and excluded from discourse, whom the daughter needed to 'murder' in order to access the symbolic structures, namely a mother who cannot act as a mediator for the daughter's entry into the world. The fact that Walker and other black women writers such as Toni Morrison offer lit-

2. Mother-blaming permeates women's writings throughout the 1970s even when they are sympathetic to the maternal figure (see, for instance, Dinnerstein 1976, Hammer 1976, Arcana 1979, Herman 1989). See Nice 1992 for a systematic exposure of the entrapment of researchers into patriarchal assumptions about mother–daughter relationships, and Caplan 1989 for a constructive attempt at overcoming mothers' self-hate and daughters' mother-blame and at healing the mother–daughter relationship.
3. Suleiman 1985 provides a psychoanalytic–sociological account of the ambivalence of mothers who write towards their vocation; she reviews writers and theorists who propose, in various ways, motherhood as the source of, and means of access to, creativity.

erary representations of conflictual mother–daughter relationships in opposition to the maternal celebration expressed in their essays should not be seen as a contradiction. Rather it is a consequence of the difficulty of charting ways of 'articulating maternal subjectivity' (Hirsch 1989: 197) to which these writers are committed.

Lack of 'subjectivity' – the ability to assume a position of enunciation, of saying 'I' – is both the origin and the consequence of women's traditional exclusion from 'culture' and of their confinement to the realm of 'nature'. It is on this exclusion that theorists have concentrated in France. 1974 saw the publication of Luce Irigaray's *Speculum, de l'autre femme* (*Speculum of the Other Woman*, 1985a), in which she deconstructed the intellectual structures and institutions of psychoanalysis and philosophy underpinning female exclusion from language and, consequently, from the public discourses of culture and society. *Speculum* was the beginning of Irigaray's monumental critique of Western phallocentric culture and its erasure of sexual difference, which she sees as the first step towards the construction of a sexed world representing women as well as men. The condition of the construction of the new order advocated by Irigaray is the acknowledgment of our debt to the mother. She posits matricide at the heart and origin of patriarchy, to counter Freud's placing of the murder of the father by the sons at the beginning of culture (Freud 1912–13), by deploying alternative Greek myths to Freud's myth of Oedipus. From her readings of Aeschylus' *Oresteia* – the tragedies dealing with Orestes' murder of his mother Clytemnestra with the collaboration of his mother-hating sister Electra – and of Sophocles' *Antigone*, emerges the notion of a female/maternal genealogy which has been destroyed or repressed for the sake of establishing patriarchal order. Women must reconstruct and find their place in this genealogy:

> We must also find, find anew, invent the words, the sentences that speak the most archaic and most contemporary relationship with the body of the mother, with our bodies, the sentences that translate the bond between her body, ours, and that of our daughters. We have to discover a language [*langage*] which does not replace the bodily encounter, as paternal language [*langue*] attempts to do, but which can go along with it, words which do not bar the corporeal, but which speak corporeal. (Irigaray 1991: 43)

This passage, with its emphasis on language, encapsulates the seemingly impossible task facing women. How can they symbolise the mother's body and their repressed bond with her while they are imprisoned in a masculine conceptual system – the symbolic order – which deprives them of the tools to do so?

In Jacques Lacan's revision of Freud, the acquisition of language is the consequence of a splitting of the subject, when the union with the mother is ruptured and the child perceives itself as 'other'. The ability to say 'I' marks the child's entry into the symbolic, the realm of the father, what Lacan calls the Law- or the Name-of-the-Father (Lacan 1977). Entry into language, and into the (patriarchal) social system which we internalise through language, must occur at the expense and repression of the mother. Moreover, women, who exist only as an idealised male fantasy through which men attempt to fulfil their desire for the lost mother, are granted only a negative position in the symbolic.[4] Crudely summarising the complex theories which Irigaray elaborated in her 1980s writings by means of an anti-academic, poetic, experimental, and subversive style, one may say that the challenge facing women is how to bring to consciousness and represent what the current systems of representation do not recognise and moreover obliterate by consigning it to the unconscious, namely, the 'maternal–feminine' and the mother–daughter relationship. At present, women find themselves in a condition of 'dereliction' (*déréliction*) – a state of loss, abandonment, helplessness, and ultimately homelessness – in being unable either to access the symbolic or to return to the original home of their mother's body (Irigaray 1993: 67–69). It is important to emphasise that Irigaray does not advocate a regression to the pre-Oedipal – she states very clearly that confusion with the mother leads to psychosis – but that her intellectual enterprise is about searching for ways of enabling women to create a home for themselves in an alternative symbolic which acknowledges sexual difference and the mother, the waste or residue of the current male symbolic.

This alternative female symbolic is closely interwoven with a new female imaginary, the latter constituting the content of the former which structures it: a female symbolic cannot come about if the imaginary does not provide it with material/matter for its representations. Although the women's movement initiated the process of recovering and/or creating representations of relations between women, there are still 'too few figurations, images, or representations' by which women can represent themselves (Irigaray 1985a: 85). Once again expressing very simply Irigaray's discourse on the complex interplay between the imaginary, the symbolic, and the social, one can say that she believes that it is possible to intervene upon the unconscious and feed it with alternative interpretations or representations. Even though at the moment women can only take the position of subject by identifying with the Law-of-the-Father and therefore by repudiating the mother, they can work towards the goal of creating forms of female-to-female intersubjective communication, starting from the mother–daughter relationship.

4. I am not concerned here with the issue of whether Irigaray, and other feminist theorists, have misread Lacan's statements that 'woman is a symptom of man' and 'woman does not exist' as a negation of woman's ontological consistency (a definition, that is to say, of woman as lack, as inherently unable to access the symbolic, and as incapable of *jouissance* outside the phallic economy). The correct interpretation would be that man's ontological consistency resides in woman (for a concise illustration of the issue, see Žižek 1992: 425–26). Here I follow Irigaray's own line of argument. My outline of Irigaray's theories is indebted to Whitford 1991.

Irigaray's project of inscription of femininity in culture is normally grouped with those of two other theorists working in France: Hélène Cixous and Julia Kristeva.[5] All three focus on language as that which shores up patriarchal order as well as constituting the site for the disruption of this order. All advocate a feminine, maternally-connoted, embodied language which will destabilise the norms of the masculine symbolic. For Irigaray this feminine language is the expression of female desire – fluid, unbounded, plural, located in the whole female body (Irigaray 1977) – and, thus, a prerogative of women. Cixous's writing is full of maternal metaphors: writing is seen as childbirth and ink as milk (Cixous 1977: 37). However, although she sees writing as a powerful weapon to reappropriate the female body, she believes that men can also write texts marked by *feminité* (femaleness) (Cixous 1976). Similarly, Kristeva's prelinguistic bodily rhythms of the pre-Oedipal fusion with the mother – the repressed 'semiotic' which ruptures through the codified representations of the symbolic in poetic expression and avant-garde artistic practices – are available to both sexes (Kristeva 1974, 1980a). In Kristeva's theorisation, motherhood is a site of resistance to phallogocentrism, since pregnancy and nurture erase the opposition between self and other, inside and outside, subject and object. However, while 'a woman as mother would be … a strange fold that changes culture into nature, the speaking into biology' (Kristeva 1986: 182, orig. 1977), the maternal remains for ever the abject, the monstrous-feminine linked to the corporeal, that which is at the same time to be expelled and impossible to eliminate: it is only through defilement of the maternal that subjectivity can be established (Kristeva 1980b). Kristeva's later work reiterates, in a way that can be seen as an involution, the necessity of symbolic matricide for individuation, lest we fall into psychic and linguistic disorders (depression, melancholia, 'asymbolia') (Kristeva 1987). She claims that the murder of the mother is much more difficult for women than for men, owing to women's identification with her, with the consequence that they suffer from psychic disorders more than men. Both Cixous's disruptive *écriture féminine* and Kristeva's theories of abjection and of 'poetic revolution' leave women and the maternal for ever in a position of liminality between the semiotic and the symbolic. Their theories have provided literary critics with interpretive strategies suitable to identify the contribution of the repressed corporeal maternal to textual production. This critical approach is particularly fruitful when applied to stylistically and structurally experimental texts. Kristeva's own literary analyses focus on texts as forms of resistance to both the paternal symbolic and a regression into the deadly maternal (Kristeva 1987).

5. All three theorists were born outside France: Irigaray in Belgium, Kristeva in Bulgaria, and Cixous in Algeria.

It appears, thus, that Irigaray is the only 'French' theorist to envisage a future of difference, a symbolisation of the maternal, and the reconstruction of the mother–daughter relationship. Her 'And the One Doesn't Stir Without the Other' (1981), an essay structured as a daughter's direct address to her mother, lays out some fundamental aspects of mother–daughter relations in the current order of Western cultures. The mother is the daughter's 'feeder' and 'food': in being nurtured, the daughter is suffocated and immobilised by her mother's love and by her own love for her mother. The merger with the mother denies personhood, while the daughter's acquisition of individuality erases the mother: 'And if I leave, you no longer find yourself. Was I not the bail to keep you from disappearing? (Irigaray 1981: 64). She concludes with a plea: 'And what I wanted from you mother was this: that in giving me life you still remained alive' (Irigaray 1981: 67). This is a lyrical rendition of the analysis of the mother, which Irigaray had already carried out in *Speculum*, as a figure perceived by the daughter as simultaneously omnipotent and lacking: in psychoanalytic terms, the phallic mother coexists with the castrated mother, both to be fled by the daughter if she is to achieve autonomy and gain value. 'And the One' reveals the current lamentable situation of missing symbolic differentiation between mother and daughter.

Irigaray does not offer a ready-made formula for bringing about the changes she advocates. She seems to appeal to women to intervene in the three following areas: to search for alternative psychoanalytic accounts of female development, to bring to light the unacknowledged mark women have left on history, to create alternative cultural representations of women. It is only an apparent paradox that she urges women to construct an alternative female identity and sexuality to the one which confines them to the maternal function prescribed by the male order, by means of recognising 'the mother in every woman' and 'the woman in every mother' (Irigaray 1991: 42). This strategy is aimed at bringing about differentiation between mother and daughter which does not require the daughter's abandonment of the mother, and thus at bringing to consciousness the daughter's forbidden desire for the maternal body, at releasing the mother's own desire, and at enabling women to use their maternal dimension to generate not only children but also to create 'images and symbols', namely artistic and intellectual creations (Irigaray 1991: 43).

Italian feminists have taken Irigaray's appeal most seriously and have succeeded in moving beyond deconstruction to a phase of (re)construction. Luisa Muraro's theory of 'the symbolic order of the mother' (1991) owes much to Irigaray but proceeded from an original feminist practice of dual relationships between women, known as 'entrustment' (*affidamento*), which was 'discovered' by the Milan Women's Bookshop Collective (*Libreria delle donne di Milano*) in the early 1980s and was subsequently debated and practised widely during that decade in many public contexts, among women lawyers, teachers in secondary schools, university students, and women taking the '150-hour' courses (for workers and adults), with visible effects on the politics of the period. Entrustment developed with the waning of *autocoscienza* ('self-consciousness', an Italian version of consciousness raising) when women realised that this practice had not helped them to gain existence in public life. Similarly, ten years of political struggle in the 1970s, which had brought about new legislation (notably divorce and the legalisation of abortion), better material living and working conditions for women, and improved personal relations between the sexes, had failed to alter the situation of isolation, estrangement, and lack of value of women in society. Entrustment was aimed at rectifying this situation: it is a vertical relationship modelled on the mother–daughter relationship, in which a woman 'entrusts' herself to another woman who is more competent than herself in a particular field, in order to assert herself in that field. Two aspects make entrustment remarkably original and productive. It was conceived as a social/political (rather than personal) practice aimed at fulfilling each woman's needs in professional and public life, and as a practice which, employed throughout the country, was meant to activate and circulate female symbolic power, thus marking the public sphere with sexual difference. This was to be achieved through female, and specifically symbolic maternal, mediation. Based on the notion of a disparity between women which evokes women's relationship with their mother, it was argued that relationships of entrustment would enable women to enter the world as two, a duality which repeats the situation at birth: just as we are born into the world with the mother, later we gain access to the world by means of female/maternal mediation. The *affidante* (the one who entrusts) is a figure of mediation enabling the *affidata* (the entrusted) to enter the exchange of female knowledge and desire, and to assert herself as a female subject from outside a patriarchal frame of reference and from within a female genealogy. From the Verona feminist philosophical community *Diotima*, led by Muraro, later came the theorisations of a maternal symbolic/authority which precedes the Law-of-the-Father and which, having been erased by the latter, can be reinstated, liberated, or activated through the words of women (Muraro 1991; Diotima 1992, 1995). Their point of departure was the incontrovertible fact that feminism and women's politics had provided women with words and, thus, with symbolic power: these words – and the philosophers of *Diotima* incessantly draw on the words of women such as Carla Lonzi, Simone Weil, Hanna Arendt, and Irigaray – in their turn make possible the return to the Mother prohibited by the Father. Entrustment and the theory of the maternal symbolic which it generated redefined and made visible the mother–daughter relationship by translating it on the symbolic plane. Maternal power was redefined as women's ability to enter into signifying relationships with other women, relationships, that is, which produce 'thought' and mark the world with female difference.[6]

Simultaneously, other Italian women's groups, also inspired by Irigaray, pursued the search for alternative cultural representations of women, by (re)appropriating mythical figures (Cavarero 1990b) and by digging into the female imaginary in order to reconstruct its archeology (Melandri 1992; Centro Documentazione Donna di Firenze 1992). Many women's groups have drawn on and combined these different strands of Italian feminist research to reflect upwards upon their relationship with their own mother and downwards upon their own experience as mothers of young daughters, thus initiating the process of making the mother–daughter relationship visible and making mothers capable of passing on positive values to their daughters. The emphasis is on the continuous interplay between a theory and a practice, both of relationships between women and of individual and/or collective writing, which feed upon and generate each other. Italian feminists have not, therefore, been concerned with constructing a priori, systematic alternative psychological/psychoanalytic accounts of female development and/or of mother–daughter relationships. For these we must look outside France and Italy to the Anglo-American context, which, on the contrary, has yielded much insight into the dynamics of the mother–daughter relationship. This scholarship has been very influential in Europe and literary critics have often combined it with Irigaray's and Rich's analyses. The next section looks at these alternative accounts, focusing on those which have had an impact on critical approaches to the mother–daughter relationship in literature.

The Search for Alternatives: Reconstructing the Mother–Daughter Bond

A psychoanalyst herself, Irigaray uncovers the bias of psychoanalysis in turning specific historical factors and philosophical notions into universal categories and timeless truths. Numerous other theorists have put psychoanalysis under scrutiny. Rather than rejecting Freud's formulations as invalid, feminist psychoanalyst Juliet Mitchell claims that his choice of the myth of Oedipus as the underlying structure of every individual's development (see Freud 1923) was the result, as well as the description, of a specific socio-historical situation (Mitchell 1974).[7] Thus, his adoption of the male child as the para-

---

6. For entrustment, see Libreria delle donne di Milano 1987 and Muraro 2000. For a survey of the Italian feminist theory of the maternal, see Giorgio 1997.
7. See also Brenkman, who states that the success of Freud's Oedipal structure/complex derived precisely from the fact that it fitted nineteenth- and twentieth-century patriarchal ideology (1992: 929), and Accati, who suggests that Freud's psychoanalysis has its foundations in the Jesuit Catholic environment of turn-of-the-century Vienna and notes the strong Catholic imprint of Lacan's ties to his mother and his Benedictine brother (1998: 272-75).

digm of the individual's psychic development, his interpretation of the feminine psychosexual development as an embracing and acceptance of a passive libidinal mode, his description of femininity solely in relation to men and as lack (of the penis/phallus) and of women as objects rather than subjects of desire (see Freud 1925, 1931, 1933), are deemed useful to understand women's oppression. Madelon Sprengnether has demonstrated, through a close reading of Freud's writings, that he formulated the Oedipus complex on the basis of his own psychoanalysis and, in particular, his maternal idealisation (Sprengnether 1990, 1995), which led him to state that a 'mother is only brought unlimited satisfaction by her relation to a son; this is altogether the most perfect, the most free from ambivalence of all human relationships' (Freud 1933: 133). It is widely accepted now that personal circumstances – individual biography, social class, historical events, contemporary ideologies including ideologies of motherhood – also determined the way Freud's successors developed or departed from his theories, and that theories have a 'subjective' and historical basis. This section will survey the most influential attempts to go beyond Freudian categories and create alternative models of female development, paying attention to the bias inherent in every account and to the increasingly greater concern of theorists with the impact of external reality and culture on the mother–daughter relationship.

While Freud theorised psychic development as the adaptation of instinct and desire to patriarchal social and cultural norms which requires maternal repression, women psychoanalysts and theorists have investigated the pre-Oedipal phase and the mother–child bond. The 'mothering' approach to child development was pioneered in the first half of the twentieth century by four women from a similar background and similar life experiences. Helen Deutsch, Karen Horney, Anna Freud, and Melanie Klein were born in German-speaking Eastern European countries, started working in either Berlin or Vienna, and, with the outbreak of the Second World War, moved to Britain or the USA, where they played leading roles in psychoanalysis. They all drew on their different experiences of daughtering and mothering to investigate the influence of the early mother–child interaction upon the individual's psychological development, an influence which had been overlooked by Freud, even after he became aware of the lasting force of the maternal bond on women's psychic lives (see Sayers 1991: 4).[8] Klein initiated in England what is known as the psychological school of object-relations, later developed by Donald W. Winnicott. Beginning with the observation of

---

8. Freud recognised the importance of the mother–daughter bond as early as 1925, but did not develop this aspect, even after he read the research of the Dutch psychoanalyst Jeanne Lampl-de Groot on the girl's continued attachment to the mother (see Freud 1925, 1931, 1933; Lampl-de Groot 1927).

her own children and moving on to play-therapy with neurotic children, Klein formulated her theory that the child's forming ego is driven by the two opposing drives of life and death, and that the child attempts to overcome its fear of death through the defence mechanism of splitting. The mother, as the first 'object' of the child's instinctual attachment – perceived as fragmented into part-objects, the prototype of which is the breast – is split into the 'good' and the 'bad' mother and is internalised as such. This gives rise to a vicious circle: envy towards the good things of the mother's body generates fantasies of aggression towards her, which in turn lead to fantasies of persecution and retaliation on the mother's part, and finally to guilt and desire for reparation.[9] The resolution of this cycle is not the breaking up of the mother–child dyad through the intervention of the father as theorised by Freud, but the infant's moving from the 'paranoid-schizoid' position to the 'depressive' position when s/he starts to develop an ability to integrate her/his split images of the mother and see her as a whole. The successful negotiation of the depressive position depends on the infant's perception of having been mothered adequately. Klein's choice of the word 'position', instead of phase or stage, reflects her finding that the mechanisms she described could persist beyond the first six months of a child's life and well into adulthood. It is not surprising, therefore, that Kleinian theory has enjoyed, and still enjoys, great popularity with literary critics approaching texts dealing with the mother–child, and especially mother–daughter, bond. Since most narratives on the mother–daughter relationship are representations of the maternal figure from the daughter's point of view, Klein's analysis of the child's internal representations of the mother provides an illuminating tool of interpretation. Klein's theory that art is an act of reparation also accounts for the self-reflexivity of many texts on mothers and daughters which dramatise the very act of narrative production.

Klein's split maternal image has influenced, often without being acknowledged, much contemporary feminist theorising. Kristeva's view of the mother as the abject, for example, can be traced back to Klein, with the suppression of the good mother and exclusive emphasis on the mother as a threatening, death-bearing monster who silences the daughter. Nancy Chodorow, like other feminists, bypassed Klein in formulating an alternative model of female self-development which is founded in object-relations theory. As a sociologist who later trained in psychoanalysis, Chodorow would not have been happy with Klein's focus on the child's inner fantasmatic projections of the mother and its innate drives to aggression/destruction and love/regret towards her. She drew, instead, on the developments of Klein's work by Winnicott who had introduced the notion of maternal agency into the pre-Oedipal mother–child

---

9. See papers written between the 1920s and the 1940s and collected in Klein 1975a and 1975b.

relationship. Winnicott's stress on the influence of the environment and maternal care upon the developing child had started a process whose point of arrival was to make 'good enough' mothering an instinctive, natural response to the child's needs, which is essential for the child's healthy separation and psychic growth (Winnicott 1967). This good enough mothering requires the mother's sacrifice of her own subjectivity and desire in order to fulfil, appropriately, the needs of the child. Winnicott paid no attention to the question of gender, focusing on a sexually undifferentiated child, or to the cultural codes which determine mothering in a particular society. The need for a differential pattern of psychosexual development is taken up by Chodorow, who, in *The Reproduction of Mothering* (1978a), argues that sexual difference is not a consequence of biology but the result of the child's internalisation of social structures, including mothering practices. Her theory that girls develop more fluid ego-boundaries than boys as a consequence of being mothered by a person of their own sex is used to explain why women develop a relational sense of self and acquire capacities for sociability, nurturing, and relatedness, which will make them desire to mother children. The consequence of this is a pattern of uninterrupted reproduction of mothering from mother to daughter. In this scenario, the girl's process of acquisition of identity remains bound up with the mother: it consists in a negotiation between the conflicting desires for attachment to and separation from the maternal body (Chodorow 1978a, 1978b). The girl turns to the father (and heterosexuality) in the first instance as a way out of the threat of dependence and merger with the mother (Chodorow 1978a: 121). Daughters also reject the mother at a later stage because they become aware of femininity as a 'negatively valued gender category' (Chodorow 1990: 14, orig. 1980). Chodorow suggests that this cycle can be broken through a more equal distribution of parenting between the two sexes – a solution already put forward by Dorothy Dinnerstein in *The Mermaid and the Minotaur* (1976).

The Reproduction of Mothering was welcomed with great enthusiasm on both sides of the Atlantic, in a cultural climate interested, in the wake of the 1970s feminist analyses of patriarchy and of the struggles for emancipation and equality, in exposing the constructed nature of sexual identity and of gender polarities. It was also highly influential in promoting a literary critical approach which found in novels a reflection of the structures of personality Chodorow and her followers theorised, and paid attention, in women's narratives, to relationships between women, especially the mother–daughter bond. It also raised the possibility of a female language and style located in the pre-Oedipal (as well as highlighting the traces of the maternal in male-authored texts) leading to specifically feminine novelistic plots and genres.[10]

10. See Hirsch 1992 for an outline of the kind of criticism generated by feminist object-relations theories.

Examples of this critical practice are Abel et al. 1983, Homans 1986, Lidoff 1986, and Kahn 1986. Their approach posits a submerged pre-Oedipal mythical female space in which the (assumed) early mother–daughter symbiosis can be recreated/relived and looks for manifestations of the daughter's longing to return to this lost realm in the language, structure, and form of women's narratives. Anglo-American object-relations theories were also combined with the critiques and revisions of Lacanian psychoanalysis carried out by Irigaray, Cixous, and Kristeva. *The (M)other Tongue* (1985) by Garner, Kahane, and Sprengnether is an example of this critical practice, which focuses on the issue of gender and representation and thus on the issue of the place of the female in language and symbolic expression. However, object-relations oriented literary criticism has privileged the child's point of view, and thus has been unable to look for alternative representations of the mother beyond the traditional pattern of idealisation/denigration while continuing to erase the maternal voice.

Chodorow was later criticised for reinforcing heterosexuality and the nuclear family (Bart 1983: 150–51), for failing to challenge the child-centred perspective of object-relations theory on which she draws and the need for selfless parental care, thus keeping the mother in the position of 'object' (Doane and Hodges 1992: 33–52), and for positing an acultural and ahistorical category of 'woman' which does not leave much space for differences between women. Carolyn Steedman, for example, underlines the insufficient attention Chodorow pays to class and ethnic differences. In her *Landscape for a Good Woman* (1986), an autobiographical narrative examined in Chapter Six, she attempts to explain how her experience of being raised in a poor English family as an illegitimate daughter influenced her choice not to become a mother. Her mother's injunction was 'Never have children dear, they ruin your life' (Steedman 1986: 85), which she obeyed in order not to reproduce a daughter like herself and become (like) her own mother. In an account of her mother's role in her life, feminist literary critic Coppélia Kahn offers evidence that Chodorow's theory is relevant to white middle-class mother–daughter relations in 1950s America, when mothers, frustrated in their bourgeois aspirations, attempted to prepare their daughters to find a better place in the bourgeois family (Kahn 1993). Thus, it appears that Chodorow provided a credible and forceful account of the role of women in perpetuating their own oppression at a particular historical time and place and within a specific social class.

These critiques should not overshadow the progressive thrust of Chodorow's work. First of all, she posits an original female/maternal identification – a primary femaleness – for both sexes, from which the male child must differentiate as not-female. She also bestows significance upon the maternal figure in the formation of women's identity, focusing interest on women's relation to mothering. If on the one hand her call for shared parenting demonstrates perhaps too naive a belief in the power of social change to affect psychic processes, on the other hand, one must not underestimate the difficulty of trying to explain one of the more inert structures of female subjectivity, namely women's continued desire to have children, even in times when motherhood is no longer their only aspiration (see Bjerrum Nielsen and Rudberg 1993: 47). This desire, which can only partially be attributed to social conditioning, has engaged theorists before and after Chodorow. Kristeva's essay 'Stabat Mater' (1986, orig. 1977), for example, is about the need for a new discourse of motherhood after the decline of religion and the cult of the Virgin Mary, a discourse capable of explaining women's desire to reproduce and of representing maternal *jouissance*, the rejoicing of the pregnant woman. The notion of 'the night child' (*il bambino della notte*), an image of a parthenogenic child, which emerges from the subconscious of little girls observed in clinical practice, is proposed by Italian psychoanalyst Silvia Vegetti Finzi as evidence of a repressed and interdicted female psychobiological generative pulsion which comes before sexual desire (Vegetti Finzi 1990). Recourse to reproductive technologies by increasing numbers of women wishing to achieve biological motherhood in the face of physiological obstacles begs the question of how far the phenomenon is 'created' by the existence and (relative) availability of these technologies (and by legislation which makes adoption just as expensive and harrowing an option as IVF in most European countries). This is especially so when the infertility which is being 'treated' has a social rather than a biological origin, when, that is, it is a consequence of changed models of procreation, with motherhood being postponed to a later age and even to the early forties, when women's reproductive capacities are severely reduced or minimal. What drives these women is something much more complex than a socially constructed desire to conform to traditional bourgeois expectations. This belated quest for motherhood – even by feminists who had rejected it to concentrate on intellectual, artistic, or political pursuits – highlights not only the social changes that have occurred in the past twenty years and the variety of life choices available to women today, both of which have affected attitudes to motherhood, but also the fact that the 'choice' of not having a child which Steedman and many other women made in the 1970s and 1980s was not entirely free. If this choice was made possible by women's newfound awareness of their ability and desire to function in society on a par with men and by the public provision of contraception and abortion (the latter was legalised in Britain as early as 1967), it was itself conditioned by new social and cultural pressures, including feminism. Furthermore, one must not disregard the influence of psychological factors upon the body that hardly make either conceiving or not conceiving a free choice. Both 'Stabat Mater', a typographically split text written in two voices which records lyrically Kristeva's own experience of motherhood alongside her analysis of the cult of the Virgin, and Vegetti Finzi's book can be seen as attempts at valorising motherhood and giving women's capacity to produce bodies a political and signifying function. Originally published in 1977, in the middle of women's struggle for the legalisation of abortion in Western European countries, Kristeva's essay opens with the statement that feminism's search for a new representation of femininity has led to 'a negation or rejection of motherhood' which leaves its representations unchanged for the great mass of people (Kristeva 1986: 161). Vegetti Finzi's book appeared alongside a theory of a maternal symbolic which seemed to eschew motherhood by turning it into a metaphor – this at a time when Italy's birth-rate was already the lowest in Europe and one of the lowest in the world.[11] In the psychological scenarios described by Kristeva and Vegetti Finzi, mothers and daughters are at war: these theorists only state the need to bring this war to the fore.

Negotiation of conflict, on the other hand, has been the main concern of the American theorists who came after Chodorow and extended her formulations. Both Jane Flax and Jessica Benjamin posit a female relational sense of self and subscribe to the notion of gendered self as the result of patriarchal family arrangements. Both theorists concentrate on the issue of the difficult balancing act, of both mother and child, between autonomy and relationality. However, whereas Flax remains within the parameters set by object-relations theory and continues to assume a pre-Oedipal mother–child symbiosis from which the child must move away in order to develop as an individual, Benjamin contests the existence of such an original situation of oneness by elaborating a theory of intersubjective recognition which is already at work in mother–child relationships at birth. It is worth summarising Flax's findings both because her description of the daughter's struggle to negotiate the conflicting desires for 'autonomy and nurturance' has been used by literary critics to enlighten textual mother–daughter relationships, and because its contradictions highlight the need for new parameters of analysis. Flax's psychotherapeutical practice shows that women's sense of continuity with the (m)other impedes their acquisition of a 'core identity' (Flax 1990: 23, orig. 1980) and that individuation – 'the development of a range of characteristics, skills, and personality traits which are uniquely one's own' – is a highly difficult process for daughters (Flax 1978: 172). This contradicts Chodorow's thesis that the acquisition of masculinity is more conflictual and problematic than that of femininity, a notion which is also overthrown by the narratives analysed in this book, which, on the contrary, represent the daughters' strife to acquire a sep-

---

11. See Bimbi 1993: 144 for birth-rates in Italy and Chamberlayne 1993 for a comparative view of abortion issues in France, West Germany, Italy, and Britain.

arate sense of self from their mother. Flax makes it adamantly clear that failure to achieve separation from the mother leads to personality disorders and psychosis (Flax 1990: 32), yet she describes a daughter's predicament which leaves no room for alternatives. She claims that the daughter's desire to return to the original symbiosis with the 'good mother' indicates that, as an infant, she received inadequate maternal nurturing (Flax 1990: 37). Winnicott's 'good enough' mothering has been replaced with 'adequate' mothering: 'In order for this phase to be adequate, the mother should be emotionally available to the child in a consistent, reasonably conflict-free way. The mother should be able to enjoy the sensual and emotional closeness of the relationship without losing her own sense of separateness. *She should be concerned about the child without smothering it*' (Flax 1978: 174, my emphasis). Flax presents two contradictory scenarios: the daughter's acquisition of autonomy is threatened by a mother who does not let her go; the daughter feels she has not been nurtured enough and does not wish to separate from the mother. She assumes a maternal figure who is narcissistically attached to the child as a result of her lack of power and her inability to satisfy her desire outside motherhood (Flax 1990: 34–35), and who therefore threatens to engulf the child. It is interesting that in order to provide a 'social' explanation for the female psychodynamics which they describe, both Chodorow and Flax resort to the notion of a mother who is dependent on her child for emotional fulfillment. Like Chodorow, Flax sees mothers as products of the same unequal sexual relationships, in the private as well as the public domain, which have produced their daughters: 'there seems to be an endless chain of women tied ambivalently to their mothers, who replicate this relation with their daughters' (Flax 1990: 37). Flax has recently appealed to theorists to look 'laterally' for a solution to the deadlock of women's inability to move away from the mother, by looking for other determinants of gender identity. In the meantime, she cautions women against the creation of a normative ideal of connectedness and relationality, against which real mother–daughter relationships, unavoidably subject to conflict, will be seen as pathological (Flax 1993).

A way of rescuing mother–daughter attachment from pathological territory is offered by Benjamin. Challenging Chodorow's and Flax's unproblematic pre-Oedipal maternal space and maternal engulfment, Benjamin focuses on the early mother–child relationship as an interaction between two subjectivities. Each member of the dyad perceives itself, from the very moment of the child's birth, as distinct from the other but is dependent on the other for recognition: 'Recognition is that response from the other which makes meaningful the feelings, intentions, and actions of the self. It allows the self to realise its agency and authorship in a tangible way. But such recognition can only come from an other whom we, in turn, recognise as a person in his or her own right' (Benjamin 1990: 12). Thus, Benjamin posits activity in both partners in the relationship. Drawing on research in neonatal abilities and play interaction in infancy, she uses the concept of intersubjectivity in order to move beyond the 'exclusively intrapsychic conception of the individual in psychoanalysis' (Benjamin 1990: 19–20). Differentiation becomes the result of a delicate balancing between self-assertion and mutual recognition which enables self and other to meet as equals. This constant tension between self and (m)other does not exclude conflict, breakdowns, or aggression, which, however, will be counteracted by repair (Benjamin 1995: 47). The breakdown of this balance results, instead, in relationships of domination and submission which destroy or negate the other.[12] Thus Benjamin moves away from a child-centred psychology and psychoanalysis, which reduce the mother to an object of the child's needs and desires, and at the same time opens the space for a maternal subjectivity which is not totally invested in the child.

The need for such a move has been recognised in the wake of feminism, but has hardly been attempted. Chodorow and Contratto stressed, as early as 1982, how the 'fantasy of the perfect mother' plagues feminism itself, in the guise both of feminist daughters' expectations from the maternal figure and of their guilt towards their own children for pursuing separation and self-expression (see also Suleiman 1985). Benjamin argues that mutual recognition is a psychological need ('not a social need or a normative ideal'), and that failure to satisfy it will lead to psychic damage (Benjamin 1995: 21). Resolution of the emotional knot between mother and daughter resides, thus, not in the intervention of a third term, but within the relationship itself, when each overcomes the desire for omnipotent control over the other and acknowledges the other's independent existence. While the desire for controlling the other belongs to the realm of fantasy,[13] the capacity for mutual recognition resides in a shared reality. In Benjamin's formulations, the two psychic registers of control/fantasy and recognition/reality coexist already in the so-called pre-Oedipal phase and continue throughout life, with the latter performing the role of keeping the former in check: the tension between them is a permanent organising issue, 'becoming intense with each fresh struggle for independence, each confrontation with difference' (1995: 84–86, 94). Intersubjective interaction between mother and child creates the symbolic space which in Oedipal theory is created, instead, by

---

12. In 1807, Hegel theorised recognition as the need of the self for an other who acts as a vehicle for self-certainty and absolute independence, which inevitably leads to domination and the master–slave relationship (Hegel 1952). Benjamin draws on Hegel to study the dynamics of sado-masochistic relationships (see Chapter Two, 'Master and Slave', pp. 51–84, in Benjamin 1990).
13. These are fantasies nurtured by both the mother and the child: the latter's fantasy of maternal omnipotence leading to a desire to retaliate and assert its own omnipotence (the Kleinian child's inner projections) and the mother's fantasy of her own perfection as a mother (a socially-constructed desire).

the rupture of the mother–child dyad through the father's intervention.[14] Maternal subjectivity is, thus, not denied.[15]

Consequently, Benjamin's version of relationality does not posit an innate harmonious connectedness in women that distinguishes them from and makes them superior to men. Neither does it invoke indifferentiation between mother and daughter or a blurring of the differences between individuals. Benjamin's symbolic space is not a reversal of traditional polarities – not an elevation of the maternal over the paternal – but a space of tensions in which 'we recognise, feel, and symbolically represent the subjectivity of real others' (Benjamin 1995: 86). This enables us to reformulate traditional identifications, with the possibility of both placing the father in the maternal position and, alternatively, creating a third term that can be 'unlinked from its association with the father' (Benjamin 1995: 105–6). Mother–child intersubjective recognition, present at birth and carrying on in adult life, provides a model capable of encompassing changes which have already occurred in the social and cultural position of women. The mothers represented in the narratives examined in this book occupy a wide range of positions between the mother who, lacking in sexual desire and social power, invests herself completely in the child she nurtures, and the modern career woman who pursues a masculine ideal of detachment and impersonality which denies the need for others – a stereotypical polarisation drawn by Benjamin herself in her earlier work (1990: 78, 83). Similarly, feminist and postfeminist women occupy a variety of positions also as daughters. Benjamin's formulations also offer a way out of gender binarism to make space for alternative family models and new and emerging sexualities and identities beyond male and female, heterosexual and homosexual.

That 1970s feminism has had an enormous impact upon women's lives in Western Europe has been taken for granted by my discussion so far. The feminist movements which developed in parallel in Western Europe, though with an emphasis on different issues at different times and with different theoretical premises, pushed gender relations onto public agendas. The feminist battles for divorce, contraception, and abortion opened the way to the

---

14. Paternal authority as an antidote to, and rescue from, maternal engulfment has been invoked differently by theorists of different schools, either as a structural/cultural necessity or as a consequence of sociosexual arrangements which can be changed (see Chasseguet-Smirgel 1970; Chodorow 1978a, 1990; Dinnerstein 1976; Flax 1978; Klein 1975a; Kristeva 1980b, 1986; Mitchell 1974, 1982).
15. Other theorists have been concerned with the issue of taking the mother out of the repressed pre-Oedipal, by either making the maternal body the locus of difference and the origin of human subjectivity (Sprengnether 1990: 326), or by theorising a Symbolic mother who acts within the Oedipus complex as an alternative mediator between mother and child to the Symbolic father (Silverman 1988). Silverman's Symbolic mother recalls Muraro/Diotima's maternal symbolic, but a comparison between the two is perhaps not productive, because of the Italian philosophers' lack of systematic engagement with psychoanalysis/psychology.

debates and the campaigns for reform which took place in the following decades and influenced social policy in three main areas: sexuality, work, and political representation. In the area of sexuality, the issues of rape, domestic violence, harassment, prostitution, and pornography have been central. In the area of work, women have fought for access to employment and for equal rights as well as for the legal recognition of their reproductive work – housework and caring for children and disabled and/or old relatives – and for legislation which encourages and enables men to share in this work. The policies and legislation which have been introduced have not always been satisfactory for a variety of reasons: the conflicting theoretical standpoints of different feminist and women's groups, the intrinsic difficulty of taking up positions and drawing up policies which do not damage, marginalise, or patronise women (or certain women at the expense of others), and the policy-makers' manipulation of women's issues for their own political ends. However, although on certain issues and in some countries only small steps have been taken to remove gender divisions and provide equal opportunities, feminist discourses have had an enormous influence upon practices and attitudes in everyday life, leading to a broadening of women's own aspirations and desires. As a result the lives of women born in the 1940s and 1950s have been dramatically different from those of their mothers. Opportunities and choices of lifestyles beyond marriage and motherhood have increased significantly in the last quarter of the twentieth century, widening the gap between maternal expectations (normally for the daughter to follow the mother's own life path) and daughters' desires. It would be impossible to describe here the different itineraries of each country's feminist movement/s and the social, political, and juridical changes which they have determined or helped to achieve, or to summarise the impact these changes have had on women's lives in any particular country.[16] These specific scenarios emerge in the chapters below, where we attempt to place the mother–daughter relationships portrayed in the texts within the contexts which have generated them, paying particular attention to the historical, ideological, social, political, and cultural factors which determine views, and indeed prescribe standards, of mothering and daughtering at a given time and place. What must be stressed here is that, if the potential for difference and conflict between mothers and daughters has never been higher than in the period with which this book is concerned – the feminist daughter being the one most at odds with her mother – the factors that have made this potential so high are the very ones which have made possible the recuperation of the maternal figure: echoing the Italian philosophers, feminism has given women the words to make the return to the mother possible. This explains both the

---

16. Lovenduski 1986, Lewis 1993, and Kaufman et al. 1997 provide comparative perspectives on women and social policies in Europe.

emergence of the mother in the literatures of some European countries during first-wave feminism in the late nineteenth century and the upsurge of interest in the mother–daughter relationship among women writers and theorists in the wake of second-wave feminism.

Benjamin's symbolic space of intersubjective communication is relevant in this context because it can be seen as the site where the historical and ideological differences between mothers and daughters are played out. These differences can be seen to conspire to impede mutual recognition and break the delicate balance on which acknowledgment rests. The analysis of these differences is, therefore, crucial to explain relationships which are articulated in different historical periods and, during the same period, in different socioeconomic and cultural contexts. Consequently, the investigation of mother–daughter relationships in literature must encompass these contexts.

We need an approach which brings together the material, psychological, and symbolic aspects of the mother–daughter bond.

Contextualising Mother–Daughter Relationships: Cultural and Literary Representations

In the chapters which follow we have attempted to combine a sociocultural approach which situates the mother–daughter relationship in its specific historical, racial, ethnic, sexual, religious, political, and economic contexts, with a linguistic/textual approach that teases out the problematics of representing it. On both fronts, textual and contextual, it is necessary to look at the tension between the power of existing structures, institutions, and discourses to keep mothers and daughters under erasure, and the agency – both conscious and unconscious – of mothers and daughters in resisting this power and inscribing their relationship in culture. In view of the cultural and linguistic exclusion of mothers and daughters, it is not surprising that the texts analysed in this volume are self-reflexive in varying degrees, dramatising the difficult process of symbolisation and representation of the relationship in the absence of existing representations or in contexts which allow only negative representations. In our analyses we pay attention to the genres, styles, and narrative strategies deployed in the texts which show the battle between tradition and innovation, without, however, assuming that experimental narrative modes automatically subvert cultural notions. Women writers have used their narratives on mothers and daughters as a forge for the creation of new writing modes. They employ a wide variety of strategies, ranging from free-flowing experimental styles close to the *écriture féminine* invoked by Cixous, to the subversion and contamination of established genres, and the inversion or rewriting of traditional plots to counter Freud's (male) Family Romance (Freud 1909).

In contrast, many writers have chosen more representational modes of writing, often with the intention of warding off the risk of uncommunicative experimentation. We have not shunned these texts to avoid reproducing traditional literary hierarchies which assume a superiority of experimental writing over realist writing.[17] Realism has traditionally been the domain of women writers, as a consequence, it has been recently argued, of women's special concern with reality, that external reality which cannot be reduced to thought (Diotima 1990). Unfortunately the realist choice is a trap, as the female self who observes and selects the reality to be represented inevitably becomes the carrier of the values and interpretations of that reality, which excludes, erases, and devalues that very self (Villa 1990: 41–43). If, as Cixous claims, novelists are the allies of a representationalism which erases sexual difference (1976: 880), the answer is not to dispose of realism but to find ways of making women's relationship with and attachment to things capable of producing and signifying sexual difference. Narratives on mothers and daughters by definition produce a reality which signifies difference: putting the mother at the centre of a daughter's quest for Self means to adhere to the most real fact of one's life, namely the fact of being born a woman out of a woman's body, even though this means discovering and struggling against the 'atopicality' of birth and the mother in discourse (Cavarero 1990a). This means that mother–daughter stories draw attention, one way or another, to the difficulty of disinterring and representing their own subject-matter. As Benjamin has indicated, a woman's dual search for recognition by the mother and of the mother cannot but take place in reality, because, as the narratives themselves demonstrate, this search requires peeling off the layers of cultural and social conditioning that envelop both the mother and the daughter's view of her. Hence the thrust towards 'truth' of our narratives, which, proceeding mostly from the daughter, very often enact the process of contextualisation of the maternal figure which I have advocated. The texts on which we focus are, therefore, varied both formally and thematically. Any attempt at summarising the individual chapters would result in generalisations which would undercut the premises on which this book rests. With this proviso in mind, I move on to identify a number of stylistic and thematic strands running through the chapters.

It appears that the daughter's point of view still dominates literary representations of mother–daughter relations. In different cultural contexts maternal representations are bound in a pattern of idealisation and defilement. Defilement is the daughter's response to the fantasy of maternal omnipotence and an inversion of her adoration/idealisation – the child's defence against its

---

17. Searching for ways of breaking the stronghold of patriarchal language, Kristeva and Cixous have engaged almost exclusively with experimental male writers, thus proclaiming women's (paradoxical) exclusion from 'feminine' writing modes and further devaluing their contribution to literature to date (Kristeva 1974, 1987; Cixous 1976).

dependency upon the mother and its dread of her power – and/or an expression of the child's contempt for her lack of value. The process towards contextualisation and intersubjectivity serves to move beyond this polarisation. The chapters which follow engage more or less explicitly with the textual process of overcoming such a dichotomy. Writing, often fragmentary and elliptical, acts as a therapy aimed at unravelling a variety of mother–daughter knots, mostly after the mother's death, and at integrating the good and bad mother. In Catholic contexts, the Madonna constitutes an entrenched ideal of self-effacing, perfect motherhood, which women are expected to emulate. The fact that the Virgin Mary is one of the few female figures to have risen to the status of myth is a measure of her normative power (see Warner 1976 and Kristeva 1986). In Italian and Irish narratives, mothers are gigantic individuals – precisely because they are incarnations of the Supernatural Mother – even while they lack authority and social value (although this is not always the case). While the Irish narratives focus on the negative force of maternal power, the Italian ones portray daughters locked up in mechanisms of maternal idealisation which displace wickedness on to the daughters. In the narratives of Austria, Germany, and England, daughters break the taboo surrounding maternal violence, abuse, and exploitation (while they also provide an analysis of the systems that have made mothers what they are). Whereas in English texts this helps to expose the oppressive aspects of motherhood behind the myth and to challenge the 'naturalness' of maternal instinct and filial love, one wonders whether in Germany and Austria the representation of maternal aggression by means of more realistic modes of writing does not contribute to perpetuating the long-standing misogynistic discourse responsible for such 'aberrant' maternal behaviour. In the German narratives in particular, the spectres of historical events like Nazism, war, and the division of Germany into two states, affect the protagonists' family life and create gaps between mothers and daughters which are impossible to bridge. Conversely, the comic-grotesque narrative modes and Gothic plots adopted extensively by English narratives, and to a lesser extent by Irish ones, place the readers at an ironic distance from the figures of baleful and wicked mothers who must be crushed and expelled. In the English narratives, the figure of the bad daughter emerges in reaction to and as a counterpoint to that of the bad mother.

In Spain and Ireland, maternal politics has been subordinated to nationalist political agendas, creating a repressive maternal imaginary with which the daughter must necessarily come into conflict. However, the Spanish narratives demonstrate women's resistance to such politics as early as the 1940s, whereas the mother–daughter bond has only recently become the site of contestation of Irish maternal mythography. Conversely, in Italy – in a culture where representations of family relations are dominated by the icon of the Madonna with male child – religious imagery is subverted to create an alternative family configuration that excludes the father. Italian daughters attempt to create on the page the missing mother–daughter intersubjective communication, and thus seek recognition and legitimation from a maternal figure who neglects them in order to pursue other love objects. It is interesting, therefore, that while in France and England, and to a lesser extent in Ireland, there is a switch from matrophobic narratives to narratives which attempt to recuperate the maternal figure, in Spain and Italy there is no distinct matrophobic phase. Younger Italian writers, on the other hand, are moving towards comic-grotesque narrative modes and plots which attempt to break the hold of the idealised powerful mother.

A plot which is variously employed in texts across the spectrum of national literatures is the myth of Demeter and Persephone. Predating patriarchal myths, it is resurrected and rewritten to either draw attention to and grieve for the missing mother/mother–daughter story or to create positive figures of female identification.[18] In Spanish narratives, it is also used to represent a democratic Motherland which has been displaced by Franco's masculinist and totalitarian Fatherland. Here this 'prehistoric' plot is deployed to create not a space of mother–daughter indifferentiation, but a site of interaction between daughters and natural or surrogate mothers, both engaged in a search for alternative symbolic knowledge. Many texts across the chapters present themselves as allegories of writing, with the mother–daughter bond becoming the means of access to and the matter of creativity.

The maternal figure is often a metaphor of origins, encompassing not only kinship but also race, ethnicity, and language. She comes to represent the ethnic roots which the daughter wishes simultaneously to repress in her search for assimilation to the dominant culture, and to preserve in order to remain loyal to the values and memories of her community. This applies equally to the black South African daughter who leaves her country, to the daughters of the immigrant Indian or Asian communities in Britain, to Neapolitan/Southern Italian daughters within the wider Italian context, and to Jewish daughters across various countries. French narratives provide the perspective of both the colonised and the coloniser: that of the daughters of Franco-Algerian immigrants in France who are subjected to the patriarchal rules of their culture of origin enforced by their mothers (who act as obstacles to modernity) and that of French daughters in the context of colonial patriarchy outside France. The narratives set in French colonial contexts throw into relief the imbrication of middle-class women in colonial patriarchy leading to maternal madness and imbalanced, pathological mother–daughter relations.

---

18. On the recovery of ancient female myths and rituals, see Harding 1971, Hall 1980, Rabuzzi 1988, and Herman 1989.

The mother's influence on the daughter's sexuality is, as expected, an important theme in the texts that we have analysed. In a society which has regulated maternal sexuality, mothers normally act as regulators of the daughters' sexuality, mainly as models of repressed (hetero)sexuality. While lesbian daughters start to appear in these texts, the daughter's sexual desire for the mother, the taboo of all taboos, unrecognised as opposed to the recognised taboo of the son's incestuous desire for her, is a strong undercurrent of many narratives, but becomes an explicit theme in only a few. The entire body of texts analysed in this book attests to the fact that the daughter's desire for the mother's body continues alongside, and often in conflict with, the desire for the father. This is not a desire to identify with the mother, in order to obtain the mother's phallus/lover or husband, but a desire to occupy the place of the mother's husband/lover. These narratives afford a glimpse into the potential for revolution intrinsic in the reinstatement/renewal of mother–daughter relationships, namely the potential to challenge the most entrenched institution of all cultures, heterosexuality, and break through the taboos of homosexuality and incest (see Rich 1980 and Irigaray 1977, 1980, 1985b).

We should ask at this point how far contemporary texts have gone in articulating maternal subjectivity. In 1989, Hirsch hypothesised – on the ground of narratives by Afro-American writers that speak with a dual voice – that if daughters should speak in the mother's voice, while waiting for mothers to find their own, they would have to articulate maternal anger. Anger – at their inability to affirm themselves outside the maternal function, at the difficulty of combining motherhood with the pursuit of creativity or work in the public sphere – is indeed one of the sentiments voiced by daughters when they become aware of their mothers' own oppressed condition. This is a projection of their own anger which they attribute to their mothers when they unearth a maternal past of frustrated desires. When these daughters speak of themselves as mothers, they voice their fears of motherhood, which they experience as stifling and engulfing. They convey the same fearful ambivalence towards their own daughters that they experience in relation to their mothers; the balancing act between self and other. Women writers have described this balancing act extensively from the daughter's point of view, but they are still reticent in relating it from the point of view of the mother of daughters. Still in the grip of their unresolved knot with their own mother, they are unwilling to put themselves in their mother's place for fear of discovering, perhaps, that they have become (like) her.[19] Their

---

19. Women who write about their experience of motherhood do so in relation to the male child, as if, it has been suggested, 'the crisis for feminism must always be about the masculine and how it enters our bodies' (Segal 1992: 268). Examples are Kristeva in 'Stabat Mater', Rich 1976, and Arcana 1979 and 1983, the latter two being the authors of well-known texts on the mother–daughter relationship. While this is probably a consequence of biographical circumstances, we should still ask why women, novelists as well as theorists, do not write about mothering daughters.

protagonists are more interested in reconstructing female genealogies backwards, with the aim of finding a place for themselves in their matrilinear heritage, to counter the estrangement to which they have been subjected. However, they often offer the story of their relationship with their mother to their daughters as a gift of a new language in which to articulate future mother–daughter relationships and a legacy that can help daughters to find their way in the world. Some of these narratives still predicate the daughter's autonomy upon the mother's effacement and death, whereas others give us an insight into the possibility of realising relationships of reciprocal and enabling recognition.

The rich corpus of narratives analysed in this book proves that if the dark continent of the mother–daughter relationship is not completely lit up, at least it is being explored, and in increasingly greater depth. If we think of literature as a reflection of reality, then the texts reveal that this relationship has already become part of current discourse. If we believe in the power of literature to shape reality by providing new matter for the imaginary, then these narratives have a crucial role in the process of symbolic inscription of the mother–daughter relationship. The fact that this relationship is considered, at present, a commercially viable topic by the publishing industry, which is also serving it up in a variety of popular cultural products,[20] also indicates its relevance and appeal to a large audience. One must only hope that this widespread interest is not a symptom of its impending demise in a world marked by fast social changes and ongoing scientific and technological discoveries which are dramatically changing our perception of, and relationship with, reality and the biological foundations of life itself.

During the last twenty years, most European countries have seen increases in divorce rates and in the number of unmarried couples, children born outside of wedlock, gay couples, and one-parent families (normally single mothers). Britain and Ireland have also registered a rise in teenage pregnancies. These changes in social norms have affected household composition and living arrangements, creating alternative family models to the nuclear family and new parental figures.[21] The current (supposedly) high incidence of infertility and the parallel development of a variety of IVF

---

20. See, for example, *From Mother and Daughter to Friends: A Memoir* (1999) by Nancy Aniston, on her relationship with her daughter Jennifer, a popular actress.
21. I am forced to make very general points because of the considerable variations among European countries. It is ironic that Ireland has a high percentage of unmarried mothers and lone parents deriving from marital breakdown, with births outside marriage constituting 10% of all births in 1993 (see Jackson 1993: 84). For changes in Italian family patterns, see the notion of 'multiplied family' in Ventimiglia 1988. Contrary to the representations of teenage motherhood by the media and policy makers as a new phenomenon, Allen and Bourke Dowling (1998) point out that teenage births in Britain have declined steadily from 10.5%

techniques to 'treat' different types of infertility have engendered a fragmentation of motherhood into separate maternal functions – biological, gestational and social – which can be performed by a number of women in relation to one and the same child (when, for example, an embryo obtained *in vitro* from a donated egg is implanted into the womb of another woman who carries the pregnancy to term on behalf of a third woman). The combinatorial potential of IVF has forced a reexamination of the concepts of motherhood and parenting at many levels, with heated debates often being initiated by controversial legal cases, when, for example, surrogate mothers have refused to give up the baby they carried for another woman/couple. A trend is now emerging which attempts to give value and existence to these new 'maternal' figures: after the baby's birth some couples continue to be in touch with the surrogate mother, who is recognised by the child as such. This is not so different from what used to happen in the past, especially in rural communities (in Southern Italy, for example), when children who were breastfed by a wet nurse or a relative grew up recognising this person as a second mother. In such contexts, biological motherhood and fatherhood were integrated, completed, or replaced by symbolic family ties.[22]

---

of all births in 1975 to 6.5% in 1995 (interestingly, half of the mothers of the teenagers who were interviewed were themselves teenage mothers). The increase concerns births among teenagers outside marriage, in line with the increase in births outside marriage for the whole population (from 9% in 1975 to 34% in 1995). Among teenagers this increase has been most dramatic, rising from 32% in 1975 to 86% in 1995 and showing an upward curve still in 1996, as a consequence of the fact that marrying (or moving in with) the baby's father is not the obvious choice. Many young mothers either continue to stay with, or move back in with, their parents, sharing parental responsibilities with the latter, and finding an important source of emotional and practical support in their mothers. The changes in the child's parental identifications in such households are highlighted by a grandmother: 'I wouldn't say it has been a bed of roses but I think it's worked out fairly well. She has got a lot of support here. The baby's got his grandfather as a father figure. He's got his uncle as a plaything and he's got two mums. What more could you want?' (Allen and Bourke Dowling 1998: 149). The United Kingdom has a high rate of teenage pregnancies compared to other European countries.

22. There are a few examples of this practice in my own family. After my mother's mother died in childbirth, the surviving baby was entrusted to a wet nurse, who was referred to, within the family, as my uncle's 'peasant mother', and whom my uncle visited regularly throughout his life. My mother breastfed a relative's baby girl after losing her own first-born daughter at birth. This baby grew up knowing my mother as her 'milk mother'. She has had an important role in my mother's later life providing the support which my mother did not obtain from her 'emancipated' natural daughters, and which she had liked to believe she would have received from the daughter she lost. My own sister had an alternative family who took care of her during the day when she was ill while my mother was at work and who 'adopted' her as their daughter (they only had a son). I have dwelt on these autobiographical details because my family was not an exception, and these and other nonbiological family ties, including the godparents one acquires at different stages in one's life, were a normal part of the social fabric in which I grew up. I am not aware of the existence of any study on this fascinating subject.

Changes in the social and economic structures have eliminated these alternative possibilities of fulfilling people's desire to mother and father, contributing to generating the need for reproductive technologies and the desire for biological motherhood. The effects which the existence of new family arrangements, reproductive technologies, and the ensuing mismatching and multiplication of parental figures will have on mother–daughter relationships are not clear and have yet to be explored in the mainstream narrative.

Women's science fiction, however, has long demonstrated a keen interest in the theme of motherhood and reproduction, imagining, like Naomi Mitchison's *Memoirs of a Space Woman* (1962), alternative biological and social relationships between mother and child. An older generation of women science fiction writers, for example the American Judith Merril in *Daughters of Earth* (1953), created mothers who act as important role models for their daughters from within the traditional structure of heterosexuality. In contrast, 1970s feminist postcataclysmic utopias of women-only communities tackled mothering and the mother–daughter relationship from within the search for nonoppressive, nonhierarchical, and nonexploitative familial and social arrangements that exclude men. Shulamith Firestone's proposal, in *The Dialectic of Sex: The Case for Feminist Revolution* (1970), that technology has the potential to free women from the tyranny of child bearing and rearing, appears to have been influential in generating a cluster of American feminist science fiction narratives in the 1970s and 1980s which, being concerned with power and the social construction of gender, either displace males and masculine values to the margins of women's communities or relegate them to history. Joanna Russ's *The Female Man* (1975), Marge Piercy's *Woman on the Edge of Time* (1976), Suzy McKee Charnas's *Motherlines* (1978), Sally Miller Gearhart's *The Wanderground* (1979), Pamela Sargent's *The Shore of Women* (1986), Joan Slonczewski's *A Door into Ocean* (1986), and Sheri Tepper's *The Gate to Women's Country* (1988) are some examples of such narratives (see Lefanu 1988: 57–59; 148). Many of these narratives were reissued in Britain, in a new science fiction imprint launched by the Women's Press in 1985, with the aim of presenting 'exciting and provocative feminist images of the future that will offer an alternative vision of science and technology' (as the manifesto printed at the front of each title explains). Both the birth of the series and the choice of texts are significant, as the dawn of the 1980s had been marked by the controversy over the new reproductive technologies following the birth of the first 'test-tube baby', Louise Brown, in England in 1978, followed by the first successful IVF procedures with a donor's egg in 1983 and with a frozen embryo in 1984 in Australia. These events generated public debate on the social, medical, and ethical implications of reproductive technologies around the world.[23]

The science fiction narratives mentioned above took up or anticipated many of the issues debated at the time. In Charnas's *Motherlines*, a society of Riding Women (a revisitation of the myth of the Amazons) who can reproduce without the male seed is organised in households/families of women from different 'Motherlines', strings of blood relations consisting of mothers, daughters, sisters, and daughters of sisters. Babies are raised by the blood-mother together with the other women of the household, the so-called 'share-mothers', among whom the adolescent daughter will chose the 'heartmother', the one towards whom she feels more affinity. This shared mothering highlights the importance of nurture and the need to take mother–daughter relationships out of the oppressive blood bond, whereas the existence of a heartmother underlines the need for women to choose symbolic mothers according to their needs and desires. The text cleverly suggests the nonexistence of mother–daughter relationships in the reader's reality by showing three different social set-ups. The Women are contrasted with the 'fems' and the 'free fems'. The world of Holdfast, where the 'fems' are enslaved to men and are deprived of their daughters at weaning when they are taken away to be trained as slaves, is evoked through the memories of the fem Alldera, after she has escaped from it. The 'free fems', who have also escaped from Holdfast, live in the wilderness but separately from the Women. Their community imitates that of Holdfast, being founded on competitiveness, hierarchy, and domination. Here there are no mothers or daughters as the free fems are unable to conceive without men and are doomed to extinction. Alldera is rescued by the Women and nurtured until she gives birth to the child she had conceived through rape before her escape because she brings the possibility of a new Motherline. Alldera's feelings towards her daughter are ambivalent: relief at being able to keep at a distance from her and jealousy at having to share her

---

23. Most European countries set up commissions with the remit to propose policies. Their reports led to legislation in some countries: 'The Warnock Report' in the United Kingdom (1984), 'The Santosuosso Report' in Italy (1985), 'The Benda Report' in West Germany (1985), and the French report to the *Conseil d'État* of 1988. The Glover Report to the European Commission followed in 1989 (see Glover et. al. 1989). 1984 also saw the publication of *Test-Tube Women: What Future for Motherhood?*, a book produced through the efforts of the international feminist network with the aim of assessing, fourteen years after Firestone's optimistic take on technology, the meaning, for women, of the (male) manipulation of women's bodies and reproductive function: 'is this liberation, or oppression in a new guise?' (Arditti, Duelli Klein, Minden 1984: 2). One strong concern of the authors was the increased possibilities for prenatal sex selection offered by the new techniques, which could lead to more effective prenatal femicide in countries like India where it was practised widely. Another concern was the possibility of a general reinforcement of the patriarchal preference for male progeny and the further devaluation of daughters and, consequently, of women.

with the other mothers. The daughter's upbringing as a Riding Woman sets her apart from her bloodmother, whose inability to speak her daughter's language can be taken as a metaphor for the gap between mothers and feminist daughters in the 1970s: 'Barvaran [the heartmother] began to speak softly to the child in the quick, fluid slang of the childpack. Alldera felt a startling stab of jealousy. If she were to address the child in Holdfastish, there would be no understanding between them. Never mind, she thought; what would I have to say to her?' (*Motherlines*: 392). The rest of the story is about mother and daughter moving towards a desire to know and find things to say to each other. Charnas emphasises choice and the importance of healing the mother–daughter bond with the help of the women's community.

Motherlines is the second book in a trilogy which was never completed. Its ending suggests that the third novel might have been about Alldera and her daughter returning to Holdfast to free the fems. Charnas explained in 1980 that the expected conservative turn of American society in the following decade made it impossible for her to write it (in Wolmark 1993: 84). It appears that she, and her characters, were unable to tackle the (re)encounter with patriarchy conceptually. Feminist utopias of the 1970s have been criticised for failing to engage with patriarchy and move beyond traditional polarised gender roles (Wolmark 1993: 81–86). Thus, if Charnas is able to imagine how to reconstruct mother–daughter relationships in a world without men, she is incapable of ensuring their survival when men reappear. A cursory review of the criticism of women's science fiction which destabilises received notions of gender identity and articulates more complex forms of identity – by employing characters who are humans, humanoids, aliens, and cyborgs whose sex may be indeterminate or mutant – indicates that it is not concerned with reformulating the mother–daughter bond.[24]

In a world where the traditional sexual divides are already being exploded, the fast advances in biotechnologies, genetic engineering, and cybernetics in recent years will by necessity further alter interpersonal relationships. The gap between reality and science fiction is narrowing, meaning that the imagined realities of science fiction require less and less of the audience's suspension of disbelief. At present no great flight of fancy is needed to imagine the embryo

---

24. See, for example, Le Guin's *The Left Hand of Darkness* (1969), Butler's *Xenogenesis* series (1987–89), and Piercy's *He, She and It* (1991) (reissued in 1992 as *Body of Glass*). A systematic reading of these texts posing different research questions might of course yield different answers. Unfortunately, the field is too wide to tackle here and, since it is dominated by American authors, it falls outside the scope of this book. It appears that there is no tradition of Italian women's science fiction. The Italian feminist journal *Donnawomanfemme* devoted a whole issue to women's science fiction in 1991, but it deals almost exclusively with the American texts available in Italian (*Aliene quotidiane*, 13/14). The few pages concerned with the Italian scene emphasise the lack of such a tradition and mention only a handful of names.

created in the test tube as a monster, 'the germ of a possible genetic mutation of the species' (Boccia and Zuffa 1998: 128), and one which for certain sectors of society has value and rights as a human and legal subject which override those of the woman who carries it in her womb. The emphasis placed on conception rather than birth has made the maternal body only a means and a container for the 'life' created by men in the lab. Are the concepts of 'birth' – to be brought into the world by the mother – and 'mother' – she who brings us into the world – doomed to disappear? At the moment, a human being can already be conceived 'without' the mother – in a test tube – and born without the biological mother – like baby Elisabetta born from a frozen embryo in Italy in 1995, two years after her mother's death. Yet, the embryo produced in the test tube still needs a woman's body to become a human being and to be brought into the world. Conversely, conception that dispenses with the sexual act makes paternal contribution to the creation of life marginal. The most ambitious goal of science is to create the artificial womb and, thus, dispense completely with the maternal body, an enterprise which is still deemed impossible to realise.[25] At the moment women's primacy in procreation is still unchallenged: as long as children are brought into the world by a woman, the mother will continue to be fundamental to the child's psychical and social formation. And as long as children are born of different sexes, the mother–daughter relationship will continue to exist and to matter. Let us hope that women writers will not abandon the project of further illuminating its many, intricate and intriguing, facets.

25. Ironically, the artificial womb, which had been invoked by Firestone and given imaginative existence in Piercy's *Woman on the Edge of Time* as the ultimate liberation of women from their biological destiny, is now seen by women as the final dispossession of their bodily experience of motherhood. It is doubly ironic that reproductive technologies do enable some women to exercise their 'right' to that experience.

Bibliography

Abel, Elizabeth, Marianne Hirsch, and Elizabeth Langland (eds) (1983) *The Voyage In: Fictions of Female Development*. Hannover and London: University Press of New England.

Accati, Luisa (1998) *Il mostro e la bella. Padre e madre nell'educazione cattolica dei sentimenti*. Milan: Raffaello Cortina.

Allen, Isobel and Shirley Bourke Dowling (1998) *Teenage Mothers: Decisions and Outcomes*. London: Policy Studies Institute.

Aniston, Nancy (1999) *From Mother and Daughter to Friends: A Memoir*. Amherst, New York: Prometheus.

Arcana, Judith (1979) *Our Mothers' Daughters*. Berkeley, Ca: Shameless Hussy Press (London: The Women's Press, 1984).

——— (1983) *Every Mother's Son*. New York: Anchor/Doubleday.
Arditti, Rita, Renate Duelli Klein, and Shelley Minden (eds) (1984) *Test-Tube Women: What Future for Motherhood?* London: Pandora.
Bart, Pauline (1983) Review of Chodorow's *The Reproduction of Mothering*, in Joyce Trebilcot (ed.) *Mothering: Essays in Feminist Theory*. Savage, Maryland: Rowman and Littlefield, 147–52 (first published in *Off Our Backs*, 11, no 1, January 1981).
Beauvoir, Simone de (1949) *Le Deuxième sexe*. Paris: Gallimard. *The Second Sex*, trans. H.M. Parshley. New York: Bantam, 1952.
Benjamin, Jessica (1990) *The Bonds of Love: Psychoanalysis, Feminism, and the Problem of Domination*. London: Virago (orig. 1988).
——— (1995) *Like Subjects, Love Objects: Essays on Recognition and Sexual Difference*. New Haven and London: Yale University Press.
Bimbi, Franca (1993) 'Gender, "Gift Relationship" and Welfare State Cultures in Italy' in Lewis (ed.) 1993, 138–69.
Bjerrum Nielsen, Harriet and Monica Rudberg (1993) 'Whatever Happened to Gender? Female Subjectivity and Change in a Generational Context' in Mens-Verhulst, Schreurs, and Woertman (eds) 1993, 44–53.
Boccia, Maria Luisa and Grazia Zuffa (1998) *L'eclissi della madre. Fecondazione artificiale, tecniche e norme*. Milan: Nuova Pratiche Editrice.
Brenkman, John (1992) 'Family, Community, Polis: The Freudian Structure of Feeling' in *New Literary History*, 23, 923–54.
Bull, Anna, Hanna Diamond, and Rosalind Marsh (eds) (2000) *Feminisms and Women's Movements in Contemporary Europe*. Basingstoke and London: Macmillan.
Butler, Octavia (1987–89) *Dawn: Xenogenesis I* (1987), *Adulthood Rites: Xenogenesis II* (1988), *Imago: Xenogenesis III* (1989). London: Victor Gollancz.
Caplan, Paula J. (1989) *Don't Blame Mother: Mending the Mother–Daughter Relationship*. New York: Harper and Row.
Cavarero, Adriana (1990a) 'Dire la nascita' in Diotima 1990, 93–121.
——— (1990b) *Nonostante Platone: figure femminili nella filosofia antica*. Rome: Editori Riuniti. *In Spite of Plato: A Feminist Rewriting of Ancient Philosophy*, trans. Serena Anderlini-D'Onofrio and Áine O'Healy, intr. Rosi Braidotti. Cambridge: Polity Press, 1995.
Centro Documentazione Donna di Firenze (1992) *Verso il luogo delle origini*. Milan: La Tartaruga.
Chamberlayne, Prue (1993) 'Women and the State: Changes in Roles and Rights in France, West Germany, Italy and Britain, 1970–1990' in Lewis (ed.) 1993, 170–93.
Charnas, Suzy McKee (1989) *Walk to the End of the World and Motherlines*. London: The Women's Press (*Walk to the End of the World*: orig. New York: Ballantine, 1974; *Motherlines*: orig. New York: Berkley, 1978).
Chasseguet-Smirgel, Janine (1970) 'Feminine Guilt and the Oedipus Complex' in Chasseguet-Smirgel (ed.) *Female Sexuality: New Psychoanalytic Views*. Ann Arbor: University of Michigan Press, 94–134 (orig. 1964).
Chodorow, Nancy (1978a) *The Reproduction of Mothering: Psychoanalysis and the Sociology of Gender*. Berkeley: University of California Press.

—— (1978b) 'Mothering, Object-Relations, and the Female Oedipal Configurations' in *Feminist Studies*, 4, no 1, 137–58.

—— (1990) 'Gender, Relation, and Difference in Psychoanalytic Perspective' in Eisenstein and Jardine (eds) 1990, 3–19 (orig. 1980).

Chodorow, Nancy and Susan Contratto (1982) 'The Fantasy of the Perfect Mother' in Barrie Thorne and Marilyn Yalom (eds) *Rethinking the Family: Some Feminist Questions*. New York: Longman, 54–75.

Cixous, Hélène (1976) 'The Laugh of the Medusa', trans. Kieth Cohen and Paula Cohen, in *Signs*, 1, 4, 875–93 (orig. 'Le Rire de la Méduse' in *L'Arc*, 61, 1975, 39–54). Reprinted in Elaine Marks and Isabelle de Courtivron, *New French Feminisms*. Brighton: Harvester, 1980, 245–64.

—— (1977) 'La Venue à l'écriture' in Hélène Cixous, Madeleine Gagnon, and Annie Leclerc, *La Venue à l'écriture*. Paris: Union Générale d'Editions, 10/18, 6–62.

Dinnerstein, Dorothy (1976) *The Mermaid and the Minotaur: Sexual Arrangements and Human Malaise*. New York: Harper and Row.

Diotima (1990) *Mettere al mondo il mondo. Oggetto e oggettività alla luce della differenza sessuale*. Milan: La Tartaruga.

—— (1992) *Il cielo stellato dentro di noi: l'ordine simbolico della madre*. Milan: La Tartaruga.

—— (1995) *Oltre l'uguaglianza. Le radici femminili dell'autorità*. Naples: Liguori.

Doane, Janice and Devon Hodges (1992) *From Klein to Kristeva: Psychoanalytic Feminism and the Search for the 'Good Enough' Mother*. Ann Arbor: University of Michigan Press.

Eisenstein, Hester and Alice Jardine (eds) (1990) *The Future of Difference*. New Brunswick and London: Rutgers University Press (orig. 1980).

Firestone, Shulamith (1970) *The Dialectic of Sex: The Case for Feminist Revolution*. New York: Morrow.

Flax, Jane (1978) 'The Conflict between Nurturance and Autonomy in Mother–Daughter Relationships and within Feminism' in *Feminist Studies: Toward a Feminist Theory of Motherhood*, 4, no 2, 1978, 171–89.

—— (1990) 'Mother–Daughter Relationships: Psychodynamics, Politics, and Philosophy' in Eisenstein and Jardine (eds) 1990, 20–40 (orig. 1980).

—— (1993) 'Mothers and Daughters Revisited' in Mens-Verhulst, Schreurs, and Woertman (eds) 1993, 145–56.

Freud, Sigmund (1909) 'Family Romances' in *The Standard Edition of the Complete Psychological Works of Sigmund Freud*, ed. and trans. James Strachey, vol. 9. London: The Hogarth Press, 1959, 236–41.

—— (1912–13) 'Totem and Taboo' in *Standard Edition*, vol. 13, 1955, 1–161.

—— (1923) 'The Ego and the Id' in *Standard Edition*, vol. 19, 1961, 12–59.

—— (1925) 'Some Psychical Consequences of the Anatomical Distinction between the Sexes' in *Standard Edition*, vol. 19, 1961, 248–58.

—— (1931) 'Female Sexuality' in *Standard Edition*, vol. 21, 1961, 225–43.

—— (1933) 'Femininity' in *Standard Edition*, vol. 22, 1964, 112–35.

Friday, Nancy (1977) *My Mother/Myself: A Daughter's Search for Identity*. New York: Delacorte Press.

Garner, Shirley Nelson, Claire Kahane, and Madelon Sprengnether (eds) (1985) *The (M)other Tongue: Essays in Feminist Psychoanalytic Interpretation*. Ithaca and London: Cornell University Press.

Gearhart, Sally Miller (1979) *The Wanderground: Stories of the Hill Women*. Watertown, Mass: Persephone Press. London: The Women's Press, 1985.

Giorgio, Adalgisa (1997) 'Real Mothers and Symbolic Mothers. The Maternal and the Mother–Daughter Relationship in Italian Feminist Theory and Practice' in Gino Bedani, Zygmunt Barański, Anna Laura Lepschy, and Brian Richardson (eds) *Sguardi sull'Italia*. Leeds: Society for Italian Studies, Occasional Paper no 3, 1997, 222–41. Revised as 'Mothers and Daughters in Italian Feminism: An Overview' in Bull, Diamond, and Marsh (eds) 2000, 180–93.

Glover, Jonathan and others (1989) *Fertility and the Family: The Glover Report on Reproductive Technologies to The European Commission*. London: Fourth Estate.

Hall, Nor (1980) *The Moon and the Virgin: Reflections on the Archetypal Feminine*. London: The Women's Press.

Hammer, Signe (1976) *Daughters and Mothers: Mothers and Daughters*. New York: Signet.

Harding, Esther (1971) *Woman's Mysteries*. New York: G.P. Putnam's Sons.

Hegel, G.W.F. (1952) *Phänomenologie des Geistes*. Hamburg: Felix Meiner Verlag (orig. 1807). *The Phenomenology of Spirit*, trans. A.V. Miller. Oxford: Oxford University Press, 1977.

Herman, Nini (1989) *Too Long a Child: The Mother–Daughter Dyad*. London: Free Association Books.

Hirsch, Marianne (1989) *The Mother/Daughter Plot: Narrative, Psychoanalysis, Feminism*. Bloomington and Indianapolis: Indiana University Press.

——— (1992) 'Object-Relations Oriented Criticism' in Wright (ed.) 1992, 280–84.

Homans, Margaret (1986) *Bearing the Word: Language and Female Experience in Nineteenth-Century Women's Writing*. New Haven and London: Yale University Press

Irigaray, Luce (1974) *Speculum, de l'autre femme*. Paris: Editions de Minuit.

——— (1977) 'Ce Sexe qui n'en est pas un' in *Ce Sexe qui n'en est pas un*. Paris: Minuit. *This Sex Which Is Not One*, trans. Catherine Porter with Carolyn Burke. Ithaca, NY: Cornell University Press, 1985.

——— (1980) 'When Our Lips Speak Together', trans. Carolyn Burke, in *Signs*, 6, 1, 69–79 (orig. 'Quand nos lèvres se parlent' in Irigaray 1977).

——— (1981) 'And the One Doesn't Stir Without the Other', trans. Hélène Vivienne Wenzel, in *Signs*, 7, I, 60–67 (orig. *Et l'une ne bouge pas sans l'autre*. Paris: Minuit, 1979).

——— (1985a) *Speculum of the Other Woman*, trans. Gillian C. Gill. Ithaca, NY: Cornell University Press.

——— (1985b) 'Female Hom(m)osexuality' in Irigaray 1985a, 98–104.

—— (1991) 'The Bodily Encounter with the Mother', trans. extract David Macey, in Margaret Whitford (ed.) *The Irigaray Reader*, intro. Whitford. Oxford: Blackwell, 34–46 (orig. *Le Corps-à-corps avec la mère*. Montreal: Éditions de la pleine lune, 1981; reprinted in Irigaray, *Sexes et parentés*. Paris: Minuit, 1987).

—— (1993) *An Ethics of Sexual Difference*, trans. Carolyn Burke and Gillian Gill. Ithaca, NY: Cornell University Press (orig. *Ethique de la différence sexuelle*. Paris: Minuit, 1984).

Jackson, Pauline Conroy (1993) 'Managing the Mothers: The Case of Ireland' in Lewis (ed.) 1993, 72–91.

Kahn, Coppélia (1986) 'The Absent Mother in *King Lear*' in Margaret W. Ferguson, Maureen Quilligan, and Nancy J. Vickers (eds) *Rewriting the Renaissance: The Discourses of Sexual Difference in Early Modern Europe*. Chicago and London: University of Chicago Press.

—— (1993) 'Mother' in Gayle Greene and Coppélia Kahn (eds) *Changing Subjects: The Making of Feminist Literary Criticism*. London: Routledge, 157–67.

Kaufman, Franz-Xaver, Anton Kuijsten, Hans-Joachim Schulze, and Klaus P. Strohmeier (eds) (1997) *Family Life and Family Policies in Europe*. Oxford: Clarendon Press.

Klein, Melanie (1975a) *Love, Guilt and Reparation (The Writings of Melanie Klein, Vol. 1)*. London: The Hogarth Press.

—— (1975b) *The Psycho-Analysis of Children (The Writings of Melanie Klein, Vol. 2)*. London: The Hogarth Press (orig. 1932).

Kristeva, Julia (1974) *La Révolution du langage poétique*. Paris: Seuil. *Revolution in Poetic Language*, trans. Margaret Waller, intr. Léon S. Roudiez. New York: Columbia University Press, 1984.

—— (1980a) *Desire in Language: A Semiotic Approach to Literature and Art*, ed. Léon S. Roudiez; trans. Alice Jardine, Thomas A. Gora, and Léon S. Roudiez. Oxford: Blackwell.

—— (1980b) *Pouvoirs de l'horreur*. Paris: Seuil. *Powers of Horror: An Essay on Abjection*, trans. Léon S. Roudiez. New York: Columbia University Press, 1982.

—— (1986) 'Stabat Mater' in Toril Moi (ed.) *The Kristeva Reader*. Oxford: Blackwell, 161–86 (orig. published as 'Hérethique de l'amour' in *Tel Quel*, 74, Winter 1977, 30–49; reprinted as 'Stabat Mater' in Kristeva, *Histoires d'amour*. Paris: Denoël, 1983).

—— (1987) *Soleil Noir. Dépression et mélancholie*. Paris: Gallimard. *Black Sun: Depression and Melancholia*, trans. Léon S. Roudiez. New York: Columbia University Press, 1989.

Lacan, Jacques (1977) *Écrits: A Selection*, trans. Alan Sheridan. London: Tavistock.

Lampl-de Groot, Jeanne (1927) 'The Evolution of the Oedipus Complex in Women' in Robert Fliess (ed.) *The Psychoanalytic Reader*. New York: International Universities Press, 1973, 180–94.

Lefanu, Sarah (1988) *In the Chinks of the World Machine: Feminism and Science Fiction*. London: The Women's Press.

Le Guin, Ursula (1969) *The Left Hand of Darkness*. New York: Ace.

Lewis, Jane (ed.) (1993) *Women and Social Policies in Europe: Work, Family and the State*. Aldershot: Edward Elgar.

Libreria delle donne di Milano (1987) *Non credere di avere dei diritti: la generazione della libertà femminile nell'idea e nelle vicende di un gruppo di donne*. Turin: Rosenberg e Sellier. *Sexual Difference: A Theory of Social-Symbolic Practice*, trans. Teresa De Lauretis with Patrizia Cicogna. Bloomington: Indiana University Press, 1991.

Lidoff, Joan (1986) 'Virginia Woolf's Feminine Sentence: The Mother–Daughter World of *To the Lighthouse*' in *Literature and Psychology*, 32/3, 1986, 43–59.

Lovenduski, Joni (1986) *Women and European Politics: Contemporary Feminism and Public Policy*. Brighton: Wheatsheaf.

Melandri, Lea (1992) 'L'eredità contesa' in *Lapis*, 16, 1992, 5–12.

Mens-Verhulst, Janneke van, Karlein Schreurs, and Liesbeth Woertman (eds) (1993) *Daughtering and Mothering: Female Subjectivity Reanalysed*. London and New York: Routledge.

Merril, Judith (1953) *Daughters of Earth* in *The Best of Judith Merril*. New York: Warner Books, 1976.

Mitchell, Juliet (1974) *Psychoanalysis and Feminism: Freud, Reich, Laing and Women*. London: Allen Lane.

—— (1982) 'Introduction' to Mitchell and Jacqueline Rose (eds) *Feminine Sexuality: Jacques Lacan and the 'école freudienne'*. New York: Norton, 1–26.

Mitchison, Naomi (1962) *Memoirs of a Space Woman*. London: Gollancz. London: The Women's Press, 1985.

Muraro, Luisa (1991) *L'ordine simbolico della madre*. Rome: Editori Riuniti.

—— (2000) 'Love as a Political Practice: the Example of the Love for the Mother' in Bull, Diamond, and Marsh (eds) 2000, 79–85 (orig. published as 'L'amore come pratica politica: l'esempio dell'amore per la madre' in Paola Bono (ed.) *Questioni di teoria femminista*. Milan: La Tartaruga, 1993, 187–93).

Nice, Vivien E. (1992) *Mothers and Daughters: The Distortion of a Relationship*. Basingstoke and London: MacMillan.

Piercy, Marge (1976) *Woman on the Edge of Time* New York: Knopf. London: The Women's Press, 1979 and 1987.

—— (1991) *He, She and It*. New York: Fawcett Crest. Reissued as *Body of Glass*. London: Michael Joseph, 1992.

Rabuzzi, Kathryn Allen (1988) *Motherself: A Mythic Analysis of Motherhood*. Bloomington: Indiana University Press.

Rich, Adrienne (1976) *Of Woman Born: Motherhood as Experience and Institution*. New York: Norton (London: Virago, 1977). *Nato di donna*. Milan: Garzanti, 1977. *Nacida de mujer*. Barcelona: Noguer cop., 1978; *Nacemos de mujer: la maternidad como esperienza e institución*. Madrid: Catedra, 1996. *Von Frauen geboren: Mutterschaft als Erfahrung und Institution*. München: verl. Frauenoffensive, 1979. *Naître d'une femme: la maternité en tant qu'experience et institution*. Paris: Denöel-Gonthier, 1980.

—— (1980) 'Compulsory Heterosexuality and Lesbian Existence' in *Signs*, 5/4, 1980, 631–60.

Russ, Joanna (1975) *The Female Man*. New York: Bantam. London: The Women's Press, 1985.
Sargent, Pamela (1986) *The Shore of Women*. New York: Crown. London: Chatto and Windus, 1987.
Sayers, Janet (1991) *Mothering Psychoanalysis. Helene Deutsch, Karen Horney, Anna Freud, Melanie Klein*. Harmondsworth: Penguin.
Segal, Naomi (1992) 'Motherhood' in Wright (ed.) 1992, 266–70.
Silverman, Kaja (1988) *The Acoustic Mirror: The Female Voice in Psychoanalysis and Cinema*. Bloomington: Indiana University Press.
Slonczewski, Joan (1986) *A Door into Ocean*. New York: Arbor House. London: The Women's Press, 1987.
Sprengnether, Madelon (1990) *The Spectral Mother: Freud, Feminism, and Psychoanalysis*. Ithaca: Cornell University Press.
—— (1995) 'Reading Freud's Life' in *American Imago*, 52, 1995, 9–54.
Steedman, Carolyn (1986) *Landscape for a Good Woman: A Study of Two Lives*. London: Virago.
Suleiman Susan (1985) 'Writing and Motherhood' in Garner, Kahane, and Sprengnether (eds) 1985, 352–77.
Tepper, Sheri S. (1988) *The Gate to Women's Country*. New York: Doubleday. London: Bantam, 1989.
Vegetti Finzi, Silvia (1990) *Il bambino della notte. Divenire donna, divenire madre*. Milan: Mondadori.
Ventimiglia, Carmine (ed.) (1988) *La famiglia moltiplicata*. Milan: Franco Angeli.
Villa, Luisa (1990) ' "Mettere al mondo il mondo": appunti sul realismo femminile tra filosofia e psicoanalisi' in *Nuova Corrente*, 37, 1990, 39–74.
Walker, Alice (1984) 'In Search of Our Mothers' Gardens' (written 1974) in *In Search of Our Mothers' Gardens: Womanist Prose*. London: The Women's Press, 231–43 (orig. 1983).
Warner, Marina (1976) *Alone of All Her Sex. The Myth and the Cult of the Virgin Mary*. London: Weidenfeld.
Whitford, Margaret (1991) *Luce Irigaray: Philosophy in the Feminine*. London: Routledge.
Winnicott, Donald W. (1967) 'The Mirror-Role of Mother and Family in Child Development' in *Playing and Reality*. London: Tavistock, 1971, 111–18.
Wolmark, Jenny (1994) *Aliens and Others: Science Fiction, Feminism and Postmodernism*. New York and London: Harvester Wheatsheaf (orig. 1993).
Wright, Elizabeth (ed.) (1992) *Psychoanalysis and Feminism: A Critical Dictionary*. Oxford: Blackwell.
Žižek, Slavoj (1992) 'Symptom' in Wright (ed.) 1992, 423–27.

Chapter Two

Towards a Female Symbolic

Re-Presenting Mothers and Daughters in Contemporary Spanish Narrative by Women

Christine Arkinstall

Introduction: Maternal Politics in Spain

Until the late 1970s, representations of mother–daughter relationships in contemporary Spanish literature by women are fraught with difficulties. This is hardly surprising, given that the Franco dictatorship endeavours to impose, from 1939 to 1975, a patriarchal culture in which women, officially equated with a maternal function that grants them identity solely as mothers, are hindered in forming relationships as individuals. It is thus only in the post-Franco period, critics have argued, that portrayals of mothers and daughters manifest more positive connotations. While, to a certain extent, this is true, my analysis will contend that contemporary women's narrative pertaining to the relationship between mother and daughter is at all times engaged in a quest for representations of both figures that question and often subvert cultural prescriptions.[1]

My point of departure is an overview of the cultural and always political conflicts surrounding the diverse constructions of the maternal in contemporary discourses. In late nineteenth-century Spain and the first decades of the twentieth century it is various workers' parties which articulate some of

---

1. A study just appeared that outlines the importance of the maternal trope and a symbolic mother–daughter relationship in contemporary Spanish narrative written by women is that by Elizabeth Ordóñez 1998.

the most progressive statements regarding motherhood, while in 1900 it is the state that introduces labour laws to protect the interests and health of mother and child (see Nash 1983: 57–58). The part played, however, by any feminist movement prior to the Spanish Civil War is minor. Tending to be based, as Mary Nash indicates, on 'the social projection of motherhood and gender roles' (1994: 167), Spanish feminism is rendered ineffectual by conservatism and passivity.[2]

In the early 1930s, however, the short-lived Second Republic introduces major advances in women's rights, such as women's suffrage in 1931, divorce in 1932,[3] and abortion in 1936 (see Scanlon 1986: 274, 265, 308). These initiatives, indebted to a more liberal government than to any women's movement, form the prelude to a revolution in women's roles with the outbreak of the Civil War in 1936, which incorporates women into the war effort, behind the scenes on the Nationalist side and in a more active capacity on the Republican side (see Ackelsberg 1991, Alcalde 1996, Graham 1995b, Mangini 1995).

Upon the victory of the Nationalist forces in 1939 the ensuing Franco dictatorship returns women to a social, cultural, and legal situation regulated by the 1889 Civil Code, which was in turn based on the Napoleonic Code from the early nineteenth century (see Scanlon 1986: 320–28). For almost forty years the body of the mother becomes the dominant element around which sanctioned concepts of femininity, gender, and nationhood are organised. Falangist doctrine and Spanish Catholicism are blended to produce the powerful political ideology of the Franco dictatorship known as National-Catholicism. The relationship of the political leader or 'Caudillo' with his feminised people, founded on hierarchical concepts of difference and gender, is reproduced in family dynamics, through the legal authority of husband over wife and children. At the same time, the relationship between State and citizen is perceived as identical to that between mother and son, with State and Church belying their patriarchal premises by representing themselves as feminised bodies: the *Madre Patria* (Maternal Fatherland) and *Santa Madre Iglesia* (Holy Mother Church) respectively. Consequently, the filial relationship privileged by the régime is that of mother and son, heavily imbued with Marian-Christological connotations.

---

2. For an overview of the feminist struggle in Spain and twentieth-century feminist writers, see Davies 1991. For the struggles, triumphs, and adversities of Spanish feminism between 1868 and 1974, see Scanlon 1986. Other valuable texts are Borreguero et al. 1986, Capmany and Alcalde 1970, and Folguera 1988.
3. In spite of the fact that the divorce law is progressive for its time, the unjust situation in which divorced mothers might find themselves is attested to in the autobiographical short story, 'Bodoque' (1945, In Relief) by Mercedes Formica (born Cádiz 1918), and in the first part of her memoirs, *La infancia* (1987, My Childhood) (see Alborg 1993: 142–44).

With women's lives inscribed by the Falangist axiom 'For woman her family is the nation' (Primo de Rivera 1944),[4] the patriarchal family becomes an integral aspect of a gendered politics which subordinates motherhood to pronatalist policies (see Nash 1994: 160). If inadequate mothers are cast as the cause of the Civil War, maternity is now represented as the feminine vocation or 'mission' that transforms women into mothers of the nation and angels of their home (see Martín Gaite 1987b: 49, 60; Formica 1967: 191).[5] The entity responsible for the formation of the Francoist ideal of *mujer-madre* or woman-mother is the Falangist-inspired middle-class organisation of the *Sección Femenina* (Women's Department), the effects of which have continued to be felt in Spanish society until recently (see Barrachina 1991, Gallego Méndez 1983, Sánchez López 1990). The consequences of daring to be a mother outside of marriage and a socially sanctioned femininity are emphasised in 1943 by the régime's utilisation of the sensational case of Aurora Rodríguez Carballeira, who ten years previously had killed her eighteen-year-old feminist daughter Hildegart.[6]

Although Francoist rhetoric affords mothers an enormous symbolic significance, it grants them little official power over their families, bodies, and actions. The married mother has no *patria potestas* or legal jurisdiction over her children until 1970 (see Telo 1986: 83). Divorce, considered 'a matter for reds' (Martín Gaite 1987b: 21) and abolished in 1939 by the Nationalists, is not again legalised until 1981. Adultery and cohabitation outside of marriage remain criminal offences until 1978. Until 1963 Spanish manhood has the right to 'cleanse his honour with blood' if it is considered that the maternal vessel has been contaminated by another (Telo 1986: 91–93, 84): a situation denounced in Mercedes Formica's novel, *A instancia de parte* (1954, Appeal for the Defence). It is not until the end of the 1960s that any adequate education regarding pregnancy and birth is offered mothers-to-be by Social Welfare (see Parra 1986: 64–65), in an attempt to eliminate the kind of harmful taboos and superstitions which abound in Mercè Rodoreda's novel *La Plaça del Diamant* (1962, *The Time of the Doves* 1983).

However, in spite of the efforts of officialdom to promote maternity as the sole admissible option for women apart from a religious vocation, in

---

4. All translations are my own, except where published translations of primary texts are indicated.
5. Regarding such a vision of Spanish motherhood, see Jiménez 1938: 12, 32; Delgado Capeans 1941, Révesz 1946, Treviño 1963. For an analysis of the social censure befalling women who did not marry, see Martín Gaite 1987b: 36–53. The concept of motherhood is also deployed subversively by dissident writers; examples are the poet, Angela Figuera, who adopts the persona of a *mater dolorosa* or mother in mourning for Spain (see Arkinstall 1997), as does Dolores Ibárruri (Gallarta 1895–1989), alias Pasionaria, leader of the Spanish Communist Party, in *El único camino*, first published in English due to Francoist censorship (1992, *They Shall Not Pass*, 1966).
6. Regarding Aurora and Hildegart, see Guzmán 1972. Regarding the régime's representation of this mother–daughter relationship, see Martín Gaite 1987b: 71.

many cases women's concern for the economic survival of the family unit in the first two poverty-stricken decades of the régime prevails over state insistence on maternal duty (see Graham 1995a: 192; Nash 1994: 174). Furthermore, Spain's economic revival in the 1960s, with the ever-increasing incorporation of the female population into the workforce of an expanding consumer society, leads to a progressive dissociation of the concepts of woman and mother. Such a conceptual change is also facilitated by contraceptives becoming more widely, although illegally, available in the late 1960s through the dedicated efforts of women's organisations (see Parra 1986: 65–68). Nevertheless abortion, as Rodoreda's novel *Isabel i Maria* reveals, has always existed in a clandestine fashion, threatening the health and lives of those women unable to terminate their pregnancies due to state policies and religious doctrine.

The seven years of so-called transition to democratic government following Franco's demise in 1975 see demands for the right to family planning continue to be made by feminist groups, with the majority acting independently of official government bodies (see Parra 1986: 65–68).[7] Their efforts contribute to the decriminalisation of contraceptive methods in 1978 (see Capel Martínez 1986a: 19) and the polemical legalisation of abortion in July 1985 by the then Socialist government (see Telo 1986: 91n).[8] Fruit of this climate is *La razón feminista* (1981–1982, Feminist Reason) by Lidia Falcón (born Madrid 1935), a treatise in which the second volume meticulously examines issues pertaining to the institution of motherhood. Throughout the next decade of its legislation the Socialist Party (PSOE) makes great progress in guaranteeing women their rights as mothers and workers (see Vallejo and de Micheo 1994): a factor also reinforced by Spain's entry into the European Union in 1986 and the need to implement European policies on equality (see Nash 1991: 384). Since 1995, when the centre-right *Partido Popular* (Popular Party) is elected to power, much publicity has been given to the question of Spain's declining birth-rate, the result of a complex alignment of factors (see Capel Martínez 1986b: 24–26).

Just how the varied trajectory of Spain's maternal politics informs the mother–daughter relationships portrayed in women's narratives and how their texts might resist the same is the focus of the ensuing pages. The second section of my chapter takes up the theme of missing mothers, and to a lesser extent, daughters, which dominates women's writing in the 1940s and 1950s. Although reference is made to a number of texts, the major focus of the analysis falls on *Memorias de Leticia Valle* (1945, *Memoirs of Leticia Valle* 1994) by

7. Regarding the debate over the right to contraception, see Balaguer 1977 and Larraburu 1977.
8. For further details regarding debates over birth control since then, see 'Qué dice la Ley' and Criado 1993.

Rosa Chacel (Valladolid 1898–Madrid 1994). In the third section I examine the pervasive preoccupation with the patriarchal ideal of the 'good enough' mother and daughter, which conflicts with women's expression of their sexuality. Here greater emphasis is placed on *Isabel i Maria* (1991, Isabel and María) by Mercè Rodoreda (Barcelona 1908–Gerona 1983) and *El mismo mar de todos los veranos* (1978, *The Same Sea As Every Summer* 1990) by Esther Tusquets (born Barcelona 1936). A fourth section privileges the theme of writing mothers and daughters, exemplified by a variety of texts but especially by *Nubosidad variable* (1992, *Variable Cloud* 1995) by Carmen Martín Gaite (Salamanca 1925–Madrid 2000). Mothers and daughters as historical subjects are the focus of the final section, in texts concerned with the writing of maternal genealogies and the strategic mythification/demystification of the mother. Particularly highlighted will be the revaluing of the mother in aspects formerly consigned to invisibility, as is evident in *La fuerza del destino* (1997, The Force of Destiny) by Josefina Aldecoa (born La Robla, León 1926).

Although the theoretical framework of the chapter is eclectic, the prominence afforded the woman writer in the majority of texts invites a more specific and contextualised deployment of Luce Irigaray's theories regarding the need for women to elaborate a 'female symbolic': that is, to refigure the mother–daughter relationship outside of a masculine system of meaning or symbolic economy. Thus, the relationship between women, language, and the writing process as the principal means of reimagining the symbolic is of primary importance in this chapter, as it is in contemporary women's narrative in Spain.

Missing Mothers and Daughters

Narrative written by women during the first two and a half decades of the Franco régime stands out for the virtual absence of mothers (see Truxa 1982: 81; Jones 1983: 127). In a peculiar inversion of the Demeter–Persephone myth, it is almost invariably not the mother who laments the abduction of the daughter, but the latter who mourns the lack, and frequently death, of the maternal figure. Such a situation lends itself to political readings. It does not only mirror the matricide on which patriarchy erects itself (see Irigaray 1993a: 36). More specifically for the Spanish postwar period, it bears witness to the eradication of a motherland, embodied in the former more liberal Second Republic, by the masculine right-wing ideology of the Francoist Fatherland. Furthermore, the preponderance of daughters in mourning may well signal the fact that the only legal position granted women is that of 'dutiful daughter': a role which, by disavowing a maternal genealogy, renders impossible the existence of the daughter outside of a patriarchal framework. Patriarchy's dependence on its forced severance of the mother–daughter relationship and the disastrous fate befalling women discontent with being dutiful daughters are features stressed in *Caza menor* (1951, Small Game) by Elena Soriano (Fuentidueña del Tajo, Madrid 1917–Madrid 1996). The daughter Ana's attempt to return to her mother without her husband's approbation results in her death, which heralds the advent of chaos in the form of the Civil War.

When mothers are present in women's narrative in the first decades of the dictatorship they are frequently repressive figures who, having internalised patriarchal mores, become the defenders and transmitters of an oppressive system. The oft-cited text in this regard is *Primera memoria* (1959, *School of the Sun* 1963) by Ana María Matute (born Barcelona 1926). It portrays a family mainly of women in which the masculinised matriarch imposes a régime of authority and silence on her daughter, grandson, and granddaughter (see Mayans Natal 1991: 32–34, 46–50). A contemporary precursor of this kind of phallic mother is the maternal figure, murdered by her son, in *La familia de Pascual Duarte* (1942, *The Family of Pascual Duarte* 1964) by Camilo José Cela (born Iria Flavia, La Coruña 1916).

These exceptions notwithstanding, the principal theme in texts written by women during the early Franco dictatorship is the elegy for the missing mother, exemplified in the little-known *Cinco sombras* (1947, Five Shadows) by Eulalia Galvarriato (born Madrid 1905). The family home itself is defined by the absence of the mother, being termed by the father 'a house without a woman' (*Cinco*: 12; see Mayans Natal 1991: 34); even though his five unmarried daughters reside in it, they lack all social meaning unless they are wives and mothers. The Demeter–Persephone myth is evoked when one of the daughters, Rosario, laments in her diary the death of her mother, equated with sun, spring, and love, and who leaves forever in her place 'the deepest and blackest darkness' (*Cinco*: 219; see Alborg 1993: 32–40).

In *Escribo tu nombre* (1965, I Write Your Name), a first-person narrative by Elena Quiroga (born Santander 1921), the protagonist, Tadea Vásquez, whose mother is dead, turns for direction to the Prioress of her convent school. However, this symbolic Mother, whose notion of liberty is constrained by Church doctrine, cannot satisfy Tadea's search for freedom in a society on the verge of Civil War. Another daughter whose mother has perished, this time in the Civil War, is Andrea, the protagonist of *Nada* (1944, *Nada* 1993) by Carmen Laforet (born Barcelona 1921). In her quest for a 'model of woman, wife, and mother' (Ordóñez 1991: 40), Andrea turns to the mother of her friend Ena. Similarly, Rodoreda's best-known text, *La Plaça del Diamant*, emphasises how the death of Natàlia's mother has left her in the world without maternal support and advice. It is through metaphors of maternity that Natàlia's oppression by patriarchal structures, her rebellion against them, and her eventual psychic rebirth are recounted (see Carbonell 1994).

Yet another daughter who suffers the loss of a loved mother is the rebellious protagonist of *Memorias de Leticia Valle*, by the modernist writer, Rosa Chacel. Although published in Buenos Aires in 1945, its first Spanish edition does not appear until 1971. Since this first-person narrative focalised exclusively through the daughter has been read as a precursor of Vladimir Nabokov's 1959 *Lolita* (see Glenn 1991b, Villena 1987), critics have stressed the relationship of seduction between an older male, here don Daniel, and younger female: the eleven-year-old Leticia. However, Leticia's precociousness, both in terms of her desires and her intellectual capacity,[9] is symptomatic of Chacel's own authorial struggle between the need to identify with and differentiate herself from authoritative conceptual models, especially those of the Spanish philosopher José Ortega y Gasset, Chacel's reputed mentor (see Bordons and Kirkpatrick 1992, Lázaro 1994, Mangini 1987).

The other theoretical father read extensively by Chacel is Freud (see Scarlett 1994: 90–93). Chacel's *Memorias* both duplicates and challenges features that define the Freudian 'Family Romance' (see Freud 1909). Firstly, the triangular relationship established by Leticia with her surrogate parents, don Daniel and his wife, Luisa, appears to take up what Marthe Robert terms the 'Foundling' plot of the Freudian paradigm, whereby the child, disillusioned by his natural parents, rejects their authority and imagines himself to be a stepchild or adopted child (see Robert 1980: 28, Kaplan 1992: 65). Like Freud's male child, Leticia rejects the paternal model offered her by her alcoholic natural father, thus inserting herself within the conflict between paternal authority and filial independence seen by Freud as characteristic of relations between father and son, due to the boy's stronger imagination. Chacel's text thus stresses the power of Leticia's imagination and the presence of female literary creativity.

The second component of the Freudian family romance revolves around what Robert calls the 'Bastard' story (1980: 28). Here the child's fantasy that the mother is an adulteress and that his origins are thus uncertain clears a space for the recreation of the self free from constraints of predetermined origin. The imaginary moral fall of the mother is concomitant with the child's elevation of the paternal figure to the status of royalty, and consequently, with his own social reinvention (see Hirsch 1989: 55–56). These elements are present in *Memorias*, but are given different inflections that subvert the Freudian model. In Chacel's text it is the paternal genealogy which is questioned and found lacking. Perceived deficiencies in the natural father, Colonel Valle, lead the daughter to choose and idealise a surrogate father, don Daniel, compared by her to a 'Moorish king' (*Memoirs*: 31; *Memorias*:

---

9. In 1900, just eleven years prior to when Leticia is writing, over 71% of Spanish women are illiterate (see Nash 1991: 396); see also Capel Martínez 1986a.

37), but whose own moral fall ultimately leads to his death. Similarly, the reason suggested for Leticia's natural mother abandoning husband and daughter is indeed adultery. However, while the Freudian model attempts to debase and erase the maternal figure, Chacel's text bears witness to Leticia's quest, forever unsatisfied, for this lost mother, who epitomises for her daughter a quintessential love disavowed by others: 'if they have all felt it why don't they talk about it?... They talk about the way mothers love ... and I always say deep inside me: that was love' (*Memoirs*: 5; *Memorias*: 11).

The mother that does fall in status is Leticia's surrogate mother, Luisa, who literally falls on her polished floor and fractures her knee. It is her forced confinement to bed that facilitates the development of Leticia's ambiguous relationship with don Daniel, symbolic of the daughter's desire to transgress societal norms. Such a differentiation between two countervailing maternal figures makes the lost adulteress mother a model for a nonconforming self, in opposition to another model, embodied by Luisa, which represents the woman confined by patriarchal society to her maternal function, and whom the creative daughter must ultimately reject in order to survive. Moreover, this privileging of the natural mother over the symbolic one suggests that the daughter's matrophobia is culturally induced, severing a 'natural' bond between mother and daughter.

As a result, the Chacelian narrative insists that behind the Oedipal struggle which confirms the child's allegiance to the father lies an unacknowledged power struggle between mother and father for the child's possession, of which the latter is conscious. *Memorias* thus documents a process of acculturation in which differences become defined through strategies of manipulation and force, evident in the constant confrontations between Luisa and don Daniel over the nature of Leticia's education (*Memoirs*: 51–52; *Memorias*: 58). This paternal figure, guardian of the Simancas historical Archive, is jealous and possessive, systematically devaluing the material, sensual world of the mother, represented by Luisa's music and cooking, and demanding the child's abandonment of the same. Of relevance is the fact that Leticia's incorporation of Luisa's world is represented in positive terms, with communication and identification between 'mother' and 'daughter' frequently occurring outside language, governed by sensorial impulses (see *Memoirs*: 98; *Memorias*: 104). Furthermore, the kind of instruction that Luisa offers Leticia is effortlessly absorbed by the latter (see *Memoirs*: 144; *Memorias*: 150). However, the transmitting of knowledge from mother to daughter must be hidden from the father and denied by both; as Leticia observes: 'I would pick up all the exercises and papers before he [don Daniel] came back at midday and Luisa was as careful as I not to mention it' (*Memoirs*: 145; *Memorias*: 151). Conversely, the pedagogical methods employed by don Daniel are designed to obstruct his 'daughter's' learning, creating in her the poison of self-doubt: 'I walked home carrying all those enigmas inside of me, as irremediably as someone who has swallowed a poison and knows there is no way to get rid of it or keep it from invading the body' (*Memoirs*: 108; *Memorias*: 114). The intellectual sustenance he provides constitutes a debilitating milk that fosters impotence and self-annulment rather than empowerment (see *Memoirs*: 95–96; *Memorias*: 114–15).

Leticia's resistance to a politics of feminine cultural castration is illustrated in her quest for an ideal symbolic mother who might also be accepted as legitimate within her patriarchal context. To this end she evaluates different models of female teachers that contribute to her intellectual development. The figure of Margarita Velayos, Leticia's teacher from Valladolid and originally her ideal, is apparently the epitome of the New Woman of *fin-de-siècle* culture. Described as 'very mannish' (*Memoirs*: 19; *Memorias*: 26), she reveals, however, that acceptance as an equal in worlds dominated by a masculine ethos demands the repression of the female body and its sexuality (see *Memoirs*: 116–17; *Memorias*: 123–24).

The patriarchal ideal of femininity is epitomised by the teacher from Simancas, expert in the art of embroidery considered necessary for a girl's education (see Martín Gaite 1987b: 59). At the beginning of their relationship Leticia admires her knowledge in this sphere and resolves to learn all that she can from her (see *Memoirs*: 20; *Memorias*: 27). It is only subsequent to her meeting don Daniel that Leticia resolves to abandon her needlework studies (see *Memoirs*: 43–44; *Memorias*: 49–50). He makes her aware of a different system of values whereby all that is feminine is objectified and devalued, evident when don Daniel caresses Leticia's ringlet as if 'judging the quality of a piece of cloth, without realizing that the curl was connected to my temple' (*Memoirs*: 31; *Memorias*: 37).

The possibility of reconciling gendered bodies of knowledge is presented to Leticia by Luisa, a gifted music teacher who in many aspects also seems to embody the maternal ideal: when Leticia first meets her, Luisa has one child holding on to her skirts and another in her arms, and her role as mother takes precedence over her professional interests, with her unable to resume teaching *solfeggio* until the infant has been weaned (see *Memoirs*: 25; *Memorias*: 31). At the same time, she is perceived by Leticia as being 'worldly', a quality defined as participating actively in the world (see *Memoirs*: 26; *Memorias*: 32). For Leticia, however, this movement is inhibited by Luisa's maternal role (see *Memoirs*: 28; *Memorias*: 35). Maternity is described as a barrier that symbolically differentiates the sexes, preventing women from transcending the demands of the corporeal, as is evident in Leticia's following reference to the Christmas Eve dinner: 'I … moved over to her [Luisa], at the corner opposite from the talkers. The arrival of the child had wound up isolating us, and I said to myself desperately: If he hadn't come, maybe we would have moved over there too' (*Memoirs*: 62; *Memorias*: 69).

Just as Leticia equates infancy with an undesirable dependency and lack of knowledge detrimental to self-autonomy, so too does she perceive the maternal function as keeping women dependent in patriarchal society, as perpetual symbolic daughters. Luisa comes to stand for an earlier generation of intellectual women who, like Chacel's own mother (see Lázaro 1994: 75, 128), subordinate their artistic talents and personal ambitions to husband and family (see *Memoirs*: 101; *Memorias*: 108). Immobilised by her role as the Madonna-like angel of the home (see *Memoirs*: 64; *Memorias*: 71), Luisa's anger may only be expressed circuitously (see *Memoirs*: 133–34, 140; *Memorias*: 140, 146–47). Unlike Leticia as writing subject, Luisa does not succeed in liberating her voice to contest patriarchal strictures.

With Leticia despatched by her natural father to Switzerland at the conclusion of *Memorias*, in order to protect her honour, she may not appear to fare much better. Likewise, her proclaimed adaptation to her new context (see *Memoirs*: 160; *Memorias*: 166) seems to contradict her declaration of resistance at the very beginning of the text (see *Memoirs*: 3; *Memorias*: 9). Ambiguity such as this, however, is common to the resolution of other female *Bildungsromane* written during the period immediately following the Civil War, in which the character appears to adapt externally to the world while maintaining an internal opposition (see Riddel 1988: 96). What is ultimately relevant is that whom Leticia erases from her life and text is don Daniel, whose suicide is barely referred to. The survivors are the natural and surrogate maternal figures and the daughter, Leticia.

'Good Enough' Mothers and Daughters

The patriarchal ideal of the 'good enough' mother that haunts Chacel's *Memorias* is dominant in a considerable number of texts dealing with the mother–daughter relationship. An extraordinary amount of ink is dedicated to the topic by Francoist ideologues, for whom it assumes, as already discussed, definite political connotations. In many respects, the premises espoused by the object–relations paediatrician, D.W. Winnicott, creator of the 'good enough' mother theory in the years subsequent to the Second World War, resemble those privileged by the Franco régime. The mother performs a social role which is essentially moral in that, by ensuring the mental health of her child, she also safeguards that of the community. The satisfactory development of the child as a creative being depends on the 'good enough' mother's 'almost complete adaptation' to its needs (Winnicott 1971: 10). Such devotion is conceived of as 'natural', with Winnicott emphasising the mother's intuitive understanding. Winnicott's essentialist vision is, moreover, particular to 'a traditional white, middle-class patriarchal structure' (Garner

1991: 80), unmindful of variations of race, class, and sexuality. His premises allow no room for the mother as a sexual being, nor do they recognise the possibility of her ambivalence and feelings of aggression towards her child (see Kahane 1993: 287), formulated as they are from the child's point of view.

In this section I propose to analyse three texts which privilege the 'good enough' mother theme, exacerbated by National-Catholicism and constantly reproduced according to different cultural interests (see Warner 1995: 3–23): *Isabel i Maria* (1991) by Mercè Rodoreda, *Adolescente* (1957, Adolescent) by Carmen Barberá (born Cuevas de Vinromá 1927) and Esther Tusquets' *El mismo mar de todos los veranos* (1978). All texts share the common context of upper-middle-class society pertinent to Winnicott's formulation of motherhood, but contrast society's ideal of the maternal with the lived reality of its mothers. They also highlight aspects of motherhood repressed by official representations and Winnicott's account: issues of female sexuality, the reality of maternal aggression, and the awareness that inherent in the 'good enough' mother syndrome is that of the 'good enough' daughter and woman's 'natural' lack. In recent years the theme of the 'good enough' mother and daughter has been given new resonances in two short stories by Almudena Grandes (born Madrid 1960): the fiercely parodic 'Amor de madre' (1996a, A Mother's Love) and the moving 'La buena hija' (1997, The Good Daughter) (see Arkinstall 2001).

Rodoreda's *Isabel i Maria*, published posthumously in 1991, is a dark narrative in which the voices of both mother and daughter, respectively named in the title, figure prominently. Begun by Rodoreda in the mid-1940s and unfinished at the time of her death in 1983, this 'matrix' or 'embryo' of her literary production (Arnau 1991: 11, 19) has a tripartite structure: firstly, a section in which different voices, including that of the mother, Isabel, alternate direct speech with interior monologue; secondly, the diary of Maria the daughter, which does not conform to a traditional diary structure; and thirdly, a much shorter epilogue, also focalised through Maria.

In *Isabel i Maria* the themes of adultery and imagined illegitimacy visible in Chacel's text are not only reworked in terms of the 'good enough' mother and daughter; here also the seduction by and of the daughter is transformed into her legalised abduction, with elements of the Demeter–Persephone myth. Isabel's story is revelatory of the social and legal obstacles confronting women born in the late nineteenth century into the propertied Catalan upper-middle class, obsessed with patrilineage and the preservation of male property rights. On the birth of her daughter Maria, Isabel has no legal redress against her husband Joaquim, who, suspecting that the infant has been fathered by his brother Lluís, exercises his official *patria potestas* and deprives her of any contact with the child until his death twelve years later. Isabel's lack of legal rights over her children, both born and unborn, is further stressed when Dr Riera, representative of the authority of the medical profession, refuses her the abortion that she desires on two occasions.[10]

By contravening the bourgeois marriage contract whereby a husband has exclusive legal rights to his wife's body (see Pateman 1988: 58), Isabel automatically forfeits all legitimate claim to her daughter. It is the very essence of adultery that disqualifies Isabel as a suitable mother, since 'an unfaithful wife, and usually by implication a bad mother, is an unassimilable conflation of what society insists should be separate categories and functions' (Tanner 1979: 12). Once her daughter has been removed from her care, Isabel loses all social meaning, with Riera commenting on her physical and psychic disintegration: 'I couldn't explain what kind of change had taken place. In a very short time she became as she is now: insignificant, as if trapped' (*Isabel i Maria*: 91). Such a statement confirms Jane Flax's point that the mother 'will cease to exist when her daughter leaves because she cannot be a mother without her reciprocal partner, a child' (1980: 33).

Just after Maria's birth Isabel's role as mother is usurped by Joaquim and the two brothers forbid her to see her daughter (see *Isabel i Maria*: 132–33). Irrespective of the fact that Lluís is as much to blame as Isabel in causing his brother moral injury, he is granted a weekly access to the child that the natural mother is not. The presence of this fraternal contract in Rodoreda's text serves to interrogate the paradigm of the Freudian family romance by pushing its precepts to their logical extreme. As in Chacel's text, behind the supposedly natural abandonment of the mother by the girl child and her voluntary identification with the father lies a power struggle that defends men's access to women, whether as fathers or husbands. Thus Joaquim tells Maria as an infant: 'Your mother is bad' and informs her later that her mother died on giving birth to her (*Isabel i Maria*: 119, 188). The influence of the brothers, concerned that the mother might 'taint' her daughter (see *Isabel i Maria*: 100, 140), ensures that the rift between these women is never surmounted. Nevertheless, the text still succeeds in undermining masculine authority by casting doubt on Maria's paternity, with her insisting as a young girl: 'I don't have a father, but I have two uncles, and my mother is dead' (*Isabel i Maria*: 189). Later, she significantly affirms her maternal origin (see *Isabel i Maria*: 105).

If the Freudian narrative is written from the child's point of view, eliding how the mother perceives her abandonment (see Hirsch 1989: 169), Rodoreda's text restores the maternal voice to the plot. Isabel's pain at the loss of her daughter is palpable in her following declaration: 'So as not to suffer, I tried to become indifferent, and I succeeded ... And after a few years ... I can't explain the delirium that overwhelmed me to have my daughter, my longing for her, my tenderness for that child' (*Isabel i Maria*: 133). Implicit in

10. For a summary of the legal and social restrictions pertaining to the married woman in the context relevant to Isabel, see Scanlon 1986: 126–37.

such an abduction of the daughter, protected by patriarchal law, is the myth of Demeter and Persephone. Rodoreda's tale is similar to that mythical account, where the grieving mother attempts to regain her lost daughter by denying humankind grain and thus the means to continue living.[11] In the case of Isabel, a modern Demeter, the 'food' essential for the continuation of the bourgeois family plot and line is the son by Lluís that Isabel vengefully aborts. There is another purpose to this action: keeping intact the family inheritance for Maria, Joaquim's legitimate daughter, and preserving a female economy at the expense of the male's. Thus Isabel states with regard to Lluís: 'Do you know why I haven't wanted to have your son? Because you don't love Maria … you'd like all this money … not to go to her. That is why I've aborted this after-thought that you so wanted' (*Isabel i Maria*: 149). Another Greek myth evoked by Isabel's action is that of Medea, whose anger against her husband leads to the killing of his children.[12]

The difficulties for women who desire to create their own stories counter to the patriarchal plot are manifest in both mother and daughter. Dr Riera's allegation that Isabel lacks principles is juxtaposed with his estimation that she is 'a little fanciful' or 'novel.lesca' (*Isabel i Maria*: 85). To be 'novel.lesca', Martín Gaite explains, is considered especially censurable in the case of the married woman, in that her fictitious embellishment of her life expresses her dissatisfaction with and covert rebellion against a physical and psychic cultural incarceration. Her 'loose' imagination and adulteration of reality equate her with the figure of the adulteress, as exemplified by Gustave Flaubert's heroine, Emma Bovary (see Martín Gaite 1985: 79–81). In Rodoreda's literary production this theme of the fallen woman is closely connected to the emergence of the woman artist or writer. While Isabel's transforming of her life into a novel, as Riera so disapprovingly states, is her only means of evading mediocrity (see *Isabel i Maria*: 85), the generation represented by Maria has a greater opportunity to engage in artistic expression. Apart from her aspirations to become a painter in Paris, Maria not only reads the stories of others, as is intimated by the familiarity with which the novel vendor greets her in Bordeaux (see *Isabel i Maria*: 254), but more importantly, as evident from her diary, she also writes. That this hesitant venturing of the woman artist into the public domain is perceived by patriarchal society as a threat and categorised as a dubious activity is symbolised by Maria's prostitution in Bordeaux. Adultery and prostitution constitute two ways, albeit restricted, of expressing disconformity with the principles of female containment upheld by the bourgeois family.

11. For feminist readings of the myth, see Grosz's exegesis of Irigaray (1989: 165); Hirsch 1989: 5–6, 34–36; Rich 1977: 238–40.
12. Another text that rewrites the myth of Medea from a feminist perspective is Soriano's short novel 'Medea' (1986).

Maria's removing of herself from her familial context with mother and uncle aligns her with those female modernist writers who, like Rodoreda herself, depart for Paris in 'a flight from the implicit expectation of marriage and motherhood' (Benstock 1989: 28). Her earlier rejection of potential motherhood, manifest in the episode in which she destroys the eggs of breeding pigeons (see *Isabel i Maria*: 173),[13] is an act that permits her to give birth to herself rather than to others. Thus she exclaims in Bordeaux: 'I have been my own mother. A mother who has adored her daughter, who has permitted her to do all she has desired … who has spoilt her to the point of vice, who has brought her up badly' (*Isabel i Maria*: 255). Through her former imaginary denial of paternal authority and her present repudiation of the principle of a judgemental phallic mother, Maria's fantasies, like Leticia's, seem to enable her, as within the paradigm outlined by Hirsch, to 'constitute a new self, free from familial constraints' (1989: 56).

However, as Maria's experiences in Paris and Bordeaux prove, changing countries does not enable her to escape patriarchal society. Although prostitution involves the contracting out of what appears to be that ultimate property in the person, the body, it also exemplifies the original sexual contract, in that, as Carole Pateman insists, 'the law of male sex-right is publicly affirmed' (1988: 208). Maria's departure for France resituates her within a masculine modernist economy that casts Paris as the prostitute that will offer men relief from 'a tyrannical feminine' (Benstock 1989: 27). Evidently, such gendered conceptual models cannot provide women with a different space.

Female sexuality is also the linch-pin in the treatment of the mother–daughter relationship developed in *Adolescente* by Barberá. This text is a little-known first-person narrative of the ambivalence and resentment felt by an adolescent daughter, Fernanda, towards her mother, Inés, who, making her daughter into a projection of herself, fails to provide her with adequate emotional support (see Mayans Natal 1991: 112). Such a situation exemplifies Nancy Chodorow's belief that an excessive empathy between mother and daughter may result in too stifling a relationship (Chodorow 1978). Abnegation can lead the mother to live her life through her daughter, whereas the daughter's fear of maternal omnipotence may provoke her repudiation of the maternal figure in order to forge an autonomous self (see Hirsch 1989: 131–34).

It is Fernanda's awakening sexuality, together with her inability to confide in her mother regarding her uncontrollable impulses, due to cultural proscriptions, that cause her to eschew both her mother as a sexual being and her own sexuality. Where Barberá's text proves especially interesting is in the attention given to the role played by a patriarchal symbolic in constructing a

---

13. This episode reappears in *La Plaça del Diamant* (1962) with Maria recast as Natàlia.

maternal model that erases the mother–daughter relationship. As María Jesús Mayans Natal indicates, within Fernanda's social context the generic word 'woman' implies potential mother, which in turn paradoxically foregrounds a female sexuality that contravenes cultural norms of feminine modesty (see 1991: 142). Thus Fernanda observes:

> To say 'women' was equivalent to acknowledging to my mother my future maternal condition. And also to letting her understand that I understood the natural processes behind my birth… It seemed shocking to me that, by means of one word, the bonds of affection linking us both could be wiped out; that is, that we ceased to be mother and daughter to become females. (*Adolescente*: 225)

The solution offered by the text conforms to the cultural exigencies for Spanish women in the late 1950s as well as anticipating more recent texts in which mother–daughter relationships are restored, rather than permanently ruptured. On the one hand, marriage is finally accepted by Fernanda as the means by which she may legitimately reconcile the conflict surrounding the issues of sexuality and maternity. On the other hand, she at last understands that her mother's lack of vital illusion is rooted in the cultural demand of feminine self-sacrifice. The narrative concludes with the inversion of the mother–daughter relationship as Fernanda adopts, for the first time, a protective role towards her mother. Significantly, it is through writing her story that Fernanda may be seen as representative of that second generation of post-civil-war women who begin to challenge the ideal that 'from the mother/will the daughter learn/to be suffering and patient' (Morales 1944: 63).

The figures of the 'good enough' mother and daughter, problematised by female sexuality, become more complex when eroticised by narrative written from a lesbian perspective. Within the conceptual boundaries of patriarchy love between mother and daughter is only permissible if subordinated to their allegiance to the father. Lesbian narrative, however, challenges this framework by reinstating women as one another's primary love object and theoretically privileging a relationship based on reciprocity rather than dominance. As a result, if Western patriarchal culture constructs itself in opposition to feminised bodies used in its interests, even more subject to repression will be the lesbian body, for contravening an institutionalised 'compulsory heterosexuality' (see Rich 1983).

In Tusquets' *El mismo mar de todos los veranos*, the theme of the female quest highlighted by critics (see Zatlin 1987, Lee-Bonanno 1988) is developed specifically in studies by Elizabeth Ordóñez (1984) and Mirella Servodidio (1987) in terms of the quest of mother and daughter for one another. Neither critic, however, explores in depth how such a search relates to the theme of lesbian sexuality evident in the relationship between the narrator, an anonymous middle-aged female literature teacher, and her adolescent student, Clara. Indeed, few analyses have engaged directly with the issue at all, in spite of the fact that this densely coded text presents a plethora of themes and symbols associated with lesbianism.

From the beginning of her first-person narrative, the protagonist (whom I shall call X) is described as constituting the 'twisted link in an irreproachable chain' (*The Same*: 14; *El mismo*: 22), a crooked element in the 'straight' world of a patriarchal, linear history dependent for its continuity on the allegiance of its mothers and daughters. Never 'good enough' for a mathematician daughter, Guiomar, who despises the humanities (see *The Same*: 110; *El mismo*: 140), nor for a mother who is a modern 'goddess of light, Athena tonans' (*The Same*: 17; *El mismo*: 26),[14] X identifies with the opposing figure of Demeter through her deprivation of filial and maternal love (see *The Same*: 24; *El mismo*: 34). Moreover, it is relevant that Demeter, as another name for the pre-Hellenic Triple Moon-goddess worshipped by the Amazons (see Graves 1972: 92–93), represents an autonomous female sexuality threatening to patriarchal order.

In her search for a maternal genealogy that might support rather than enchain her, X retreats to her childhood home, her beloved dead grandmother's apartment. This space, with which she identifies completely, obstinately preserves its tellurian character, reminiscent of J.J. Bachofen's disappeared matriarchal culture (see Rich 1977: 88), in spite of X's mother's successive renovations: 'both of us, the house and I, mute, passive, dark, stubborn, offered her [my mother] a doubly ferocious resistance, filled with sickly shadows, with unhealthy hidden dampnesses, with incredibly tender, secret underground places, with forbidden Dionysian pleasures' (*The Same*: 16; *El mismo*: 25). X's desire to recover her origins is discernible in her symbolic entrance into the home through an 'endless hallway, so long and dark' (*The Same*: 9; *El mismo*: 16–17). Reminiscent of the vaginal passage, it signals her hoped-for rebirth in an environment that not only constitutes a prolongation of her own body, but also a reencounter with a green, fertile world which has characteristics of the sea: 'I open the three balcony windows that face the avenue. It is like looking down from an unknown and craggy island … onto a slightly rough sea of tender green colors … if I half close my eyes … I see some remnant of the submerged city appear' (*The Same*: 9–10; *El mismo*: 17). Such a medium fuses two cogent symbols of humankind's origin and of lesbian identity: the sea and an Edenic green world (see Zimmerman 1990: 79–82). More important still, the implied darkness of the depths, whether subterranean or submarine, of this house/body, once again permits a linking of the theme of the mother–daughter relationship and lesbianism:

---

14. This mother closely resembles that in Tusquets' short story 'Carta a la madre' (1997, Letter to the Mother).

if Irigaray refers to the mother–daughter relation as 'the "dark continent" *par excellence* ... in the shadows of our culture' (1993a: 35), for Rich the 'lesbian possibility' constitutes 'an engulfed continent' (1983: 155). X's return to the homes of her past represents an attempt to salvage this vanished prehistory with its abandoned daughters and mothers.

Consequently, this particular female quest maps a path back to a womb-like space and time: from the lonely 'adolescent's bed' in the grandmother's apartment (*The Same*: 18; *El mismo*: 27), to the 'twin beds' in the children's bedroom shared with Clara in the grandmother's seaside house (*The Same*: 124; *El mismo*: 156), to known landscapes metamorphosed into mythical origins such as the Minotaur's labyrinth, monsters' caves and undines' grottoes (see *The Same*: 109, 121; *El mismo*: 139, 155), all of which are metaphors for the female sexual and reproductive organs. The emphasis on a sexual relationship between women paralleling that between mother and daughter does not here desexualise the lesbian relationship through a regression to the mother–infant relationship. Rather, it charges it with an intensity and agency denied it by masculine psychoanalytic theories, and reaffirms the 'lovable or desirable female body' which patriarchy obliges mother and daughter to renounce (Grosz 1995: 158, 165).[15] Moreover, although Clara has been seen as functioning solely as symbolic daughter in this lesbian couple (see Smith 1992: 102), both X and Clara perform the roles of mother and daughter at different narrative moments (see, for example, *The Same*: 120, 148; *El mismo*: 154, 189). Similarly, metaphors of gestation and birth abound with reference to the relationship between the two women (see *The Same*: 91, 145, 157; *El mismo*: 116, 184–85, 199).

The quest by X and Clara for a cultural geography that might reunite women with their bodies rather than alienating them – a theme also developed in Martín Gaite's *Nubosidad variable* in the following section – is articulated through the very structure and symbolic texture of this narrative. Considered to epitomise the features of *l'écriture féminine* or 'writing through the body' (see Cixous 1986, Guild 1993, Tsuchiya 1992), its meandering, syntactically complex sentences constitute a kind of formal experimentation which offers, Leigh Gilmore suggests, 'a way to make a lesbian subject position visible and not to disguise it' (1994: 207). Through her emotional and sexual relationship with Clara, X reclaims a language that not only articulates a previously unvoiced and unrecognised sexuality, but which is also particular to the context of mother and daughter:

> I lull her with incredible, strange words, words I never said ... not even to Guiomar when she was little ... words which I myself didn't know were in me, crouching in

---

15. For an example of how maternal imagery operates also on a sexual level in *El mismo mar*, see 103–7, orig. 132–37.

some dark corner of my consciousness, quietly waiting to be … spilled out thickly and sweetly in an unrecognizable voice that most certainly has to be mine … an unlearned language … [which] doesn't originate first in thought, next to be turned into sound by the voice: it is born from deep inside, and is already a voice. (*The Same*: 108, 123–24; *El mismo*: 138, 158)

The dénouement, whereby X returns to her husband and Clara leaves for Colombia, not only marks the differences between an older generation of women unable to break with a political and cultural past and a younger group, poised to move beyond the Franco régime three years after the dictator's death and embrace international activism (see Ordóñez 1991: 123). It also presents the more sobering message that, in order to assume openly a lesbian identity at that particular moment, it is necessary to leave Spain. The sexual identities of real and symbolic mothers and daughters cannot survive in a social climate which fails to give lesbianism adequate cultural validation (see Gould Levine 1983: 304–5).[16]

Writing Mothers and Daughters

One of the recurrent themes in women's writing from the 1970s onwards, with their participation in the workforce now a common reality, is the conflict arising over the possible reconciliation of motherhood and a profession, frequently one involving writing. As Susan Suleiman has stipulated in 'Writing and Motherhood', women's concerns revolve around 'motherhood as obstacle or source of conflict and motherhood as link, as source of connection to work and world' (1985: 362).[17] The complex nuances of these attitudes towards maternity and work are explored in women's narratives, exposing a situation which has culturally fragmented women to a greater or lesser degree depending on diverse historical moments, making them less of a mother if they work and less of a person in a competitive consumer society if they choose to mother exclusively.

One such text is Martín Gaite's *Retahílas* (1974, Enumerations), a precursor in many ways of *Nubosidad variable*. Via the characters of Eulalia, a childless woman, and Lucía, a mother, the choice of professional interests versus

---

16. For a summary of the evolution of social attitudes towards lesbianism in Spain, see Prieto 1983. Same-sex relationships were not granted legal recognition in Spain until 1994 (see *La Nueva España*, 3 April 1994: 36). For an interesting point of comparison with Tusquets' text, see 'Primer Amor' (1997, First Love) by Cristina Peri Rossi (born Montevideo 1941).
17. The conflict surrounding literary production versus reproduction is an outstanding feature in the work of Soriano, manifest in her interviews, fictional narrative, and her autobiographic/biographic *Testimonio materno* (1985, Maternal Testimony), where her own creative life is read in the context of the life and death of her son. Regarding Soriano, see Arkinstall 1991.

motherhood is debated, fictionalising, as Catherine Davies puts it, 'the gap between the theory and the practice of women's liberation' (1991: 211). Rejecting the tendency, represented by Eulalia, to consider motherhood an outdated, and even politically suspect, option for women, given the significance it assumes during the dictatorship, Martín Gaite revindicates it as a valid choice, as the following exchange between Eulalia and Lucía makes clear: ' "In Spain, Lucía, we all know full well, you cannot do the two things, either you're a mother or a person". But she was outraged by such a dogmatic alternative ... we could invent something different from what we saw around us, that was the wonderful thing, a way of being a mother that had no need to exclude being a person' (trans. Davies 1991: 211, *Retahílas*: 145–46). By challenging the dogmatism of the 'either/or' solution advocated by the feminist Eulalia, reminiscent of a climate of political intolerance, Martín Gaite speaks for a pluralism that does not limit women's lives by equating mother with 'non-person'.

A more problematic vision of the demands of motherhood is presented in *La enredadera* (1984, The Vine) by Josefina Aldecoa, published ten years later. The title itself symbolises women's maternal potential, as Aldecoa's following comment makes clear: 'I have endeavoured to portray one of the most pressing problems of the feminine condition: woman's very femininity, her very ability to be a mother is her own vine' (Aldecoa in Alborg 1993: 206). By means of its two protagonists, Clara and Julia, the text examines the similarities and differences in the attitudes of these women towards motherhood, framed by their distinct historical periods: late nineteenth-century and contemporary Spain, respectively. Given that Julia, a sociologist and writer, is the mother of a son, the mother–daughter relationship is pursued solely with regard to Clara and her daughter Lucía.

From the beginning of her first-person narrative, Clara's attitude towards her daughter is coloured with a culturally engendered ambivalence. Although loved by her older husband, Clara is the victim of a patriarchal society that values male offspring over daughters. Her feeling of failure at having produced a female child contributes to her postpartum depression, which Aldecoa's text documents explicitly (see *La enredadera*: 41). Furthermore, the mother giving birth perceives her child as a parasite that inflicts violence on her host and threatens her with nonexistence, evidenced in the abrupt slippage from the first-person 'I' to the third person of 'being' in the following passage: 'I had a vague premonition that I was going to die. It seemed to me that that tearing of flesh, that brutal beginning of a new life, could only lead to the death of the being that had sheltered, fed and created it at her own expense' (*La enredadera*: 40). At no point in the narrative does Lucía offer her perspective, remaining silent. Clara's words, however, provide another possible reason for Lucía's attraction to a religious life apart from the estrangement existing between mother and daughter: nuns, although sharing the encloistered condition of all women under patriarchy, are perceived by the mother as beings 'who aren't women ... who haven't allowed their bodies to be seized, torn, destroyed internally and then abandoned' (*La enredadera*: 172–73).

Perhaps the text which best illustrates the theme of writing mothers and daughters is Martín Gaite's best-seller, *Nubosidad variable* (1992). Its coprotagonists, Sofía and Mariana, reinitiate a lost friendship through the medium of writing and, in so doing, begin a journey towards a recovery of selves devastated by acting as mirrors for others. In Sofía's case, it is her unhappy marriage and patriarchally written maternal function that reduces her to being 'a full-length mirror that reflected them back' (*Variable*: 30; *Nubosidad*: 40), robbing her of her individuality; in Mariana's, her profession as a psychoanalyst demands that she operate within masculinist theoretical structures which leave her internally fragmented and unable to effectively 'mother' the derelict beings attending her clinic.

The writing generated by Sofía and Mariana for one another constitutes a dialogue reinforced by the very format of the novel, primarily in the second person singular and reliant on the so-called 'feminine' discourses of the journal, diary, and letter. It fulfils Irigaray's vision of a female symbolic with the power to acknowledge the feminine, and consequently the body of the (m)other, based on, as Margaret Whitford puts it, 'a dynamic exchange between interlocutors which can transfigure flesh and blood' (Whitford 1991: 49).[18] Such a language created by women and revelatory of their specificity would give them, Irigaray considers, a 'space-time' and 'house of language' or shelter that they might inhabit on their own terms (Irigaray 1993c: 116, 107). Thus language itself, rather than woman, would become the object of exchange, enabling women to function as subjects in, rather than sacrifices to, the social order (see Whitford 1991: 52). Distinguishing between a form of expression specific to the speaker (*langage*) and a masculine discourse (*langue*), Irigaray stresses: 'We have to discover a language [*langage*] which does not replace the bodily encounter, as paternal language [*langue*] attempts to do, but which can go along with it, words which do not bar the corporeal, but which speak corporeal' (Irigaray 1993a: 43).

In *Nubosidad variable*, the patriarchal attempt to 'bar the corporeal' is present on both a literal and a symbolic level. Sofía's entry into the adult world,

---

18. It should be noted that the relationship between Sofía and Mariana is both similar and dissimilar to the Italian practice of *affidamento* or entrustment (see Giorgio 1997: 222–41). Whereas *affidamento* stresses a vertical relationship between a more powerful symbolic mother and disciple daughter that would give women the status of subjects, *Nubosidad* stresses that the relationship in question is horizontal and reciprocal (a factor stressed by Whitford 1991: 78 in her exegesis of Irigaray), and privileges the role of a female symbolic in women's acquisition of an active, desiring subjectivity. See also Irigaray (1993e: 193–95) for her views on *affidamento*.

marked by her confrontation with the male mathematics teacher, demands that she abandon her free experimentation with a language specific to her in favour of a metalanguage of rigid formulae (Irigaray's *langue*) which reduce the subject to object, immobilising the body within an economy of death and decay: 'Now, if I say "logarithm", "digit", "square root" or "equation", I see a lot of little grey, articulated sticks creeping across the carpet like a procession of worms ... they seethe at my left side (overwhelmed, I've lain down on the carpet)... I can't move, I'm surrounded' (*Variable*: 104; *Nubosidad*: 115).

The Irigarayan concept of a language specific to its user is evident in Sofía's recounting of the linguistic games she used to play as a child, where meaning and identity are transformed through a redistribution of formal elements and contexts. Particularly relevant is her description of such experimentation in terms of different combinations of feminine dress: 'She used to enjoy inventing words and taking to pieces words she'd heard for the first time, making different combinations with the dismantled pieces... Long words were like dresses with a bodice, waistcoat and skirt' (*Variable*: 103; *Nubosidad*: 114). Here the topos of language as clothes for the mind assumes special significance with regard to the concept of the creation of a female symbolic, reinforced by the child's emotional and physical identification with the philologist or lover of words: 'And she gave wings to the words because she was their friend, and because being someone's friend means wanting them to be able to fly. She drew another, more detailed version of the philologist and this time [she] had blond plaits. Behind [her] stood an angel ... who was pinning a pair of silvery wings on [her] shoulders' (*Variable*: 103; *Nubosidad*: 114).[19] That the recreation of a linguistic form in one's own corporeal image empowers its bearer or 'wearer' to fly evokes the kind of feminine Imaginary envisioned by Hélène Cixous: 'the site ... of identifications of an ego no longer given over to an image defined by the masculine ... but rather inventing forms for women on the march, or ... "in flight", so that ... women will go forward by leaps in search of themselves' (Cixous 1981: 52). If, in *Nubosidad variable*, words become butterflies caught by the philologist or 'butterfly-catcher' (*Variable*: 103; *Nubosidad*: 114), they are also a 'paper plane' (*Variable*: 286; *Nubosidad*: 301) which, once released, transports its traveller to unknown destinations, borne by the uncontrollable force of the writing process (see *Variable*: 265; *Nubosidad*: 278).

Linguistic invention and narration constitute a magic refuge and land of friendship for the younger Mariana and Sofía (see *Variable*: 138, 204; *Nubosidad*: 150, 216). Years later, literature becomes a similar refuge for an unhap-

---

19. Given Sofía's re-creation of the philologist in her own image, the subversive implications of the text become more apparent if the translator's masculine pronouns and possessive adjectives are replaced by my feminine ones, indicated in the square brackets.

pily married Sofía and her small daughter, Encarna, whose very name, 'Incarnate', evokes the concept of embodiment. Their bond is founded not so much on physical factors as on a shared love of words (see *Variable*: 276; *Nubosidad*: 290). It is, however, an imaginary world into which Sofía cannot fully enter, due to her responsibilities as an adult and her relationship with her husband, creating a situation corroborative of the double consciousness of the mother, who experiences a 'split self-image' when negotiating her interests with husband and child (Ferguson 1984: 163). Threatened by a world of social roles, the exclusive nature of the love between Sofía and Encarna, as with the mothers and daughters in Chacel's and Tusquets' texts, must be kept hidden, resulting in their using a coded language (see *Variable*: 277–78; *Nubosidad*: 291).

The relationship between Sofía and her own mother, also named Encarna, is even more fraught with difficulties. Encarna feels imprisoned by her socially legitimate roles of wife and mother, which produce in her a feeling of worthlessness and sterility (see *Variable*: 332; *Nubosidad*: 348). Her return from the dead as a ghost parallels the status of women in life as the 'shadowy nurses' of patriarchy alluded to by Irigaray (1993d: 83). In an inversion of the daughter's lament for and inculpation of the mother penned by Irigaray (1981: 60–61), Encarna acknowledges that her treatment of her daughter has been dominated by an icy coldness, adversarial surveillance, and excessive preoccupation with time (see *Variable*: 333–34; *Nubosidad*: 347–50). Contrary to the Irigarayan account, however, Encarna and Sofía do succeed, one in an after–life and the other through her dreams, in finally understanding and loving each other, with Sofía describing their reconciliation in terms of her giving birth to her own mother (see *Variable*: 364; *Nubosidad*: 381).

Just as pregnancy and motherhood are institutions that precipitate Sofía into a loveless marriage with Eduardo and mark the moment from which she ceases to write (see *Variable*: 188; *Nubosidad*: 201), it is with her abandoning of the marital bed for a room of her own that the writing process once more begins to flow. Frequent forays into the open space of the street finally culminate in her leaving her husband's house for her dead mother's home, bequeathed to her own daughter Encarna. Known as the 'refuge', it witnesses Sofía's above-mentioned spiritual reconciliation with her mother and estranged daughter (see Chapter XVII). It is from this physical and psychic point that Sofía will travel to the seaside town of Cádiz in the mythical South, to meet with Mariana and continue their written dialogue in person. A similar series of displacements traces Mariana's trajectory towards self-fulfillment. Her struggle against an excess of analytical thought in her professional life materialises in her increasingly frustrated attempts to write an academic essay on the subject of the erotic: a process which demands the hierarchical relationship of mind over body. Consequently, Mariana rejects her 'room with the couch' (*Variable*: 207; *Nubosidad*: 219) in the metropolis of Madrid and embarks on a physical and metaphorical journey in search of her buried past.

That the recreation of a language inseparable from the body is, fundamentally, an erotic process, intent on uncovering a hidden emotional and linguistic corpus, is captured in Mariana's description of her writing process as a 'solitary strip-tease' in front of a mirror (*Variable*: 116; *Nubosidad*: 128). The concept of writing as represented by Mariana is, however, neither essentialist nor transcendental. On the contrary, writing constitutes the subject and her inner space, in a sensual act of self-possession that is in no way predetermined and always provisional: '[It] allows me to advance more easily through a territory which I define and choose at the same time as I touch and explore it, which involves exploring myself … For this territory is revealed and takes shape as I write … with my writing I engender my own homeland, undisputed, albeit subject to change' (*Variable*: 118; *Nubosidad*: 130).

An imaginary space in which women may live involves creating a corpus of signification founded on the specificity of the female body. In *Nubosidad variable* it is the medium of literature that effects the transformation experienced by Sofía and Mariana, with language described as acting both as birth canal and bridge, giving them life at the same time as reconnecting them: 'Copying out fragments of a novel that still illuminates your dreams, Sofía … would be another channel [birth canal] open between you and me … an aerial bridge linking our memories' (*Variable*: 300; *Nubosidad*: 316). Their writing relationship has led to their becoming subjects who, like Rosi Braidotti's figuration of the nomad (see Braidotti 1994), may elaborate a space which enables them to set up house anywhere. Such a concept is manifest in the epilogue in their engrossed discussion on the Cádiz shores of one another's narratives: a process which will result in the text of *Nubosidad variable* itself.

It is also the reciprocal symbolic mother–daughter relationship between the two women that has empowered Sofía, just prior to this episode, to repair the estrangement experienced with her own mother and daughter. The latter's childhood dream that she might be her mother's 'captain' and take her to a 'fairy-tale house' by the sea to live from writing stories (see *Variable*: 282–83; *Nubosidad*: 296), although symbolically fulfilled in the concluding scene through Mariana, has also partially materialised when Encarna informs her mother that she has had a book accepted for publication. There is the suggestion that Encarna becomes the mother of her own mother, as much through her emotional support of her as through Sofía's hope, evident in her following words, that Encarna's mind will be the metaphorical womb which will preserve her story through writing: 'I … stay there for a few moments with my head pressed against her young belly, in which the continuation of these memoirs may one day build its nest' (*Variable*: 362; *Nubosidad*: 379). It is such a reforging of the bond between women that constitutes the prerequisite for another system of signification that will recognise patriarchy's unacknowledged debt to the mother (see Irigaray 1993b: 127): a feature that is specifically addressed by the narratives examined in the following section.

Mothers and Daughters as Subjects in History

From the early 1970s onwards, and with increasing momentum after Franco's death in 1975, there appears a proliferation of texts engaged in recovering women as historical subjects. Indebted to second-wave feminism in Spain, this current is also contemporaneous with the development of scholarship on women's history as outlined by Mary Nash, who documents the concern with remedying a 'historical amnesia on women' and with 'including women as active collective agents in the dynamics of historical change' (Nash 1991: 382). In general terms, in women's narratives that portray mother–daughter relationships, those produced from the 1970s to the early 1980s address more specifically women's relationship with history, in the form of biographical studies and family sagas that establish a female genealogy or matrilinear identity. The early 1990s witness a greater impetus to rewrite myths pertaining to mothers and daughters, with a tendency to represent them as heroic saviours of humanity. A more recent development has been a demythification of maternal stereotypes hitherto eschewed.

Texts representative of a more specific engagement with the female historical subject are two biographies by Mercedes Formica which respectively privilege the figures of daughter and mother: *La hija de don Juan de Austria* (1973, The Daughter of don Juan of Austria) and *María de Mendoza. Solución a un enigma amoroso* (1979, María of Mendoza. Solution to a Love Mystery) (see Alborg 1993: 129–36). These women are not so much presented in terms of their kinship, but as historical subjects who negotiate, to the best of their ability, the power politics of their era. Formica's accounts reveal how the ideologies that shape the feminine during the sixteenth and seventeenth centuries continue to pervade her own society (see Leggott 1998).

The histories of three generations of middle-class women from Barcelona, all called Ramona or Mundeta, are set against the historical events of late nineteenth- and twentieth-century Spain in *Ramona, adéu* (1972, Goodbye Ramona) by Montserrat Roig (Barcelona 1946–1991). With the intimist first person marking the grandmother's account, presented in diary form, the third person generally given to the mother, and a mixture employed for the granddaughter, the novel is but one example of many in Roig's work of a 'matrilineal and matronymical her-story' (Davies 1994:

28).[20] Defined by one critic as a 'contrasaga', another describes it as an 'exaltation of genealogy as a testimony of women's pasts hidden within private writings and memory' (Dupláa 1996: 114). The lives of the grandmother and mother are beset by unrealised potential and rebellions frustrated by marriage and societal norms. Only the granddaughter will bid farewell, like Tusquets' Clara, to a patriarchal Spain, so as to avoid repeating a similar pattern. The limitations with which the women must contend are reinforced by lack of communication among them, preventing them from forming the kind of alliance that liberates Mariana and Sofía, and which is partially realised in the following text.

The heterogeneity of women's voices in history, stressed by a title which foregrounds the collective rather than the individual, is the subject of *Otras mujeres y Fabia* (1982, Other Women and Fabia) by Carmen Gómez Ojea (born Gijón 1945). The protagonist, Fabia, is a thirty-six-year-old former teacher of literature who leaves her profession on becoming financially independent. Through her observations of her female working-class neighbours, and middle-class friends and relatives, Fabia's open-ended text revindicates 'women's work', giving domesticity its own history by documenting the rich detail of mothers' lives. Its iconoclastic, poetic style accords special attention to the oral accounts told by women to their children. Unrecognised by History, such narratives form a 'history from below' (Stuart 1994: 56), an 'umbilical cord' which conveys 'an untampered-with history ... more instructive and revealing than a hundred round tables' (*Otras mujeres*: 80). With fixed patriarchal frames and canons under constant revision, Fabia becomes a symbolic mother who brings her female ancestors back to life in order to return to them their own voice. Her story records not only a 'literary heritage' but also her 'literal genealogy' (Castillo 1990: 106), which stretches back to the Great Mother herself (see *Otras mujeres*: 17). Similarly, a symbolic mother–daughter relationship occurs in *La única libertad* (1982, The Only Freedom) by Marina Mayoral (born Mondoñedo, Lugo 1942), where the protagonist engages in reconstructing her family history in Galicia (see Zatlin 1987: 31). Yet another text focalised through a daughter who defends her mother in nontraditional terms (see Cipljauskaité 1988: 77) is the lyrical *Toda la casa era una ventana* (1983, All the House Was a Window) by Emma Cohen (Barcelona, date of birth unknown).

20. Another text by Roig which deals with the mother–daughter relationship is *L'hora violeta* (1980a, The Violet Hour), while the first short story in *Molta roba i poc sabó ... i tan neta que la volen* (1971, Lots of Washing and Not Much Soap) focuses on the recovery of a grandmother's life by her granddaughter (see Davies 1994: 61, 29–30 respectively). More recently, a similar text in which a granddaughter collaborates in recording the memories of her literary grandmother is Paloma Ulacia Altolaguirre and Concha Méndez's *Memorias habladas, memorias armadas* (1990, Spoken Memories, Assembled Memories).

A prevalent theme from the 1990s onwards is the rewriting of patriarchal myths of femininity so as to restore the agency of the mother–daughter relationship and recover maternal power. An earlier instance of this recoding of foundational texts is *Os habla Electra* (1975, Here Speaks Electra) by Concha Alós (born Valencia 1922), where the first-person narrative by the daughter, Electra, recalls a lost and fertile world embodied by her mother, 'the archetypal Great Mother' (Lee-Bonanno 1987: 95), whose land is destroyed by patriarchal agents. From initially turning to the figure of the father to grant her legitimacy in this new order, Electra comes to identify with her mother through her own sexuality and pregnancy, reinstating her as a 'protean, mythical, and even divine creature' and reasserting her 'matrilinear identity' (Ordóñez 1991: 108, 110). Although the eventual destruction of the patriarchal world seems to bring with it the promise of recreating a matriarchal society, this hope is short-lived. Electra emerges as the sole survivor facing an uncertain destiny.

Striking resemblances to Alós' text may be observed in the best-seller *Temblor* (1990, Quivering) by Rosa Montero (born Madrid 1951). Forced to abandon, with the onset of menstruation, the home of her mother, murdered to facilitate this rupture, the protagonist Agua Fría enters the hierarchical society of the Talapot. Ruled by priestesses who found their 'natural' superiority on women's ability to be 'mothers ... creators of life' (*Temblor*: 53), this gift, however, has been subordinated to their desire for power over all those categorised as other, including men (see Gascón Vera 1992: 21). Escaping from the Talapot, Agua Fría sets forth to save a world which is being consumed by 'mists of nonexistence and forgetfulness' (*Temblor*: 85), engendered by the Talapot's denial of historical change, and the real and metaphorical death of the mother (see *Temblor*: 223). That contact and cooperation with the other, and not its mutilation and assimilation, holds the key to the renewal of the world is stressed with Agua Fría's pregnancy, the result of her union with Zao, member of the patriarchal tribe of the primitive Uma. The novel concludes with the protagonist bringing about the fall of the Talapot, but leaving once again, with her soon-to-be-born child, to effect an ongoing revolution on the margin of established social structures.[21]

The mother/daughter as saviour of the world reappears in a different guise in *Gabriel: Coda final* (1991, Gabriel: Final Coda) by María Dolores Boixadós (Sort, Lérida, date of birth unknown). Originally written in 1969 with the title 'La madre' (The Mother), the novel narrates how an older woman, herself a mother and grandmother, rescues children from abuse and death (see Alborg 1993: 186–89). With the work of this archetypal figure facilitated by wings, her quasi transformation into an angel reworks the

---

21. For further studies of *Temblor*, see Davies 1994: 150–61, Glenn 1991a, Zatlin 1992.

nineteenth-century feminine ideal of the angel in the home, with woman's traditional ministering qualities here denouncing state indifference to disadvantaged others. Boixadós' text thus advocates the kind of premises espoused by Sara Ruddick, for whom 'maternal thinking' involves a treasuring of lives and a 'preservative love' intrinsically opposed to the abuse and destruction of others (Ruddick 1984a, 1984b). More recently, the association of the angel with the mother–daughter relationship has been given original nuances in 'La niña sin alas' (1997, The Girl Without Wings) by Paloma Díaz-Mas (born Madrid 1954).

Perhaps the writer whose work most consistently investigates and demythifies the mother–daughter relationship to date is Josefina Aldecoa, author of a trilogy dealing with the Spanish female historical subject in the twentieth century. The first volume, *Historia de una maestra* (1990, Story of a Schoolteacher), has been described by Martín Gaite as 'a story of maternity' in which the love of the mother, Gabriela, for her daughter Juana, 'is ever-present' (1993a: 237). It constitutes a narrative written by Gabriela for Juana so that the daughter might understand, from her mother's perspective, the momentous events of the Second Republic and Civil War, survived only by the women in the family (see also Alborg 1993, Soliño 1995). Not guilty of any 'representative slippage from "mothers" to "women"' (Daly and Reddy 1991: 1), Aldecoa's *Historia* examines the mother as woman also, in all her multiple facets, devaluing neither the one nor the other. The dialogue between mother and daughter that implicitly structures Aldecoa's *Historia* is made explicit in the second volume of the trilogy, *Mujeres de negro* (1994, Women in Black), which alternates the voices, in first person, of Gabriela and a now adult Juana. Its context is the aftermath of the Civil War for those who supported the Republicans, the exile of mother and daughter in Mexico, following Gabriela's second marriage to Octavio, and the return of Juana to Francoist Spain. The last novel in the trilogy, *La fuerza del destino* (1997, The Force of Destiny), continues this dialogic principle in that the voices of mother and daughter frame or embrace the entire novel.

What makes *La fuerza* such an extraordinary text, however, is that it privileges the voice of the ageing, and later dying, mother. By so doing, it contravenes powerful cultural prejudices that render women, and old women in particular, invisible and unheard. As Rachel Josefowitz Siegel has signalled, '*Old woman* is *mother* and *mother* is *old*; *old woman* is other. *Old woman* is a role, an image, a stereotype – she is not a person. *Old woman* is Crone, Old Witch, Old Hag... *Old woman* is not me; *old woman* is not what I want to be' (1990: 90). If in 1991 Brenda Daly and Maureen Reddy write that 'few fictional or theoretical works *begin* with the mother in her own right, from her own perspective, and those that do seldom hold fast to a maternal perspective' (1991: 2–3), Aldecoa's first-person account may be seen as indicative of an incipient move in recent Spanish narrative by women to represent the older woman so as to express the realities of her embodied experience. Thus *La fuerza* is symptomatic of a shift from matrophobia and somatophobia, even amongst feminist mothers and daughters, to a genuine wish to engage with the figure of the mother.[22]

To a greater extent than its predecessors, *La fuerza* is unusual also for Gabriela's detailed analysis of her relationship with her own mother and daughter. Breaching canonical divisions between private and historical, personal and collective, Gabriela's narrative creates a text in which maternity is not confined to female experience but becomes emblematic of the engendering of a democratic nation: 'The day on which the Republic was proclaimed ... our hope bore a double meaning, the birth of our daughter and that of a new historical period' (*La fuerza*: 157). Similarly, Gabriela's death coincides with the 1982 victory of the Socialist Party in Spain, with the newly born democracy serving to continue her life and ideals.

Gabriela's political dissidence against the Franco régime is carried over to her private life, in her frank discussion of her sexuality and desire. Aldecoa's text challenges images of maternity that disacknowledge the mother as an agent of desire, to address the type of questions raised by Flax: 'Yet what of the mother's desire? How does it shift between child and (adult) lover? ... What images do daughters have of their mothers as sexual beings, of passionate attachments that exclude ... them?' (Flax 1993: 150). Aldecoa's text privileges both the mother's and the daughter's attitude towards such 'passionate attachments'. On the one hand, the close relationship between Gabriela and the young Juana, acknowledged in the mother's statement that 'my daughter was my anguish and my happiness. An obsession' (*La fuerza*: 89), is marred by Gabriela's love for Octavio, which arouses feelings of jealousy in Juana. Although Octavio lavishes care and attention on his stepdaughter, it is the physicality of his love for Gabriela, as she herself points out, that separates daughter from mother (see *La fuerza*: 122). On the other hand, Gabriela's reiterated reminiscences of her sexual pleasure with Octavio are a testimony to the fact that women's desire for love and pleasure is not incompatible with old age nor conditional on their reproductive ability: 'If I had loved arms encircling my body. If I had a mouth clasped to mine, why would I need the horizon and sun? ...Only my lover and I ... plunged into the abyss of our prodigious company' (*La fuerza*: 140).

The mother–daughter relationship in *La fuerza* problematises other myths pertaining to the maternal. These mythifications either present women's dif-

---

22. Regarding matrophobia and somatophobia, see Hirsch 1989: 165–66. For other texts contemporaneous with Aldecoa's that present the theme of the ageing mother, but from the daughter's perspective, see Martín Gaite's *Lo raro es vivir* (1996, The Strangeness of Life) and 'La hija predilecta' (1997, The Favourite Daughter) by Soledad Puértolas (born Zaragoza 1947).

ferences as a source of alienation among them or threaten to elide these differences by stressing that all women are essentially the same. What is a complex dynamics of continuity and difference is successfully negotiated in the mother–daughter relationship between Gabriela and Juana. At one point Gabriela exclaims with regard to herself and Juana: 'How similar and yet how different our lives are!' (*La fuerza*: 44). The most marked similarities and differences lie not in their attitudes towards love, sexuality, and maternity, but in their political beliefs. Although Juana clearly continues Gabriela's struggle for a democratic Spain, where mother and daughter diverge is in their vision of how best to achieve such an aim (see *La fuerza*: 62). By openly presenting the differences existing between Gabriela and Juana, even within a common political ground, *La fuerza* opens up for debate 'the simplistic claims that the gender-based continuity of identity between mother and daughter is relatively unproblematic or positive' (Flax 1993: 151), and qualifies the feminist utopia of a sisterhood between women, irrespective of generation, race, class, and other socio-historical factors.

Neither is Juana nor Gabriela presented in a unilateral position as exclusively daughter and mother. While Juana is daughter to Gabriela and mother of Miguel, Gabriela also describes herself as daughter, grandmother, and prospective great-grandmother. The survival of Gabriela's ideals that this genealogy affirms shows the mother to be the powerful guardian of the links between the generations, the protector of an unbroken symbolic umbilical cord defying patriarchal castration; thus Gabriela declares: 'There is an umbilical cord which I have never cut and which joins the three of us, Juana, Miguel and Gabriela. And which one day will join me, without my seeing it, to Miguel's children and grandchildren' (*La fuerza*: 112).

Indeed, pervading Gabriela's recollections is her own dead mother, whose words, presence, and tenderness still sustain her in life: 'Even now, I can hear my mother's steps on the stairs of this house ... I can hear her footsteps, the caress of her soft fingers tucking me up ... Even now' (*La fuerza*: 36). As an ageing woman, however, her evocations of her mother are also tinged with guilt in that she now recognises the debt, ignored by patriarchy, that she owes, and regrets her inability to establish a relationship of equality founded, not on duty, but on pleasure: 'I have a debt with my mother. I never gave her anything but work. I asked her for help, company. But I never gave her back anything happy, a party, a trip' (*La fuerza*: 92). It is due to her own physical decline that Gabriela, as dependent as a child in the geriatric clinic and fed by another kind of bottle, this time intravenous, can acknowledge her intense need of her long-dead mother, repaying her debt to her mother through her narrative: 'I will never again be able to move by myself ... I need a woman. I can't find her ... My mother. Mummy, Mummy' (*La fuerza*: 218). In this sense, Adrienne Rich's affirmation that childbirth may serve as a common bridge of understanding between mothers and daughters (see 1977: 220) is expanded to include aspects of existence formerly little expressed in literature and avoided within the wider narratives of our lives. Gabriela thus becomes a hero representative of all human beings, who must enter into the inevitable and unequal battle with diminishing physical powers and death.

Postcript

In 1997 an anthology entitled *Madres e hijas* (Mothers and Daughters) and edited by Laura Freixas (born Barcelona 1958) sees its tenth edition in just one year. Conceived on the occasion of the birth of Freixas' daughter, this collection is valuable in that it offers a range of texts that specifically address different features of the relationship between mothers and daughters. Above all, it stands as proof of the increasing prevalence, importance, and popularity in Spain of issues that open up for debate the complex dynamics of this relationship. These pages have attempted to outline a genealogy of the mother–daughter theme that might serve as an introduction to this little-researched topic in Spanish women's narrative. It is hoped that it will sow the seeds for further studies, with poetry and theatre written by women constituting other fertile fields of investigation.

Note

My heartfelt thanks to Adalgisa Giorgio and Mercedes Maroto-Camino, symbolic mothers during the gestation of this chapter.

Bibliography

Ackelsberg, Marsha (1991) *Free Women of Spain: Anarchism and the Struggle for the Emancipation of Women*. Bloomington: Indiana University Press.
Alborg, Concha (1993) *Cinco figuras en torno a la novela de posguerra*. Madrid: Libertarias.
Alcalde, Carmen (1996) *Mujeres en el franquismo*. Barcelona: Flor del Viento.
Aldecoa, Josefina (1984) *La enredadera*. Barcelona: Seix Barral.
——— (1990) *Historia de una maestra*. 2nd ed. Barcelona: Anagrama.
——— (1994) *Mujeres de negro*. 1st ed. Barcelona: Anagrama.
——— (1997) *La fuerza del destino*. 1st ed. Barcelona: Anagrama.
Alós, Concha (1975) *Os habla Electra*. Barcelona: Plaza y Janés.

Altolaguirre, Paloma Ulacia and Concha Méndez (1990) *Memorias habladas, memorias armadas*. Madrid: Mondadori España.

Arkinstall, Christine (1991) 'Elena Soriano y la recreación de la historia' in *Alaluz*, Year xxiii, no. 2, 1991, 59–66.

――― (1997) 'Rhetorics of Maternity and War in Angela Figuera's Poetic Work' in *Revista Canadiense de Estudios Hispánicos*, vol. 21, no. 3, 1997, 457–78.

――― (2001) '"Good-Enough" Mothers and Daughters in Almudena Grandes' Short Fiction' in *Anales de la Literatura Española Contemporánea*, vol. 26, no. 2, 2001, 1–23.

Arnau, Carme (1991) 'Pròleg' in Rodoreda 1991, 11–31.

Balaguer, Soledad (1977) 'Contracepción a la española: Todas somos delincuentes' in *Vindicación Feminista*, no. 7, 1, January 1977, 41–43.

Barberá, Carmen (1957) *Adolescente*. Barcelona: Plaza y Janés.

Barrachina, María (1991) 'Ideal de la mujer falangista. Ideal falangista de la mujer' in *Las mujeres y la Guerra Civil Española*. Madrid: Ministerio de Asuntos Sociales, Instituto de la Mujer, 211–17.

Benstock, Shari (1989) 'Expatriate Modernism' in Mary Lynn Broe and Angela Ingram (eds) *Women's Writing in Exile*. Chapel Hill and London: The University of North Carolina Press, 20–40.

Boixadós, María Dolores (1991) *Gabriel: Coda final*. Barcelona: Hogar del Libro.

Bordons, Teresa and Susan Kirkpatrick (1992) 'Chacel's *Teresa* and Ortega's Canon' in *ALEC*, no. 17, 1992, 283–99.

Borreguero, Concha, Elena Catena, Consuelo de la Gándara, and María Salas (1986) *La mujer española: de la tradición a la modernidad (1960–1980)*. Madrid: Tecnos.

Braidotti, Rosi (1994) *Nomadic Subjects. Embodiment and Sexual Difference in Contemporary Feminist Theory*. New York: Columbia University Press.

Capel Martínez, Rosa María (1986a) *El trabajo y la educación de la mujer en España (1900–1930)*. Madrid: Ministerio de Cultura, Instituto de la Mujer.

――― (1986b) 'Historia de los cambios políticos y sociales en España' in Borreguero et al., 17–27.

Capmany, María Aurèlia and Carmen Alcalde (1970) *El feminismo ibérico*. Barcelona: Oikos-Tau.

Carbonell, Neus (1994) 'In the Name of the Mother and the Daughter: The Discourse of Love and Sorrow in Mercè Rodoreda's *La Plaça del Diamant*' in Kathleen McNerney and Nancy Vosburg (eds) *The Garden Across the Border. Mercè Rodoreda's Fiction*. Selinsgrove: Susquehanna University Press/London and Toronto: Associated University Presses, 17–30.

Castillo, Debra A. (1990) 'Frame Tale: Carmen Gómez Ojea's *Otras mujeres y Fabia*' in Noël Valis and Carol Maier (eds) *In the Feminine Mode. Essays on Hispanic Women Writers*. Lewisburg: Bucknell University Press/London and Toronto: Associated University Presses, 101–12.

Cela, Camilo José (1962) *La familia de Pascual Duarte* in *La obra completa de Camilo José Cela*. 13th ed. Barcelona: Destino (orig. 1942).

――― (1964) *The Family of Pascual Duarte*, trans. and intro. Anthony Kerrigan. London: Weidenfeld and Nicolson.

Chacel, Rosa (1985) *Memorias de Leticia Valle*. 1st ed. Barcelona: Lumen (orig. 1945). *Memoirs of Leticia Valle*, trans. and afterword Carol Maier. Lincoln and London: University of Nebraska Press, 1994.

Chodorow, Nancy (1978) *The Reproduction of Mothering: Psychoanalysis and the Sociology of Gender*. Berkeley: University of California Press.

Ciplijauskaité, Biruté (1988) *La novela femenina contemporánea (1970–1985). Hacia una tipología de la narración en primera persona*. Barcelona: Anthropos.

Cixous, Hélène (1981) 'Castration or Decapitation?', trans. Annette Kuhn, in *Signs*, Autumn 1981, vol. 7, no. 1, 41–55 (orig. 1976, 'Le Sexe ou la tête?' in *Les Cahiers du GRIF*, no. 13, 5–15).

―――― (1986) 'The Laugh of the Medusa', trans. Keith Cohen and Paula Cohen, in Elaine Marks and Isabelle de Courtivron (eds and intro.) *New French Feminisms. An Anthology*. Sussex: The Harvester Press (orig. 1980), 245–64 (orig. 1975, 'Le Rire de la Méduse' in *L'arc*, no. 61, 39–54).

Cohen, Emma (1983) *Toda la casa era una ventana*. Madrid: Debate.

Criado, Azucena (1993) 'El Congreso de los Diputados rechaza una propuesta para comercializar la píldora abortiva en España' in *El País*, 15 March 1993.

Daly, Brenda O. and Maureen T. Reddy (1991) 'Introduction' in Daly and Reddy (eds) 1991, 1–18.

Daly, Brenda O. and Maureen T. Reddy (eds) (1991) *Narrating Mothers: Theorizing Maternal Subjectivities*. Knoxville: The University of Tennessee Press.

Davies, Catherine (1991) 'Feminist Writers in Spain Since 1900: From Political Strategy to Personal Inquiry' in Helena Forsås-Scott (ed.) *Textual Liberation. European Feminist Writing in the Twentieth Century*. London and New York: Routledge, 192–226.

―――― (1994) *Contemporary Feminist Fiction in Spain. The Work of Montserrat Roig and Rosa Montero*. Oxford and Providence, USA: Berg.

Delgado Capeans, R.P. (1941) *La mujer en la vida moderna*. Madrid: Bruno del Amo.

Díaz-Mas, Paloma (1997) 'La niña sin alas' in Freixas (ed.) 1997, 159–68.

Dupláa, Christina (1996) *La voz testimonial en Montserrat Roig*. Barcelona: Icaria.

Falcón, Lidia (1994) *La razón feminista*. Madrid: Vindicación Feminista (orig. 1981–1982).

Ferguson, Ann (1984) 'On Conceiving Motherhood and Sexuality: A Feminist Materialist Approach' in Trebilcot (ed.) 1984, 153–82.

Flax, Jane (1980) 'Mother–Daughter Relationships: Psychodynamics, Politics, and Philosophy' in Hester Eisenstein and Alice Jardine (eds) *The Future of Difference*. Boston, Mass.: G.K. Hall and Co, 20–40.

―――― (1993) 'Mothers and Daughters Revisited' in Janneke van Mens-Verhulst, Karlein Schreurs, and Liesbeth Woertman (eds) *Daughtering and Mothering. Female Subjectivity Reanalysed*. London and New York: Routledge, 145–56.

Folguera, Pilar (ed.) (1988) *El feminismo en España: Dos siglos de historia*. Madrid: Pablo Iglesias.

Formica, Mercedes (1945) 'Bodoque' in *Revista de Occidente*, no. 51, 1945, 5–65.

―――― (1967) 'Spain' in Raphael Patai (ed. and intro.) *Women in the Modern World*. New York and London: The Free Press, 176–91.

—— (1973) *La hija de don Juan de Austria*. Madrid: Revista de Occidente.
—— (1979) *María de Mendoza. Solución a un enigma amoroso*. Madrid: Caro Raggio.
—— (1987) *La infancia*. Jérez: Cátedra Adolfo de Castro.
—— (1991) *A instancia de parte*, ed. María Elena Bravo. Madrid: Castalia (orig. 1954).
Freixas, Laura (ed.) (1997) *Madres e hijas*. 10th ed. Barcelona: Anagrama (orig. 1996).
Freud, Sigmund (1909) 'Family Romances' in *On Sexuality. Three Essays on the Theory of Sexuality and Other Works*, trans. James Strachey. The Penguin Freud Library, vol. 7. London and Harmondsworth: Penguin, 1977, 217–25.
Gallego Méndez, María Teresa (1983) *Mujer, falange y franquismo*. Madrid: Taurus.
Galvarriato, Eulalia (1967) *Cinco sombras*. 4th ed. Barcelona: Destino (orig. 1947).
Garner, Shirley Nelson (1991) 'Constructing the Mother: Contemporary Psychoanalytic Theorists and Women Autobiographers' in Daly and Reddy (eds) 1991, 76–93.
Gascón Vera, Elena (1992) *Un mito nuevo: La mujer como sujeto/objeto literario*. Madrid: Pliegos.
Gilmore, Leigh (1994) *Autobiographics. A Feminist Theory of Women's Self-Representation*. Ithaca and London: Cornell University Press.
Giorgio, Adalgisa (1997) 'Real Mothers and Symbolic Mothers: The Maternal and the Mother–Daughter Relationship in Italian Feminist Theory and Practice' in Gino Bedani, Zygmunt Barański, Anna Laura Lepschy, and Brian Richardson (eds) *Sguardi sull'Italia*. Leeds: Society for Italian Studies, Occasional Paper no 3, 1997, 222–41.
Glenn, Kathleen (1991a) 'Fantasy, Myth, and Subversion in Rosa Montero's *Temblor*' in *Romance Languages Annual*, vol. 3, 1991, 460–64.
—— (1991b) 'Narration and Eroticism in Chacel's *Memorias de Leticia Valle* and Nabokov's *Lolita*' in *Monographic Review/Revista Monográfica*, vol. 7, 'Hispanic Marginal Literatures', 1991, 84–93.
Gómez Ojea, Carmen (1982) *Otras mujeres y Fabia*. 1st ed. Barcelona: Argos Vergara.
Gould Levine, Linda (1983) 'The Censored Sex: Woman as Author and Character in Franco's Spain' in Beth Miller (ed.) *Women in Hispanic Literature. Icons and Fallen Idols*. Berkeley and London: University of California Press, 289–315.
Graham, Helen (1995a) 'Gender and the State: Women in the 1940s' in Graham and Labanyi (eds) 1995, 182–95.
—— (1995b) 'Women and Social Change' in Graham and Labanyi (eds) 1995, 99–116.
Graham, Helen and Jo Labanyi (eds) (1995) *Spanish Cultural Studies. An Introduction. The Struggle for Modernity*. Oxford: Oxford University Press.
Grandes, Almudena (1996) 'Amor de madre' in *Modelos de mujer*. Barcelona: Tusquets, 125–34.
—— (1997) 'La buena hija' in Freixas (ed.) 1997, 185–224.
Graves, Robert (1972) *The Greek Myths*, vol. 1. Harmondsworth: Penguin (orig. 1955).

Grosz, Elizabeth (1989) *Sexual Subversions. Three French Feminists*. Sydney, Wellington, London, and Boston: Allen and Unwin.

—— (1995) *Space, Time, and Perversion. Essays on the Politics of Bodies*. New York and London: Routledge.

Guild, Elizabeth (1993) '*Écriture féminine*' in Wright (ed.) 1993, 74–76.

Guzmán, Eduardo de (1972) *Aurora de sangre. (Vida y muerte de Hildegart)*. Madrid: G. del Toro.

Hirsch, Marianne (1989) *The Mother/Daughter Plot: Narrative, Psychoanalysis, Feminism*. Bloomington and Indianapolis: Indiana University Press.

Ibárruri, Dolores (1966) *They Shall Not Pass: The Autobiography of La Pasionaria*, trans. unknown. London: Lawrence and Wishart.

—— (1992) *El único camino*, ed., intro., and notes María Carmen García-Nieto París and María José Capellín Corrado, prol. Irene Falcón. Madrid: Castalia/Instituto de la Mujer (orig. 1962).

Irigaray, Luce (1981) 'And the One Doesn't Stir Without the Other', trans. Hélène Vivienne Wenzel, in *Signs*, Autumn 1981, vol. 7, no. 1, 60–67 (orig. *Et l'une ne bouge pas sans l'autre*, Paris: Minuit, 1979).

—— (1993a) 'The Bodily Encounter with the Mother', trans. David Macey, in Whitford (ed.) 1993, 34–46 (orig. *Le Corps-à-corps avec la mère*. Montreal: Éditions de la pleine lune, 1981; reprinted in Irigaray, *Sexes et parentés*. Paris: Minuit, 1987).

—— (1993b) 'An Ethics of Sexual Difference' in *An Ethics of Sexual Difference*, trans. Carolyn Burke and Gillian C. Gill. Ithaca, New York: Cornell University Press, 116–29 (orig. *Ethique de la différence sexuelle*, Paris: Minuit, 1984).

—— (1993c) 'The Limits of the Transference', trans. David Macey with Margaret Whitford, in Whitford (ed.) 1993, 105–17 (orig. 'L'Amour du transfert' in *Etudes freudiennes*, 19/20, 1982; reprinted in *Parler n'est jamais neutre*. Paris: Minuit, 1985).

—— (1993d) *Sexes and Genealogies*, trans. Gillian C. Gill. New York: Columbia University Press (orig. *Sexes et parentés*. Paris: Minuit, 1987).

—— (1993e) 'Women-Amongst-Themselves: Creating a Woman-to-Woman Sociality', trans. David Macey, in Whitford (ed.) 1993, 190–97 (a trans. of 'Créer un entre-femmes' in *Paris-Feministe*, 31–2, September 1986, 37–41, orig. 'Sorella donna, libera nos' in *Rinascita*, 28 September 1985, extracts from an interview Irigaray gave in 1985 in Bologna).

Jiménez, Vicente (1938) *Engrandecimiento de la Patria por las madres españolas*. Cádiz: Salvador Repeto.

Jones, Margaret E.W. (1983) 'Del compromiso al egoísmo: la metamorfosis de la protagonista en la novelística femenina de postguerra' in Janet W. Pérez (ed.) *Novelistas femeninas de la postguerra española*. Madrid: José Porrúa, 125–34.

Josefowitz Siegel, Rachel (1990) 'Old Women as Mother Figures' in Jane Price Knowles and Ellen Cole (eds) *Motherhood: A Feminist Perspective*. New York and London: The Haworth Press, 89–97.

Kahane, Claire (1993) 'Object-relations theory' in Wright (ed.) 1993, 284–90.

Kaplan, E. Ann (1992) *Motherhood and Representation. The Mother in Popular Culture and Melodrama*. London and New York: Routledge.

Laforet, Carmen (1992) *Nada*. 16th ed. Barcelona: Destino (orig. 1944). *Nada*, trans. Glafyra Ennis. New York: Peter Lang, 1993.

La Nueva España, 3 April 1994, 36.

Larraburu, Carmen (1977) 'Cuarenta años de oscurantismo ginecológico' in *Vindicación Feminista*, no. 16, 1 October 1977, 30–31.

Lázaro, Reyes (1994) 'Indecisiones y seducciones familiares: Rosa Chacel, Ortega y la generación del noventayocho.' PhD thesis. University of Massachusetts Amherst. Ann Arbor, UMI.

Lee-Bonanno, Lucy (1987) 'Concha Alós' *Os habla Electra*: The Matriarchy Revisited' in *Anales de la Literatura Española Contemporánea*, vol. 12, nos. 1–2, 1987, 95–109.

——— (1988) 'The Renewal of the Quest in Esther Tusquets' *El mismo mar de todos los veranos*' in Roberto C. Manteiga, Carolyn Galerstein, and Kathleen McNerney (eds) *Feminine Concerns in Contemporary Spanish Fiction by Women*. Potomac: Scripta Humanística, 134–51.

Leggott, Sarah J. (1998) 'Women and Historicity in the Works of Mercedes Formica' in *Confluencia*, Spring 1998, vol. 13. no. 2, 30–39.

Mangini, Shirley (1987) 'Women and Spanish Modernism: The Case of Rosa Chacel' in *Anales de la Literatura Española Contemporánea*, vol. 12, nos. 1–2, 1987, 17–28.

——— (1995) *Memories of Resistance: Women's Voices from the Spanish Civil War*. New Haven: Yale University Press.

Martín Gaite, Carmen (1985) 'Las mujeres noveleras' in *El cuento de nunca acabar*. Barcelona: Destino, 69–81 (orig. 1983).

——— (1987a) *Retahílas*. 4th ed. Barcelona: Destino (orig. 1974).

——— (1987b) *Usos amorosos de la postguerra española*. Madrid: Anagrama.

——— (1993a) 'De tú a tú' in *Agua pasada*. Barcelona: Anagrama. 236–38.

——— (1993b) *Nubosidad variable*. 14th ed. Barcelona: Anagrama (orig. 1992). *Variable Cloud*, trans. Margaret Jull Costa. London: The Harvill Press, 1995.

——— (1996) *Lo raro es vivir*. Barcelona: Anagrama.

Matute, Ana María (1973) *Primera memoria*. 7th ed. Barcelona: Destino (orig. 1959).

——— (1963) *School of the Sun*, trans. Elaine Kerrigan. New York: Pantheon.

Mayans Natal, María Jesús (1991) *Narrativa feminista española de posguerra*. Madrid: Pliegos.

Mayoral, Marina (1982) *La única libertad*. Madrid: Cátedra.

Montero, Rosa (1990) *Temblor*. 7th ed. Barcelona: Seix Barral.

Morales, María Pilar (1944) *Mujeres (Orientación femenina)*. Madrid: Nacional.

Nash, Mary (1983) *Mujer, familia y trabajo en España (1875–1936)*. Barcelona: Anthropos.

——— (1991) 'Two Decades of Women's History in Spain: A Reappraisal' in Karen Offen, Ruth Roach Pierson, and Jane Rendall (eds) *Writing Women's History. International Perspectives*. London and Hampshire: MacMillan, 381–415.

——— (1994) 'Pronatalism and Motherhood in Franco's Spain' in Gisela Bock and Pat Thane (eds) *Maternity and Gender Policies. Women and the Rise of the*

European Welfare States, 1880s–1950s. London and New York: Routledge, 160–77.

Ordóñez, Elizabeth J. (1984) 'A Quest for Matrilineal Roots and Mythopoesis: Esther Tusquets' *El mismo mar de todos los veranos*' in *Crítica Hispánica*, no. 6, 1984, 37–46.

——— (1991) *Voices of Their Own. Contemporary Spanish Narrative By Women*. Lewisburg: Bucknell University Press/London and Toronto: Associated University Presses.

——— (1998) 'Multiplicidad y divergencia: Voces femeninas en la novelística contemporánea española' in Iris M. Zavala (ed.) *Breve historia feminista de la literatura española (en lengua castellana)*, vol. 5. Barcelona: Anthropos, 211–37.

Parra, Isabel (1986) 'El control de la natalidad' in Borreguero et al. 1986, 61–70.

Pateman, Carole (1988) *The Sexual Contract*. Stanford: Stanford University Press.

Peri Rossi, Cristina (1997) 'Primer amor' in Freixas (ed.) 1997, 95–106.

Prieto, Enrique (1983) *La homosexualidad femenina*. Madrid: Ediciones UVE.

Primo de Rivera, Pilar (1944) 'Prólogo' in Morales 1944.

Puértolas, Soledad (1997) 'La hija predilecta' in Freixas (ed.) 1997, 117–38.

'Qué dice la Ley' in *Cambio 16*, no. 1, 122, 24 May 1993, 37.

Quiroga, Elena (1965) *Escribo tu nombre*. Barcelona and Madrid: Noguer.

Révesz, Andrés (1946) *Así son ellas*. Madrid: José Janés.

Rich, Adrienne (1977) *Of Woman Born: Motherhood as Experience and Institution*. London: Virago (orig. 1976).

——— (1983) 'Compulsory Heterosexuality and Lesbian Existence' in Elizabeth Abel and Emily K. Abel (eds) *The Signs Reader. Women, Gender and Scholarship*. Chicago and London: The University of Chicago Press, 139–68 (orig. 1980).

Riddel, María del Carmen (1988) 'La escritura femenina en la postguerra española: Análisis de novelas escogidas de Carmen Martín Gaite, Ana Mª Matute y Elena Quiroga.' PhD thesis, Ohio State University. Ann Arbor, UMI.

Robert, Marthe (1980) *The Origins of the Novel*, trans. Sacha Rabinovitch. Brighton, Sussex: The Harvester Press (orig. *Roman des origines et origines du roman*. Paris: Gallimard, 1972).

Rodoreda, Mercè (1962) *La Plaça del Diamant*. Barcelona: Club dels Novel.listes.

——— (1984) *La Plaza del Diamante*, trans. Enrique Sordo. 1st ed. Barcelona: Edhasa (orig. 1965).

——— (1983) *The Time of the Doves*, trans. and intro. David Rosenthal. New York: Taplinger.

——— (1991) *Isabel i Maria*. 1st ed. Barcelona: Institut d'Estudis Catalans.

——— (1992) *Isabel y Maria*, trans. Basilio Losada. Barcelona: Seix Barral.

Roig, Montserrat (1971) *Molta roba i poc sabó ... i tan neta que la volen*. Barcelona: Edicions 62. *Aprendizaje sentimental*, trans. Mercedes Nogués, Barcelona: Argos Vergara, 1981.

——— (1972) *Ramona, adéu*. Barcelona: Edicions 62. *Ramona adiós*, trans. Joaquim Sempere. Barcelona: Argos Vergara, 1980; Barcelona: Plaza y Janés, 1987).

——— (1980a) *L'hora violeta*. Barcelona: Edicions 62.

——— (1980b) *La hora violeta*, trans. Enrique Sordo. 1st ed. Barcelona: Argos Vergara.

Ruddick, Sara (1984a) 'Maternal Thinking' (orig. 1980) in Trebilcot (ed.) 1984, 213–30.

——— (1984b) 'Preservative Love and Military Destruction: Some Reflections on Mothering and Peace' in Trebilcot (ed.) 1984, 231–62 (orig. 1982).

Sánchez López, Rosario (1990) *Mujer española, una sombra de destino en lo universal: trayectoria histórica de Sección Femenina de Falange (1934–1977)*. Murcia: University of Murcia.

Scanlon, Geraldine (1986) *La polémica feminista en la España contemporánea (1868–1974)*, trans. Rafael Mazarrasa. Madrid: Akal (orig. 1976, 'The Feminist Debate in Modern Spain', PhD thesis).

Scarlett, Elizabeth (1994) *Under Construction. The Body in Spanish Novels*. Charlottesville and London: University Press of Virginia.

Servodidio, Mirella (1987) 'A Case of Pre-Oedipal and Narrative Fixation: *El mismo mar de todos los veranos*' in *Anales de la Literatura Española Contemporánea*, vol. 12, nos 1–2, 1987, 157–74.

Smith, Paul Julian (1992) 'The Lesbian Body in Tusquets's Trilogy' in *Laws of Desire. Questions of Homosexuality in Spanish Writing and Film 1960–1990*. Oxford: Clarendon, 91–128.

Soliño, María Elena (1995) 'Tales of Peaceful Warriors: Dolores Medio's *Diario de una maestra* and Josefina Aldecoa's *Historia de una maestra*' in *Letras Peninsulares*, Spring 1995, 27–38.

Soriano, Elena (1985) *Testimonio materno*. Barcelona: Plaza y Janés.

——— (1986) 'Medea' in *Mujer y hombre*. Barcelona: Plaza y Janés, 191–303 (orig. 1955).

——— (1992) *Caza menor*, ed. Concha Alborg. Madrid: Castalia (orig. 1951).

Stuart, Mary (1994) 'You're A Big Girl Now: Subjectivities, Feminism and Oral History' in *Oral History*, Autumn 1994, 55–63.

Suleiman, Susan (1985) 'Writing and Motherhood' in Shirley Nelson Garner, Claire Kahane, and Madelon Sprengnether (eds) (1985) *The (M)other Tongue. Essays in Feminist Psychoanalytic Interpretation*. Ithaca and London: Cornell University Press, 352–77.

Tanner, Tony (1979) *Adultery in the Novel. Contract and Transgression*. Baltimore and London: The Johns Hopkins University Press.

Telo, María (1986) 'La evolución de los derechos de la mujer en España' in Borreguero et al. 1986, 81–94.

Trebilcot, Joyce (ed.) (1984) *Mothering. Essays in Feminist Theory*. Totowa, New Jersey: Rowman and Allanheld.

Treviño, J.G. (1963) *La mujer*. Madrid: Ediciones Studium.

Truxa, Sylvia (1982) *Die Frau im spanischen Roman nach dem Bürgerkrieg*. Frankfurt am Main: Klaus-Dieter Vervuert.

Tsuchiya, Akiko (1992) 'Theorizing the Feminine: Esther Tusquets's *El mismo mar de todos los veranos* and Hélène Cixous's *écriture féminine*' in *Revista de Estudios Hispánicos*, vol. 26, no. 2, May 1992, 183–99.

Tusquets, Esther (1978) *El mismo mar de todos los veranos*. 1st ed. Barcelona: Lumen.
—— (1990) *The Same Sea As Every Summer*, trans. and afterword Margaret E.W. Jones. Lincoln and London: University of Nebraska Press.
—— (1997) 'Carta a la madre' in Freixas (ed.) 1997, 75–93.
Vallejo, María Dolores and J. Luis de Micheo (1994) *Mujer: trabajo, familia y finanzas. Todos sus derechos*. Madrid: Temas de Hoy.
Villena, Luis Antonio de (1987) '*Memorias de Leticia Valle*: La seducción inversa' in *Rosa Chacel. Premio Nacional de las Letras Españolas*. Madrid: Biblioteca Nacional, 41–44.
Warner, Marina (1995) 'Monstrous Mothers' in *Six Myths of Our Time*. New York: Vintage, 3–23 (orig. 1994).
Whitford, Margaret (1991) *Luce Irigaray. Philosophy in the Feminine*. New York and London: Routledge.
Whitford, Margaret (ed.) (1993) *The Irigaray Reader*, intro. Whitford. Oxford: Blackwell, 1993 (orig. 1991).
Winnicott, D.W. (1971) *Playing and Reality*. New York: Basic Books.
Wright, Elizabeth (1993) *Feminism and Psychoanalysis. A Critical Dictionary*. Oxford: Blackwell (orig. 1992).
Zatlin, Phyllis (1987) 'Women Novelists in Democratic Spain: Freedom to Express the Female Perspective' in *Anales de la Literatura Española Contemporánea*, vol. 12, nos. 1–2, 1987, 29–44.
—— (1992) 'Gothic Inversion of the Future: Rosa Montero's *Temblor*' in *Romance Notes*, vol. 33, no. 2, Winter 1992, 119–23.
Zimmerman, Bonnie (1990) *The Safe Sea of Women. Lesbian Fiction 1969–1989*. Boston: Beacon Press.

Chapter Three

'The Horror of the Unlived Life'

Mother–Daughter Relationships in Contemporary Irish Women's Fiction

Anne Fogarty

Introduction

Adrienne Rich has declared that the cathexis between mother and daughter is 'the great unwritten story' in British and American literature (1977: 225). A cursory analysis of contemporary Irish literature would appear to further reinforce this claim. A predominantly patriarchal view of culture has relegated women's writing to the margins, rendering it almost invisible, and concerned itself solely with tracing lines of continuity between male artists. The cathexis of mother and daughter is, hence, in the first instance, an unwritten story in Ireland because it is largely uncharted, hidden in the obscured domain of women's fiction. As this chapter intends to demonstrate, the many plotlines that form the narratives of the female portrayal of relationships between mothers and daughters can, however, be recovered from the rich but silenced archive of contemporary Irish women's writing and opened up for critical scrutiny and evaluation.

It will be proposed that these fictions constitute a space of alternative imaginings in which the conflicts between mothers and daughters are enacted, dissected, and portrayed. However, although they allow the possibility of seeing things otherwise, they do not proffer, except in rare cases, any idealised delineations of or utopian solutions to the intergenerational bonds between women. Instead, the works under review depict the links between mothers and daughters in Irish society as tempestuous, problem-laden, and fraught with multiple tensions. Many recent critics have contended that twentieth-century Irish literature has been peculiarly dominated by Oedipal plots because they permit an exploration of the unstable operations of power in a colonial culture.[1] In a society which does not have political self-governance, it is the nullity of paternal power rather than its depredations that constitutes a problem. By the same token, however, it must be recognised that the lines of continuity between mothers and daughters in modern Irish writing are similarly broken and problematic.[2] The figure of the mother also becomes associated with the trauma of a past that can neither be buried nor resolved and with the struggle of the daughter to create an identity in the face of an overwhelming sense of illegitimacy and disempowerment.

Both Marianne Hirsch and Luce Irigaray have pointed to the problems entailed in recovering the silenced and troubled narratives of mothers and daughters in patriarchal culture. Hirsch shows that recent feminist reworkings of the tale of Oedipus have concentrated on the figure of the Sphinx but have failed to address a still more glaring omission, the untold story of the other woman, the mother, Jocasta (1989: 1–5). Her findings indicate the difficulties which have to be faced in excavating and reconstructing the otherness of the mother's point of view and the resistance to her perspective even within feminism. Irigaray contends that the story of Clytemnestra which encompasses the unsettling themes of maternal anger and jealousy, filial matricide, and daughterly madness is a much more telling narrative than that of Oedipus because of its capacity to emplot the way in which a male-dominated culture struggles to sever the links between women, to silence mothers and daughters, and to curb the workings of female desire (1991a: 36–38). However, the disturbing nature of this alternative female-centred mythology suggests that the process of reconstituting the voices and histories of mothers and daughters will involve unleashing explosive hostilities as part of the endeavour to discover the reciprocal bonds between them.

Ironically, as Irigaray claims, the production of women 'as a silent substratum' especially in their roles as daughters and mothers depends upon a

1. For a discussion of the figure of the discredited father in Irish literary works, see Kiberd 1995: 380–94. For a related study which attributes the voicelessness of women in Irish theatre to the prevalence of the 'male double act', that is the exploration of the intimate but damaged relations between fraternal pairings of men, see Roche 1994.
2. For a suggestive interpretation of family connections in *Ulysses* that notes the relegation of the daughter but probes this absence in order to explore the links between fathers and daughters and the profound lability of sexual desire in Joyce's text, see Valente 1996/1997. Valente indicates that the seeming disappearance of the daughter in Irish fiction may be due to the fact that her role is introjected by the male protagonist.

proliferation of voices and texts which claim to speak to and about them (1991c). In Ireland, religious and political discourses in particular have constructed highly ambivalent and restrictive views of maternity. The resonant mythography revolving around the figure of Mother Ireland in nationalist representations appropriates maternity in the cause of debates about empowerment and disenfranchisement, freedom and tyranny, community and servitude. The images of Ireland as a hapless abandoned maiden, a homeless crone, an exacting, tutelary spirit who needs to be propitiated, and as a melancholic mother who demands unceasing sacrifice and devotion from her children and is herself defined by an unswerving propensity to self-immolation generated by nationalist literature continue to inflect the ways in which femininity is construed in the country today and endows women writers in particular with a problematic and constraining legacy.[3]

The hegemonic control exercised by the Catholic church until recently further ensured that maternity was seen as the essence of womanhood and that it was associated with purity, asexuality, and self-denying devotion to others. The national constitution drawn up in 1937 further indemnified this assumption that motherhood formed the very basis of women's social and political identity. Famously, article 41 of this document recognises the importance of maternal work, and promises that the state will endeavour to ensure that mothers will not be forced 'by economic necessity to engage in labour to the neglect of their duties in the home'.[4] While setting out to acknowledge the contribution of mothers to the well-being of the state, the constitution also severely delimits and restricts their ambit. The veneration of women in their role as mothers ironically has the effect of diminishing their power; well-intentioned paternalism paves the way for social oppression.[5]

Recent sociological studies have borne this out by revealing that women, while receiving official sanction for their work as carers by both state and church alike throughout the twentieth century, were materially and economically disadvantaged for undertaking such labour.[6] It seems then no coincidence that in the numerous court cases about infanticide, abortion rights, teenage pregnancy, and sexual abuse which have caught the public attention in Ireland in recent years, many of the most virulent moral and ethical battles

3. For analyses of the ambivalent legacy of nationalist icons of the female and the maternal, see Patrick Keane 1988, Boland 1989, Longley 1990, Meaney 1991, and Kearney 1997.
4. *Bunreacht na hEireann (Constitution of Ireland)* 1937: 136–38.
5. The paragraph confining women to the home is routinely denounced as an example of the malign practices of Irish patriarchy. See, however, Clear 1995 who finds that Eamonn De Valera inserted these provisos after reading Ivy Pinchbeck's study of maternal ill health and infant mortality in early industrialisation. Such well-intentioned, paternalist solicitude, however, had the effect of reinforcing conservative views of women.
6. See Coakley 1997 and Mary Daly 1997, who both argue convincingly that the pronatalism and familism of the Irish state did not bring any political or social dividends for women.

have hinged on issues of women's rights and female sexuality.[7] The ideals of femininity and maternity set up in the constitution as a bulwark against social disorder and the ills of modernity are now fiercely contested in contemporary Ireland in the continuing upheavals caused by the clash between entrenched patriarchal values and an advancing feminist ethos.[8]

This chapter sets out to explore how such tensions between conservatism and feminism, traditionalism and modernity may be traced in the many mother–daughter plots that occur in recent Irish women's fiction. In comparing representative texts from 1950 to the present, my aim is to investigate the way in which the changing perspectives on the status of women are mirrored and refracted in these narratives. It will be argued that these texts succeed in undermining seemingly timeless ideological verities about female behaviour by highlighting the historical, emotional, and material dimensions of the cross-generational links between women. The figures of mother and daughter act, consequently, as sites of contestation in which notions of female identity are put to the test, aspects of patriarchal oppression are unearthed, and unresolved conflicts within the female psyche are enacted. All of the texts examined depict relationships between mothers and daughters as inveterately divided and strained. The emphasis on struggle in these works effectively counters the calcified, static, and outmoded images of maternal completion and wholeness insisted on by patriarchal culture. However, it also indicates that the ambiguities and divisions which define female subjectivity cannot easily be banished. While the identities of succeeding generations of women are shown to be interwoven and mutually implicated, the quest for autonomy and selfhood is depicted to be eternally at odds with the female experience of filial dependence and the maternal prerogative to nurture.

My exploration of the mother–daughter plots constructed by contemporary Irish women writers will also demonstrate that these texts manipulate the conventions of the realist novel in order to topple the questionable and oppressive icons of femininity current in patriarchal culture. Despite their outward compliance with the conventions of the romance plot and of the *Bildungsroman*, these works are also concerned with composing a new vocabulary and mythography of the feminine. As will be seen, motifs such as those of the omnipotent mother and the devouring daughter are deconstructed and reformulated to yield new meanings and symbolic patterns. Above all, these texts return obses-

---

7. For accounts of some of the most notorious of these recent incidents including the so-called 'Kerry Babies' tribunal in 1985 in which a woman was accused of infanticide, the death in childbirth of the fifteen-year old Ann Lovett in an outdoor grotto in Granard, and the X case in 1992 in which a fourteen-year-old rape victim was prevented by a High Court injunction from leaving Ireland for an abortion, see McCafferty 1985 and 1992, and Smyth 1992.

8. A history of the different phases of Irish feminist activism in the twentieth century is outlined in Beaumont 1997, Connolly 1997, Shannon 1997, and Smyth 1993.

sively to the scene of the mother's death and deploy it as a narrative marker which gives a definitive shape to the daughter's story. The various ways in which this moment of crisis is envisaged may be used as a guide to the changing relations between women in the forty-year period investigated in this chapter and also as a means of mapping out and differentiating the multifarious narrative structures and devices adopted. However, it will also be argued that the compulsive necessity to confront the spectre of maternal demise is one of the chief characteristics of the mother–daughter plots set in motion by recent Irish women writers. Daughterly dereliction and melancholia, and maternal neediness, oppression, and longing are the twin but warring energies which determine the contours and trajectories of these narratives.

In her analysis of mother–daughter plots in nineteenth- and twentieth-century novels, Marianne Hirsch has noted a progression from matrophobic narratives in which the development of the daughter depends upon the silencing and negation of the mother's point of view to feminocentric plots that explore the multiple points of connection rather than merely the tensions between women in different generations (1989). The texts examined in this chapter provide evidence of a similar pattern whereby fictions highlighting the gulf between mothers and daughters give way to narratives that find equal space for stories of filial protest and escape and the otherness of maternal discourse. In the light of this feminist typology, the recurrent invocation of the awesome but destructive powers of the mother in contemporary Irish women's writing seems retrograde. However, it will become evident that the searing portrayals of maternity that abound in their work act not only as a way of capturing the pervasive female sense of dispossession in a patriarchal society but also of charting the dark but potent forces historically linked with the feminine in Irish society. Like the sovereignty goddess in Celtic mythology, the mother in these texts is endowed with ambivalent elemental and social powers. She is at once associated with destruction and sorrow as well as fertility and plenitude.[9] The very turbulence of the mother–daughter bond becomes paradoxically the means by which feminine identity with all its painful intergenerational entanglements can be reimagined.

The Reproduction of Mothering: Female Interdependence in the Fiction of Mary Lavin

Throughout her long career, Mary Lavin (1912–1996) has written consistently about the theme of motherhood and examined the conflicts that beset

---

9. Analyses of the complex symbolism of Celtic sovereignty goddesses may be found in O'Crualaoich 1988, Herbert 1992, and Green 1995.

successive generations of women. Although she invariably privileges the viewpoint of the mother, her fictions consistently probe the way in which female identity is both fashioned and incapacitated by matrilinear dependence. Her first novel, *Mary O'Grady*, provides a useful starting point as it tells the life story of its eponymous maternal heroine caught between traditional and modern notions of femininity in early twentieth-century Dublin.[10]

Lavin's novel insistently instates the mother as subject but it also subtly defamiliarises her point of view.[11] In this manner, the contradictions underlying the otherworldly ideal of motherhood by which the heroine sets her lights are deftly exposed. The asexual spirituality to which she aspires is consistently shown to be at odds with the obdurate physicality of her sufferings. Equally, her naivety and often seeming insentience are ironically counterpointed with the supposedly deep-seated, immemorial wisdom which is part and parcel of what Julia Kristeva calls the 'consecrated' ideal of motherhood (1987: 234). Lavin, in fact, uses two aspects of Marian iconography in order to point to the divergence between the superhuman archetype of maternity and the misfortunes which befall her heroine. The latter is portrayed as embodying opposing facets of the Virgin Mary, in her aspect as sublime divinity on the one hand and in her persona as sorrowing mother on the other. The constant 'arrowy pangs of sundering' (*Mary O'Grady*: 29) which she suffers when her children leave her correspond to a recognised pattern of maternal sorrows which were part of the lot of the *mater dolorosa*. The tears and physical pain of the Virgin grieving over the loss of her son were seen, as Marina Warner explains, as having a purifying and sanctifying force (1976: 221–23). Lavin's heroine struggles constantly to transform her misfortunes into precisely such a mode of transcendence. However, the unremitting nature of her suffering is such that it is impossible for her to transmute it into a triumphant story of maternal self-sacrifice. In addition, her desertion of her rural home and reluctant assumption of an urban existence demonstrate her failure to live up to the time-honoured ideal of empowered female nurturance exemplified by her memories of the potent protectiveness of her own mother on the family farm in Tullamore. The novel intimates that the pressures of modernity dissipate the sacred potency of the mother in Irish society.

The lines of division between Mary and her three daughters, Ellie, Angie, and Rosie, are even more marked as they embrace urban life and lead independent existences. The melodramatic death of the two oldest daughters and

10. *Mary O'Grady* was first published in 1950; all references will be to the 1986 Virago edition.
11. *Mary O'Grady* has been inexplicably neglected by criticism. Kelly 1980 concentrates on Lavin's short stories and hence mentions it only in passing while Weekes 1990 simply reiterates without demur Lavin's own dismissive views of her early writing. For a sympathetic reading of the novel that adeptly pinpoints its idiosyncrasies and subtleties, see Martin 1986.

their fiancés in an aircrash halfway through the novel serves as a violent enactment of the power struggles between generations of women and underlines the futility of a belief in the salvationary force of maternal love. While the decision of Ellie and Angie to take a trip in a plane is depicted as a gesture of defiance, the accident is also portrayed as a terrible and literal realisation of Mary's fears. On the one hand, the calamity functions as an image of the daughter's desperate struggle to achieve individuation and free herself of maternal control, while on the other it symbolises the horrifying retributive power of the omnipotent mother who proves her superior strength by going to the extreme of destroying her offspring.[12]

The latter half of the novel gives particular prominence to Mary's strained involvement with her youngest daughter, Rosie. Her desire to confine her daughter within the safe arena of childhood harmony and primary narcissism is pitted against the latter's need to declare her difference and to achieve a separate identity. Both goals, as the narrative illustrates, are doomed. In the final pages, Rosie's announcement that her marriage has irrevocably failed appears to bring the sufferings of Lavin's ill-starred protagonist to a pinnacle. The sudden discovery that her daughter is expecting a child opens up a final possibility of hope. It is, however, also suggested that the experience of motherhood is symbolic of the mirroring self-cancellations of female history rather than of its shared unities. The daughter's attempt at advancement is merely a reenactment of the inescapable story of maternal pain and loss. Mary's death in the final pages of the narrative seems an aptly ironic culmination of her doctrine of self-denying maternal love. The novel leaves us with the anguished perspective of the daughter who in witnessing the demise of her mother has been dealt, we are told, 'the greatest blow life could have given her' (*Mary O'Grady*: 382) and the recognition that intergenerational female identities are destined to be forever sundered. Even though Rosie is now ready to assume Mary's mantle, the text indicates that her fateful repetition of the maternal role will lead not to an experience of oceanic oneness but to a renewed cycle of division, loss, and conflict.

Many of Lavin's later short stories consider the way in which daughters are indelibly scarred by what Christiane Olivier terms 'the imprint of the mother' and struggle to resist the compulsion to duplicate or reproduce her life (Olivier 1989).[13] In these works, the friction between mothers and daughters is shown to be the result not just of the asphyxiating sameness of filial and maternal identities but also of the impossible otherness of the figure

---

12. Jung 1959 provides an account of the conflicting aspects of the archetype of the mother. Her power to nurture and sustain life also endows her with a terrifying and potentially deadly omnipotence.
13. Several of Lavin's early short stories also explore the mother–daughter relationship: see 'Lilacs' (1942) and 'The Nun's Mother' (1944).

of the mother in Irish culture. If, as Olivier argues, the woman within male-dominated culture is 'someone who cannot find herself' because she is constantly persuaded to move away from herself towards others, then the daughter's plot in which she asserts her difference while probing the meaning of her mother's history is an effort to thwart the nullifying effects of such restriction (1989: 122). For Lavin the dismantling of the stereotypes of maternal power and of daughterly submission results inevitably in pain and betrayal as well as a sense of restitution. In 'A Family Likeness' (Lavin 1985), Ada, a grandmother, relives her disappointment with her own mother while attempting to muster sympathy for her daughter's current struggle with the demands of young parenthood. The culminating image of the woman's granddaughter at the end of the tale playing with a cow pat acts both as a comic release from the piqued misunderstandings that had formed the basis of the conversation between mother and daughter throughout and as a symbol of the way in which ancestral rivalries between women are constantly dug out and reenacted. The momentary insight gained by the protagonist into the reality of her own mother's life is uneasily balanced against the overwhelming sense of ongoing conflict between generations of women in the present.

In 'Happiness' (Lavin 1969), a similar reckoning of the unequal fates and conflicting vantage points which make up the discontinuities of female familial histories occurs. The story tracks a daughter's attempt to understand the cryptic definition of happiness which her mother has declared to be her life philosophy. In taking stock of this defiant maternal protagonist, the narrative uncovers a world in which female emotional economies dangerously feed off and cannibalise each other. The attempt by the maternal protagonist to achieve an elusive *jouissance* is threatened, on the one hand, by the ravening dissatisfaction of her own mother and, on the other, by the gnawing envy of her daughter. Despite the scepticism of the daughterly narrator, the story still manages to construct a complex maternal discourse which refuses to be pinned down or easily contained and to counteract the stereotype of the inaudibility of female suffering. Her mysterious courage is a sign, not of the ineffable nature of maternity, but of her contradictory humanity.

The narrative ends with a harrowing description of the mother's battle against death. Only when her youngest daughter grants her leave to die does she relinquish her anguished battle against life. The story, thus, concludes with a sense that the mother and her two daughters have reached an uneasy truce with each other. 'Happiness' portrays the daughterly struggle for liberation as predicated on the uncovering of the mother's story. However, there is also a suggestion that the questioning of the otherness of the maternal subject still does not allow for a full dialogue between generations of women to emerge. The discovery of the autonomy of the mother does not release the daughter in Lavin's fictions. Rather it reinforces her sense of lack and powerlessness. The by-product of the melancholic regressiveness of bereavement, female understanding is depicted as necessarily partial and clouded.

In addition, maternal experience still seems in Lavin's writings to be lost in an unattainable privacy despite her attempts to demystify it. Although the action of *Mary O'Grady* coincides with many of the most explosive events in Irish history at the beginning of the century, these occurrences never impinge on the narrative. Such deliberate exclusions illustrate, on one level, Lavin's concern to give prominence to the stories of women that are usually omitted in political histories of the period. However, on another level, they indicate that maternal subjectivity remains curiously resistant to narrativity, locked in the obdurately ahistorical space of private reflection. The death of the mother in *Mary O'Grady*, 'A Family Likeness', and 'Happiness' may be seen, hence, as a sign not of closure or even of crisis but as a complex register of the ideological, emotional, and historical impediments that prevent the daughter's attempt to achieve wholeness or to forge a separate, enabling identity of her own.

Memory and Conflict: The Revolt of the Daughter in Julia O'Faoláin's *The Irish Signorina* and Molly Keane's *Good Behaviour*

Julia O'Faoláin's (born 1932) *The Irish Signorina* (1984) is similarly concerned with the ambivalences which come to the fore in the process of reconstructing a female genealogy and of unlocking what Irigaray terms 'the deadly silence' of maternal history (1991a: 44). Like Lavin, she utilises the conventions of the *Bildungsroman* and of the realist novel in order to probe the way in which matrophobia colours and distorts the relations between women.[14] The protagonist, Anne Ryan, visits Tuscany in the aftermath of her mother's death with the objective both of overcoming the trauma of this recent loss and of piecing together and giving some coherence to the fragmented family records and memories that she has inherited. In going to Italy, she is deliberately retracing past events as she has been invited to stay as a guest at the villa of the ageing Marchesa Niccolosa Cavalcanti in whose household her mother had once served as governess. The duality of the heroine's persona is emphasised throughout as is the impossibility of fully severing and dissociating maternal and filial identities. Anne's view of the present is constantly mediated by her recall of maternal reminiscences on the

---

14. Beckett (born 1926) in 'Failing Years' (1980) and 'Under Control' (1990), Boylan (born 1948) in *Home Rule* (1992), and Ita Daly (born 1944) in *Ellen* (1986) and *A Singular Attraction* (1987) explore antagonistic relationships between mothers and daughters.

one hand and her own negative memories and appraisal of her mother on the other. The degree to which daughter and mother are coextensive and act as mutual uncanny doubles is also evident in the response of others to the heroine. They see her both as an individual in her own right and as a reincarnation of the woman they had once known.

The protagonist's desire to find out more about her mother's past is instigated by her dismissal of the latter's reprehensible capitulation to the humdrum anonymity of married life and her failure to act on the passion of a fleeting affair. The incomplete, nostalgic remembrances about her life in Italy, which her mother imparted to her in that 'cocoon of nervy intimacy' (*Irish Signorina*: 14) that united them before her death, frustrate her daughter because they seem so abortive and pointless. Above all, they dishearten her because they fail to achieve happy endings. The story of thwarted female desire that she inherits from her mother is marked by disillusionment and the cancellation of death. By contrast, Anne is convinced of the necessity of pursuing one's passions and of the imperative to avoid at all costs what she terms 'the horror of the unlived life' (*Irish Signorina*: 16). In order to side-step the female fate of incompletion, O'Faoláin's heroine relives her mother's life and improves upon it in accordance with the operations of fantasy described by Freud as the 'Family Romance' (1909). In such imaginary projections, the child invents a substitute family with a higher status than his actual one in order to correct and escape from the tensions and hostilities of the actual one. For Freud, the family romance is fuelled by the rivalry between fathers and sons and the disruptive excess occasioned by the male child's desire for the mother. Ultimately, he argues that the child's fantasies allay these dangerous tensions by exalting the father and denigrating the mother through casting her in the role of adulteress or traitor. O'Faoláin's version of the family romance has aspects both of the male-identified Freudian model and of feminist displacements of this patriarchal template which have been identified by Marianne Hirsch (1989: 125–61). Such revisionary narratives create, Hirsch contends, a separate all-female realm which is dominated by the fluid connections between women.

O'Faoláin's heroine is torn between her wish to denounce and discard her mother and her unwilling discovery of hidden affinities with her. The opulent world of the Italian villa provides her with a fantasy and substitute home, while the imperious, dying Marchesa acts as an aggrandised and revivified version of her dead mother. This surrogate mother bequeaths to her not just threadbare memories but the villa that she owns thus ensuring the heroine's future. In this manner, the family romance produces an exalted version of her mother simply by replacing and rejecting her. However, in reliving her mother's life, Anne is also forced drastically to revise her opinions of her actions. She discovers that her mother's affair with Guido, the son of the Marchesa, was broken off by his cowardice and family interference and not because of failure of nerve on her part. The heroine's castigation of her mother for being a 'sour nag' and 'a dispirited slattern' falters in the face of her discovery of her mother's youthful dreams and her lost capacity for happiness (*Irish Signorina*: 74, 107). Her bid to define herself in opposition to the past is further called into question by her passionate affair with her mother's former lover. The daughter's desires, despite her attempt to separate from the painful emotional legacy of her upbringing, are circular and fatally moulded by her maternal inheritance. In allowing her to live out with impunity the passions that she felt her mother had wrongly denied, O'Faoláin rewards but also highlights the dark amorality and lawlessness of her heroine.

At one point in the novel, Anne asks Guido whether he is using her mother to seduce her or using her to revive her mother; he answers by telling her that she fulfils 'an old promise' (*Irish Signorina*: 110). On one level, the novel suggests that the sins of the past are cancelled out by the composite, cooperative nature of female desire. Anne assuages her grief for her mother's death and anger at her 'unlived' life by completing her passionate affair for her. The daughter's surrogacy is at once an act of rebellion and defiance and an acknowledgment of the inescapable affiliative links between generations of women. However, on another level, O'Faoláin suggests that in order to evade the deadening values of the conformist and passionless world which her mother inhabited she is forced to act in accordance with the repressed scripts of incestuous, Oedipal desire. Rejection of the mother means acceptance of the law of the father. Anne, at the end of the novel, it is intimated, is quite literally about to marry her father. The daughter in this novel reproduces her mother's role by ousting her and commandeering her love, by insisting on her right to lead a life of radical difference, and by entering into an unorthodox sexual relationship and remaking her family history for herself. She arrives at a partial insight into that maternal subjectivity which she abhors, but the bitterness which she harbours about the wasteful vacancy of her mother's life means that a reconciliation of their perspectives is impossible. Only the distancing vision of permanent exile from Ireland and the fantasmatic space of the family romance allow for momentary, uneasy points of contact between mother and daughter to emerge. However, even this place of utopian wish fulfillment impedes the links between them and reroutes their love in the direction of the father. Thus, the daughter's conscious subversion of Oedipal desire in *The Irish Signorina* by actively seducing the paternal lover Guido in her mother's stead disrupts the conventions of familial love but also dangerously reproduces them.[15] The fragmented

---

15. Gallop argues that the desirability of the daughter and the possibility that she might seduce the father are censored in the Freudian explication of the Oedipus complex because it would disrupt the paternal right to possess and exchange his offspring in the larger community of men (1982: 56–79).

narrative of maternal loss and incompletion threatens to engulf and undermine the daughterly plot of rebellion and individuation.

Molly Keane's (1904–1996) *Good Behaviour* (1981) also uses the figure of the lawless daughter but in an even more extreme form. In a defiant departure from the proprieties of the realist novel, it draws upon the anarchic resources of Gothic and grotesque modes of imagining in order to tell the story of the mendacious, manipulative, and voracious Aroon St Charles, the only heir to the ramshackle, impecunious Anglo-Irish estate of Temple Alice. Social satire and black comedy unite in this narrative, which outlines the tale of a daughter's revenge on her mother and her seemingly triumphant defeat of an adversarial world.[16] The text opens with a description of Aroon's macabre murder of her mother through feeding her to death. In a parodic inversion of maternal nurturance, the monstrous and recalcitrant daughter serves up rabbit *quenelles*, a dish which Mrs St Charles loathes, as an expression not of love but of unremitting hatred. The narrative retrospective which opens up after the rupture of this melodramatic beginning provides us with Aroon's highly unreliable and prejudiced account of her upbringing and family life. Keane depicts the dysfunctional relations of the St Charles family as symptomatic of the decadence of the social class to which they belong. The emotional degeneracy of the household mirrors the shabby and degraded existence of this failing outpost of landlordism. Elizabeth Bowen has noted that sexlessness and a sublimated infantilism are the peculiar identifying traits of the protagonists of the Irish Big House novel (1986: 101). Both such qualities may be attributed to Aroon who lives in a regressive world of uncontrolled appetites and impulses in which the greatest erotic gratification is derived from food and not from sex. Even the family home, Temple Alice, bears the name of the archetypal Victorian fantasy created by Lewis Carroll of the young girl who remains permanently locked in the chaotic and inverted anti-world of childhood.

Aroon's hatred of her mother is provoked by the latter's cold-blooded neglect of her children who are banished to the comfortless oblivion of the nursery and exposed to the maltreatment of countless successive nurses and nannies. Aroon's apparently artless and sympathetic assessment of her mother's motives for such behaviour is an undisguised attack on her failure to care for her offspring:

> I don't blame Mummie for all this. She simply did not want to know what was going on in the nursery. She had had us and she longed to forget the horror of it once and for all. She engaged nannie after nannie with excellent references, and if they could

---

16. Several other novels by Keane also explore the grotesque relations between monstrous mother figures and perverted daughters: see *Loving Without Tears* (1988a, orig. 1951) and *Loving and Giving* (1988b).

not be trusted to look after us, she was even less able to compete. She didn't really like children; she didn't like dogs either, and she had no enjoyment of food, for she ate almost nothing. (*Good Behaviour*: 13)

Emotional starvation and lovelessness are associated in this passage with physical abstinence. The daughter's boundless appetites and rapacity, it is suggested, are simply a reactive response to the unnatural antipathy of her mother to her. Her physical engorgement reflects in the negative the mother's emotional iciness and withdrawal. In effect, however, in the comically overdetermined world created by Keane, Aroon and her mother mirror each other's monstrosity. Mrs St Charles's contempt for her daughter is matched by the latter's loathing of her. Confined by economic circumstances to the same household, they become inveterate and intimate enemies. Keane skilfully exploits the extremism of the stereotypes of the phallic, castrating mother and of the devouring daughter in order to expose the moral bankruptcy and sheer nastiness of the manipulative power games that dominate the day-to-day order in Temple Alice. In the absence of a positive sense of maternal identity, Irigaray argues that the distanceless proximity between women leads to irremediable voracity and the flaying of one woman by the other (1991b: 107). Aroon's 'grotesque, sentimental fixation' (*Good Behaviour*: 45) on her uncaring mother leads to just such a situation of deadly immediacy in which both opponents are locked in an unyielding and lacerating struggle. Each reduces the other to a worthless object. 'Mummie', as Aroon announces with macabre emphasis in the opening pages, 'is my doing' (*Good Behaviour*: 5). By finally reducing her mother to the powerless infantilism of the invalid she has triumphantly reconstructed her in her own image and created the perfect target for her ravening affections.

The novel exposes in exquisite detail the horrors of dependent and captive love. This world of surfaces, in which outward proprieties and good behaviour are paramount, is ironically full of perverse and abusive relationships which mirror the sadism of the mother–daughter bond that dominates the plot. Aroon's father is an incurable philanderer who conducts affairs with every available woman in his vicinity. The destructiveness of his indiscriminate sexuality is particularly borne out by the suicide of Mrs Brock, the rotund, warm-hearted, clairvoyant governess whom Aroon had, with customary intensity, adopted as a substitute mother. The narrator's ingenuous and vindictive viewpoint ruthlessly exposes the sexual violence of the world around her while always denying its traces. She portrays Mrs Brock's friendship with her father as a betrayal of her possessive love for the governess but feigns ignorance of the affair between the two and is apparently blind to the patent cruelty of the rejection of a servant who has been made pregnant by a heartless employer. The tragedy of the governess's fate is commuted in the unreliable and uncomprehending egotism of Aroon's narrative into a further instance of the treachery of maternal love. Thus, her initial devotion to Mrs Brock allows her the fleeting pleasure of the illusion of harmonious oneness. The sublimated eroticism of her description of the powerful expansiveness of this maternal being who acts as an affirmative reflection of the fleshy cumbersomeness of Aroon herself is obvious in the following passage:

> We screamed and spattered in the breaking waves while Mrs Brock took her real swim. I watched her fat body, a frilled torpedo in the black bathing costume, standing balanced and poised, ridiculous on a rock, before she dived – a joyous plunge into the deep water. Then she struck out into the bay with the strength and buoyancy of a seal; indeed, when the black bathing dress was sleeked by the water onto her body she had all the armoured rotundity of a seal – the same easy glory and enjoyment of an element that frightened me. (*Good Behaviour*. 50)

After maternal love is deflected, however, from the daughter to the father, the governess instantly falls in the narrator's estimation and is seen not as powerfully invigorating but as cold and rejecting. Mrs Brock's attempts to tell her charge in a coded way about Mr St Charles's mistreatment of her, and her consequent unhappiness, by discussing the sexual practices of the white mice in the nursery are wilfully misconstrued by Aroon as a rupture of the bonds between them. The jealous voracity of daughterly love turns the story of the unfortunate servant woman into a further example of a mother figure 'who had frightened me and failed me and now left me alone' (*Good Behaviour*. 64). Maternal abandonment rather than male cruelty is the inappropriate moral that she derives from her distorted record of warped affections.

The novel contains many other instances of the displacement of the daughter and of Aroon's purblind inability to read the signs of the relationships around her. She imagines herself to be in love with her brother's friend, Richard Massingham, and purportedly fails to notice that the two men are in fact romantically attached to each other. Aroon comically interprets an episode in which her putative lover hides in her bed and places his head on her 'enormous bosoms' as a scene of sexual initiation and a sign of devotion on his part. Hubert, Aroon's brother, Richard Massingham, and Aroon herself are all united by the fact that for a spell they enjoyed the positive, maternal tutelage of Mrs Brock. The text suggests that her benign nurturance produces the polymorphous pleasures of same-sex love which are however censored as perversion in this social world, which is dominated by the corrupt double standards of heterosexual good behaviour. Mrs Brock had been dismissed from her previous post for mollycoddling her male charges and because of an improper devotion that she had harboured for her mistress. Her suicide seems a punishment not just for the contretemps of her affair but for the all-embracing eros of maternal love which licenses same-sex as well as heterosexual love. Equally, the relationship between Hubert and Richard is depicted as unspeakable and doomed. Hubert is killed in a car crash thus cancelling the enormity represented by a gay relationship in this unamenable milieu where all positive forms of love are poisoned and degraded.[17]

Aroon's single-minded campaign to defeat her mother is not merely a retaliation for neglect but also for the denial of the oceanic fullness of the love between mothers and daughters. The substitution of the picture of the abandoned servant drowning herself in lonely despair for the image of the commanding power of Mrs Brock swimming seal-like out to sea acts as an index of the way in which the effects of maternal desire are ruinous rather than enhancing in the deleterious household of Temple Alice. In the latter half of the novel, Aroon struggles to gain a kind of vicarious power by taking over command of the household finances through entering into secret arrangements with the family solicitor behind her mother's back and fighting for control of her father when he becomes an invalid following a stroke. She finds herself simultaneously locked in combat with her mother, with Rose, the supremely efficient housekeeper who is her father's lover, and with an officious Nurse. In a parody of family relations, all of them battle to win the love of and assert their rights over the father who, although paralysed and mute, continues his drinking and pursuit of extramarital pleasure even while in his sickbed. In the rancorous fights which ensue, Aroon sets herself up as a moral censor who desperately tries to prevent her father's drinking and Rose's attempts to provide him with physical comfort. The decline of Mr St Charles from an heroic war veteran and amputee and virile country squire to an ineffectual Lothario and incapacitated invalid further charts the degeneration of the family. His debilitation also acts as an ironic commentary on the futile and destructive nature of female power games and on the perverted nature of daughterly and maternal love. Aroon who, as she declares, derives enjoyment from 'other people's disasters'(*Good Behaviour*: 174) relishes the battles in the sickroom and gains particular pleasure from the tasty food that is available there, which she always happily demolishes.

The novel ends with an account of the simultaneous humiliation and triumph of Aroon. She disgraces herself by her undisguised drunkenness on the day of her father's funeral, but later feels vindicated when it is announced that she is to inherit the family estate. The father's legacy dispossesses the mother in favour of the daughter. Aroon who has constantly smarted under her mother's baiting insinuations about her unmarried status and lack of money is now in a position to avenge herself. She jubilantly concludes that

---

17. For an analysis of the complex role of lesbianism and homosexuality in Keane's fictions, which argues that same-sex relations are seen as both anarchic and perverted in her writing, see Breen 1997.

'Papa loved me the most' and exults in the fact that she feels 'empowered' by this posthumous declaration of affection (*Good Behaviour*. 243, 244). Aroon's inheritance is of symbolic rather than material importance as the family fortunes have long since been squandered. Her advancement to head of the household neatly reverses relations between herself and her mother. Aroon is now in the position of maternal omnipotence while her mother occupies the place of filial dependence as is indicated by the final sentence which describes the latter's stricken appearance, which resembles that of 'a child warding off a blow' (*Good Behaviour*. 245).

Molly Keane's comic *tour de force* both stages and dismantles the stereotypes of the castrating mother and of the devouring daughter.[18] The plot gleefully uses the matrophobia and misogyny linked with these constructs in order to describe the declining fortunes and ultimate dissolution of an Anglo-Irish family and the internecine conflicts which underlie the polite surfaces of civilised good behaviour. It would be wrong, however, to view this text as operating simply within the confines of political allegory or social satire. Rather, Keane, in constructing a mother–daughter plot that delights in the monstrous excesses of female conduct, succeeds in demolishing many of the pieties enshrined in the religious and cultural images of motherhood prevalent in Irish society. Her text defiantly lays the ghost of the sentimental cult of maternity and also rejects the virtues of submissive female silence and forbearance. Aroon's story is a tale of outrageous female impropriety as well as being a dissection of the injustices borne by women in a corrupt society and an exploration of the pathology of possessive love. *Good Behaviour* makes the daring move of using the motif of the death of the mother to comic effect. Its anarchic humour feeds off the bitterness of the entrenched conflicts between mothers and daughters thus defusing some of their malignity. With hyperbolic verve, the text playfully exposes the fictionality of received views of female identity within patriarchy while also mocking the idealised depiction of relations between women that frequently forms the basis of feminist fictions of matrilineage.[19] Aroon, the unreliable daughterly narrator, is the vehicle for a narrative which is patently fallacious and self-deceiving. Her autobiographical self-defence is both affecting and specious. The artistry of Keane's irreverent novel resides in its ability to both captivate us and lay bare its own devices and strategies. *Good Behaviour* encourages us to see the mother–daughter plot as a complicated narrative game in which dangerous fantasies may be unleashed that expose and also exorcise some of the dark truths about cross-generational female connections.

18. Benjamin 1994 reviews the ramifications of the myth of the all-powerful mother.
19. Davidson and Broner 1980 have assembled various accounts of this recent tradition of matrilinear fictions which are characterised by their desire to explore aspects of female history and heritage.

Violent Truths: Incest and Desire in Deirdre Madden's *The Birds of the Innocent Wood* and Edna O'Brien's *Down By The River*

The themes of incest and violence also surface in recent feminocentric narratives that set out to reimagine familial relations and to rethink the symbolic deadlock of mother–daughter plots that force women in Irish society into antagonistic rivalries or trap them in endless cycles of duplication. Both Deirdre Madden (born 1960) and Edna O'Brien (born 1930) expose the incestuous involutedness of the traditional family, but they also indicate, however faintly, that the violent pathologies bred in such an environment are not just an index of the self-perpetuating losses welding successive generations of women together, but also a route by which the daughter might be freed from oppression and powerlessness.[20] In Madden's *The Birds of the Innocent Wood* (1988) matrophobia, the turmoil caused by the haunting incompletion of female desire, and the yearning to struggle free from the deadly secrets locked at the heart of family life, shape the emotions of two generations of women who endeavour to establish a sense of identity in the wake of maternal loss.[21]

The novel begins by telling the story of Jane who is left an orphan after her parents are burnt to death in a house fire while she herself is in hospital. Madden, thus, redefines the orthodox structures of the family by endowing her heroine with a macabre past and a Gothic sensibility. Jane, it would appear, is tragically but providentially delivered from the constrictions of traditional daughterly submissiveness and at liberty to construct a self outside of the depleting legacy of the family romance. The opening sentence of the novel draws explicit attention to the complex possibilities inherent in the heroine's predicament and the peculiar self-reflexiveness with which it seems to endow her, 'The circumstances of Jane's early life were so tragic and romantic that at one time she drew solace from thinking that it all might be an elaborate fiction and that a happier truth would one day be revealed' (*Birds*: 1). The early loss of her mother, however, while it frees her from normality, also irrevocably scars her. Although she enjoys distressing her school mates by narrating her disturbing life story 'with a daemonic combination of eloquence and detachment' (*Birds*: 5), she herself becomes increasingly detached and icy. The absence of a relationship with a familial and a mater-

---

20. Lentin's (born 1944) *Songs on the Death of Children* (1996) may also be cited as an instance of a feminocentric narrative that uses the theme of violence, in this case the Holocaust and recent Israeli history, in order to explore the troubled connections between a mother and her daughter.
21. The strained relations between a mother and her daughters also form part of the plot of Madden 1996.

nal past leads to a sense of inner depletion. Her perpetual, unspoken state of mourning is a consequence of the absence rather than the pain of memory.

Jane laments the fact that the fire in which her parents had died also destroyed all family mementos. In particular, the erasure of the image of the mother leaves her unable to develop a separate or secure sense of self: 'She would look at and touch her own body, telling herself that her mother had once existed in just such a form, but she could never really understand this. If only she could remember or imagine a swathe of scented hair, or a warm hand webbed with fine blue veins, then everything would have been so different' (*Birds*: 7). Her desire to revivify her dead mother stultifies her because of her lack of a language with which to realise this aim. The nuns in the boarding school, horrified by the effects of her chilling personal tales, prevent her from pursuing this ghoulish mode of communication. Thus, this outlawed and unspeakable story of the dead mother becomes both a sign of the disturbing depths hidden beneath the placid surfaces of the conventional Irish community in which Jane lives and of the dangerous explosiveness, as well as stifled potential, of the familial bonds between women.[22]

Jane's feelings of incompletion and hunger for affirmation lead her to her husband James who supplies her with those things in which she feels deficient. The family farm by a lake on which he works both attracts and repels her; it seems at once alien and redolent of the certainties and fixed values of rural life and of domestic existence for which she yearns. The natural sounds and images linked with this pure but glacial landscape, particularly the eerie cries of wild birds, punctuate the narrative and become associated with the repressed language of pain and desire, which the heroine intuits but never masters. The lost link with the mother appears to be the fundament of a female identity that revolves around a paralysing sense of estrangement and difference.

Structurally, the novel mimics this tacit feminine syntax of misrecognition and Gothic emotion by interweaving the story of the battle of Jane's twin daughters, Catherine and Sarah, to lay the ghost of their mother by unearthing buried family secrets with an account of her marriage, her nervous breakdown following the stillbirth of her first child, the emotional conflicts she experiences with her husband, and her eventual death. With its overlapping but never fully convergent narratives, the novel thus enacts the painful intergenerational struggle between women, and tracks the way in which their emotions clash and interpenetrate even after death. Indeed, the battle against the suffocating lure and overwhelming dread of the dead mother is the most significant point of continuity between the three female

---

22. Williams 1995 discusses the way in which the female plots and language of Gothic fictions threaten to destabilise the structures of the patriarchal family.

protagonists. While walking on a cliff's edge during her honeymoon, Jane attempts to wrestle with her inner demons by violently banishing the all-commandeering domain of Gothic memory:

> She wished she could stop believing still that her parents lived in such a light. They above all were what she wanted to forget; and yet now they seemed to be everywhere, as they had been when she was a child. That presence had then been a comfort, but it was no comfort now to feel her mother's eye in the hot sun above her, or to sense her in the musty smell which emanated from the hotel's dank cupboards and clung to her clothes. *Look then*, thought Jane fiercely. *Just look at me, I've made a life for myself after all. I'm going to be happy. I hope that you can see me for every second of every day.* (*Birds*: 44–45, Madden's emphasis)

Julia Kristeva has argued that although 'the call of the mother' can be used by women to shatter the symbolic order of patriarchy, it also has a deadly potential (1986: 156–57). In the absence of an alternative female system of signification, the ghostly maternal domain often expresses itself through hallucinations, voices, and madness. It leads to disintegration rather than to coherence. Madden's intersecting maternal and filial protagonists appear to be hampered by just such an impasse. Jane can never free herself from the hallucinatory knowledge of maternal loss. Her twin daughters in turn seem to be caught up in further involutions of female pain and mourning. Catherine is oppressed by the realisation that she has inherited certain ways of feeling from her mother and by the discomfiting recognition that her death brings in its wake not just grief but also 'a great sense of lightness' (*Birds*: 30). Sarah, too, shares this sensation of release which unexpectedly follows on the death of the mother. She, like Catherine, knows that the bonds of familial love simply caused her to suffer. Her retrospective vision of 'the poor misshapen shell of her mother's life' (*Birds*: 33) affords her the benefit of empathetic understanding but it does not permit her to disengage herself from the fatality of the feminist family romance which is just as incapacitating as the Oedipal one. Throughout the novel, she pursues a passionate but blighted affair with Peter, the son of Ellen, a former family friend who lives close by. This liaison seems in part motivated by Sarah's compulsion to disregard her mother's antagonism towards this woman and by her half-recognised sense of affinity with this man. The disruptive effects of female memory, however, assert themselves despite the daughter's attempt to struggle free because as the novel hints, but never directly admits, Peter is in fact the half-brother of these emotionally interdependent sisters. Catherine constantly skirts but never fully voices this truth in her ruminations. She dreads the effect of this sinister subliminal knowledge and associates the panic it induces with her fearful memories of Jane, her mother, and with her own sense of inner vacancy. Her desperate attempts to keep a diary are a ploy to avoid the rupture of this female mode of recall which threatens to blot out and destroy her identity. The painfulness of her faltering but unending memories of the mother whose face she has forgotten is paralleled with the equal distress caused by her sense of connection with Sarah, her sister, who seems to be 'herself divided' (*Birds*: 89).

In keeping with the carefully etched but reticent mode of female consciousness which Madden projects, the novel avoids any simplistic attempts at resolution. In fracturing the conventions of realism and its strategies of containment such as closure, the illusion of the bounded subject, and the insistence on narrative coherence, Madden reveals the troubled and sedimented layers of meaning and disruptive desire that mark the trajectory of the mother–daughter plot. The family secrets that are tantalisingly evoked, such as the suicide of Peter's supposed father shortly after his birth, and the fact that Jane's first child had died, remain tentative and indeterminate. Although revelation seems impossible in this claustrophobic feminocentric world, it is also shown to be unnecessary as the lines of connection between the characters facilitate the transmission of elusive but essential truths. The narrative maintains a subtle ambiguity: Jane's daughters at the end appear to have made both an uneasy peace with each other and to be indelibly marked by the unspoken language of maternal sorrow and desire. The invisible birds crying out at night remind them simultaneously of the death of their mother and of the melancholic loneliness which is the hallmark of the coextensive being of mothers and daughters in the novel. The daughters' pained consciousness of things appears to be a terrible exaction on the part of the vengeful, dead mother, and a sign of their ability to transcend the inheritance of matrilinear loss. The pattern of reticent disclosure remains the signature of Madden's narrative to the very end. In the final chapter, Catherine buries the knowledge of her sister's impending death as they both tremulously celebrate Easter. Their closeness seems at once a positive token of the permeable intimacies of female familial bonds and a sinister portent of the deadly momentum of the mother–daughter relationship.

Edna O'Brien's *Down By The River* (1996) similarly depicts the fate of her heroine as a fateful extension and unavoidable continuation of her mother's passive suffering. To this extent, the plot of the novel continues themes initiated in O'Brien's early work *The Country Girls Trilogy* (1960–1964) in which her heroine, Kate, is ultimately driven to suicide because of the propensity for unhappiness and quiescence which she inherits. Throughout this sequence of novels, the heroine's inner thoughts incessantly intermarry with those of her mother, indicating both the closeness and the suffocating nature of the link between them. The tragic drowning of her mother, who 'was more dead than anyone I ever heard of' (*Country Girls*: 45), has a double import for her: it inscribes itself as a haunting Gothic horror and as an insuperable loss. Insufficiency and lack form the very basis of her being and hamper her attempts to achieve an independent identity. The young Kate both desires reunion with her dead parent and dreads seeing her ghost. The mother in the imaginings of O'Brien's emotionally incapacitated heroine is unremittingly linked with the realm of the abject. For Kristeva, abjection is a state which is associated with the repugnance evoked by physical functions, bodily fluids, decay, and the sight of the corpse. She argues that its archaic and strange economy 'simultaneously beseeches and pulverises the subject' because of the fact that it refuses to remain banished or separate and constantly advertises its presence at the very heart of selfhood (1982: 5). Such is the situation of O'Brien's first female protagonist. She attempts to assuage the horror of maternal loss by turning into a social rebel and becoming an active, albeit hapless, participant in the sexual revolution of Ireland in the 1960s. Her wounded identity and capacity for suffering, especially at the hands of her lovers, seem, however, a product of her maternal inheritance. Her interiority is likewise depicted as an echo chamber in which she constantly relives her relationship with her mother and invokes her opinions and values. This filial empathy is both a source of strength and an incapacitating legacy. Kate, when she finds herself slipping involuntarily into her mother's role, is horrified by the resemblance, as she is adamant that she does not want to reenact her 'doleful' and tragic history (*Country Girls*: 77). Her dogged but doomed pursuit of romantic love fails either to expiate or erase 'the commonplace sacrifice' which was the sum total of her mother's existence (*Country Girls*: 203). Her affairs with Mr Gentleman and Eugene are blighted because they fall short of the all-sustaining totality of maternal love. The coextensive nature of the mother–daughter bond makes it impossible for Kate to find pleasure in the present and increases her sense of alienation and of self-estrangement. Above all, O'Brien's heroine is handicapped by her inability to find a voice. The atavism of maternal memory and longing gags the daughter and condemns her to the inexpressive mutuality of female experience. Kate's belated discovery of her hatred of her mother and her 'sponge-soft, pamper love' (*Country*: 477) does not free her; it submerges her even more fully in the subversive but disabling domain of feminine abjection. Her equivocal death by drowning, after she has lost custody of her child and undergone a voluntary sterilisation, sums up her existence in which she is 'alone and covert as always' (*Country Girls*: 524), as her friend Baba tartly notes. However, the symbiotic links between mother and daughter are depicted by O'Brien not only as death-laden and self-destructive but also as a necessary and saving dimension of female existence. Kristeva argues that abjection allows the ego to explore the abominable limits of the domain of drives, death, and maternal anguish from which it must separate in order to survive (1982: 53–55). In O'Brien's trilogy of novels, her duo of heroines, the victimised Kate and the indomitable Baba, succeed in battling against the social and sexual oppressiveness of Irish society, not only by rebelling against the religious values and sexual repressiveness that had trammelled previous generations of women but also by exploring what Kristeva terms the 'topology of catastrophe' (1982: 9) which interlinks the forfeited existences of mother and daughter. Kate's tragic submersion in the negative potency of the maternal element is at once a defeat and a defiant embrace of the otherness of female identity. Her capitulation to the deadliness of maternal power is, moreover, counterpointed by Baba's mocking and acerbic commentary upon things and her unswerving determination to survive and refusal to mourn the death of her friend. Thus, *The Country Girls Trilogy* depicts its twin but opposing heroines as achieving an uneasy balance between daughterly resistance and engulfment by the abjection of the dead mother and her ambivalent power.

O'Brien has been taken to task for her predilection for doomed, sacrificial women and for her construction of the Irish female psyche as necessarily submissive and self-lacerating.[23] Such strictures, however, wrongly assume that her fictions are simply sociological documents or written in a strictly realist vein. Although her novels consistently stress the oppressed position of women in Irish society, they aim not so much at verisimilitude as at a densely symbolic representation of female subjectivity. The evocative richness of the author's style acts as a counterpoint to the mute, internalised sufferings of her heroines and gestures at the possibility of locating a feminine language that is not simply trapped in the silenced sphere of abjection. Her most recent novel, *Down By The River* (1996), is a fictionalised reworking of some of the details of the X case, during which a young girl was prevented from having an abortion by various pro-life groups. O'Brien's teenage protagonist, Mary, becomes pregnant after a long period of violent sexual abuse by her father. Her attempt to have an abortion in England is foiled by legal interventions and the hostile attitudes of the multifarious Catholic organisations which try to commandeer her. A miscarriage, however, saves her from the fate that has been willed upon her both by her family and Irish society at large. Significantly, the novel ends with a description of the resonance of Mary's singing. Unlike many of O'Brien's earlier protagonists, the beset heroine of this novel thus ultimately manages to find a voice which allows her to break through the muteness of her subjection: 'Her voice was low and tremulous at first, then it rose and caught, it soared and dipped and soared, a great crimson quiver of sound going up, up to the skies and they were silent then, plunged into a sudden and melting silence because what they

---

23. For recent analyses of O'Brien's deployment of negative female figures, see O'Hara 1993, Shumaker 1995, Rooks-Hughes 1996, and Lynch 1996.

were hearing was in answer to their own souls' innermost cries' (*Down*: 297–98). Mary's experience of abuse replicates and continues her mother's bruised existence, as she too is regularly the victim of domestic violence and allows herself to be molested by the local doctor. The daughter's uncomprehending disempowerment is shown to be part and parcel of her ambivalent intimacy with her mother, Bridget:

> You can think more than one thing about the same person at exactly the same time. You can think oodles of things and they are all different and they are all true. Her mother was a plantation of evening foliage and evening flowers, lush and copious, dark red dahlias; her mother was that bit of stone wall with stained-glass windows that no one could see through; her mother was the Chinese lady in the picture with the dagger in her hair and pursed knowing lips, her mother was the woman who sat on the table when that doctor came and made free with her, was allowed to swing her legs, then feel her calves, then slip off her shoes and she being told in a strained voice to go off and play. You can think more than one thing about a person at the same time and they are all true, but one thing seems to be truer, the clandestine thing. (*Down*: 9–10)

Thus, Mary's feelings of helplessness and recoil at her father's behaviour are in a complex fashion bound up with her love for her mother and anger at the latter's fickleness and weakness. Her self-loathing is a facet of her problematic, merged identity with her mother. However, like 'the clandestine thing', that is the abusive sexual relations that are secretly at the heart of the overtly harmonious family romance, her divided emotions remain unvoiced at the beginning of the novel. Irigaray argues that the mother–daughter bond is disallowed by the male-centred Freudian economy of desire and driven into an unremitting silence outside of the patriarchal symbolic order. Consequently, women, she contends, are forced to subsist in a permanent state of *déréliction* or abandonment resulting from the sense of lack that is caused by the nonsymbolisation of the daughter's relation to the mother and her body (1993: 67–69).[24] In O'Brien's novel the guilty secret of sexual abuse acts not just as an indictment of the way in which the traditional patriarchal family destroys women's lives but also as a violent marker for the unspokenness that both cruelly unites and divides them.

The failure of Bridget, Mary's mother, to speak out about the abuse that is taking place in her household seems but a further corroboration of the painful, censored texture of female consciousness in the novel. Mary's reaction to the sexual violation by her father expresses itself in attacks of mutism in which she feels that her 'tongue had become an enemy' and in her desire to 'have no body' and thereby to dissociate herself from physical existence completely (*Down*: 31, 38). Her mother's death involuntarily mimics her daughter's current travail but also in a veiled manner anticipates her recovery.

---

24. For a discussion of Irigaray's definition of this term, see Whitford 1991: 77–82

Before she dies, Bridget attempts to sing a romantic lament only suddenly to have her voice cancelled by 'a great cataractic gush' (*Down*: 58) from her body prior to her demise. The final encounter between mother and daughter is also punctuated by the terror of the unspoken world of meaning that envelops them. Mary insists on viewing her dead parent in her coffin because she is impelled by an urge to communicate something vital to her. The sight of the latter's face, however, inspires such horror that it prevents her from uttering whatever she had come to say:

> The new nails positioned upright along the white paint of the mantelshelf were like a host of insects, and the coffin lid aslant against the window, a tall, stern onlooker. For a moment its bulk had made the room dimmer and then her eyes adjusted and Mary let out a little shriek when she saw her mother's expression, a more alive than dead determining in it. There was a snarl at the corner of her mouth, her upper lip raised in a helpless and grotesque curl. She wanted to put her hand there and press the two lips together but she was afraid. Her mother had striven to speak unfinished words. And she, she now would not be able to say that which she had come to say. (*Down*: 64)

Mary's mother becomes associated here with the unspeakable terror of the abject. Her very helplessness seems to be an aspect of the malign power she wields over her daughter; her silence is as damaging as the abuse that she witnesses but never acknowledges.

Although she seems condemned to reenact her mother's part after her death by becoming a housekeeper for her father and by passively subjecting herself to his ever more violent attacks, Mary succeeds in breaking out of the sphere of 'unfinished words'. She runs away from home and in doing so slowly finds a means of rescuing herself from the servility and misery which had been her mother's lot. The experience of pregnancy terrifies her and alienates her even further from her body. However, it also provides her with a deeper insight into her world. Kristeva claims that the abject and the sacred are contiguous; the purification rituals that aim to exclude objects of pollution nonetheless depend on the dark forces that they expel (1982: 17). O'Brien's heroine in *Down By The River* harnesses the powers of horror linked with the abject and finds thereby a tentative form of liberty for herself. In particular, language enables her to overcome the vicissitudes of her existence. Her diary, for example, is used to indict her father. Complementing her mother's unfinished performance of a ballad about 'a great deserted house where banquets were no more' (*Down*: 58), Mary's song dwells on future possibility and romantic longing. In a passage that recalls the ending of James Joyce's 'The Dead', her singing is described as an emanation of a bleak but strangely auspicious landscape:

> Across the land the snow is falling, the silver-thorn flakes meshing and settling into thick, mesmerising piles, sheeting the country roads, looping the winter hedges to a

white and cladded stillness and down at home their house is empty, the vacant rooms waiting for life to come back into them, for windows to be lit up again and the sloshing crowd waiting too, the way she is waiting for the face to materialize, the face that she will sing the words to, sing regardless, a paean of expectance into the gaudy void. (*Down*: 297)

In O'Brien's rewriting of the family romance, the home has become vacant, the father is exposed as a brutal tyrant, and the censored tragedy of the mother's oppression and her unfulfilled desires are made good by the daughter's cathartic language. The fact, however, that her projected future continues to revolve around the house which was the source of all her suffering suggests that the daughter's attempt to struggle free of maternal abjection and of male domination will never finally be effected. Earlier, Mary realised that 'she had loved her mother too much and not enough' (*Down*: 64). At the end of the novel, the ambivalence of the cross-generational bond between women continues to exert its force. It is uncertain whether Mary will be drawn back into the vortex of violence at the heart of the family romance or whether she faces a future that will be an advance on the life which her mother had led. The feminocentric narratives which O'Brien composes, however, open up the possibility of rethinking the conflictual relationships between mothers and daughters by freeing the daughter in part from the burden of her matrilinear inheritance.[25] Unlike Kate, whose maternal devotion had turned to hatred by the end of *The Country Girls Trilogy*, Mary, in the final pages of *Down By The River*, reaches a new understanding of her mother's doomed quest for love. Although it is unclear to what extent this reconciliation can cancel out the detrimental effects of sexual violence and abuse, the hard-won empathy of O'Brien's heroine dispels some of the assumptions of matrophobia while still recognising the split emotions that continue to divide the generations. The repudiation of the mother is no longer a necessary facet of the daughter's advancement, even though her lethal power continues to mark the latter's existence.

The Feminist Family Romance: Reconstructing the Mother–Daughter Relationship in Mary Morrissy's *Mother of Pearl*, Maeve Kelly's 'Orange Horses', and Lia Mills's *Another Alice*

The final section of this chapter will consider some recent feminocentric narratives, all of which attempt to move beyond the prominence granted to

---

25. O'Brien's 'A Rose in the Heart of New York' 1984 (orig. 1978) insists, however, on the unremitting silence that perpetually divides mothers and daughters.

the daughter's perspective in feminist writing and the consequent relegation of the mother's point of view by inventing plots that interweave the multiple, divergent perspectives of both generations. Elaine Tuttle Hansen has noted that matrilinear plots have recently been expanded in a new direction to make space for the story of the mother without child (1997). Mary Morrissy (born 1957) in *Mother of Pearl* (1996) constructs a postmodern fable that focuses upon this latterday theme of thwarted motherhood.[26] The novel is divided into four sections which revolve around the tales of two mothers and the daughter they share. The first two parts tell the story of Irene Rivers, a woman who snatches a baby, Pearl, from a hospital as a realisation of the fantasy child she has willed into existence during a phantom pregnancy, and of Rita Golden, the young mother whose newborn daughter is stolen away before she has even made her acquaintance as a retribution, she feels, for her apathy towards her. The penultimate chapter is focalised through the daughter who, when restored to her original family, is denied knowledge of the past and is consequently haunted by the memory of Jewel, her lost sister. The final pages return to the original protagonist, Irene Rivers, who refuses to relinquish the fantasy of the child who was briefly hers and continues to draw sustenance from her unabating vision of her phantom daughter.

In knitting together the twin themes of abandonment and ghostliness, Morrissy uses her fragmented narrative to explore the imagined realities that interlink mothers and daughters. In this manner, she firmly undermines the notion that the biological family indelibly determines our identity. Instead fantasmatic relations between mothers and daughters hold sway for the course of the novel. All three chief protagonists are bound together by a ghostly web of interconnected longings. Their self-identity is predicated on the absences and doublings of female desire. Irene searches for the 'pickled ghost' (*Mother of Pearl*: 55) of her imagined daughter to satisfy her deep-felt need for a baby, and continues to nurture dreams of this filial wraith after the kidnapped child has been taken away from her. Her belief that Pearl 'is not lost but merely waiting to be found again' (*Mother of Pearl*: 223) remains with her long after the story of the kidnapping has been forgotten. Rita Golden, the second mother in the novel, finds herself unable to relate to the 'ghost of a lost baby' (*Mother of Pearl*: 161) who is restored to her. Biological kinship reveals itself to be an insecure basis for maternal affection in the novel. Like Irene, Rita has to resort to fantasy in order to make sense of the child she has suddenly recouped. She invents a story of a first born infant, 'a Cupid child' (*Mother of Pearl*: 170) who had died before the birth of her second daughter, Stella, and the rediscovery of her abducted baby.

26. For other texts that also address the issue of infertility or use the image of the abducted child to critique traditional views of motherhood, see Boylan, 'A Model Daughter' (1989) and O'Donnell (born 1954), 'Breath of the Living' (1991).

The restored daughter, called Pearl by her adopted mother and Mary by her birth mother, is thus bequeathed an identity which revolves around a series of doublings. Plagued by a sense of her own ghostliness, she clings to the tale of a lost sister whom she christens Jewel and is consumed by fantasies about her which are at once terrifying and spellbinding. Eventually she abandons these vivid daydreams, which were in fact rooted in the other existence she had led as an abducted child in Irene's household. Thus, all three of Morrissy's protagonists invent ghostly daughters or sisters through whom they attempt to allay, and also to voice, the many anxieties and fears that subtend the mother–daughter relationship. In this postmodern fable, imagined relations replace biological bonds, thus destabilising filial and maternal identities and rendering them more elastic and expansive. The female ability to create exclusionary others, and also to weave ghostly alternative selves into their emotional economies, offset some of the conflicts that seem an irreducible part of the mother–daughter dyad. The dark core of intergenerational relations remains nonetheless an important aspect of Morrissy's reimagining of female interconnections. The fantasmatic inner space of her characters also provides leeway for the reenactment of primal fears about maternal omnipotence and neglect and the destructiveness of the devouring daughter. As in the fiction of Deirdre Madden and Edna O'Brien, the relationship between mothers and daughters remains precariously balanced between a sense of symbiotic completeness and of insuperable loss, but it now seems feasible to realise these conflicts in ways that side-step the overwhelming negativity of matrophobia.

Many recent fictions make an even more marked attempt to reenvisage the positive as well as the destructive dimensions of mother–daughter bonds.[27] In Maeve Kelly's (born 1930) 'Orange Horses' (1990), Elsie, a travelling woman who is trapped in a violent and loveless marriage, suddenly gains a vivid insight into the frustrations and desires of her estranged daughter, Brigid, after the latter recklessly breaks a communal taboo which forbids women to ride the mounts owned by the men in the camp. The daughter describes her feelings of exhilaration when she galloped away on a horse that had been transfigured, in her eyes, into a magical, orange creature by the sunset. Mother and daughter fall asleep in one other's arms after this moment of sublime surrender in which Brigid's impassioned ride is transmuted into an image of total freedom. As Elsie realises, 'an orange horse that

---

27. Significantly, the possibility of a reconciliation between mother and daughter is given particular thematic prominence in the work of a new generation of women writers including Devlin (born 1951), Ní Dhuibhne (born 1954), and Donoghue (born 1969). This positive reassessment of familial connections between women is also evident in the recent work of longer-established writers such as Beckett and Ita Daly. See Devlin 1986, Daly 1989, Beckett 1990 ('Inheritance'), Ní Dhuibhne 1991, and Donoghue 1997.

never was could be the greatest secret of all' ('Orange Horses': 41). However, there seems to be no way of translating this intuition of a vertiginous female sublime into everyday reality. In the closing moments of the tale, both protagonists are burnt to death in their caravan, cancelling out all traces of themselves. The intensity of the shared love between mother and daughter is such that it eludes the world. Kelly's story subtly shifts between realist and mythic dimensions in order to imagine a space in which a reconciliation can be effected between mother and daughter and eternally sustained. Ultimately, only the violent conflagration of a joint death ensures the durability of this belated and precarious intimacy between a mother and her daughter.

Lia Mills's (born 1957) *Another Alice* (1996) tells the story of Alice Morrissy who has to undergo a devastating but restorative therapy in order to dredge up the repressed memories of sexual abuse at the hands of her father. Her self-hatred is accompanied by embittered rejection of her mother, Elaine, whom she regards as a hostile stranger and an evil accomplice in her degradation. It is only when her mother dies that she realises that she has squandered the opportunity of making peace with her by talking over the past. Having used emotional withdrawal as a means of containing the pain of her childhood years, Alice is forced to recognise the necessity of confronting her buried memories when she discovers that she is in danger of siphoning this unexpressed anger into her relationship with her young daughter, Holly. Having survived the emotional and physical trauma of the self-excavation that is part of the therapeutic process, at the end of the novel the heroine is in a position to begin life anew with her child. In the final pages, mother and daughter set out together on a joyous car journey through a landscape that is no longer haunted but 'limitless' (*Another Alice*: 392). Mills uses the form of the *Bildungsroman* to chart the passage of Alice from wounded denial and inner loathing to self-knowledge and acceptance. While the progressive recovery of her heroine constitutes one of the trajectories of the narrative, the novel alters the usual concern of such plots with self-development and advancement by highlighting the intense involvement of the heroine with her daughter. Her self-growth is shown to enhance rather than to be at odds with the mutuality of her relationship with Holly. Equally, in locating the roots of her own inner torment she learns to forgive her mother whom she had condemned as heartless. The desires of the mother and the needs of the daughter merge in this text. The findings of feminist psychoanalysis implicitly inform the dialogues of Mills's central protagonist with herself. By looking at the archetypes of the monstrous mother and of the rebellious daughter in this manner, the novel succeeds in making the fates of competing generations of women less embattled. Matrophobia is revealed as a psychic malaise that can be scotched. Alice, in remaking herself, also rethinks her view of her mother and renegotiates her relationship with her daughter. The feminocentric world of *Another*

Alice works its way through the female inheritance of pain and conflict in order to conceive of the possibility of mutual support and love between Alice and Holly. As with 'Orange Horses', the conclusion of the novel subtly shifts from the realist into the mythic mode. A fairy-tale ending is conjured up in order to reinforce the sense of wish-fulfilment and harmonious completion. However, unlike Kelly's short story, Mills's novel is much more decided in its affirmation of the joyous connection between mothers and daughters and in its anticipation that this positive energy can be sustained.

Conclusion

The various fictions examined in this chapter illustrate the extent to which mother–daughter relationships are freighted in an Irish context with apparently insurmountable prejudices about the malign force of maternal power. Matrophobia haunts these texts and is invoked even by feminist writers such as Mary Lavin, Julia O'Faoláin, Molly Keane, Lia Mills, and Edna O'Brien in order to depict the desperate struggle of the daughter to avoid the trap of female subjugation and the calamity of duplicating maternal experience. Repudiation of the mother coexists, however, in the work of contemporary Irish women writers with an intense melancholia inspired by the fatal lack on which mother–daughter relationships are founded. Despite the desire to break loose from traditional familial and psychic impediments, the urge to recover the history of the mother seems in many of these fictions a necessary concomitant of the daughter's quest for fulfilment and self-knowledge. A frequent battle is consequently enacted between the imperative to unleash the terrible force of maternal power and the equally urgent compulsion to escape its devastating hold. The death of the mother is a motif that tellingly interlinks all of these narratives focusing on the intergenerational struggles between women. It acts not just as a barometer of female oppression in Irish society, but also as a means of conjuring up and harnessing the ambivalence of the mother–daughter bond. Moreover, the emphatic portrayal of the conflictual nature of relationships between women in the writing of Deirdre Madden, Julia O'Faoláin, Maeve Kelly, and Mary Morrissy provides a necessary counterweight to the sentimental and restrictive ideals of motherhood promoted by a patriarchal society.

All of the mother–daughter plots in Irish women's fiction from the 1950s onwards are clearly concerned with probing the charged symbolism that surrounds the figure of the mother. The works produced in the late 1980s and 1990s in particular provide evidence of a hard-won shift of consciousness. The denigration of the mother which was such an unremitting feature of earlier texts has ceded to attempts at effecting a reconciliation between the generations. The rejection of the male-centred, Oedipal family romance in favour of a feminocentric view of personal relations coincides with the deployment of narrative strategies that undermine the fixities of the realist novel. Madden, O'Brien, Mills, and Morrissy fracture the inherited codes of realism with the object of rethinking the seemingly inescapable hostilities embedded in the mother–daughter plot. The mother remains, however, an ominous and disturbing figure even in these fables of feminist reconciliation. Painful rapprochements and intractable tensions continue to be the fulcrum of Irish fictions that focus on the complex ambiguities of the mother–daughter relationship.

Bibliography

Beaumont, Caitriona (1997) 'Women and the Politics of Equality: The Irish Women's Movement 1930–1943' in Maryann Gialanella Valiulis and Mary O'Dowd (eds) *Women and Irish History: Essays in Honour of Margaret MacCurtain*. Dublin: Wolfhound Press, 1997, 173–83.

Beckett, Mary (1980) 'Failing Years' in *A Belfast Woman*. Dublin: Poolbeg.

——— (1990) 'Inheritance' and 'Under Control' in *A Literary Woman*. London: Bloomsbury.

Benjamin, Jessica (1994) 'The Omnipotent Mother: A Psychoanalytic Study of Fantasy and Reality' in Donna Basin, Margaret Honey, and Meryle Mahrer Kaplan (eds) *Representations of Motherhood*. New Haven: Yale University Press, 129–46.

Boland, Eavan (1989) *A Kind of Scar: The Woman Poet in a National Tradition*. Dublin: Attic Press.

Bowen, Elizabeth (1986) '*Uncle Silas* by Sheridan Le Fanu' in *The Mulberry Tree: Writings by Elizabeth Bowen*, selected and introduced by Hermione Lee. London: Virago, 100–113.

Boylan, Clare (1989) 'A Model Daughter' in *Concerning Virgins: A Collection of Short Stories*. London: Hamish Hamilton.

——— (1992) *Home Rule*. London: Hamish Hamilton.

Bradley, Anthony and Maryann Gialanella Valiulis (eds) (1997) *Gender and Sexuality in Modern Ireland*. Amherst: University of Massachusetts Press.

Breen, Mary (1997) 'Sexuality in the Novels of Mollie Keane' in Éibhear Walshe (ed.) *Sex, Nation and Dissent in Irish Writing*. Cork: Cork University Press, 202–20.

Bunreacht na hEireann (Constitution of Ireland). Dublin: Government Publications Office, 1937.

Byrne, Anne and Madeleine Leonard (eds) (1997) *Women and Irish Society: A Sociological Reader*. Dublin: Beyond the Pale Publications.

Clear, Caitriona (1995) ' "The Woman Can Not be Blamed": The Commission on Vocational Organisation, Feminism and "Home-makers" in Independent Ireland in the 1930s and '40s' in Mary O'Dowd and Sabine Wichert (eds)

Chattel, Servant or Citizen: Women's Status in Church, State or Society. Queen's University of Belfast: Institute of Irish Studies, 179–86.

Coakley, Anne (1997) 'Gendered Citizenship: The Social Construction of Mothers in Ireland' in Byrne and Leonard (eds) 1997, 181–95.

Connolly, Linda (1997) 'From Revolution to Devolution: Mapping the Contemporary Women's Movement in Ireland' in Byrne and Leonard (eds) 1997, 552–73.

Daly, Ita (1986) *Ellen*. London: Jonathan Cape.

——— (1987) *A Singular Attraction*. London: Jonathan Cape.

——— (1989) *Dangerous Fictions*. London: Bloomsbury.

Daly, Mary E. (1997) '"Oh, Kathleen Ní Houlihan, Your Way's a Thorny Way!": The Condition of Women in Twentieth-Century Ireland' in Bradley and Valiulis (eds) 1997, 102–26.

Davidson, Cathy N. and E.M. Broner (eds) (1980) *The Lost Tradition: Mothers and Daughters in Literature*. New York: Frederick Ungar.

Devlin, Anne (1986) 'Life Lines' and 'The Way-Paver' in *The Way-Paver*. London: Faber.

Donoghue, Emma (1997) *Kissing the Witch*. London: Hamish Hamilton.

Freud, Sigmund (1909) 'Family Romances' in *On Sexuality: Three Essays on the Theory of Sexuality and Other Works*. The Pelican Freud Library, vol. 7, trans. James Strachey. London: Penguin, 1977, 217–25.

Gallop, Jane (1982) *Feminism and Psychoanalysis: The Daughter's Seduction*. London: Macmillan.

Green, Miranda (1995) *Celtic Goddesses*. London: British Museum Press.

Hansen, Elaine Tuttle (1997) *Mother Without Child: Contemporary Fiction and the Crisis of Motherhood*. Berkeley: University of California Press.

Herbert, Máire (1992) 'Goddess and King: The Sacred Marriage in Early Ireland' in Louise Fradenburg (ed.) *Women and Sovereignty*. Edinburgh: Cosmos Yearbook of the Traditional Cosmology Society 7, Edinburgh University Press, 264–75.

Hirsch, Marianne (1989) *The Mother/Daughter Plot: Narrative, Psychoanalysis, Feminism*. Bloomington and Indianapolis: Indiana University Press.

Irigaray, Luce (1991a) 'The Bodily Encounter with the Mother', trans. extract David Macey, in Whitford (ed.) 1991, 34–46 (orig. *Le Corps-à-corps avec la mère*. Montreal: Éditions de la pleine lune, 1981; reprinted in Irigaray, *Sexes et parentés*. Paris: Minuit, 1987).

——— (1991b) 'The Limits of the Transference', trans. David Macey with Margaret Whitford, in Whitford (ed.) 1991, 105–17 (orig. 'L'Amour du transfert' in *Etudes freudiennes*, 19/20, 1982; reprinted in *Parler n'est jamais neutre*. Paris: Minuit, 1985).

——— (1991c) 'Women-Mothers, the Silent Substratum of the Social Order', trans. David Macey, in Whitford (ed.) 1991, 47–52 (originally published in *Le Corps-à-corps avec la mère*. Montreal: Éditions de la pleine lune, 1981).

——— (1993) *An Ethics of Sexual Difference*, trans. Carolyn Burke and Gillian C. Gill. London: Athlone Press (orig. *Éthique de la différence sexuelle*. Paris: Minuit, 1984).

Jung, Carl G. (1959) 'The Mother Archetype' in *The Archetypes and the Collective Unconscious, The Collected Works of C.G. Jung*, vol. 9, Part I, trans. R.F.C. Hull. London: Routledge and Kegan Paul, 80–83 (orig. 1954).
Keane, Molly (1981) *Good Behaviour*. London: Abacus.
────── (1988a) *Loving Without Tears*. London: Virago (orig. 1951).
────── (1988b) *Loving and Giving*. London: André Deutsch.
Keane, Patrick J. (1988) *Yeats, Joyce, Ireland and the Myth of the Devouring Female*. Columbia: University of Missouri Press.
Kearney, Richard (1997) 'Myths of Motherland' in *Postnationalist Ireland: Politics, Culture, Philosophy*. London: Routledge, 108–21.
Kelly, A.A. (1980) *Mary Lavin, Quiet Rebel: A Study of Her Short Stories*. Dublin: Wolfhound Press.
Kelly, Maeve (1990) 'Orange Horses' in *Orange Horses*. London: Michael Joseph.
Kiberd, Declan (1995) *Inventing Ireland: The Literature of the Modern Nation*. London: Jonathan Cape.
Kristeva, Julia (1982) *Powers of Horror: An Essay on Abjection*, trans. Léon S. Roudiez. New York: Columbia University Press (orig. *Pouvoirs de l'horreur*. Paris: Seuil, 1980).
────── (1986) 'About Chinese Women' (orig. 1974), trans. Séan Hand, in Toril Moi (ed.) *The Kristeva Reader*. Oxford: Basil Blackwell, 138–59.
────── (1987) 'Stabat Mater' in *Tales of Love*, trans. Léon S. Roudiez. New York: Columbia University Press, 234–63 (orig. *Histoires d'amour*. Paris: Denoël, 1983).
Lavin, Mary (1944) 'The Nun's Mother' in *The Long Ago and Other Stories*. London: Michael Joseph.
────── (1978) 'Lilacs' in *Tales from Bective Bridge*. Dublin: Poolbeg (orig. 1942).
────── (1969) 'Happiness' in *Happiness and Other Stories*. London: Constable.
────── (1985) 'A Family Likeness' in *A Family Likeness and Other Stories*. London: Constable.
────── (1986) *Mary O'Grady*. London: Virago (orig. 1950).
Lentin, Ronit (1996) *Songs on the Death of Children*. Dublin: Poolbeg.
Longley, Edna (1990) *From Cathleen to Anorexia: The Breakdown of Irelands*. Dublin: Attic Press.
Lynch, Rachel Jane (1996) ' "A Land of Strange, Throttled, Sacrificial Women": Domestic Violence in the Short Fiction of Edna O'Brien' in *The Canadian Journal of Irish Studies*, vol. 22, 1996, 37–48.
Madden, Deirdre (1988) *The Birds of the Innocent Wood*. London: Faber.
────── (1996) *One by One in the Darkness*. London: Faber.
Martin, Augustine (1986) 'Afterword' in Lavin 1986, 383–91.
McCafferty, Nell (1985) *A Woman to Blame: The Kerry Babies Case*. Dublin: Attic Press.
────── (1992) 'The Death of Ann Lovett' in Smyth (ed.) 1992, 99–106.
Meaney, Gerardine (1991) *Sex and Nation: Women in Irish Culture and Politics*. Dublin: Attic Press.
Mills, Lia (1996) *Another Alice*. Dublin: Poolbeg.
Morrissy, Mary (1996) *Mother of Pearl*. London: Jonathan Cape.

Ní Dhuibhne, Eilís (1991) 'Needlework' in *Eating Women Is Not Recommended*. Dublin: Attic Press.
O'Brien, Edna (1984) 'A Rose in the Heart of New York' in *A Fanatic Heart: Selected Stories of Edna O'Brien*. London: Weidenfeld and Nicolson (orig. 1978).
—— (1988) *The Country Girls Trilogy*. London: Penguin (orig. 1960, 1962, 1964).
—— (1996) *Down By The River*. London: Phoenix.
O'Crualaoich, Gearóid (1988) 'Continuity and Adaptation in Legends of the Cailleach Bhearra' in *Béaloideas*, vol. 56, 1988, 153–78.
O'Donnell, Mary (1991) 'Breath of the Living' in *Strong Pagans and Other Stories*. Dublin: Poolbeg.
O'Faoláin, Julia (1984) *The Irish Signorina*. London: Penguin.
O'Hara, Kiera (1993) 'Love Objects: Love and Obsession in the Stories of Edna O'Brien' in *Studies in Short Fiction*, vol. 30, 1993, 317–26.
Olivier, Christiane (1989) *Jocasta's Children: The Imprint of the Mother*, trans. George Craig. London: Routledge (orig. *Les Enfants de Jocaste*. Paris: Denoël, 1980).
Rich, Adrienne (1977) *Of Woman Born: Motherhood as Experience and Institution*. London: Virago (orig. 1976).
Roche, Anthony (1994) *Contemporary Irish Drama: From Beckett to McGuinness*. London: Gill and Macmillan.
Rooks-Hughes, Lorna (1996) 'The Family and the Female Body in the Novels of Edna O'Brien and Julia O'Faoláin' in *The Canadian Journal of Irish Studies*, vol. 22, 1996, 83–97.
Shannon, Catherine B. (1997) 'The Changing Face of Cathleen Ní Houlihan: Women and Politics in Ireland, 1960–1966' in Bradley and Valiulis (eds) 1997, 257–74.
Shumaker, Jeanette Roberts (1995) 'Sacrificial Women in the Short Stories by Mary Lavin and Edna O'Brien' in *Studies in Short Fiction*, vol. 32, 1995, 185–97.
Smyth, Ailbhe (1992) 'Sadistic Farce: Women and Abortion in the Republic of Ireland' in Smyth (ed.) 1992, 7–24.
—— (1993) 'The Women's Movement in the Republic of Ireland 1970–1990' in Ailbhe Smyth (ed.) *Irish Women's Studies Reader*. Dublin: Attic Press, 245–69.
Smyth, Ailbhe (ed.) (1992) *The Abortion Papers Ireland*. Dublin: Attic Press.
Valente, Joseph (1996/1997) 'A Child is Being Eaten: Mourning, Transvestism, and the Incorporation of the Daughter' in *The James Joyce Quarterly*, vol. 34, Fall 1996/Winter 1997, *Special Double Issue: Joyce's Women*, 21–64.
Warner, Marina (1976) *Alone of All Her Sex: The Myth and Cult of the Virgin Mary*. London: Picador.
Weekes, Ann Owens (1990) *Irish Women Writers: An Uncharted Tradition*. Lexington: University of Kentucky Press.
Whitford, Margaret (1991) *Luce Irigaray: Philosophy in the Feminine*. London: Routledge.

Whitford, Margaret (ed.) (1991) *The Irigaray Reader*, intro. Whitford. Oxford: Basil Blackwell.

Williams, Anne (1995) *Art of Darkness: A Poetics of Gothic*. Chicago: University of Chicago Press.

CHAPTER FOUR

THE PASSION FOR THE MOTHER

CONFLICTS AND IDEALISATIONS IN CONTEMPORARY ITALIAN NARRATIVE

Adalgisa Giorgio

Introduction

At the Tirrenia festival of the Italian Communist Party in 1986, Luce Irigaray delivered a lecture on the theme of female genealogies during which she invited the party officials to use their power to disseminate images of mothers and daughters in public places throughout the country (Muraro 1994: 51). The meaning of such a proposal is clear to those who are familiar with Irigaray's critique of Western philosophy and psychoanalysis: it was a strategic move aimed at making visible, indeed creating, a new icon and generating, at the level of symbolic and imaginary structures, a relationship which is an 'un-thought' in contemporary Western cultures. Irigaray's suggestion becomes more poignant when one considers that it was made in the context of a culture with a strong Catholic matrix, whose most representative icon is the Madonna with child. Recent anthropological studies on the emergence of such an iconography in relation to the development of religious doctrine during the past nine centuries, show how, with the Counter Reformation and the Council of Trent (1545–1563), Mary's role as Mother of the Son overshadowed her role as Spouse of the Father, and she became the symbol of the Church as mother of the faithful, and, finally, the essence of all mothers. Within the Holy Family, Christ and Mary share power, but the Mother is subordinate to the Son. This pattern was reproduced in the secular family, where women's position reflected the changes in the cult of the Madonna and the mother–son dyad eclipsed all other family relationships (Accati 1995, 1998).

The Catholic cult of the Madonna as Virgin and Mother found fertile ground in the pre-Christian myth of the Great Mediterranean Mother (Bachofen 1967, Neumann 1963), a myth which persists in contemporary Italian culture (Parenti 1989). In the past one hundred and fifty years the cult of the Madonna has developed in parallel with economic, social, political, and cultural changes which have assigned women the roles of procreators, carers, and educators of children, and of custodians and transmitters of the highest moral, religious, and patriotic values. This occurred first during the Risorgimento, then continued during the early decades of the new Italian nation, and finally during the Fascist régime (Bravo 1997, Koch 1997, Oppo 1997, Scattigno 1997). Womanhood has been erased by motherhood, and motherhood has primarily meant generating and nurturing the male child. The archetype of the powerful, self-sacrificial, possessive, suffering, resilient Italian mother, who is the pillar of the family and demands lifelong exclusive loyalty and affection from her children in exchange for her devotion, is a mother whose amorous gaze is directed at the male child (Bravo 1997: 139–40). Within this set-up, the daughter has no independent status: she is trained to become the mother/wife of the son/husband. Any Italian daughter searching for autonomy and individuality must negotiate this powerful maternal imaginary. Centuries of patriarchal religious and lay discourses have made the Italian mother an ambivalent figure who simultaneously encompasses authority and subordination, chastity and sexuality, the sacred and the profane. In particular, she is a figure who, although overpoweringly present within the family, is invisible in public life.

When a new wave of feminism swept over Italy in the 1970s and challenged women's traditional roles – even more successfully than in other European countries, also because of the deeply patriarchal nature of Italian society (Chamberlayne 1993: 188) – daughters discovered the importance of the mother in their lives, but found no positive elements of identification in her. Within the consciousness-raising groups, women attempted to recreate the lost union with the mother by establishing horizontal relationships between women which excluded conflict and aggression (Minetti 1982; Molfino 1987). However, this practice also excluded the mother. The realisation that it was impossible to eliminate the differences between women led to the elaboration, from the mid-1980s onwards, of new feminist practices and theories that have attempted to turn the negative value traditionally granted mothers into positive difference. On the basis of a new practice of relationships between women modelled on the mother–daughter relationship known as *affidamento* (entrustment), the Milanese feminist collective

Libreria delle donne (Women's Bookshop Collective) and the Verona feminist philosophical community *Diotima* have theorised a symbolic maternal authority which legitimates women's existence, beyond and despite the conflicts which characterise real mother–daughter relationships (see Chapter One). While these groups have concentrated on women's access to language and thought through maternal symbolic mediation, other groups and individuals have focused on the reconstruction of the repressed maternal imaginary. This has involved an emphasis on women's corporeal and psychic experiences, as well as on the historical, cultural, and social stratifications which affect these experiences, in particular motherhood and the mother–daughter relationship.[1]

The emergence of the theme of the mother–daughter relationship in Italian women's narratives in the early 1980s is undoubtedly a consequence of the feminist 'discovery' of the daughter's primary relationship with the mother in the 1970s (without implying that the writers were involved in the feminist struggle or were aware of the theoretical debates). However, the way it has been articulated over the past thirty years reflects the anthropological context that I have outlined. The theme was already lurking during the 1970s, at the same time as writers as diverse in their aesthetic and ideological commitment as Oriana Fallaci (born 1930), Gina Lagorio (born 1930), Dacia Maraini (born 1936), and Lidia Ravera (born 1951) took centre stage with texts focusing on women's roles and on motherhood from the mother's viewpoint.[2] *La porta dell'acqua* (1976, The Gate in the Water) by Rosetta Loy (born 1931) and *La bambina* (1976, The Little Girl) by Francesca Duranti (born 1935) concentrated, instead, on the young daughter's painful separation from and loss of the mother. These early novels by two writers who came to prominence in the 1980s prefigure the narratives on mothers and daughters of the next decade, which focus on the daughter's quest for identity in relation to the mother and articulate alternative plots to the Oedipal one.

This chapter examines a selection of narratives produced in Italy during the last two decades of the twentieth century from the double perspective of the way the daughter experiences and resolves (or does not resolve) her primary attachment to the mother, and attempts to establish a textual space of interaction with her. My analyses employ an eclectic approach which incorporates much of the theoretical material discussed in Chapter One. In particular, Jessica Benjamin's theory of mother–child intersubjectivity offers a useful interpretative key for a set of texts in which the daughter is forever reaching out towards a mother who is perceived as indifferent to her and in

---

1. See Libreria delle donne 1987, Cavarero 1990b, Muraro 1991, Diotima 1992, Centro Documentazione Donna di Firenze 1992. For an overview, see Giorgio 1997a.
2. See Lagorio 1969 and 1977, Fallaci 1975, Maraini 1975, Ravera 1979.

which the daughter's act of writing or narrating is aimed at creating the space of communication necessary for mother–daughter recognition (Benjamin 1995). Since recognition is a two-way process, the daughter's longing for maternal recognition must be accompanied by her ability to recognise the mother as an individual. Since this can only happen within the register of reality, and not of fantasy, the daughter's search for maternal recognition goes hand in hand with a process of stripping aimed at seeing the mother in her reality, which means seeing her in the reality in which she functions and by which she has been produced, and discovering her individuality beyond the maternal role. Adriana Cavarero's 'philosophy of narration' offers an insight into another recurrent aspect of these Italian narratives, namely their metanarrative structure and the intertwining of the mother's voice with the daughter's. She proposes, and demonstrates through the analysis of a variety of classical narratives, that human beings can understand who they are – namely the particularity and uniqueness of their individuality – only through becoming aware of the story of their origins. Like Oedipus, we will understand who we are and the significance of our actions and our life only when we understand who our mother is. Taking the cue from Hanna Arendt's claim that personal identity always, and by necessity, posits the other, Cavarero further maintains that we gain an understanding of ourselves only through the words and gazes of the other (Cavarero 1997). The daughters' narratives with which this chapter is concerned bear testimony to these claims and illustrate the intricate nature of the two-way exchanges between mothers and daughters by which they legitimate each other both emotionally and symbolically. Particular attention will be paid to the way the texts transform the physical and psychic magma of the mother–daughter bond into exchanges, signs, and words that help the daughter to be in the world.

The Daughter's Furious Attachment to the Maternal Body

That a daughter never relinquishes her primary attachment to the mother is a widely accepted psychological/psychoanalytic notion, which is borne out by women's narratives of different cultures. In the output of Italian writers, the daughter's lasting attachment clashes with maternal indifference, which, paradoxically, binds her irremediably to the mother. The texts which are analysed in this section stage the daughter's difficult process of elaboration of the loss of the mother's body and acceptance of her desire – for the husband, the son, or simply her own female *jouissance* – from which she feels excluded. Before examining the two texts which exemplify this typology, *Althénopis* (1981a, *Althénopis*, 1988) by Fabrizia Ramondino (born 1936) and *L'amore molesto* (1992, A Disturbing Love) by Elena Ferrante (born 1945), I offer a reading of an earlier novel, *Menzogna e sortilegio* (1948, *House of Liars*, 1951) by Elsa Morante (1912–1985), as a paradigmatic representation of the daughter's condition of 'dereliction' – *déréliction* is her condition of loss, abandonment, and 'homelessness' in the symbolic (Irigaray 1993: 67–69) – within the psychological, social, religious, cultural, and affective set-up described above.

Prompted by the death of her adoptive mother Rosaria, twenty-five-year-old misanthropic Elisa reconstructs her family history in search of an answer to the question 'Who is this Elisa?', a question which cannot be answered without also asking 'Who is Anna?', Elisa's natural mother (*Menzogna*: 11).[3] The game of 'loves me loves me not' mentioned in the poem dedicated to Anna which opens the novel, reveals that the crux of Elisa's narrative and predicament is her unfulfilled passion for her mother (*Menzogna*: 7). The story of her family, whose hallmarks are the clash between desire and a reality which continuously frustrates its fulfilment and the self-delusions with which her parents dressed up reality, is enclosed within a metanarrative that underscores the most bitter truth among the truths which Elisa sets out to expose: the impossibility of the mother's love for the daughter and the latter's inability to relinquish her love for the former. To this passion for her mother, Elisa attributes her unhappy life and her current physical and psychical isolation.

Elisa belongs to a progeny of unloved daughters, embittered by their failed dream of romantic love and social advancement through marriage. On the contrary, the male protagonists, Francesco and Edoardo, are the offspring of successful (if not happy) unions, and of mothers who gain social and personal value precisely through having brought a son into the world. Elisa's longing for her mother clashes with the latter's subjection to the myth of love embodied not by her husband Francesco, who is poor and ugly, but by Edoardo, her rich, blonde, and blue-eyed cousin, to whose sadistic games of possessive jealousy and indifference Anna had willingly submitted during a brief liaison in adolescence. Elisa must compete against her mother's lifelong obsession with Edoardo, who displaces her not only as Anna's lover but also as her child, the son whom Anna had asked him to give her before he abandoned her and who was meant to replace Edoardo himself: 'this child, she would name him Edoardo and she would revere and love him like a husband' (*Menzogna*: 179). Elisa has no place in Anna's passions. At the height of her mother's folly – when she learns of Edoardo's death, Anna becomes alienated from reality, writes love letters to herself pretending to be him, and 'consummates' her passion for him hysterically – Elisa begs her not to die

---

3. Since there exists only an abridged English translation of Morante's novel, I provide my own translations from the 1994 edition. Among the texts examined in this chapter, only *Althénopis* has been translated into English. All translations of quotations from other texts are mine.

until she is old too, when the three of them (Anna, Edoardo, and herself) can be united in eternity. But Anna cruelly and mockingly answers: 'Ah, next to me and him, there is no place for you, poor Elisa!' (*Menzogna*: 608). Unable to displace him, Elisa turns Edoardo into her own love object. She often talks about her 'incurable partiality' (*Menzogna*: 282) towards him, and identifies in turn with Anna, loving him as a son/lover, and with Edoardo himself, in order to take his place in Anna's heart (*Menzogna*: 129, 567). By transferring her impossible love for her mother upon the latter's object of love, Elisa perpetuates the erasure of the mother–daughter dyad, which is allowed to surface only in her dreams and fantasies of daughters who conquer their mothers' love through difficult tests and great sacrifice (*Menzogna*: 501).

One of these is a reworking of the Greek myth of Demeter and Persephone, adapted to Elisa's socioeconomic situation (unlike Demeter, the mother of Elisa's fantasy has no power to upset the world order and counter the authority of the father) and reflecting the sentimental and melodramatic quality of her imagination. A mother and a daughter who roam the earth begging are separated by a knight who falls in love with the daughter, takes her away, and turns her into a princess. The mother, desperate because of the loss of her beloved daughter, searches for her for seven years until the daughter appears to her in a dream and shows her the way to her kingdom. On arrival, seven years later, the mother is made queen. The dream is a plea for the simultaneous existence of the marital couple and the mother–daughter dyad. Maternal recognition is thus articulated only in Elisa's subliminal life, symptomatically through recourse to forms of representation from the Greek imaginary, a repressed substratum in Western culture, predating the Judaeo-Christian one. By contrast, representations of the mother–son dyad proliferate in the novel in the form of natural as well as symbolic ties: Francesco and Edoardo with their respective mothers, and Edoardo with his sister, with Anna and, as we have seen, with Elisa herself. The mother–son bond is also evoked through references to the Catholic icon of the Madonna with child (*Menzogna*: 563; see Vannocci, 1990: 420–23).

Elisa remains tied to her mother as a servant to her master (*Menzogna*: 442), reflecting the mechanism of domination and subservience which characterises the relationships between her father and her mother, between her father and Edoardo, and between her mother and Edoardo. Her fantasy of a wicked daughter who is changed into a snake and will regain her human form only after she conquers her mother through heroic deeds and servile acts is a projection of her resentment towards her mother, of her guilt for nurturing these feelings, and of her wish to be recognised by her mother (*Menzogna*: 502). Thus, if her insistent declarations of love for Anna are not genuine, they should not be attributed, as has been proposed, to an unresolved Oedipus – namely to Elisa's attempt to conceal her hatred for her mother with whom she competes for her father's love (see Scarano 1990: 149–52, Bardini 1990: 205) – but to the fact that Elisa is unable to see her mother as an autonomous individual who can choose (or let herself be chosen) by other partners than herself. In the only episode of physical union between Anna and Francesco recounted in the novel, Elisa suffers because she has been banished from the marital bed which she has always shared with her mother. If she falls in love with Edoardo, she only does so as a consequence of her desire to possess her mother's body.

Lost as she is in her insane and frustrated desire for Edoardo, Anna unknowingly exasperates her daughter's desire for her, paradoxically through her neglect and through making Elisa her accomplice in her project of 'becoming' Edoardo. Anna's death coincides with her only act of recognition (her last seduction) of her daughter. Just before expiring, she invokes her daughter's name and clutches her hand in an act of complicity, which causes immense joy in ten-year-old Elisa, but also sanctions her bondage to her mother's mythical memory for the next fifteen years, despite her adoptive mother's tender love: 'my life stops at the day which saw me ... enter this place [Rosaria's house] for the first time' (*Menzogna*: 17). The physical symptoms Elisa experiences on her mother's death indicate a final expulsion from the womb. She is sucked out of the bed chamber/maternal womb by the gelid wind of the external world, a repetition of birth, which does not connote liberation, but definitive and irreparable loss.

The massive labour of introspection which the writing of her family history has entailed has enabled Elisa to unveil the family romances of all the actors in her story, including her own, and thus to cut down to size her potent imago of Anna.[4] However, if at the end of her narrative she has achieved rest from strife, she has not come out of her isolation, and is content with living in the sole company of cats. Elisa's writing enterprise does not succeed in creating a space of intersubjective communication with her mother. Anna does not speak to Elisa. She only speaks in Edoardo's voice: in order to say 'I', she takes on his identity and constructs herself as his love object in the letters that she writes and sends to herself. Introspection unsustained by interaction with the (m)other, Cavarero reminds us, leads to estrangement from the world and one's own self (1990a: 100). If Elisa manages to dispel the pretence of magic and grandeur in her family's ambitions, desires, and mystifications, she does so by weaving an alternative, but no less

---

4. Freud's *familienroman* (1909) is the attempt of the neurotic and the highly gifted people to 'correct' reality by replacing, in their fantasy, their real parents with others of a higher status. In that it combines psychological drives and socioeconomic desires to explain the relationship between parents and offspring, it has been a productive category by which to interpret Elisa's project of unmasking both the delusions of her family members and her own (see Bardini 1990).

unreal and exalting, romantic plot. It has been said that Elisa's project to write realism is undermined by her defective linguistic and narrative competence, which has fed itself on legends, melodrama, and serialised romantic fiction (Lugnani 1990: 63–69). It is significant that at the end of the novel she is unwilling to leave the enclosure of Rosaria's house to meet, for the first time, her paternal grandmother, her last living relative and the only one who, in her own belief, had lived according to a healthy sense of reality.

The story of the passions of Elisa's family is stripped of all direct references to historical events and places. Thus, it appears to belong to a mythical and static time, even though Morante portrays a Southern Italian feudal/rural society in evolution. As a consequence, Elisa's predicament as a daughter takes on a typicality which precludes change. Sharing a Southern setting with *Menzogna e sortilegio* are *Althénopis* and *L'amore molesto*, two texts which throw into relief the socio-historical determinants of their protagonists' stories. The protagonist of *Althénopis* finds herself at the intersection of old and new models of bourgeois femininity, which causes her both to identify with and reject her female heritage. The protagonist of *L'amore molesto* goes through a similar process of identification with and rejection of the proletarian model of female sexuality embodied by her mother. Both daughters are immersed in a dynamic process of 'becoming' and receive a legacy from their dead mothers which helps them to redefine their selves.

The importance of the female heritage in *Althénopis* is underlined by the positioning of the grandmother and the mother respectively at the beginning and end of the narrative. The grandmother leads, through numerous other strong and powerful female figures, to the mother, whose death is portrayed as an opening up to a future of new generations. The grandmother–mother–daughter triad displaces the Freudian triangle of father–mother–child as the term of reference for the young girl and then adolescent searching for her identity. In the chapter devoted to the family triangle, the father is granted very little attention, whereas the mother occupies the foreground. More than half of the novel is set during the Second World War, and the father, who works at a ministry in Rome, is removed from the family, who have been evacuated from Naples to a village in the Neapolitan coastal countryside. During his rare appearances, he is seen through the eyes of the young daughter as a defeated man, a dull stranger caught in ridiculous acts, as the enforcer of a discipline and an etiquette whose irrelevance in times of war – when the social and political order he represents is crumbling – he is unable to see. The narrative subsequently omits the times when the family members are reunited, after the war and before the father's death. This event is mentioned by the adult narrator only in passing for its financial effects on the family and it is overshadowed by the death of the grandmother, which occurs immediately after and coincides with the onset of menarche in the protagonist. After the third chapter, for two hundred and thirty pages of the novel the mother also remains in the background, a longed-for and unreachable presence, the forbidden object of desire. The young girl's gaze lingers on the difference between grandmother and mother, and on the images of femininity and desire they embody. The former is exuberant, carefree, creative, inclined to excess, especially in preparing food; the latter is unhappy, distant, controlled, even cynical, trapped in her worries and migraines, miserly with food and caresses (the language of love which must be repressed), weighed down by class pride, lack of money, and the inability to keep up an upper-middle-class lifestyle. Only during their rare excursions to the wood does the mother come out of her 'realm of duties and *bienséances*' (*Althénopis*: 44; 39),[5] forgets her 'thoughts', gets rid of her migraines, and becomes a carefree child herself. The daughter remembers these moments as happy times of fusion with her mother and nature, a respite from her vain efforts to draw her mother into the adventurous and free life she can lead outside the constrictions of her class and in contact with the peasant children from the area. The daughter's pining for her mother introduces a strong melancholy undercurrent into a narration otherwise glorious, solar, vibrant in Mediterranean colours, scents, and tastes. As she approaches adolescence, her free, genderless childhood is threatened by the prospect first of a gendered, oppressive model of Southern bourgeois femininity, to which she is destined by her class, and later of an apparently free, nongendered Northern model of personhood based on money and career. The young woman rejects the first, and having tried the second, abandons that too.

In the short final part of the novel, the adult daughter returns home in a neurotic state of mind after a failed excursion (omitted from the text) into an unspecified North. The search for self resumes, but from within the confines of her relationship with her mother, now old and fragile: 'At that door, recently re-varnished, the umbilical cord was cut a second time. It was necessary to learn to breathe in a different way, and the Daughter fell sick in her breathing ... Defeated she had come back to the Mother, almost as if to ask her the reason for living' (*Althénopis*: 232–33; 234–35). The style of the narration changes for this part, with the first person of the previous two parts becoming a distancing third person. This reduces mother and daughter to the status of characters who are talked about and cannot speak to each other. The fluid and dazzling descriptions of places and people, the baroque sentence structure, the luxuriant language (incorporating Neapolitan dialect) turn into hard, short sentences punctuated by words with capital initials such as Manners, Order, Family, Mother, Daughter, Man, Widowhood, connoting the

---

5. I provide the page references for both the English translation and the Italian original, in this order.

difficult and painful communication between mother and daughter. The daughter's eyes record the mother's forlorn and hollow existence within a claustrophobic Neapolitan flat which is a simulacrum of the worn-out bourgeois values and rites for which she had lived and to which she had expected her daughter to reinstate her. The sumptuous dining room in which meagre meals are served is described as a mother who denies nourishment to her children and is compared to the mother herself. The gulf between them widens, and the mother withdraws 'ever further into her own entrails, as water into the depths of the earth' (*Althénopis*: 240; 242), where the daughter cannot reach, 'the secret union which had preceded her birth, broken then for ever by impatient rejection, was remote as buried waters' (*Althénopis*: 254; 256). Communication occurs only on the mother's deathbed, in the form of a passing on of the seed of life. The dying mother keeps touching her pubis and repeats: 'I am a baby girl, I am a baby girl' (*Althénopis*: 261; 264). A little girl is born from the old woman's body, and the daughter receives her mother's gesture as a handing over of generative power: 'That gesture which had remained buried for so many years alighted in her lap, to … enter the soul of her who grasped it, to lift the ban and make her fertile, that others born of woman might see the light' (*Althénopis*: 261; 264). The mortal female body becomes the generator of the immortal continuum of life.

Most of *Althénopis* was written by Ramondino after her mother's death while she was pregnant. She had originally been inspired to write by two dreams in which her grandmother, appearing as she is described in the opening pages of the novel, encouraged her to write stories on her behalf. Ramondino has often said that she gave birth to twins: a book and a daughter.[6] Therefore, if in the novel she tells the story of a daughter in exile from the maternal, the writing itself serves to establish a line between mother and daughter and between generations. Women's generative power, which the mother hands down to the daughter in the text, has been put to the service of bringing into the world not only human beings, but also, as Irigaray advocates, language and art (Irigaray 1991: 43).

In *L'amore molesto*, the daughter's desire for the mother is structured by the codes controlling the female body and sexuality in Neapolitan proletarian culture. Forty-five-year-old Delia returns to her native town after her mother, Amalia, drowns. In an attempt to reconstruct the last two days in her life and find a motive for her apparent suicide, Delia stumbles onto a set of clues which implicate herself: Amalia's telephone calls during which she had giggled obscene words in dialect to her daughter, an identity card where her photograph had been touched up to look like Delia, new clothes intended as a birthday present for Delia which Amalia had worn before drowning, and

---

6   See Ramondino 1981b and 1987: 53, Guacci 1987, Giorgio 1991.

her death on Delia's birthday. If 'to take one's life is to force others to read one's death' (Higonnet 1986: 68), this daughterly narrative fulfils the mother's desire to have her life interpreted through her death. Psychoanalysis views suicide by drowning as the fulfilment of the wish to bear a child (Freud 1920: 162n). Amalia's suicide by drowning on her daughter's birthday communicates her wish to kill the Delia who had both betrayed her as a child and rejected her as an adult, and to give birth to a new Delia.[7] The daughter's investigation makes it apparent that her mother Amalia had 'engineered' her death to help Delia find herself.

During the course of her search, Delia is forced to face her repressed past and rejected origins. As she moves through Naples and comes across places, people, smells, and noises from her past, the present fades into fragmented visions from her childhood, which yield a picture of a family bound by passion, jealousy, and violence. As a child, Delia experiences severe anxiety every time her mother goes out, and vows to kill her on her return. Her reaction to maternal otherness is shaped by a culture and a language that associate love with violence and death.[8] She models her love for and rage against Amalia upon the obsessive jealousy and abuse through which her father tries to control his wife's mind and body. Delia's recollections also conjure up an independent, exuberant, and sensual woman, who does not succumb to her husband's attempts to contain her pleasure in life and in her own body. Amalia is 'the victim who is not annihilated' by 'the bogeyman who does not scare' (*L'amore*: 92). When she receives anonymous presents, she accepts them, thus fuelling her husband's suspicions that she betrays him with his friend Caserta. Amalia's piecework – the family's only stable source of income – empowers her to defy her husband and eventually leave him, taking her three daughters with her.[9]

Young Delia is baffled by her mother's ambiguity. She recalls how at the cinema Amalia would lean her head on her husband's shoulder looking happy, while launching furtive glances laterally from behind his arm, which he erected as a fortification between her and other men: 'That double movement used to tear me inside. I did not know in which direction to chase my fleeing mother, whether along the axis of her eyes or along the parabola that her hair drew against her husband's shoulder' (*L'amore*: 126). Her parents' sexual power games influence Delia's view of her mother. Her desire to possess and control her gives rise to her desire to *become* her. She contemplates

---

7. Freud also tells us that people find the mental energy required to commit suicide by turning against oneself a death wish originally directed against another (1920: 162).
8. See Niola for the association, in Neapolitan dialect, of the idea of killing with desire: 'I want to beat you to death', 'I want to kiss you to death' (1994: 101).
9. See Goddard 1996 on Neapolitan proletarian women's position vis-à-vis work, sexuality, and family relations.

biting off Amalia's 'extraordinary' finger, sporting a nail pierced by the needle of the sewing machine, in order to destroy that which makes her mother different from her, because she cannot gather the courage to offer her own finger to the needle in order to make herself like her.

Delia's identification with Amalia is the key to her present life and to the mystery of her mother's death. Her search culminates in a revelatory and liberating sequence, during which she disinters the repressed memory of when she had told her father that she had seen Amalia make love with Caserta, and reconstructs the psychological process which had led her to say what she had only imagined: 'childhood is a fabrication of lies' (*L'amore*: 117). She recalls herself engaged in sexual games with Caserta's young son, Antonio, in the shop belonging to Caserta's old father, imagining being Amalia and behaving as she imagined Amalia to behave outside her husband's gaze:

> I pretended not to be me. I did not want to be 'I', unless I was Amalia's I... I was I and she. I-she would meet with Caserta. Indeed I did not see Antonio's face ... but what there was of his father's adult face in his face.
> I loved Caserta with the same intensity with which I imagined my mother loved him. And I detested him, because the fancy of that secret love was so vivid and concrete, that I felt I could never have been loved in the same way: not by him, but by her, Amalia. Caserta had taken everything which was mine by right'. (*L'amore*: 118)

A second memory surfaces, with Caserta's father running his hands up Delia's legs while telling her obscene words. Once again the old man's face dissolves into Caserta's and Delia becomes Amalia. But the identification is not perfect: 'It was Amalia who experienced all the pleasure: I was left only with terror ... and in the meantime Amalia played to be her real self who knows where ... Caserta was undoubtedly elsewhere, with my mother' (*L'amore*: 119–20). Angry and distraught, she runs home and tells her father a transfigured version of reality, a defence mechanism which enables her to disown her sexual curiosity by attributing it to Amalia and to deny her experience of sexual abuse, as well as a revenge against Amalia because she cannot be (like) her.

Delia's 'lie' represents a symbolic murder of Amalia, after which she had slowly eradicated from herself any gesture, mannerism, or preference of Amalia's, including her city and dialect, both associated with obscenity and a disturbing and aggressive sex (*L'amore*: 96). Frigidity had been her answer to her fantasies of maternal sexuality: 'None of the kisses [men] had given me had seemed like the kisses I had imagined Caserta had given Amalia ... I felt no more than that diffused pleasure, pleasant but lacking in urgency ... I remained worn-out and dissatisfied' (*L'amore*: 80–81). Now Delia realises the wretchedness of her efforts to shed 'one by one, any reason to be like [Amalia]' (*L'amore*:126), and sets out to reverse the process. In the crumbling shop, she finds her mother's old suit which Caserta had taken in a last attempt to possess Amalia, and wears it, 'the ultimate narration which my mother had left me' (*L'amore*: 121). Although it is too large, she feels it fits her perfectly. She walks away in it under Caserta's eyes, taking Amalia with herself. She decides that her mother's death was not an accident, but an act to free herself from the two men who had attempted to expropriate her throughout her life (*L'amore*: 116). Amalia was a 'woman who had somehow invented her story until the end' (*L'amore*: 92).

At the end of the narrative, Delia draws her mother's hairdo around her face on her identity card photograph: 'I looked at myself, I smiled at myself. That old-fashioned hair style ... suited me. Amalia had been there. I was Amalia' (*L'amore*: 126). This act and these words, on which the novel ends, complete Delia's response to Amalia's offer of reconciliation. She realises that the obscene words which her mother had giggled on the phone – the same words Caserta's father had whispered to her while he abused her which she had then repeated to her father as the words that Caserta had told Amalia – were meant to help her overcome the past, accept her mother's desire, and open the way to her own desire: 'Perhaps she wanted simply to prove to me that also those words were speakable and that, contrary to what I had believed throughout my life, they could also not hurt me' (*L'amore*: 120). After 'having abandoned me in the world to play alone with the words of mendacity, without measure, without truth' (*L'amore*: 120), Amalia had finally given Delia the key to her life by means of her death.

Luminal (1998, Luminal), a novel with eighteen-year-old 'bad girls' as protagonists, by one of Italy's most transgressive young writers, Isabella Santacroce (born 1967), offers an insight into the daughter's erotic desire for the mother's body, which finally breaks through the unconscious. The narrative is an explosive and desecrating mixture of religious and sexual images, conveyed through outrageous language and a rhythm which, by contrast, imitates that of a prayer:

> Magnificent virgin inside a blazing new shaved body at the centre of the universe I the tightrope walker before leaving you mother-candyman I have passed again the razor blade gathering the hair in your pill-case I have desired the penis of your lover who like you did not know about me hidden under your bed ... from there I would watch your gothic cunt and the creativity of your head on the cocks you went up and down rhythmically on your knees you would part the fucker wide lowering yourself your buttocks would open showing orifices I have had orgasms out of your copulations trained daughter without your knowing I have learned noble positions. (*Luminal*: 91)

The image of the Virgin merges with the unbearable image of the mother as a desiring body. The daughter displaces upon her own body, by means of a brutalising sexuality, both her sexual desire for her mother and her desire to punish her for giving her body to other lovers. The ambivalent maternal image which was discussed in the introduction to this chapter still has a powerful hold on Italian daughters, even while they lift the taboos surrounding maternal sexuality and the daughter's incestuous desire for the mother.

Illegitimacy and Maternal Apotheosis:
The Daughter as Hero

Marie Maclean's study of illegitimate French literary figures shows that bastardy goes hand in hand with myth-making. The lives of the illegitimate protagonists of *Madre e figlia* (1980, Mother and Daughter) by Francesca Sanvitale (born 1928) and *Passaggio in ombra* (1995, Passage in the Dark) by Mariateresa Di Lascia (1954–1994) are guided by a similar desire to turn their lives into a myth and themselves into heroes. Since their project as narrators is to identify the patterns which run through their lives in order to extract from them the deeper meaning of their existence, they become aware of their 'myth-making', though not of the mechanisms of legitimation at work in their self-construction. Their lives display many variants of the motifs of the hero tale.[10] The hero is a figure of liminality who becomes 'legitimated not by the name of the Father in a human genealogy, but by supernatural, extra-human forces, which can only be activated by his own efforts' (Maclean 1994: 18). Our protagonists legitimate themselves through an appeal to divine origins and a miraculous birth. This entails attributing divine or extraordinary powers to themselves or to their mothers, which turns their narratives into an apotheosis of the latter. The mother's early death in Di Lascia's novel ensures that her protagonist remains tied to an awesome, static, and therefore detrimental image of her mother, whose deeds she cannot match. Therefore, she wavers between maternal and paternal affiliations and remains in the limbo of semi-madness. The daughter/writer in Sanvitale's novel constructs and deconstructs herself and her mother by exposing and inverting the process through which she turned herself into a hero, in order to counteract her mother's loss of value and to revalorise her. The lifelong *corps-à-corps* is resolved in a productive symbolic exchange between mother and daughter.

Like Morante's Elisa, the narrator of Di Lascia's *Passaggio in ombra* embarks upon telling the story of her family on the death of her adoptive mother, her paternal great-aunt Peppina, to explain her current isolation, neurosis, and accidia. Also Chiara's narrative project is to expose her own and her family's illusions and delusions. In what appears to be a rewriting of Morante's story

---

10. Maclean lists the following: illegitimate birth, an absent or hostile father, upbringing by foster parents, the mother's persecution or suffering because of the illegitimate child, the conquest of a kingdom, and the death as a hero (1994: 19).

offering an alternative mother–daughter plot, Chiara, unlike Elisa, had been granted beauty and the love of two mothers.[11] Born from a liaison between a twenty-five-year-old midwife newly arrived in a Southern village after the outbreak of the Second World War, and a local young man, Francesco, on leave from the war, Chiara lives the first three years of her life in complete happiness in the 'amorous nest' (*Passaggio*: 16) of her mother's body: 'my mother and I lived alone for a long time, in love with each other without remedy' (*Passaggio*: 14). She talks of her birth as a miraculous event proceeding from her mother only. The fact that Anita, the stork that brings all the babies in the village, 'had also brought me all by herself' sanctions Chiara's superiority in the eyes of the other children (*Passaggio*: 99). Anita's authority as a life-giver makes her bastard daughter cherished by the community and later by Francesco's female relatives. Eighteen pages into the story, Francesco's return from the war destroys the mother–daughter dyad for ever and brings separation, uncertainty of identifications, and suffering. Within a year Francesco has contrived to seduce his daughter and to claim her by giving her his name. This act of renaming – a natural completion of a process of paternal appropriation initiated by Anita herself when she had named Chiara after Francesco's dead mother – marks the beginning of Chiara's destruction. It is her entry into a deadly Oedipal plot.

Chiara's life from now on is marked by the physical and psychic disorder that her father brings to her life, and the search for a new rooting. Her story is presented as a progressive fall from a superior height linked to the failure of her dream of full legitimation, to be realised first through Anita's marriage to Francesco (which never takes place because of his cowardice), and then, after her mother's death (also presented as a consequence of Francesco's intrusion into her life) and her father's disappearance, through the dream of marrying Saverio, the ostracised and disowned bastard son of her father's sister Giuppina. Saverio opens new suggestive possibilities of identifications for Chiara. Her dream of (semi-incestuous) union with him, sustained by the awe that he inspires for being even less than a bastard and a foundling, disguises her desire to reinforce both her affiliation to the paternal and her ex-centricity to her father's family and the local community: 'He is my cousin: the farthest and nearest point in my own family; that which takes me out of it, and into its most secret and darkest heart! I will marry him and will mix our names ... "D'Auria twice!"' (*Passaggio*: 245). But she is forced to give up Saverio by her aunts. The dream of paternal recognition having shattered, Chiara is also incapable of pursuing the route to subjectivity indicated by her mother's example. First she is unable to defy social conventions as her mother had, and give herself to

---

11. There are extraordinary correspondences between *Passaggio in ombra* and *Menzogna e sortilegio*, which I cannot investigate here. It is intriguing that Di Lascia denied having read Morante's novel (see Marchi 1995: 45–46).

Saverio. Later she fails to complete her studies to become a doctor and thus further her mother's profession. Life after Saverio is a passive wait for the extraordinary event that will bring about the fabulous destiny predicted for her by her female relatives (*Passaggio*: 226), ultimately leading to her alienation from the world and from herself. However, even this path is not pursued fully. She remains a 'border creature' (*Passaggio*: 22), unable to find her freedom in either death or folly in order to become a truly divine creature: 'In other places … in other times … the insane were celebrated as divine creatures' (*Passaggio*: 117).

Chiara's present condition is the final stage of a degradation started when she had been propelled into the Father's realm and seduced to identify with an apparently heroic but in fact weak paternal. Chiara's love for Saverio also necessitates her social exclusion, at a time when her symbolic integration through education is under way. Her linguistic and expressive competence must be checked if she wants to communicate with Saverio who is barely literate (*Passaggio*: 208). Her failure in the world is a consequence of her living in a void of figures of mediation with the world. With Anita's death, Chiara loses a positive figure of female mediation. Anita is replaced and displaced by other mothers, Francesco's aunt and sister – interestingly, they bear the same name – who have little value in a society which has denied their desire, both as women and as mothers.[12] This new female genealogy offers Chiara protection and financial support, but at the same time entraps her in a hypocritical and patriarchal Southern society which destroys her through the arcane fascination of its interdictions. At the time of the narration, Chiara has succeeded in seeing her father as an ordinary man (*Passaggio*: 22–23), but she can still only think of Anita with the awe that one experiences before 'the unexpected apparition of a temple erected for a pagan divinity, or of a terrifying and wondrous natural event: an earthquake or a deluge. Such was the force of my mother' (*Passaggio*: 17). The perfect maternal imago becomes an opaque, repressed, silent figure who cannot speak to Chiara.

The narrator of Sanvitale's *Madre e figlia*, on the other hand, presents the incandescent matter of her relationship with her mother, which alone can sustain a living image of the latter. The mother–daughter *corps-à-corps* is encapsulated in the vision which opens the novel. Marianna emerges, luminous, from the shadow of the baroque arch of a palace door, unaware that a crowd is waiting to attack her: 'Only my shoulders and my open arms hold them from punishing her superficiality and past riches, from gushing into the door, from raiding the palace, knocking her over and crushing her, preventing her from being herself and my secret joy when I imagine her in Vienna

---

12. Donna Peppina had become sterile after contracting syphilis from her husband. Unmarried teenager Giuppina is forced to keep secret her pregnancy and to give up Saverio at birth, after which she does not succeed in conceiving again.

dancing the Lehar waltz in the ballroom with the mirrors' (*Madre*: 3). The crowd is a projection of Sonia's resentment for her mother's inability to take her life into her own hands, her childlike irresponsibility, her unknowing indifference to her daughter's anguish, her disruption of the latter's efforts to build a dignified life for them both, for demanding her attention by means of her illnesses: 'I am the war that is looking for her in order to kill her' (*Madre*: 6). Sonia attempts to recreate on the page the fabulous past of young countess Marianna in *fin-de-siècle* Northern Italy, before the events that turned her into a victim unable to name the world: the break of her engagement by her fiancé, her father's death, her elopement with a married army officer, and Sonia's birth. The visions of an adolescent Marianna, dressed in lace, covered in jewels, dancing gracefully, alternate with the reality of the gaping, oozing wound on her old woman's chest, of her paralysed and enlarged eye, of a frail woman slovenly dressed in black. Love for that body – 'even though old, even dead, even decomposed. Only my mother's body is for me a body to love' (*Madre*: 4) – guilt, and the desire for reparation drive fifty-year-old Sonia's narrative, which attempts to extricate the threads of their entangled lives four years after Marianna's death.

The text we read dramatises Sonia's struggle to recompose these lives by linking her memories of the past with the images that emerge from past and present fantasies and dreams, and then making everything fit within the chronology of history. The novel's temporal planes are continually twisted and superimposed, while the first-person narration by Sonia, constituted as a speaking subject, alternates with the third-person of an impersonal narrator, who focuses on Sonia and Marianna as characters in plots written for them. The narrative refuses to be subjected to the rigid structures of chronology, following instead the vagaries of memory and the logic of the unconscious and taking on the form of a collage organised around epiphanies, often enlisting the reader's participation to tease out interpretations through a second-person direct address.[13] The alternation between different modes of narration creates an effect of confusion between mother and daughter, symbolic of their con-fused identities and voices.

If the metanarrative in which the fragmented mother–daughter story is embedded details Sonia's struggle to recapture the past and give it a meaningful order on the page, it is the mother who acts as the starting point of the narrative, offering the daughter the means to initiate her process of reparation through the written word. Towards the end of the novel we are told that, close to death, signora Marianna had got into the habit of thinking aloud and speaking like an automaton about her early life: 'Sonia looked at her mother as one looks at the nutshell turning into a gold carriage and as one looks at

---

13. On the novel's structure and use of time, see Blelloch 1990 and Wright 1993.

this gold carriage, attached to little mice which become white horses' (*Madre*: 218). Standing by in the shadow, the daughter becomes a 'vase in which precious sighs, words or images were decanted' (*Madre*: 218), which she will use to transform Cinderella into a princess. Writing acts as the daughter's restitution of both life and symbolic competence to the mother, that symbolic competence which, significantly, she had relinquished as Sonia had started learning to read and write. Sonia's life will be spent in the pursuit of giving her mother her life and voice back.

As Sonia undertakes her journey through fragments of dreams, memory, and history with the aim of laying bare the patterns underlying her life, a number of plots emerge. The story of how she had turned herself into a martyr and a hero who would rescue her mother from poverty, pain, and disease, is intertwined with another subtext that functions as a narrative of legitimation through maternal archetypes. Marianna's name, made of 'the two most beautiful names, those of Jesus' mother and grandmother' (*Madre*: 8), summons an alternative family romance to the Holy Family, the maternal trinity of St Anne, Mary, and child of the apocryphal Gospels, a cult begun at the end of the fifteenth century which became an archetype and a 'figurative equivalent of the family ruled by the mother' (Maclean 1994: 51). When Sonia is born in May, the month consecrated to the Madonna, she is hailed as 'a precise copy of the Child Jesus' (*Madre*: 21). At the age of six, she identifies hysterically with Christ on the cross and his agony (*Madre*: 22), while at the age of eight she receives the message from the effigy of Christ with an open chest that 'sorrow is a safe route, joy lies in covering it all the way until your hands are marked by the stigmata, and your bleeding heart is surrounded by rays' (*Madre*: 55). In the Catholic school which she attends, eleven-year-old Sonia acts, in a school play, the part of a woman, Dolores, who offers her life in exchange for that of another woman, Maria, who has been condemned to death and whose life must be preserved because she is a mother. Sonia's perfect rendition of her character is a premonition of her later masochistic desire to shoulder the burden of her mother's life, and give up her life in order to expiate the guilt of her existence.

Guilt and punishment are also thrown into relief by a passing reference to the biblical figure of Hagar. When Sonia evokes Marianna's early life in the enchanted family palace, her attention is captured by pregnant Hagar, represented in the frescos on the ballroom walls while running away from the storm towards God's punishment. In the biblical story, the servant Hagar gives birth to Abraham's illegitimate child, Ishmael, who is accepted by barren Sarah as her son. However, when the latter is blessed with a son of her own at the age of ninety, Hagar is persecuted and expelled into the desert with her child. Like Hagar and Ishmael, Marianna and Sonia are two fugitives doomed forever to wander outside the community, continually moving house and city in order to hide from Sonia's father's wife who, allegedly, wants to kill her.[14] They are banned from a social and political order which is in the hands of four men, Father, King, *Duce*, and Pope: 'Their clothes moved like waves, their steps produced no noise, their bodies had no volume. They passed over the street and the city almost like shadows... They were delinquents, hunted by the law and by revenge' (*Madre*: 23). Marianna withdraws into silence at the same time as Sonia understands the importance of naming the world with precision, in order to counter a masculine order that is erasing their existence: 'Signora Marianna was losing the use of many words day by day... there was no "pan", "jug", "frying pans", "lid", "teapot", "coffee-maker", "kettle", "sieve" and so on. Every object belonging to the kitchen, remained fixed in an unreal presence as if in a painting, and "the little pot" ... became the idea of all other lost objects and the only named one' (*Madre*: 31). On her father's death, Sonia discovers that he had formed a second illegitimate family for which he had long before left his wife. In the contest between three families – a legitimate, childless one and two illegitimate ones with offspring – the one blessed with a son wins: the mother–daughter dyad has no currency in a conservative and patriarchal system like Fascism.

Hagar's story, which has been used as a social myth of bastardy (Maclean 1994: 23), is relevant to Sonia's predicament in other ways. Ishmael was destined by God not only to be a wild man whose hand would be against every man (see Genesis XVI: 11–13) but also the progenitor of a race of princes (see Genesis XVII: 20), thus initiating the complementary myths of the evil bastard and of his divinisation (Maclean 1994: 165–66). From divine child, the adult Sonia turns herself into a hero like Orlando, Achilles, Hercules, and David, and turns her life into a series of tests set for her by the Gods (*Madre*: 116). The scene in which, at twenty years of age, she releases her father from financial responsibility for her and her mother, is preceded by a dictionary entry on the word 'hero':

Hero: valiant, strong, courageous.
Demigod, paladin, knight, warrior, great man, champion; model, example.
Character, protagonist. (*Madre*: 123)

Her mission to become her mother's saviour loses its religious connotations and takes on mythical overtones. She speaks of 'five years of labours [an allusion to Hercules] and reconstruction', during which her expectations of a

---

14. A Poussin exhibition inspired Sanvitale to put his paintings 'The Calm' and 'The Storm' into her novel. Hagar does not appear in these paintings, but in a third one by Poussin. Sanvitale was unaware of the links between Hagar's story and the myth of bastardy (private conversation: Rome, December 1998).

collaboration with Marianna leading to 'a giant future' are systematically frustrated by the latter's indifference, her neglect of the home, and her habit of incurring debt, which Sonia must repay (*Madre*: 127–28), as if to demand that her daughter repay unendingly her debts to her, for having been given life and for having ruined her (Marianna's) life. Sonia tries in vain to make her mother understand that 'she had come into the world to rescue her, she was not the executioner, she was the help sent by God' (*Madre*: 132). Her exasperated self-abnegation turns into hatred and violence. She leaves her mother, but with the determination to make her happy, even against her will: 'She was still the hero and on her insignia there were the colours of her abandoned mother' (*Madre*: 133). The bodily experiences – Marianna's cancer, Sonia's abortion and miscarriage – bring the two women together again, but the boundaries between them become blurred. When Marianna becomes ill with breast cancer, Sonia imagines herself as the 'purulent wound' which runs across her mother's thin chest (*Madre*: 153). They live in alienating interdependence, with Marianna demanding her daughter's care and Sonia thriving on the power of life and death which she believes she has over her mother. To counter her entanglement with her mother, Sonia sets up rigid boundaries between herself and her husband, and between her Self and her body, in an exasperated search for self-sufficiency and control in at least some areas. As is always the case with bastards, Sonia's emotional life is a life of excesses (Maclean 1994: 212–13). Long after her mother's death, Sonia is still on a mission to do her justice and rehabilitate her memory. In the dream with which the novel closes, Sonia sublimates her guilt, elaborates her loss, and completes the glorification of Marianna as an aged and serene queen of a secular heaven made immortal by her daughter's words.

Reconstructing the Mother–Daughter Relationship: The Daughter as Auto/Biographer

The two texts examined in this section, *Il gioco dei regni* (1993a, The Game of Kingdoms) by Clara Sereni (born 1946) and *Mia madre era una donna. Romanzo* (1996, My Mother Was a Woman: A Novel) by Amanda Knering (born 1922), share the explicit project of constructing life stories with reference to the ideologies and institutions which have both produced them and affected their textual production. While Knering's text concentrates on the mother–daughter relationship, this is not the exclusive concern of Sereni's work, even though the narrator's project to reconstruct a female genealogy provides the moving force of her auto/biographical project.

Mia madre era una donna claims simultaneously the status of novelistic discourse, essay, and auto/biography. The title makes explicit its aim of uncovering the 'who' – the individual – behind the 'what' – the functions of mother and wife. This is achieved by interweaving the (re)construction of the lives of the narrator and her mother with historical, sociological, and psychological considerations on how society and its institutions reduce women to roles. The auto/biographical project is underscored by the inclusion of photographs of Knering's mother, Josephine Ziehl, which, in providing 'material "proof" of a woman who has really existed, in bone and flesh, at a particular time and place' (Cavarero 1997: 94), draw attention to the uniqueness of her existence beyond the roles she played. However, the auto/biographer must resort to supposition and imagination to fill the 'silences and voids' between the 'crumbs' and 'fragments' which she possesses (*Mia madre*: 13, 71). This novelistic enterprise is far from straightforward in the absence of a textual tradition: 'Because it is not the lives which provide models, but the stories' (*Mia madre*: 71).

The two-page first section, placed after a photograph of sixteen-year-old Josephine and entitled 'Portrait of a memory', underlines the gap between the daughter's memory of her mother exclusively as a housewife and the individual hidden behind the role: 'I have crossed her life without meeting her: like piercing through a shadow' (*Mia madre*: 13). The second section, entitled 'Behind the portrait' and forming the main body of the text, attempts to dispel the shadow and retrieve the mother's 'true' life. The narrator alternates between an intimate and emotional second-person narrative addressed to her mother and a third-person analytical narrative. The second-person form of address tries, textually, to create the missing narration between mother and daughter:

> And which biography of you can I recount if I do not know your story?
> We never came out of our isolation...
> You locked up in your shell as a mother, I in mine, as a daughter.
> Give me your story, mother.
> You are telling me that you are a woman without a story. An anonymous woman.
> (*Mia madre*: 72)

The narrative is governed by different impulses. When the centre of consciousness is the daughter as a character, the tone is one of accusation, with the mother being blamed for her poor mothering. We are told about her anger for her husband's infidelities, her lack of concern with the psychological effects of her fighting and shouting on her children, the attention she demanded through her anorexia and Münchhausen syndrome, her delegation of the care of her children to the servants, and, consequently, the daughter's sense of having been neglected and abandoned. When the biographer takes over, the daughter looks at her mother without 'the lenses which distort every mother–daughter relationship' (*Mia madre*: 71), but armed instead with the insights of the American and French feminists (*Mia madre*: 50). This narrative contextualises and exculpates the maternal figure; the daughter then starts to make sense of her own treatment of her mother.

Echoing Adrienne Rich (1976), the narrator tells us that 'motherhood is an institution which requires from women maternal instinct rather than intelligence, which forces them to realise it according to preestablished models ... self-denial rather than self-realisation, a relationship which starts and exhausts itself in the children' (*Mia madre*: 101). The mother's life is examined with an eye to both the oppressive ideologies that shaped it and the signs of rebellion which can be gleaned from it. Born in Germany in 1900, Josephine had been brought up according to the Küche-Kirche-Kinder (kitchen, church, children) ideology. She had moved to Trentino, a border region which became Italian at the time of the narrator's birth, after marrying an Italian from that area. Fascism had banned her mother tongue, which, the narrator indirectly suggests, contributed to the distance between them: 'If my mother has never used her language with me, she has not even ever played with me' (*Mia madre*: 111). A picture emerges of a woman excluded from the local community and from her husband's heavily patriarchal family, who had fitted unwillingly into the prescribed roles of mother and wife: 'Not only Küche-Kirche-Kinder, you dreamed other roads, your dreams ran towards other ends' (*Mia madre*: 60). She recalls that, like herself, her mother wanted to become an actress, had attended high school, but had succumbed to marriage and to the values in which she had been brought up after becoming pregnant. Current psychological findings help her to see more in her mother's illnesses than a request for her husband's attention: she now links them with problems of identity and femininity. After recovering from them, her mother had travelled around Italy, most inappropriately for the times, with her brother-in-law. She had also established lifelong friendships with men. The biographer draws a woman who was religious but was not a bigot (*Mia madre*: 97), who was well-read and forward-looking, who travelled, drove a car, wore trousers, walked in the mountains at a time when all of these things were considered unsuitable for women. However, this alternative narrative is also put under scrutiny. The urge 'to draw a different portrait of you, much more human than the plastered image of my memory' (*Mia madre*: 70) does not blind the biographer to the fact that her mother, despite her rebellion at bourgeois respectability, never succeeded in evading her maternal, domestic role (*Mia madre*: 103).

The mother's entrapment in this role is at the core of the daughter's relationship with her and of her narrative. Her claim that she is 'structurally' different from Josephine in not conforming to the prescribed gender roles of housewife and mother is undercut by the contradictions and omissions which can be found in her impassioned account of their differences. These seem to amount to no more than the fact that Josephine, from early on, had no mother who could help her achieve what the narrator achieved both against her mother's will and with her support. Appearing callous in her declarations that 'I did not feel any scruples about finding my own ways of evading, about reorganising my life according to my own pleasure, my own measure' (*Mia madre*: 116) and that 'I have never felt any guilt towards her' (*Mia madre*: 127), she does not try to hide the fact that she was able to obtain a degree, although she got pregnant and married very young (as did her mother), to become involved in politics, pursue a writing career, and have numerous lovers in other cities by means of turning her mother into her own wife and leaving her children and husband in her charge. She does not make amends for having taken what she needed from her mother to fulfil her desires in life, in times which did not grant women many opportunities. Piety and female solidarity towards the mother suffuse the narrative throughout, but neither guilt nor reparation are its moving force. What the narrator does not seem to realise is how much her own life is the result of social conditioning by a societal organisation and a cultural order in which she can become an individual only by making herself different from her mother and turning herself into a copy of her father. Yet in her closing remarks on her mother's last words before dying ('You are my mother, aren't you') – which she takes as evidence that her mother had searched for her 'wholeness' in her 'strong, decisive, even hard' daughter, 'just what she, as a daughter, would have liked to find in her own mother' (*Mia madre*: 127–28) – she seems to suggest that maternal legacies must be established and passed on from mothers to daughters, if relationships of exploitation and dependence are not to be reproduced. It is a pity, therefore, that Knering's narrator has chosen not to tell us anything about her relationship with her own daughter, who receives only one passing mention. If she has broken the chain of the reproduction of mothering (see Chodorow 1978) by offering her daughter a different maternal model, we wonder whether she has not added another link to the chain of seemingly unloved Italian daughters. However, if her life had been an attempt at writing an Oedipal plot, the book is an attempt at writing a maternal one which will constitute a legacy for the daughters to come.

Clara Sereni's *Il gioco dei regni* also blends the biographical project with the novelistic one, in wishing to illumine the real persons before turning them into characters of fascinating and dramatic plots (*Gioco*: 446). Like Knering, Sereni brings to light a mother–daughter story of conflict and rejection, but from within a wider reconstruction of her family history. Using a method of composition by fragments derived from the Jewish heritage that she reclaims through the book she is writing (in Gaglianone 1996: 22–23), she sews together extracts from the writings left by her family members; exceptional men and women who had pursued high civic and political ideals at the expense of family affections. Her task is to recover the private world excluded from the words with which they had handed themselves down to posterity. It is in her mother's words that she finds the most significant excisions and silences. *I giorni della nostra vita* (1955, The Days of Our Life), the autobiography which Marina Sereni wrote as a legacy to her daughters before she died prematurely of cancer, omits every reference to her own mother, a Greek-Orthodox Russian revolutionary. The story of her life starts with her encounter with Emilio Sereni, the man who was to become her husband. In the last straightforwardly autobiographical section of *Il gioco dei regni*, Clara Sereni explains how, during a trip to Israel in search of her lost Jewish roots, she had discovered among the writings of Xenia, her maternal grandmother, a story of her relationship with her daughter. The juxtaposition of Marina's and Xenia's words yields the sad story of a daughter's lifelong rejection of her mother. The adolescent's condemnation of her mother's political activities, which she perceives as irreconcilable with the maternal function and an obstacle to her dream of a bourgeois life and marriage, continues in her adult life, after she marries one of the young men who frequent her mother's political gatherings and becomes part of his upper-middle-class Jewish family. The cruel way Marina contrives to keep Xenia out of her life, stopping her from seeing her daughters, and even banishing her to the corridor outside her hospital room while she is dying, can be explained only in part by their political differences. Awe, envy, and resentment for her mother's intellectual stature appear to prevent Marina from recognising her as a subject and from becoming one herself under her mother's eyes. Ironically, Marina devotes her own life to politics, thus repeating her mother's life. However, *Il gioco dei regni* draws a picture of Xenia which obscures Marina. The former emerges as an independent thinker and an inspiring leader, ready to take on new causes, including Zionism, which she pursues fully by moving to a kibbutz in Israel (even though she is not Jewish). A woman 'who had had an intense relationship with writing' (*Gioco*: 437), she leaves a vast amount of memoirs, letters, political essays, lecture notes, and articles. Like Xenia, Marina lives for her ideals, but they are always those, first Zionism then Communism, prescribed by her dogmatic husband.

Whereas in her mother's book Sereni had only found 'an unbridgeable distance' (*Gioco*: 441), in her grandmother's papers she finds the missing link between herself and her female Jewish heritage, the sense of belonging to 'an uninterrupted female genealogy' (*Gioco*: 446). *Il gioco dei regni* is structured precisely around this genealogy: even though the foreground is taken up by the giant figures of the three Sereni brothers, the maternal and paternal grandmothers provide a line of continuity both in the narrative and in the lives that it reconstructs.[15] *Mia madre era una donna* reflects the pre-neofeminist and

---

15. On the structure of Sereni's novel, see Chemello 1998.

neofeminist thematics of female emancipation from patriarchy and from the mother as an agent of its norms, as a consequence of the times in which the mother first and then the daughter grew up. *Il gioco dei regni* reflects the contemporary Italian Jews' search for a collective cultural identity after the crisis and collapse of ideologies of both the right and the left (Levi della Torre 1994: 8, 17–20), as well as the post-1970s feminist (and Jewish) search for a rooting in maternal genealogies.

Reconstructing the Mother's Voice

Towards the 1990s, women's narratives weave together the mother's voice with that of the daughter in a process which increasingly releases the former from linguistic/structural subordination to the latter. This results in the adoption of a variety of more or less experimental rhetorical strategies. The outcome of the 'confrontation' between mother and daughter is also varied, sometimes leading to the daughter's revision of her views on the mother – especially in the case of 'weak' mothers who are then revalorised – to the daughter's being freed from her emotional dependence on an idealised maternal figure, and/or to the daughter's acceptance of the mother as an autonomous and desiring subject. A recurrent motif is the daughter's desire to receive maternal approval and recognition for her life and achievements.

The device of the mother who narrates her life adopted by Sanvitale is also employed by Carla Cerati (born 1926) in *La cattiva figlia* (1990, The Bad Daughter) with more realistic motivations and effects. The middle-aged narrator, forced to take care of her obstinate and sullen old mother at a time of newly-won freedom from her husband and children, asks her to speak about her past in a desperate attempt to deflect their reciprocal intolerance. From the mother's long direct speech, which later, unobtrusively, becomes a third-person narrative by the daughter, a new image emerges of a resourceful and adventurous woman who had fought against paternal authority and societal conventions, and who had been the material and psychological pillar of her family of origin and of her own family through years of poverty.

La casa sulla Marteniga (1993, The House on the Marteniga) by Tina Merlin (1926–1991) is an autobiographical *Bildungsroman* which traces the narrator's early life on a farm in the Po valley, her involvement in the Resistance, her political militancy, her intellectual maturation and career as a journalist. Each chapter in the first-person, chronologically-ordered retrospective narrative ends with a section in italics recording the here and now of the narration, the process of remembering the past and the pain it entails, as borne out by the exchanges between the narrator and her mother. The daughter undertakes her work of excavation with the aim of both lightening the burden of her mother's suffering for the loss of her sons in the war, and of obtaining maternal recognition. Although the mother recognises her daughter's right to her attention, she is unable to stop grieving for her dead sons in order to take pride in the achievements of her living daughters.

When the mother is already dead at the time of the daughter's recollection, the texts foreground their own power to bring her to life through language. In the short story 'Gli Orti della Regina' (1993, The Queen's Gardens) by Marisa Bulgheroni (born 1925) the daughter gives body and voice to the fabulistic vocation of her dead mother. The two-voiced narrative – italics distinguishes the mother's words from the daughter's – is a reconstruction of facts, a construction of wefts, an artistic creation of flowers, plants, and words, aimed at unravelling an intricate tangle of passions. Mother and daughter are reunited at the intersection of nature and culture, in a garden which is presented as a female artistic creation (see Giorgio 1997b). *Lettera alla madre* (1988, Letter to My Mother), by Hungarian-born Holocaust survivor Edith Bruck (born 1932), demonstrates the life-giving power of the word. Here, a daughter who survived Auschwitz brings back the repressed memory of her mother who died there by employing an I/Thou narrative structure which engenders their reciprocal animation: 'if I do not talk to you, if I never mention you, if I never quarrel with you, I forget you, and if I do not write and do not write to you, I allow you to be forgotten' (*Lettera*: 47). The daughter is thus able to rescue her mother from oblivion and grant her a form of life after an arbitrary death, assuage her guilt for having survived her, and accept her loss, as well as seek a reconciliation with herself as a Jew.[16] Auschwitz is also at the centre of *Lezioni di tenebra* (1997, Lessons in Darkness) by Helena Janeczek (born 1964, Germany, of Jewish Polish parents), in which a daughter reconstructs her mother's past in an attempt to overcome the pain and guilt which she has inherited through her placenta. The mother's participation in the text, visible in her comments in italics, which correct and add to the facts and memories that the daughter collates, sparks off her process of elaboration of the pain for the loss of her own mother, who had been deported after she had left her to seek safety. In Janeczek's and in Bruck's novels, writing serves to reestablish a line of communication between mothers and daughters separated by guilt, sorrow, and death.

In *Benzina* (1997, Petrol) by Elena Stancanelli (born 1965) the mother is given an independent voice, after she has been silenced by her daughter and her lesbian lover, and a space for reconciliation is created. The narrative proceeds from a three-voiced interior monologue relating the unpremeditated murder of a middle-class mother by her daughter's lover

---

16. See Giorgio 1999a for Bruck's use of apostrophe, and Giorgio 1999b for her manipulation of autobiographical details.

in the service station which the two young women run. As the mother dies, her soul leaves her body and floats above the scenes that unfold before her eyes of the two young women cleaning her blood, making love, putting her body into the car boot, and embarking upon a picaresque journey around the outskirts of Rome. The lovers' attempts to dispose of the corpse produce a comic-grotesque narrative which breaks the traditional taboos surrounding the maternal figure. Unexpectedly, it is the mother's monologue (really a second-person dramatic monologue addressed to her daughter) which generates the most irony, as a consequence of the vantage point from which she observes the events. The mother's conformism is revealed by her comments on the dust and dead mosquitoes lying on the fridge, by her squeamishness at 'the indecent spectacle of my daughter thrown across a plastic table with her petrol-pump attendant busy on her genitals' (*Benzina*: 27) and at the 'indecorous farce' of the whole affair (*Benzina*: 26). Conversely, the monologues of the two lovers, their occasional dialogues, as well as what we learn about them through the mother's eyes, relate their frantic actions, their confusion, their fears, their fights and the hurt that ensues, in dealing with an event which becomes more and more intractable, both practically and emotionally. The mother's comment that 'she has done you some favour. She got rid of a mother for you and gave you in exchange a corpse so heavy that you cannot even lift it' (*Benzina*: 41) betrays her delight with the fact that her daughter will carry the burden of her death for life.

The dynamics between the three voices/characters, however, change with the unfolding of the events. As the corpse is shifted around the town, the young women talk to it and to each other, discussing and explaining their pasts, their relationships with their parents, their sexuality. The mother, who can listen but not speak, is forced to consider their point of view. She reexamines her relationship with her daughter and starts revising, with her characteristic self-irony, her ideas about love, sex, and family life: 'if I were allowed to have my life back, I would not repeat the same stupid things... I would know that a daughter can even wish you a wrench on the back of your neck if you do not pay her enough attention during her difficult adolescence' (*Benzina*: 102). We hear of her fear of pregnancy and motherhood, and of her confusion when her daughter became bulimic. She recalls her panic in realising the depth of her commitment when her daughter was born: 'When I had the very tiny hand of my daughter in my hand, and I saw her eyes which glued themselves to mine for ever, I understood that I would never make it, that it was too much for me' (*Benzina*: 140). Mother and daughter engage in a most revealing 'interior dialogue'. The mother's thoughts about her passion for handbags and her compulsion to fill them up, in order to later give them away – a reenactment of her desire for and fear of pregnancy, the yearning to be filled up and emptied out –[17] are juxtaposed with the daughter's memories of the handbags that her mother bought for her and which she regularly rejected, and of her gorging and throwing up. Past conflicts start to dissolve as each addresses the other in their self-enclosed monologues. The mother turns into the young women's helper. She uses her supernatural powers to stop her daughter's lover from being raped: 'I am so proud of myself! I would so much like to tell my husband and see him turn pale. Because I, shrinking violet, a moment ago have carried out a grand deed, a heroic exploit, the first action of which I can be truly proud since I was born' (*Benzina*: 111). In unlocking the hand brake of a car to push it against the rapists' car, she also unlocks her bourgeois emotional restraint and the wall she had erected between herself and her daughter:

> There are neither generous mothers nor devoted daughters. There is you...
> For this reason I should have loved you, in order to dig a tunnel which running beneath our lives would lead me straight to you. Like death. A silent and private tunnel, where we could hug each other without fearing to crease our souls out of embarrassment... never again I will make the mistake to believe that there is a way of being different from love. (*Benzina*: 114–15)

She starts calling her daughter's lover by her name instead of 'benzinaia' (petrol-pump attendant) and her daughter by the nickname her lover had given her, a nickname being, she realises now, a sign that two people love each other. She even works out an alibi to exculpate them of her death. There is no need for one, though. When the young women are threatened again by the same men, who now wreck their petrol station and kill their dog, they set the petrol station on fire and end their life together in a spectacular explosion in front of the police (a scene which recalls the close of the film *Thelma and Louise*). The mother now speaks in the first person plural as she tells the reader that the three of them, united in death, look down on earth and laugh.

The mother's point of view is also given in *Vuota per sempre. Appunti dall'anoressia* (1997, Empty for Ever. Notes from Anorexia), by Laura De Luca (date of birth unknown), a long letter in which a twenty-one-year-old anorexic responds to excerpts from her mother's diary. The daughter accuses her mother of having neglected her to pursue her own life and lovers. A product of 1968 – a political activist, feminist, and pop musician – the mother expresses her right to her own self, her rejection of self-sacrificial motherhood, the difficulty of stepping into roles, her confusion about whether to try to save her daughter and how, or to leave her free to die. In narratives like *Benzina* and *Vuota per sempre*, set in contemporary Italy, fea-

---

17. For women's conscious and unconscious experience of pregnancy, see Ferraro and Nunziante Cesaro 1992.

turing young protagonists and mothers who came to adulthood in the 1960s and 1970s, the spectre of the 'bad mother' rises between mothers and daughters as a category which has emanated from a new ideology of motherhood created in the 1950s and 1960s and still upheld today. This is a totalising concept of mothering which requires women's commitment well beyond the duty of biological procreation and provision of care in the early years of the child's life, to include 'the work of relational, social, and affective reproduction: the work of the "heart" and of intelligence' which carries on beyond infancy and adolescence (Saraceno 1997: 321). The work of the post-Freudian mother is subjected to the normalisation, control, and judgement of such experts as paediatricians, pedagogues, and psychologists. The mothers in *Benzina* and *Vuota per sempre* are subjected to this child-centred culture which makes them responsible for their daughters' anorexia and bulimia, and brands them as 'bad mothers'. The bourgeois mother from *Benzina* casts only faint doubt on the psychologist's diagnosis that her daughter developed bulimia as a reaction to her confusion and dismay at pregnancy and motherhood. The mother in *Vuota per sempre*, conversely, tries to uphold till the end her rejection of prescribed norms of mothering: 'Was she wearing a jumper? a good mother would have asked. Not me, who is not and does not want to be a good mother' (*Vuota*: 93). When we gain access to the mother's mind, we see women caught in the contradictory social and psychological mandate to invest all their energies and resources in 'producing', by means of their exclusive care, an autonomous individual whom they have to let go (Saraceno 1997: 323). It is not surprising that we find bafflement and anxiety.

Ramondino, the only writer among the ones examined in this chapter who has looked at the mother–daughter relationship from both perspectives, offers an insight, in her play *Terremoto con madre e figlia* (1994, Earthquake with Mother and Daughter),[18] into a mother who asks herself: 'What is a mother? Why does nobody tell me?' (*Terremoto*: 18). She relates to her adolescent daughter through her own experience as a daughter, trying to avoid old patterns: 'you become a mother only when you realise that you are making your child suffer what you suffered at the hands of your mother' (*Terremoto*: 58). As in *Vuota per sempre*, mother and daughter are divided by the watershed of 1968. Their differences and clashes are neutralised by the splitting of their voices into two: alongside the voices of ordinary interaction are those of the 'mother-bottle' and of the 'daughter-telephone', through which the alcohol-addicted mother turns to her past of political militancy and addresses her inner anguish, and the daughter projects herself towards the world outside the dyad and the future. The play is set in Naples in the aftermath of the 1980 earthquake, a situation which Ramondino exploits to

---

18. First performed in Asti, 1st July 1993, under the direction of Mario Martone.

draw a tragi-comic picture of the parallel drama of a city and a mother–daughter dyad shaken in their foundations. Ramondino presents an unprecedented picture of a mother who is aware of the social constraints imposed on motherhood, of the cultural and psychological mechanisms at work in mother–daughter relations, and of the need for continual reflection upon how to relate to her daughter, from what appears to be the perspective of a woman who chose to become a mother.

Conclusion

The mother–daughter relationship continues to exert great fascination upon women writers.[19] This is hardly surprising for the older ones who attempt to come to terms with the inevitable experience of their mother's death through writing.[20] It is also understandable why younger writers avail themselves of this theme, when one considers the centrality of the maternal figure in the Italian family, even after the recent emergence of new family models (see Saraceno 1997). Italian narratives on mothers and daughters are dominated by maternal figures who are aloof from, and indifferent to, their daughters. Whether they are strong or weak individuals, whether they are bourgeois or peasant women, whether they are working women or housewives, mothers are seen as pursuing desires – of their own choice or determined by the institutions which condition them – that exclude the daughters. Maternal power and influence are obtained through indifference and neglect, which generates the daughter's obsessive attachment to and idealisation of the mother.

The theme of the impossibility of not loving the mother runs through most narratives. When the mother is put on trial, the daughter often contrives to blame herself and justify the mother. This is the case also in texts representing highly conflictual relationships like Sanvitale's and Cerati's, which, in fact, originate in guilt and in the desire for reparation.[21]

Even the anorexic daughter of *Vuota per sempre* admits that 'I would have liked to be like you, perfect and unassailable in the obstinacy of your frenzies, in your battles', and ends her letter to her dead mother with the words

19. It has also been dealt with in psychoanalytic histories (Ravasi Bellocchio 1987), daughters' memoirs (Mori 1992), in more commercial forms of autobiographical literature (Sotis and Moratti 1991), and women's magazines (Corva 1991).
20. Petracci's *Lo sai che non moriremo più? Una storia d'affetto* (1996, Do You Know That We Shall Never Die? A Story of Affection) is an old woman's monologue addressed to her dead mother which draws, with great sensitivity, their symbiotic life together over sixty years during which all differences had been erased.
21. Cerati's title already betrays the daughter's guilt. See also the ironic title of Sereni's short story 'La figlia buona' (1993b, The Good Daughter), on the psychological violence of a (bad) daughter upon her old mother.

'I love you, mother' (*Vuota*: 63, 124). The daughter's emotional dependence on the mother and her need to be recognised and accepted by her are to be found even in such texts as *Benzina* and *Luminal*, which open the way to transgressive representations of the mother similar to those which abound in English literature. However, the unprecedented use of the comic and the grotesque by younger writers is a signal of the daughter's desire to chip the powerful maternal figure of the Italian imaginary.

Yet, the Marian model still exerts enormous influence upon daughters, as *Luminal* and the recent tour de force of Laura Bosio (born 1953) in *Annunciazione* (1997, Annunciation) demonstrate.[22] The latter is an intensely suggestive journey through Biblical sources, myths, poems, and theological scholarship around the figure of the Madonna, by a woman who searches for her dead mother and for herself in the images of Mary in the paintings of the 'Annunciazione' (*Annunciazione*: 11). It is the mystery of Mary's fear and wonderment when the Angel tells her that she is going to give birth that obsesses Bosio's alter ego, but her search does not find an answer to a question which has fascinated many others before her. The recent narratives that offer glimpses into the mother's mind suggest that, if women have deconstructed the 'institution' of motherhood, they are still baffled by the 'experience', especially when they bring daughters into the world. They seem to recognise the threat of loss of self as soon as they meet their eyes, and respond by pushing them away in order not to be engulfed. This fear is clearly also a consequence of internalised social norms and expectations associated with motherhood. Access to legal contraception and abortion and the availability of reproductive technologies, an area in which Italy has recently taken a leading role while also having the lowest fertility rate in the world,[23] have undoubtedly changed the way Italian women relate to motherhood.[24] If soci-

---

22. See also Bosio's *I dimenticati* (1993, The Forgotten Ones), the *Bildungsroman* of a twenty-one-year-old woman who goes back to her mother after a self-destroying journey of initiation into life, the agents of which are men. The mother, who becomes aphasic when the daughter reaches puberty, reawakens when she is reunited with her, in a reciprocal exchange of life and language.
23. Births dropped from over one million in 1965 to 561,000 in 1992, with a rate well under replacement level of 1.27 children per woman in 1991. Fertility rates of 1.8 and 1.68 have been estimated for women born in the mid-1950s and late 1950s respectively (Menniti et al. 1997: 226).
24. Women writers have started looking at 'difficult' motherhood. Sereni's poetic and unsentimental stories of *Manicomio primavera* (1989, Bedlam Spring), for example, deal with the frustrated desire for a child and with the mortification of not having produced the healthy and beautiful child every woman expects and desires. The light-hearted and ironic short pieces in Cornelio and Violi's *Di madre in peggio* (1995, From Mother to Worse) explore, in a witty style imitating the superficial chit-chat of everyday life, the contrast between women's inner feelings and outer attitudes vis-à-vis various aspects of pregnancy, motherhood, and mothering, including the failure to become a mother. On the contrary, the 1970s narratives on motherhood mentioned at the beginning of this chapter took for granted a woman's ability to have a child and for that child to be perfect.

ological studies of the 'great transformations in the relationships between generations' and of women's experience of mothering daughters as a consequence of the socioeconomic and cultural changes of the last thirty years are still not available (Saraceno 1997: 350–51), literature shows signs of being concerned with this exploration.

The widespread practice of incorporating the mother's voice into the daughter's narrative attests to the commitment of contemporary women writers to hear or imagine the mother's point of view. Yet, with the notable exception of Ramondino, they appear to be reluctant to abandon their position as daughters and speak as mothers of adult daughters. If it has taken Italian women centuries to start articulating representations of the mother–daughter relationship and to move beyond the deadlock of maternal idealisation and denigration, it will probably take them a few more years to start writing about their daughters. Only then can we begin to compose the full picture of the mother–daughter story.

Bibliography

Accati, Luisa (1995) 'Explicit Meanings: Catholicism, Matriarchy and the Distinctive Problems of Italian Feminism' in *Gender and History*, 7, 1995, 241–59.

——— (1998) *Il mostro e la bella. Padre e madre nell'educazione cattolica dei sentimenti.* Milan: Raffaello Cortina.

Bachofen, Johann J. (1967) *Myth, Religion and Mother Right. Selected Writings of J.J. Bachofen.* London: Routledge and Kegan Paul (orig. 1954).

Bardini, Marco (1990) 'Dei "fantastici doppi", ovvero la mimesi narrativa dello spostamento psichico' in Lugnani et al. 1990, 173–299.

Benjamin, Jessica (1995) *Like Subjects, Love Objects: Essays on Recognition and Sexual Difference.* New Haven and London: Yale University Press.

Blelloch, Paola (1990) 'Francesca Sanvitale's *Madre e figlia*: From Self-Reflection to Self-Invention' in Santo L. Aricò (ed.) *Contemporary Women Writers in Italy: A Modern Renaissance.* Amherst: University of Massachusetts Press, 124–37.

Bosio, Laura (1993) *I dimenticati.* Milan: Feltrinelli.

——— (1997) *Annunciazione.* Milan: Mondadori.

Bravo, Anna (1997) 'La Nuova Italia: madri fra oppressione ed emancipazione' in D'Amelia (ed.) 1997, 138–83.

Bruck, Edith (1988) *Lettera alla madre.* Milan: Garzanti.

Bulgheroni, Marisa (1993) 'Gli Orti della Regina' in Rosaria Guacci and Bruna Miorelli (eds) *Racconta 2.* Milan: La Tartaruga, 97–105. Reprinted in Bulgheroni, *Apprendista del sogno.* Rome: Donzelli, 1996, 91–101.

Cavarero, Adriana (1990a) 'Dire la nascita' in Diotima, *Mettere al mondo il mondo. Oggetto e oggettività alla luce della differenza sessuale.* Milan: La Tartaruga, 93–121.

―――― (1990b) *Nonostante Platone: figure femminili nella filosofia antica*. Rome: Editori Riuniti. *In Spite of Plato: A Feminist Re-Writing of Ancient Philosophy*, trans. Serena Anderlini-D'Onofrio and Áine O'Healy. Cambridge: Polity Press, 1995.

―――― (1997) *Tu che mi guardi, tu che mi racconti. Filosofia della narrazione*. Milan: Feltrinelli.

Centro Documentazione Donna di Firenze (ed.) (1992) *Verso il luogo delle origini*. Milan: La Tartaruga.

Cerati, Carla (1990) *La cattiva figlia*. Milan: Frassinelli.

Chamberlayne, Prue (1993) 'Women and the State: Changes in Roles and Rights in France, West Germany, Italy and Britain' in Jane Lewis (ed.) *Women and Social Policies in Europe*. Aldershot: Edward Elgar, 170–93.

Chemello, Adriana (1998) 'La "genealogia" riconosciuta di Clara Sereni' in Chemello (ed.) *Parole scolpite. Profili di scritttrici degli anni Novanta*. Padua: Il Poligrafo, 103–19.

Chodorow, Nancy (1978) *The Reproduction of Mothering: Psychoanalysis and the Sociology of Gender*. Berkeley: University of California Press.

Cornelio, Valeria and Tonci Violi (1995) *Di madre in peggio*. Milan: Garzanti.

Corva, Lisa (ed.) (1991) *Cara mamma, cara figlia. Lettere dall'Italia: parlano le lettrici di Grazia*. Milan: Mondadori.

D'Amelia, Marina (ed.) (1997) *Storia della maternità*. Rome-Bari: Laterza.

De Luca, Laura (1997) *Vuota per sempre. Appunti dall'anoressia*. Rome: Voland.

Di Lascia, Mariateresa (1995) *Passaggio in ombra*. Milan: Feltrinelli.

Diotima (1992) *Il cielo stellato dentro di noi: l'ordine simbolico della madre*. Milan: La Tartaruga.

Duranti, Francesca (1976) *La bambina*. Milan: La Tartaruga.

Fallaci, Oriana (1975) *Lettera a un bambino mai nato*. Milan: Rizzoli. *Letter to a Child Never Born*, trans. John Shepley. London: Arlington Books, 1975; revised trans. London: Hamlyn, 1982.

Ferrante, Elena (1992) *L'amore molesto*. Rome: Edizioni e/o.

Ferraro, Fausta and Adele Nunziante Cesaro (1992) *Lo spazio cavo e il corpo saturato. La gravidanza come 'agire' tra fusione e separazione*. Milan: Franco Angeli.

Freud, Sigmund (1909) 'Family Romances' in *The Standard Edition of the Complete Psychological Works of Sigmund Freud*, ed. and trans. James Strachey, vol. 9. London: The Hogarth Press, 1959, 236–41.

―――― (1920) 'The Psychogenesis of a Case of Homosexuality in a Woman' in *Standard Edition*, ed. and trans. James Strachey, vol. 18. London: The Hogarth Press, 1955, 146–72.

Gaglianone, Paola (ed.) (1996) *Conversazione con Clara Sereni. Donne, scrittura e politica*. Rome: Ômicron.

Giorgio, Adalgisa (1991) 'A Feminist Family Romance: Mother, Daughter and Female Genealogy in Fabrizia Ramondino's *Althénopis*' in *The Italianist*, 11, 1991, 128–49.

―――― (1997a) 'Real Mothers and Symbolic Mothers. The Maternal and the Mother–Daughter Relationship in Italian Feminist Theory and Practice' in

Gino Bedani, Zygmunt Barański, Anna Laura Lepschy, and Brian Richardson (eds) *Sguardi sull'Italia*. Leeds: Society for Italian Studies, Occasional Paper no 3, 1997, 222–41. Revised as 'Mothers and Daughters in Italian Feminism: An Overview' in Anna Bull, Hanna Diamond, and Rosalind Marsh (eds) *Feminisms and Women's Movements in Contemporary Europe*. Basingstoke and London: Macmillan, 2000, 180–93.

——— (1997b) 'Parola e passione materna: "Gli Orti della Regina" di Marisa Bulgheroni', in Zygmunt Barański and Lino Pertile (eds) *In amicizia: Essays in Honour of Giulio Lepschy*. Special Supplement to *The Italianist*, 1997, 315–26.

——— (1999a) 'Strategies for Remembering: Auschwitz, Mother, and Writing in the Work of Edith Bruck' in Helmut Peitsch, Charles Burdett, and Claire Gorrara (eds) *European Memories of the Second World War*. Oxford: Berghahn, 247–55.

——— (1999b) 'Dall'autobiografia al romanzo. La rappresentazione della *Shoah* nell'opera di Edith Bruck' in Claire Honess and Verina Jones (eds) *Le donne delle minoranze. Le ebree e le protestanti d'Italia*. Turin: Claudiana, 297–307.

Goddard, Victoria A. (1996) *Gender, Family and Work in Naples*. Oxford and Washington, D.C.: Berg.

Guacci, Rosaria (1987) 'Germania, luogo eventuale. Da Napoli a Essen Werden. Fabrizia Ramondino parla dei suoi "Taccuini tedeschi" e delle sue città' in *Il Manifesto*, 19 June 1987.

Higonnet, Margaret (1986) 'Speaking Silences: Women's Suicide' in Susan R. Suleiman (ed.) *The Female Body in Western Culture: Contemporary Perspectives*. Cambridge, Massachusetts, and London: Harvard University Press, 68–83.

Irigaray, Luce (1991) 'The Bodily Encounter with the Mother', trans. extract David Macey, in Margaret Whitford (ed.) *The Irigaray Reader*. Oxford: Blackwell, 34–46 (orig. *Le Corps-à-corps avec la mère*. Montreal: Éditions de la pleine lune, 1981; reprinted in Irigaray, *Sexes et parentés*. Paris: Minuit, 1987).

——— (1993) *An Ethics of Sexual Difference*, trans. Carolyn Burke. Ithaca: Cornell University Press (orig. *Ethique de la différence sexuelle*. Paris: Minuit, 1984).

Janeczek, Helena (1997) *Lezioni di tenebra*. Milan: Mondadori.

Knering, Amanda (1996) *Mia madre era una donna. Romanzo*. Castel Maggiore, Bologna: Book Editore.

Koch, Francesca (1997) 'La madre di famiglia nell'esperienza sociale cattolica' in D'Amelia (ed.) 1997, 239–72.

Lagorio, Gina (1969) *Un ciclone chiamato Titti*. Bologna: Cappelli.

——— (1977) *La spiaggia del lupo*. Milan: Garzanti.

Levi della Torre, Stefano (1994) *Mosaico. Attualità e inattualità degli ebrei*. Turin: Rosenberg e Sellier.

Libreria delle donne di Milano (1987) *Non credere di avere dei diritti: la generazione della libertà femminile nell'idea e nelle vicende di un gruppo di donne*. Turin: Rosenberg e Sellier. *Sexual Difference: A Theory of Social-Symbolic Practice*, trans. Teresa De Lauretis with Patrizia Cicogna. Bloomington: Indiana University Press, 1991.

Loy, Rosetta (1976) *La porta dell'acqua*. Turin: Einaudi.

Lugnani, Lucio (1990) 'Logos kai Ananke' in Lugnani et al. 1990, 9–93.
Lugnani, Lucio, Emanuela Scarano, Marco Bardini, Donatella Diamanti, and Claudia Vannocci (1990) *Per Elisa. Studi su 'Menzogna e sortilegio'*. Pisa: Nistri-Lischi.
Maclean, Marie (1994) *The Name of the Mother: Writing Illegitimacy*. London and New York: Routledge.
Maraini, Dacia (1975) *Donna in guerra*. Turin: Einaudi. *Woman at War*, trans. Mara Benetti and Elspeth Spottiswood. London: Lighthouse Books, 1984.
Marchi, Ena (1995) 'Ricordo di Mariateresa' in *Linea d'ombra*, 13, no. 104, 1995, 44–46.
Menniti, Adele, Rossella Palomba, and Linda L. Sabbadini (1997) 'Italy: Changing the Family from Within' in Franz-Xaver Kaufman, Anton Kuijsten, Hans-Joachim Schulze, and Klaus P. Strohmeier (eds) *Family Life and Family Policies in Europe*. Oxford: Clarendon Press, 225–52.
Merlin, Tina (1993) *La casa sulla Marteniga*. Padua: Il Poligrafo.
Minetti, Maria Grazia (1982) 'Alla ricerca dello specchio. Fusione e differenziazione nei gruppi delle donne' in *Memoria*, 3, 1982, 22–31. 'In Search of the Mirror: Fusion and Differentiation in Women's Groups', trans. Sharon Wood, in Paola Bono and Sandra Kemp (eds) *The Lonely Mirror: Italian Perspectives on Feminist Theory*. London and New York: Routledge, 1993, 115–27.
Molfino, Francesca (1987) 'I possibili spazi della conoscenza psicoanalitica' in Maria Cristina Marcuzzo and Anna Rossi Doria (eds) *La ricerca delle donne. Studi femministi in Italia*. Turin: Rosenberg e Sellier, 203–19.
Morante, Elsa (1994) *Menzogna e sortilegio*. Turin: Einaudi (orig. 1948). *House of Liars*, abridged trans. Adrienne Foulke. New York: Harcourt, 1951.
Mori, Anna Maria (ed.) (1992) *Nel segno della madre. Di donna in donna: tredici figlie raccontano*. Milan: Frassinelli.
Muraro, Luisa (1991) *L'ordine simbolico della madre*. Rome: Editori Riuniti.
––––––– (1994) 'Il concetto di genealogia femminile' in *Tre lezioni sulla differenza sessuale*. Rome: Centro Culturale Virginia Woolf-Gruppo B, 27–53 (orig. workshop 1988).
Neumann, Erich (1963) *The Great Mother: An Analysis of the Archetype*. Princeton, N.J.: Princeton University Press (orig. 1955).
Niola, Marino (1994) *Totem e ragù*. Naples: Pironti.
Oppo, Anna (1997) 'Concezioni e pratiche della maternità fra le due guerre del Novecento' in D'Amelia (ed.) 1997, 208–38.
Parenti, Francesco (1989) 'La duttilità transculturale della simbologia materna e le sue componenti immutabili' in Tilde Giani Gallino (ed.) *Le Grandi Madri*. Milan: Feltrinelli, 220–29.
Petracci, Franca (1996) *Lo sai che non moriremo più? Una storia d'affetto*. Milan: Longanesi.
Ramondino, Fabrizia (1981a) *Althénopis*. Turin: Einaudi (new ed. 1995). *Althénopis*, trans. Michael Sullivan. Manchester: Carcanet, 1988.
––––––– (1981b) 'In *Althénopis* ci sono tutte le mie esperienze' in *Lettere/2*, July 1981, 1–6.

―――― (1987) *Taccuino tedesco*. Milan: La Tartaruga.
―――― (1994) *Terremoto con madre e figlia*. Genoa: Melangolo.
Ravasi Bellocchio, Lella (1987) *Di madre in figlia. Storia di un'analisi*. Milan: Raffaello Cortina.
Ravera, Lidia (1979) *Bambino mio*. Milan: Bompiani.
Rich, Adrienne (1976) *Of Woman Born: Motherhood as Experience and Institution*. New York: Norton (London: Virago, 1977).
Santacroce, Isabella (1998) *Luminal*. Milan: Feltrinelli.
Sanvitale, Francesca (1994) *Madre e figlia*. Turin: Einaudi (orig. 1980).
Saraceno, Chiara (1997) 'Verso il 2000: la pluralizzazione delle esperienze e delle figure materne' in D'Amelia (ed.) 1997, 318–51.
Scarano, Emanuela (1990) 'La "fatua veste" del vero' in Lugnani et al. 1990, 95–171.
Scattigno, Anna (1997) 'La figura materna tra emancipazionismo e femminismo' in D'Amelia (ed.) 1997, 273–99.
Sereni, Clara (1989) *Manicomio primavera*. Florence: Giunti.
―――― (1993a) *Il gioco dei regni*. Florence: Giunti.
―――― (1993b) 'La figlia buona' in Maria Rosa Cutrufelli, Rosaria Guacci, and Marisa Rusconi (eds) *Il pozzo segreto. Cinquanta scrittrici italiane*. Florence: Giunti, 204–10. Reprinted in Clara Sereni, *Eppure*. Milan: Feltrinelli, 1995, 25–31.
Sereni, Marina (1955) *I giorni della nostra vita*. Rome: Edizioni di Cultura Sociale.
Sotis, Lina and Francesca Moratti (1991) *Mamma com'è difficile. Quando tra madre e figlia è meglio scriversi*. Milan: Mondadori.
Stancanelli, Elena (1998) *Benzina*. Turin: Einaudi.
Vannocci, Claudia (1990) 'La pinacoteca di Elisa: per uno studio dell'ipotesto figurato' in Lugnani et al. 1990, 409–38.
Wright, Simona (1993) 'Francesca Sanvitale: Passato e presente come strumenti narrativi' in *La Fusta*, October 1993, 241–49.

CHAPTER FIVE

WRITING MOTHER–DAUGHTER RELATIONALITY IN THE FRENCH CONTEXT

Alex Hughes

Introduction

Within the corpus of twentieth-century French-language theoretical accounts that address maternity and mother–daughter intersubjectivity – accounts that include Simone de Beauvoir's *Le Deuxième sexe* (1949) and Julia Kristeva's *Histoires d'amour* (1983) – the speculations of the feminist philosopher Luce Irigaray occupy a privileged place. In particular, three texts published by Irigaray in the late 1970s and early 1980s – 'And the One Doesn't Stir Without the Other', *Le Corps-à-corps avec la mère*, and *An Ethics of Sexual Difference* – focus on the absence, under patriarchy, of an acknowledged order of mother–daughter relations, and on the problems posed by the cultural 'erasure' of the mother–daughter tie. The readings of French female-authored narrative treatments of mother–daughter bonding proffered in the next three sections of this chapter draw on insights provided by these Irigarayan essays. Consequently, I want to begin by invoking what they have to say about mother–daughter relationality.

Currently, Irigaray affirms, an androcentric sociocultural economy remains in place, under which the bond between the mother and the daughter is devalued by virtue of the overvaluation of the male subject-as-patriarch, and in favour of the father–son connection. Within such an economy, no recognised order or history of mother-to-daughter relations (that is, no 'female genealogy') can obtain (1993: 108). Interwoven with this is a 'hom(m)osexual' symbolic order – an order of discourse, language, and knowledge – that cannot properly 'think' the feminine, except as incarnated in the reproductive function (1981b: 27), or symbolise, adequately, the mother–daughter tie (see Whitford 1989). The symbolic's 'gaps' are by no means anodyne. They hinder the female subject from conceptualising, positively, either her sexual difference or her relation to the female (m)Other, and contribute to the suppression of female subjectivity and (harmonious) female intersubjectivity.

Patriarchy's failure to legitimate any kind of feminine identity save that of the mother-as-reproducing-medium undermines, Irigaray argues, woman's subject status. Women's sociosymbolic confinement within what Irigaray conceives as a 'desubjectivised' functional role constitutes, in other words, an identitarian 'murder', to which the male subject escapes exposure (1981b: 27). Likewise, the fact that the patriarchal economy and the symbolic order it reflects accord women no sanctioned 'space'/value outside the desubjectivised maternal, and no access to, or vision of, a genealogy of their own, renders female interrelationality unworkable. For one thing, women's generic species-enclosure within the maternal function compels women 'subjects' generally (especially mothers and daughters) to compete to occupy, exclusively, the maternal place. Mother–daughter rivalry prevents women from realising reciprocal, subject-to-subject connections between themselves, and consigns them, vis-à-vis each other, to a form of 'exile' (1993: 102–3). It is initiated when the daughter, as she must under a culture that constructs women as exchange objects 'between men' and as reproducing 'machines', turns away from her mother (notably at the Oedipal stage) and moves to embrace her own maternal 'destiny'. Rivalry is not, moreover, the sole obstacle to feminine interpersonality, because, under patriarchy, mothers and daughters alike are positioned in the sphere of the (objectified) maternal; they are left vulnerable to a 'fusionality' that can be experienced as self-other overidentification, self-other asphyxiation or self-other implosion, but is never conducive to individuated subjecthood and loving female intersubjectivity (1993: 67–69; see also Whitford 1989).

Irigaray casts the absence, amongst women, of genuinely intersubjective, mediated relations as emblematic of the unethical way in which the patriarchal economy produces and regulates sexual difference. This is not to say that she views the status quo as immutable. She has suggested that by evolving revolutionary conceptualisations of the mother–daughter connection, women can modify the androcentric symbolic order, engineering sociosexual change (1981b: 86; see also Whitford 1989: 108, 117–21). Likewise, she has indicated that the linguistic realm that is the symbolic's foundation can and must admit a 'house of language' wherein women might articulate their 'love of the same in the feminine' and, armed with their own object of linguistic exchange, might achieve differentiated relations with their (m)others (1993: 104–9).

Clearly, then, Irigaray's writings do not rule out the possibility that the mother–daughter relationship – construed, consistently, as a 'lost' bond – might become (re)functional and '(re)subjectivised'. Yet much of her work focuses on the difficulties that mother–daughter interrelationality actually (and pathologically) admits – notably, the subjective nondifferentiation to which mothers and daughters are only too prone to succumb (see especially Irigaray 1981a).

Irigaray's dissections of the 'impossibilities' inherent in the mother–daughter (non)relation are the product of a post-1968, French, radical poststructuralist feminism whose propensity for highly conceptualised speculation has been much maligned, but whose founding texts include not only Lacan's hermetic rewritings of Freud but Simone de Beauvoir's empirically-grounded *Second Sex* as well. Although their publication predates the socio-sexual, intellectual revolution that took place in France in the wake of May 1968, it is certainly possible, by virtue of the sexual-political insights they afford, to associate the literary works addressed in the next section of this discussion with the feminist enterprise that Irigaray's writing emblematises. The texts in question are *Mémoires d'une jeune fille rangée* (1958, *Memoirs of a Dutiful Daughter*, 1963), the first volume of the autobiographical cycle that Beauvoir (1908–1986) brought out between 1958 and 1981, and *Ravages* (Devastation), an autobiographical novel published in 1955 by Violette Leduc (1907–1992).[1] Both privilege the daughter's perspective, and both elaborate creative visions that announce elements within the theoretical readings of female–female intersubjectivity published by Irigaray in the 1970s and 1980s. In the pages that follow, my aim is to indicate how they do so. In addition, I want to extrapolate, from the treatments of mother–daughter relationality these narratives offer, the lineaments of a possible, provisional paradigm for understanding, more generally, the manner in which, in the postwar period, French women authors have transcribed the mother–daughter bond. Then, in the following two sections, I shall measure against this putative paradigm a trio of accounts of mother–daughter relationality published between 1975 and 1990 by Marie Cardinal (born 1929), Marguerite Duras (1914–1996) and the *beur* (Franco-Algerian) writer Djura (born 1948). Like Beauvoir's *Mémoires* and Leduc's *Ravages*, these accounts make extensive use of biographical material, even if this is not always signalled openly. All three, moreover, belong to the corpus of creative writings on female identity and female intersubjectivity that burgeoned in France during the feminist 1970s and after: a corpus which symbolises the gynocentric reconfiguration of the French cultural space that occurred in the post-1968 period, treats extensively of female–female bonding, and includes works such as Monique Wittig's *Le Corps lesbien* (1973, *The*

---

1. All translations of primary texts are my own, except where published translations are indicated.

Lesbian Body 1975), Emma Santos's *La Malcastrée* (1973, The Ill-Castrated Woman), Chantal Chawaf's *Retable/La Rêverie* (1974, Retabulum/The Reverie), Jeanne Hyvrard's *Mère la mort* (1976, *Mother Death*, 1988), Hélène Cixous's *Le Livre de Promethea* (1983, *The Book of Promethea*, 1991), Annie Ernaux's *Une Femme* (1987, *A Woman's Story*, 1991), and Marie Redonnet's *Rose Mélie Rose* (1987, Rose Mélie Rose). The readings performed in these two sections of my chapter (like the discussion offered in the final section) will serve to establish how paradigmatic my mother–daughter model actually is. In other words, my readings will seek to indicate whether or not the mother–daughter discursive model delineated in the next section undergoes any sort of metamorphosis in texts produced in the aftermath of the emergence of radical, post-1968 French feminism. The fact that the narratives they address depict universes that are nonidentical to those mirrored in Beauvoir's *Mémoires* and Leduc's *Ravages* will represent a central feature of my analysis, permitting me to engage with the issue of cultural specificity. This latter phenomenon will likewise constitute a central focus of my concluding remarks.

Mother–Daughter Models

Mémoires d'une jeune fille rangée and *Ravages* not only foreground the role played in their narrator-heroines' development by the mother–daughter bond but also 'maternalise' other feminine connections, signalling the centrality of the maternal–filial relationships they chart. Likewise, both narratives highlight the kind of intersubjective phenomena my Introduction evokes. Their similarities notwithstanding, they sketch out rather different solutions to the difficulties the mother–daughter relation incorporates, bearing witness to their authors' divergent responses to the process of 'writing the mother'.

As I have argued elsewhere (Hughes 1994b), in Beauvoir's *Mémoires*, a four-part text covering the childhood, adolescence, and early adulthood of its creator, a key focus is the phenomenon of mother–daughter indistinction, and the anxiety it provokes. In the opening section of her tale, Beauvoir's mature daughter-narrator looks back not only at the bond she shared in childhood with her mother, but also at the dread its 'fusional' nature inspired (*Memoirs*: 39–41; *Mémoires*: 55–57). Except in an early segment of Beauvoir's text, however, in which her infantile eating difficulties are invoked (*Memoirs*: 7–8; *Mémoires*: 11), this dread is not signalled entirely explicitly.[2] Instead, it is

---

2. Laurie Corbin recognises the fearful aspect of the *Mémoires* in her study of mother–daughter representation in Beauvoir, Colette, and Duras, commenting that 'the passages in which Simone de Beauvoir describes her fear of a closeness or complicity between herself and her mother are notable for an almost inexplicable force in the daughter's need for separation' (Corbin 1996: 51).

intimated by Beauvoir's narrator's 'casual' inclusion, in her retrospective account, of micronarratives generated by her renarration of narratives encountered in her youth (*Memoirs*: 7–8, 51–52, 53–54; *Mémoires*: 13, 72, 74–75). Each of these micronarratives privileges issues of absorption and engulfment. Taken together, they attest to the presence within Beauvoir's autobiography of an infantile, enduring vision of the mother as a powerfully stifling entity, whose subjugatory potential must be conjured at all costs. This vision works in counterpoint to another, less 'visceral' vision of Françoise de Beauvoir, that issues out of Beauvoir's adult, politicised awareness of the class and gender inequalities of early twentieth-century France, and casts Françoise as a subaltern, powerless being, restricted by the androcentric, bourgeois universe she inhabits. The contrapuntal maternal discourses of the *Mémoires* are not, however, mutually contradictory in that, we sense, it is precisely because Françoise herself is a site of repressed subjectivity that she functions as a repressive force.

If the *Mémoires* pinpoint the deep sense of nonindividuation to which, in her earliest years, Beauvoir's narrator was subject, they also signal a key strategy she adopted in order to disentangle herself from the maternal orbit, conveying, additionally, its generally unsuccessful character. This strategy underlies the pursuit, by the child-heroine of Beauvoir's tale, of various doubles or companions, sought out as an antidote to the subjective annihilation whose spectre haunts her dealings with her mother (see Portuges 1986: 113). Its failure relates to the fact that at least two of these 'doubles', Simone's sister Poupette and her friend Zaza, are too implicated in the maternal 'empire' from which Simone longs to free herself to provide release. Zaza, especially, although she appears to incarnate characteristics such as 'hardness' and 'masculinity' that make her the antithesis of the all-embracing, invasive maternal presence evoked in the first part of the *Mémoires*, proves to represent no less subjugatory a force than Mme de Beauvoir herself, and to consign Simone to the same dependent (non)subjectivity that she experienced vis-à-vis her mother in her childhood (*Memoirs*: 39, 95, 113; *Mémoires*: 56, 131, 158).

It might appear that the 'message' of Beauvoir's *Mémoires* is, ultimately, that the daughter's thraldom to the maternal admits no resolution. This is not, however, the case. Beauvoir's autobiography privileges education and intellectual enquiry as the means whereby the female subject (notably, the bourgeois, male-identified female subject) can distance herself from maternal domination and mother–daughter overidentification (see Corbin 1996: 46–48; Hughes 1996). Further, more unexpectedly, it implies that, by 'murdering' the mother, and 'murdering' her in writing, a daughter may achieve (complete) individuation. As indicated above, Beauvoir's narrator-heroine's schoolfriend Zaza is made on one level to function in the *Mémoires* as a maternal surrogate. In the concluding part of a story whose subject becomes its heroine's conquest of an existential, intellectual freedom that includes the freedom to write, Beauvoir's narrative concentrates on Zaza's premature death – cast as a counterpoint to the liberation that Beauvoir's textual self eventually realises. Writing about Zaza's fate allows the mature author Simone de Beauvoir to express the grief, and guilt, she long wished to articulate: 'Together we had fought against the revolting fate that had lain ahead of us, and for a long time I thought I'd paid for my freedom with her death' (*Memoirs*: 360; *Mémoires*: 503). Likewise, it enables her to denounce the bourgeoisie from which she and Zaza came, and whose shibboleths she blamed for her friend's demise. Concomitantly, however, the act of 'textualising' Zaza's unexpected death at the end of a tale in which she is also 'maternalised' permits the middle-aged writer into whom the daughter-heroine of the *Mémoires* evolved to effect, inside her autobiographical narrative, a form of displaced, discursive matricide that surely connects with the freedom that is both celebrated and culpabilised within the final segment of her self-history. In other words, the conclusion of Beauvoir's *Mémoires* – for all the loving manner in which it evokes its author's lost classmate – can be taken to incorporate a belated, liberatory daughterly/writerly gesture of 'maternal' obliteration that is both occluded and rendered more emancipatory by the fact that its 'victim' is not, apparently, a mother at all. Narrative 'matricide' certainly surfaces in other Beauvoirian opuses, including *La Femme rompue* (1967, *The Woman Destroyed*, 1969).[3] Beauvoir's recourse to it, at the end of the first of her autobiographical accounts, highlights the centrally significant place occupied by the mother–daughter 'question' within a text that seems, superficially, as its narrative development progresses, increasingly unconcerned with the maternal–filial connection.

Violette Leduc's work dwells obsessively on issues of mother–daughter bonding. The mother–daughter relation is a primary focus of *L'Asphyxie* (1946, *In the Prison of Her Skin*, 1970), the first of Leduc's autobiographical novels, and is foregrounded in *La Bâtarde* (1964, *La Bâtarde: An Autobiography*, 1965), the first volume of her directly autobiographical trilogy. Her third autobiographical fiction, *Ravages* – a three-part narrative that 'maternalises' its heroine Thérèse's connection to her lesbian partner Cécile, by casting Cécile as Thérèse's mother's double (see Hughes 1994a: 40–80) – chronicles the emotional and sexual misadventures of a young woman, and is not therefore, except 'unconsciously', a tale of childhood.[4] That said, Leduc's novel resembles Beauvoir's *Mémoires* in two, key ways. First, it like-

---

3. For a fascinating discussion of this phenomenon in Beauvoir's late autobiographical writings, see Jardine 1985.
4. *Ravages* conflates the adult and the infantile/the conscious and the unconscious, and is a text that works on a number of levels. It can be approached as a symbolic rendition of female psychosexual evolution.

wise communicates the difficulties intrinsic in mother–daughter coexistence. These are highlighted by Thérèse's sense that she functions as a reflection of her authoritarian genetrix, or as an entity trapped inside a maternal mirror, and by the feelings of oppression she experiences in spaces shared with her mother and her lesbian 'mother/lover'. Second, by mapping the markedly 'Oedipal', patriarchally-legitimised movement away from her mother(s) and towards the interventionary male that Thérèse effects, *Ravages* mirrors the *Mémoires*' preoccupation with daughterly individuation.[5] Unlike Beauvoir's *Mémoires*, however, Leduc's novel offers a less than positive treatment of the phenomenon of daughterly defection – encapsulated in Thérèse's relations with Marc, the man she marries in the hope that contact with his phallic masculinity will rescue her from maternal dominion and enable her to vie for feminine/maternal supremacy (*Ravages*: 42, 53–54). The account of Thérèse's marital disappointments that *Ravages* contains signals that, under patriarchy, woman's recourse to a normative, male/'Oedipal' escape route, while it may bring release from mother–daughter indistinction and self/other specularity, also potentially exposes the female subject to sexual and domestic dependency. Further, again in contrast to Beauvoir's autobiography, *Ravages* refuses to privilege 'matricide' – whether actual, symbolic, or textual – as a means of resolving the snares of mother–daughter interrelationality. Instead, Leduc's narrative intimates that mothers and daughters should strive to overturn obstacles to female-to-female reciprocity, reversing the mother–daughter 'exile' – the state of non-functional or dysfunctional relatedness – that is, seemingly, in the 'man's world' *Ravages* documents, an intractable feature of women's existences.

Ravages ends with the illegal abortion Thérèse undergoes after her marriage collapses, in order to miscarry the son (and male 'double') her husband craves. Its conclusion suggests that, by destroying the child that emblematises the Oedipal, marital, phallocentric route into the patriarchally-inflected feminine that she has followed hitherto (and followed in order to flee the mother–daughter dyad), Thérèse is making a gesture of maternally-oriented reconciliation.[6] It intimates, in other words, that, in opting to terminate her pregnancy, Thérèse is in pursuit of (and possibly achieves) a symbolic 'return to the mother': 'I regained consciousness and my mother was at my bedside, twiddling her thumbs as she sat in their armchair. I was no longer in pain and I could see her once more' (*Ravages*: 329–30). The end of *Ravages* also implies, in passages that reproduce the hallucinations that assail the septi-

---

5. *Mémoires* also associates the movement towards the male with daughterly independence. However, the shift towards the male lover is far more 'Oedipalised' in *Ravages*.
6. *Ravages* certainly echoes Freud's account of (1) the symbolic connection between the child and the phallus and (2) childbirth/motherhood as the endpoint of a female Oedipal trajectory predicated on the daughter's shift from mother-love to phallic father-love.

caemic Thérèse and revolve around the theme of solitude, that the renewed mother–daughter relationality she chooses freely will not reexpose her to the desubjectivisation her intimacy with her maternal parent previously incorporated. This implication emerges strongly in *Ravages*'s closing lines:

> 'Come', she said.
> She pulled me into the corridor. She raised me up from the ground. I flew, I was healed. We passed before the doors of the sick. The clinic was taking its ease. My mother pushed me forward. I found myself in front of a mirror.
> 'Your nice little figure. You've got your figure back', she said.
> For the first time, her words did not resonate inside me. I was alone. Finally alone.
> (*Ravages*: 330)

Superficially, Leduc's tale might appear to imply that if women (daughters) simply turn from their maternal 'destiny' (that is, refuse to compete for the maternal place), they can abolish the divisions to which the patriarchal order – an omnipresent force in *Ravages* – subjects their mothers and themselves. While it does tacitly criticise the functional aspect of woman's reproductive role, Leduc's narrative does not, however, in reality, proffer so sweeping a message. *Ravages* dramatises, rather, the finally negative, if superficially salutary, self/other nonrelatedness to which patriarchy – incarnated in Thérèse's intrusive lover Marc – consigns mothers and daughters. It is a text that works to critique the depredations inflicted on women's intersubjective potential in an androcentric universe. In consequence, Leduc's autobiographical novel must be acknowledged as a far more polemical text than Beauvoir's matricidal – and much better known – *Mémoires*.

I suggested above that, although the Beauvoirian and Leducian narratives scrutinised here were written in the void of gender politics that was 1950s France, they intuit aspects of Irigarayan thought. My sense is that each of them announces two facets within Irigaray's elaborations of female–female intersubjectivity. Beauvoir's autobiography may not openly address patriarchy's erasure of mediated, mutual relations between women. However, its narrator's account of her struggle against mother–daughter entanglement certainly pinpoints the dangers that inhere in the patriarchally-induced phenomenon of female–female subjective indistinction; dangers cast into relief by Irigaray's 'And the One Doesn't Stir Without the Other'. (Both texts, for instance, foreground the daughter's sense of being fed/filled by her mother so comprehensively that she is deprived of subjective autonomy.) Likewise, in parallel with 'And the One', Beauvoir's *Mémoires* signal that, within a sociocultural system under which woman is desubjectivised as the disempowered (m)Other, a daughter's relation to her maternal parent will necessarily admit a fear of identificatory fusion, a desire for differentiation, and, ultimately, a willingness to commit (symbolic) matricide in order to consolidate it. *Ravages* predicts Irigaray's perception that, under patriarchy, daughters may coexist with their mothers in fusional, 'specular' mode, or cut off from them completely, in order to service the process of male self-reproduction and take the maternal place (a fate Thérèse nearly embraces),[7] but, either way, cannot easily enjoy individuated relationships *with* them. Also, although less explicitly than much of Irigaray's work, Leduc's novel's conclusion, juxtaposing as it does 'I could see [my mother] once more' and 'I was alone', illuminates the necessity for (and intimates the geography of) a sociosymbolic 'space' where differentiated but connected relations between women might emerge, displacing rivalry and fusionality as models for feminine bonding and remedying the mother–daughter 'exile' that the patriarchal, 'hom(m)osexual', Oedipal economy encourages.

Taken together, *Mémoires d'une jeune fille rangée* and *Ravages* suggest that, when daughters confront the 'problem' of mother–daughter (non)relationality and make it the focus of their literary endeavours, they may elect either to delineate and denounce the mother's damaging imbrication in the daughter's life/identity, or to mourn the unworkability of the mother–daughter connection. They intimate, further, that the woman author who opts for the first strategy will probably privilege, textually, those processes that facilitate mother–daughter differentiation, including that of (symbolic) matricide, while the daughter-writer who chooses the second will be drawn to address the phenomenon – and the modalities – of mother–daughter reconciliation. Clearly, neither Simone de Beauvoir nor Violette Leduc sets out, in writing the *Mémoires* and *Ravages*, to create 'models' of mother–daughter discourse. But, because these authors occupy a primary place within the pantheon of post-1945 French female writers, it is tempting to adopt as a provisional paradigm for the act of mother–daughter inscription the contrastive denunciation/recuperation binary that the *Mémoires* and *Ravages* foreground. If, though, we accept that these particular narratives may encapsulate potentially paradigmatic (French, postwar) modes of 'writing the mother',[8] it is manifestly necessary to test them out as such, by establishing whether they are echoed elsewhere. My project, in the rest of this chapter, is to do precisely

---

7. For Irigaray's discussions of how, under the economy of (mediated) male–male specularity that is patriarchy, women's reproductive capacities are made to serve the male subject's quest for self-perpetuation, see especially Irigaray 1985a and Irigaray 1985b.
8. For a discussion of paradigms of mother–daughter discourse that addresses a gamut of European and American narratives from nineteenth-century realism to contemporary texts by women of colour, see Hirsch 1989. In terms of the paradigms posited here, Beauvoir's *Mémoires* betray an authorial tendency to use writing to differentiate from and erase the mother that Hirsch likewise locates in many nineteenth-century women's novels, whereas Leduc's *Ravages* is not dissimilar to the 'feminist family romances' of the 1970s: texts that concentrate, Hirsch argues, on mother–daughter bonding and struggle, privilege female intersubjectivity, and foreground the pre-Oedipal.

that. In the next two sections, I want to see whether 'matricidal' and 'reconciliatory' models of discourse feature in daughterly narratives that not only belong to the contemporary, post-1968 French literary field but also situate the mother–daughter bond in contexts that are culturally peripheral to the republican, white, mainland, mainstream French 'space' that is reproduced in Beauvoir's *Mémoires* and Leduc's *Ravages*, and constitutes the arena from which Irigaray's undoubtedly universalising, acultural accounts of women's intersubjective travails draw their inspiration.[9]

Colonial Tales

In *Imperial Leather: Race, Gender and Sexuality in the Colonial Contest*, Anne McClintock comments as follows on white women's relationship to colonialism:

> Barred from the corridors of formal power, they experienced the privileges and social contradictions of imperialism very differently from colonial men... Marital laws, property laws, land laws and the intractable violence of male decree bound them in gendered patterns of disadvantage and frustration. The vast, fissured architecture of imperialism was gendered through and through by the fact that it was white men who made and enforced laws and policies in their own interests. Nonetheless, the rationed privileges of race all too often put white women in positions of decided – if borrowed – power, not only over colonised women but also over colonised men. As such, white women were not the hapless onlookers of empire, but were ambiguously complicit both as colonisers and colonised, privileged and restricted, acted upon and acting. (1995: 6)

McClintock's remarks address British imperialism and its androcentric workings; however, her account of the ambiguities intrinsic in the situation of the white colonial woman subject is not only equally pertinent to the no less patriarchally organised French colonial scene,[10] but is also endorsed, albeit in different ways, by the autobiographical fictions discussed in this section of my chapter. Marie Cardinal's *Les Mots pour le dire* (1975, *The Words To Say It* 1993) and Marguerite Duras's *L'Amant* (1984, *The Lover* 1986) evoke early to mid-twentieth-century sexually, ethnically, and socially hierarchical French colonial universes within which (bourgeois) European female subjectivity was constructed out of, and bore witness to, an admixture of racially produced 'superiority' and gender disempowerment. Like

---

9. The 'universalism' of Irigaray's work and, more generally, of Western feminist theory has been critiqued in recent years by exponents of postcolonial feminism.
10. For a study of French women's colonial experience that uses testimonials by women ex-colonials to confirm that French colonialism was also an 'affaire d'hommes', see Knibiehler and Goutalier 1985.

Ravages, neither sets up a formal autobiographical 'pact'. My intention, here, is first to assess the extent to which the mother–daughter connections foregrounded by these novels are cast as inflected by the power relations of the colonial environment, and second to evaluate whether the denunciation/reconciliation binary holds as a model for mother–daughter discourse in relation to narratives where the gendered dynamics of colonialism become an issue.

Cardinal's *Mots* focuses on its adult narrator's colonial childhood and adolescence, spent in 'French' Algeria, and on the psychoanalysis she embarks on in her thirties, when psychosomatic crises engendered by her youthful dealings with her mother Solange become untenable. In renarrating her 'talking cure', *Les Mots*'s narrator-heroine certainly acknowledges the negative influence exerted on her by the rigid cultural and gender codes favoured by *L'Algérie française*'s colonial occupiers. Arguably, however, Cardinal's text has more – and more revealing – things to say about its heroine's mother's formation as a female colonial subject.

Cardinal's narrator's mother, *Les Mots* reveals, was born into a turn-of-the-century Algerian environment whose historiography documents it as 'the "imperial man's world" par excellence' (Clancy-Smith 1992: 61). This androcentric space – territorialised by white European males who passed its land down to their white European sons (*Words*: 125; *Mots*: 153) – was home to a predominantly French colonial community that was 'as conservative in defining gender roles as traditional Muslim society' (Clancy-Smith 1992: 65), and whose conservatism confirms that, in imperial contexts, gender roles were frequently 'polarized in ways in which perhaps they [were] not in the home country' (Mills 1994: 36). It was also, Cardinal's novel infers, a locus into which, partly because nineteenth-century Algeria became the site of a Catholic, anti-Islamic crusade, the values and discourses of France's Catholic bourgeoisie had been implanted, intact.[11] Within this 'penetrated' realm, which had been 'impregnated' with 'the spirit of France',[12] the young woman into whom Cardinal's narrator's mother grew up was subjected to precisely the kind of gendered violence that McClintock's study evokes.

Les Mots makes it clear that if its narrator-heroine's divorcee mother was complicit with the codes governing the paternalistic, bourgeois colonial universe she inhabited until the fall of *L'Algérie française*, she was also their victim.[13] Cardinal's novel presents Solange as entrapped in a 'dungeon' constructed by religious, class, and gender orthodoxies which were made more rather than less repressive by their colonial dimension, and which con-

11. On colonial anti-Islamism, see Ruscio 1995: 114–19.
12. These terms are taken from a speech by the French educationalist Paul Bert, made in 1885 in relation to Algeria and cited in Ruscio 1995: 101.
13. See, especially, chapter 16 of Cardinal's narrative, and see also Lionnet 1989: 199.

demned her to various forms of privation. It portrays her as prevented, by the constraints of her racially and socially privileged, exclusionary world, from enjoying, postmaritally, either her sensual capacities or the talents she possessed: talents befitting her for the 'male', empowering professions of surgeon and architect (*Words*: 200–201; *Mots*: 236–37, 322). Finally, *Les Mots* depicts her as someone whose sole reward for her refusal to defy the sociosexual dictates of the French colonial bourgeoisie was the ersatz sense of value/authority afforded by her years of charity work amongst Algeria's indigenous poor. Also, by casting as an emblem of the paternalistic colonial régime whose dogmas violated her subjecthood the 'benevolence' that was her talisman and the source of her sense of self, Cardinal's text foregrounds not only the destructive effects of, but also the ironies intrinsic in, Solange's colonial class situation.

In invoking the background of *Les Mots*'s central maternal figure, Cardinal's narrating persona illuminates the 'gendered patterns of disadvantage and frustration' dissected in McClintock's analysis of the workings of colonial patriarchy. She does so, moreover, for a reason. By highlighting Solange's victimisation by, as well as her collusion with, a colonial order of racial/class dominion whose doxas she eventually sees through, Cardinal's self-projective narrator seeks to contextualise the unhealthy mother–daughter relationship that is the key focus of her story. This relationship, as it is disinterred by Cardinal's narrator's psychoanalytic cure and in her narrative recapitulation of it, is unremittingly emotionally arid. It exposes Cardinal's daughter-heroine to an enduring exile vis-à-vis her mother/origin that is provoked by a near total lack of maternal affective commitment, and proves acutely noxious. This exile is mourned in those segments of *Les Mots* that invoke the rare moments of mother–daughter harmony which Cardinal's heroine's childhood admitted (*Words*: 291–92; *Mots*: 339–40).[14] Measured against the theoretical paradigms elaborated in the work of Irigaray and glossed in my Introduction, it constitutes the epitome of the 'cruel' absence of loving female intersubjectivity that *An Ethics of Sexual Difference* locates as a patriarchal construct. If, however, Cardinal's narrative depicts its central mother–daughter bond as a highly defective connection, which is rendered defective by Solange's inability to love her daughter properly, *Les Mots* also signals that its defects are due to the harm done to Solange herself by the Catholic, bourgeois, masculinist colonial hegemony whose gender rules contoured her existence, and whose norms corrupted her: 'In the matter of divorce her religion made her intransigent: not to have the love of a man, not to have his strong arms to comfort and caress her … Not ever! Further, a

---

14. For an Irigarayan reading of *Les Mots* as a treatment of mother–daughter exile, which parallels Cardinal's daughter-narrator's lost access to the mother with her exile from Algeria, her 'motherland', see Le Clézio 1981.

sense of class made it prohibitive to earn a living or develop her mind beyond the acceptable limits for women' (*Words*: 201; *Mots*: 237). In other words, *Les Mots* echoes the Irigarayan notion that, as long as mothers are compelled by patriarchy to renounce their identities as sexual beings, confine themselves to maternal functionality, and abandon all pretentions to material and economic autonomy, neither enabling, authentic mother-love, nor mother–daughter harmony, can easily obtain (see Grosz 1989: 121).

Two specific phenomena stand as testaments to Solange's failure to adhere to a 'good' maternal model – a failure that generates the mental disequilibrium to which Cardinal's daughter-heroine falls victim and engenders the matrophobia she comes to feel. The first is the *saloperie* that Solange perpetrated on her child; that is, her amateur, aborted attempt, during a pregnancy rendered socially 'shameful' by her imminent divorce, to destroy her daughter/foetus, and her later, 'murderous' decision to tell her of it (*Words*: 134–41; *Mots*: 163–71). The second is the draconian, deformative gender/class training she meted out, punitively, to her resistant little girl: 'This child, the pink-cheeked postulant must – since she had not known how to die to please her mother – become what the mother had been unable to become: a saint, a heroine … I wanted to love her but in my own way. I refused to enter the alienating or macabre meanderings she proposed' (*Words*: 201; *Mots*: 237–38). These phenomena are, in turn, presented by *Les Mots*'s adult narrator as symptomatic of Solange's own madness – an affliction her daughter temporarily inherits.[15] Maternal madness is not, however, established in *Les Mots* as the root cause of the damaging mother–daughter dynamic that is its object of scrutiny. Cardinal's narrator explicitly links Solange's failure either to assume or take proper steps to avoid her (single, undesired) motherhood and the unreasonable upbringing she imposed upon her child – emblems, both, of her lack of maternal *caritas* as well as her mental imbalance – first to the restrictive Church and class dictates to which her status as a female, subaltern member of a dominant colonising group left her especially susceptible, and second to the enduring 'deformations' her internalisation of their gender-strictures produced (*Words*: 200–202; *Mots*: 236–38). And in so doing – that is, in declaring, even as she chronicles her mother's villainy, 'I know why the woman did it. I understand her' (*Words*: 141; *Mots*: 171) – Cardinal's narrator signals that the nexus of maternal inadequacy, maternal insanity, and daughterly dysfunctionality that provides the fulcrum of her story owed its existence to forces over which Solange had little control, and for whose consequences she cannot be inculpated.

---

15. On Cardinal's use of madness as an emblem of women's common, desubjectivised position in patriarchal culture, see Haigh 1994: 65.

Addressing the damning record of her mother's shortcomings that Cardinal's narrator draws up, and, more particularly, her documentation of Solange's descent into drunkenness, incontinence, and death, Françoise Lionnet alerts us to the 'matricidal' aspect of *Les Mots* (Lionnet 1989: 199–201). Yet, as Lionnet herself recognises, Cardinal's autobiographically-inflected tale is, predominantly, a vehicle for mother–daughter reconciliation. By entering and renarrating the narrative process that is psychoanalysis, Cardinal's adult daughter-narrator comes to comprehend what generated her mother's cruelty, and to forgive it. As *Les Mots*'s sixteenth chapter reveals, in forgiving her mother, textually, and reviving, *post mortem*, the love she formerly felt for her, Cardinal's narrator finally obliterates the mother–daughter divide that impelled her into self-disgust and madness. In other (Irigarayan) words (see Haigh 1994), the analytic process engenders, belatedly, a narrative 'house of language' or 'parler femme', wherein female–female connectivity is somehow revivified: 'How good it was to finally love her in the light, in the springtime, in the open, after the terrible battle from which we were delivered! Two blind people armed to the teeth, claws exposed, in the arena of our class. What blows she had struck me, what venom I had distilled. What savagery, what butchery!' (*Words*: 292–93; *Mots*: 341).

Like Cardinal's *Mots pour le dire*, Duras's *L'Amant* takes as one of its focuses a maternal madness that evolves against a French colonial (in Duras's case, Indochinese) backdrop and damages the daughter who becomes its narrator. In *L'Amant*, however, in contrast to *Les Mots*, insights into the situation of the colonial woman subject are not proffered, primarily, as exculpatory pointers to maternal 'innocence'. Concomitantly, Duras's self-referential story of her impoverished colonial adolescence – distinguished from Cardinal's narratively conventional *récit d'analyse* (psychoanalytic account) and from 'canonical' autobiography alike by its play with chronology and voice – does not single out, thematically, the mother–daughter exile that *Les Mots* foregrounds. Instead, in a manner reminiscent not only of Beauvoir's *Mémoires* but also of Irigaray's 'And the One Doesn't Stir Without the Other', it privileges the phenomenon of mother–daughter (dis)entanglement.

As my Introduction indicated, Irigaray's work affirms that the lot of the woman subject is to find herself in the place of the maternal. Women/daughters are contained within the mother's space, argues Irigaray, not only by the patriarchal order, which accords them no social recognition unless they fulfil the maternal function, but also by the mother herself, who needs her daughter/mirror to reflect her maternal identity/value back at her, and may nurture excessively in order to keep her daughter by her (Irigaray 1981a). Being 'in the mother's place' does not, Irigaray suggests, enable the daughter/woman to have a relationship with her mother. It condemns her, rather, to mother–daughter fusion and subjective subjugation, counteracting female community.

While Duras's account of her narrator's formative years does not depict nurturing excess as one of the elements that blighted her adolescence, it certainly stages the drama of being in the maternal place without a relation to the mother that Irigaray's writings cast as the daughter's portion. This drama is presented as involving three 'movements', which pertain primarily to Duras's narrator's colonial youth, but also impinge on her adult, writerly existence. These turn on (1) her efforts to escape the maternal sphere; (2) her failure to extricate herself entirely; and (3) her profound reluctance to cut loose from the mother definitively.

For Duras's daughter-narrator, being proximate to the mother means finding herself in an atemporal, locationless void that simultaneously erases her own identity and precludes authentic forms of mother–daughter encounter. *L'Amant* envisions this realm – whose tentacles reach into its narrator's maturity – as a locus that exists inside her flesh but eternally excludes her, even as it sucks her into itself and keeps her in thrall: 'What happens there is silence, the slow travail of my whole life. I'm still there, watching ... as far away from the mystery now as I was then. I've never written, though I thought I wrote, never loved, though I thought I loved, never done anything but wait outside the closed door' (*Lover*: 29; *Amant*: 34–35).[16] Less melodramatically, Duras's tale casts it as a space from which *L'Amant*'s narrator-heroine seeks, as early as her childhood years, to liberate herself, by means of the related expedients of desire and writing. Each of these expedients is signalled as potentially emancipatory; however, *L'Amant* also reveals them to be ultimately no more 'antidotal' than the doubling stategy adopted by the daughter-heroine of Beauvoir's *Mémoires*.[17]

Desire, Duras's narrative suggests, is perceived by its heroine as a vehicle for daughterly individuation not only because *jouissance* is something she can access while her mother cannot (*Lover*: 12, 43; *Amant*: 15, 50), but also because the erotic connection she forms with the Chinese lover she meets on the Mekong ferry in her sixteenth year transgresses the rules governing the white, familial fiefdom that is the mother's empire (*Lover*: 39; *Amant*: 46). Writing is likewise intuited by Duras's protagonist as a source of future liberation because a literary career, like interracial sex, countermands the mother's plans for her, and constitutes a means by which maternal dominion can be trounced (*Lover*: 26; *Amant*: 31). Neither (adolescent) eroticism nor (adult)

---

16. On Duras's mother as an absent space, against which the daughter must struggle to individuate, see Corbin 1996: 135; Hirsch 1989: 148, 150–51.
17. My sense that writing and desire do not engender separation marks off the reading performed here from that offered by Suzanne Ferrières-Pestureau, who also reads *L'Amant* as a treatment of 'la menace fusionnelle', but argues that in it, Duras presents literary activity and sexuality (and, indeed, self-phallicisation) as forces that do undermine 'la masse narcissique "fille–mère"' (the narcissistic mother–daughter mass). See 1997: 27–34, 48–49.

creative practice prove, however, to be effective sources of filial release, since neither permits Duras's narrator-heroine to elude the maternal orbit completely. Writing keeps her in the mother's thrall even in adulthood, because literary activity condemns her to a reiteration of, and enclosure within, her familial past (*Lover*: 11; *Amant*: 14). Similarly, *L'Amant* hints, daughterly desire is no counterweight to maternal entrapment because it is, in part, a maternal construct, in which the mother herself is profoundly invested because it affords her a second-hand purchase on a realm of pleasure she has not been able to penetrate (*Lover*: 97–98; *Amant*: 112–14). Duras's daughter-heroine only accedes to the place of desire because she becomes desirable – and her desirability, metonymised in the fetishistic costume she wears on the Mekong riverboat, is openly represented in *L'Amant* as (partly) a maternal invention (*Lover*: 15–28; *Amant*: 17–33). Once, moreover, she finds herself in desire's place, making 'liberatory' love to the Chinese from Cholon in his bachelor apartment (*Lover*: 43; *Amant*: 51), her mother's shadow is everywhere, rematernalising a space that is only ever superficially countermaternal.

Escaping the place of the mother appears, then, to be a feat that Duras's narrator-protagonist fails to realise, *L'Amant*'s (disingenuous) references to her 'definitive separation' notwithstanding. Moreover, the reader senses that it is not even a project to which she is fully committed. Two facets of Duras's narrative intimate that this is so. The first is its occlusion, in its closing segments, of the issue of daughterly disentanglement. This is produced by the fact that *L'Amant*'s focus becomes its heroine's parting not from her mother but, rather, from her Chinese lover. The second is Duras's account of the terror her narrator-protagonist experiences when, just before leaving colonial Indochina (geographically, the 'mother's place' *par excellence*), she hallucinates that her mother has vanished. This terror is inspired, clearly, as much by the prospect that the maternal space might actually cease to be ('I knew no one else was there in her place, but that that identity irreplaceable by any other had disappeared definitively and I was powerless to make it come back') as by Duras's heroine's sense that, if her mother disappears, she herself might inherit the madness her parent manifests (*Lover*: 91; *Amant*: 105).[18]

Maternal madness may constitute a legacy that *L'Amant*'s daughter-heroine refuses; however, it seems to be what retains her in the maternal sphere. She is, enduringly, a possessed 'spectatrice de sa mère', as fascinated by her mother's deranged state – which she nonetheless cannot properly 'see' – as her mother is fascinated by her daughter's capacity for *jouissance* (*Lover*: 34, 62; *Amant*: 40, 73).[19] If, though, it ensures that Duras's heroine remains

---

18. On *L'Amant*'s vanishing episode as emblematic of the daughter's fear of maternal inheritance, see Corbin 1996: 92–93; Hirsch 1989: 148.
19. Daughterly inability to see the mother properly, Irigaray argues in 'And the One', is symptomatic of her entanglement in mother–daughter fusionality.

riven to her genetrix, maternal insanity also wreaks the kind of harm evoked in *Les Mots*. *L'Amant* presents it as a source of the mother's tacit, exploitative prostitution of her child to the rich Chinese lover, and of the murderous violence she unleashes when she can no longer turn a blind eye to her daughter's sexual activity (*Lover*: 62–63; *Amant*: 72–74). Concomitantly, Duras's story casts motherly madness as a frightening phenomenon which may appear to constitute a vehicle for mother–daughter 'communion' – a noxious communion, predicated on mutual imbalance (*Lover*: 91; *Amant*: 105) – but which in fact, because it is a 'secret knowledge that the mother shares with her favourite elder son and with her servant but [keeps from] the daughter' (Baisnée 1997: 156), precludes mother–daughter relationality, even as it prevents the daughter from quitting the mother's place.

As indicated above, in Cardinal's *Mots*, maternal madness, and the dysfunctional mother–daughter dynamic it engenders, are contextualised in terms of colonial power relations, and contextualised in such a way as to excuse maternal inadequacy. Disculpatory contextualisation is not, however, a prominent feature of *L'Amant*. Duras's autobiographical fiction is less openly anti-colonial than her earlier *Barrage contre le pacifique* (1950, *The Sea Wall*, 1986), a novel in which material used in *L'Amant* is exploited rather differently (see Chester 1992). It is certainly not the case, though, that it neglects to illuminate the gendered workings of the French colonial scene. By pointing up, for instance, the 'objectification of the white woman by the male gaze of both colonizer and colonized' (Chester 1992: 441), as well as the erotic magnetism of the European female, *L'Amant*'s account of its heroine's sexual adventures in an Indochinese colonial space as androcentric as *L'Algérie française* does signal some of the ways in which sexual difference functions in the colonial situation. That said, Duras's text does not let either its narrator's mother or her poisonous mental disequilibrium 'off the hook', by offering the kind of detailed delineation of maternal cruelty as a colonial construct elaborated in Cardinal's narrative. Reference *is* made, in *L'Amant*, to the economic sufferings inflicted on Duras's heroine's (poor white, widowed) mother by the patriarchal network of French male administrators who ran colonial Indochina, and to the role such sufferings played in the evolution of her destructive maternity (*Lover*: 68; *Amant*: 73). However, Duras's evocations of the mother's sociosexual 'assassination' (*Lover*: 59; *Amant*: 69) are partially undercut by reminders that she is also, as a European schoolmistress, racially privileged, and are insufficiently evolved to perform an authentically exculpatory function. Their truncated aspect – evidenced by the disconcerting shift in focus from the mother's misfortunes to the social rites of wartime Paris that Duras's narrator effects in the middle of her story (*Lover*: 68; *Amant*: 79) – may reflect the elliptical narrative style employed in *L'Amant*. Equally, it may relate to the fact that Duras had already used *Un*

Barrage contre le pacifique to critique the maltreatment meted out to her mother by colonial patriarchal society. Either way, *L'Amant* manifests a wariness with regard to contextual disculpation that clearly differentiates it from *Les Mots pour le dire*.

Because *L'Amant* focuses far more closely on the nefarious effects of its narrator-heroine's mother's terrifying madness than on the forces that engendered it, it can hardly be construed as a '(re)conciliatory' daughterly opus. Rather, critics suggest, Duras's narrative constitutes a 'matricidal' production, in which the mother is not only condemned for her insane alterity – 'she ought to be locked up, beaten, killed' (*Lover*: 27; *Amant*: 32) – but is also, like the mother of Beauvoir's *Mémoires*, textually 'erased' (see Hirsch 1989: 148; Baisnée 1997: 156 and, especially, Kristeva 1987: 249–50). Maternal erasure occurs via a process of narrative silencing – the mother's voice barely features in *L'Amant* – and narrative occlusion whose *mise-en-abyme* is Duras's narrator's fantasy of maternal vanishing. *L'Amant*'s incorporation of this process transforms Duras's text into a work which may on one level combine mother-love and mother-loathing in a 'double vision' (Corbin 1996: 107) but which – as Duras's narrator herself intimates, when she says 'I think I wrote about our love for our mother but I don't know if I wrote about how we hated her too' (*Lover*: 29; *Amant*: 34) – is ultimately more inflected by the latter.

In the autobiographical novels dissected above, Duras and Cardinal both acknowledge, albeit to differing degrees, the gender-conventional, sexually hierarchical character of the French colonial, early/mid-century milieux they represent. Equally, both writers reveal these milieux to have been intensely patriarchal environments, in which colonisation was viewed as a male affair and women – notably bourgeois women such as Cardinal's narrator's mother – were discouraged from manifesting autonomy or initiative (see Knibiehler and Goutalier 1985: 147). At the same time, however, Cardinal and Duras (especially the latter) confirm that, in the colonial space, European women could accede to a manifestly problematic form of empowerment, in which ethnic privilege was paramount. (Duras's account of her heroine's liaison with her Chinese lover supports, for example, McClintock's contention that the 'rationed privileges of race' put white women in positions of dominance not only over colonised women but also vis-à-vis colonised men.) What interests me in all of this is that, even as they map French colonial realms that were undoubtedly culturally peripheral to the (equally but differently patriarchal) prewar Metropolitan domain evoked in Beauvoir's *Mémoires* and Leduc's *Ravages*, Duras and Cardinal closely reproduce the contrastive modalities of mother–daughter inscription highlighted in the previous section of this chapter. Clearly, the either/or discursive paradigm elaborated as a provisional construct in the concluding segment of my last section is validated by contemporary writings born out of at least one kind of 'marginal' modern French context. In the next part of my analysis, I shall evaluate the extent to which it is likewise endorsed by mother–daughter narrative discourse produced from within another marginal space – that occupied by France's North African immigrant community. I shall do so by assessing whether, in the 'exemplary' Franco-Maghrebian female-authored autobiographical text that provides my final key focus, a 'matricidal' (Beauvoirian/Durassian) mode of mother–daughter writing prevails over a 'reconciliatory' (Leducian/Cardinalian) model or vice versa, or whether my binarised paradigm requires modification.

The *Beur* Experience

Like many of the life-writings published by *beurs* (that is, second generation Maghrebian immigrants) in the 1980s and 1990s, Djura's *Le Voile du silence* (1990, The Veil of Silence) combines individual reminiscence with semi-documentary testimony (see Hargreaves 1991 and Bonn 1994). On the one hand, in common with other female-authored *beur* autobiographies, it foregrounds the (political, public) issue of women's oppression – namely, that experienced by Franco-Algerian immigrant females inside a community dominated by traditions imported from Islamic North Africa. On the other hand, again in a manner characteristic of the genre to which it belongs, *Le Voile* also chronicles the conflicts that set its narrator-protagonist apart from her family in the years and decades following her entry into adolescence. These conflicts relate not only to her sex, but also to the family enmity generated by her adult successes as a folk musician, and by her eventual decision, taken in the face of familial ingratitude, to stop supporting her mother and siblings. They culminate in the violent assault to which Djura's autobiographical protagonist is subjected, during pregnancy, by members of her family clan; an assault that is partly provoked by her non-marital liaison with a French partner, and is addressed at the start and end of her story.

By evoking a childhood and adolescence spent in Parisian working-class suburbs in the company of her alcoholic father, depressive mother, and burgeoning band of brothers and sisters, Djura's tale maps the subproletarian universe inhabited by the Algerian workforce 'welcomed' into France in the early 1950s. Concomitantly, her narrative denounces its profound androcentrism. The mid-century immigrant milieu, *Le Voile* insists, may have evolved inside the 'liberal' geographic space of the French Metropolis; however, it was not one in which women of Maghrebian origin could lightly cast off the yoke imposed by the sexually inegalitarian mores of Islam, or cease to be 'eternal minors' (*Voile*: 41, 100). Further, Djura affirms, if it constituted a world in which females, as a species, were treated barely less repressively than the women of their Algerian motherland, it was also one where daughters, in particular, were especially oppressed (*Voile*: 41, 54–56, 67–68). The mothers of France's growing Maghrebian community, Djura's text contends, were certainly victimised by their habitually violent, authoritarian husbands. Nonetheless, they themselves could also be authoritarian victimisers, ready to force their girl children to accept the male dominion they had already submitted to:

> You would see mothers give sticks to their youngest son, allowing him to beat his older sister, while others would hold their little girls down as the forces of fraternal justice carried out their punitive activities. These women, even though they had themselves suffered from them, perpetuated patriarchal practices, inciting their sons to terrify the opposite sex, developing their violence, their 'virility', in order to make them into 'men'. (*Voile*: 44)[20]

Their daughters, on the other hand, had no access to any form of power. As the surveillance of male relatives was a constant feature of their existences, they stood little chance of avoiding marital arrangements imposed by the latter (Djura herself resists her marital 'fate', albeit with difficulty), and had to overcome many obstacles in order to access the independence enjoyed by their French peers (*Voile*: 55–56).

Le Voile du silence is a narrative with a distinctly non-European focus/flavour, as well as a work that enjoys, as a *beur* production, a 'decentred' relationship with mainstream French cultural discourse.[21] Yet, of all of the texts considered here, it meshes most closely with the vision of the patriarchal economy proffered by Irigaray's eurocentric theoretical writings. That it does so is a function of its portrayal of France's postwar, Maghrebian immigrant world as an ultramasculinist locus governed by cultural and ideological norms that not only buried women in a reproductive servitude predicated on the production of sons (*Voile*: 24–25), but also hindered them from enjoying any connection with their female offspring, save that engendered by their common domestic enslavement (*Voile*: 48–49). To suggest that Djura's text offers a consciously 'Irigarayan' gloss on the (defective) female intersubjectivity generated within the French North African immigrant space would be to overstate the gender-political/conceptual impact of her narrative. That said, its intuitively Irigarayan aspect is confirmed by the record *Le Voile* incorporates of its author's difficult dealings with the woman who brought her into the world.

20. Djura's negative depiction of the oppressive Algerian immigrant mother is perhaps excessively harsh. Annie Krieger-Krynicki argues (1986: 68–69) that Maghrebian mothers who came to France in the 1950s often supported their daughters' efforts to emancipate themselves.
21. On the 'peripheral' nature of *beur* writing, see Laronde 1995: 29.

Djura's relationship with her mother, as it is charted in her autobiography, evolves in three phases. Each gives credence to the Irigarayan contention that mother–daughter love cannot thrive in patriarchally organised spaces where subjectivity remains the privileged province of the male, only the father–son lineage is allowed to count 'genealogically', and no adequate recognition is made of the mother–daughter relation (1993: 108). 'Phase one' begins with Djura's birth and ends with her flight from her parental home – a flight provoked by her desire for autonomy. While it admits a degree of female–female complicity generated by the paternal/marital brutality Djura and her mother mutually fear, it is characterised, above all, by an absence of mother–daughter community. This absence derives from the fact that Djura's mother, like other Muslim women of her generation, cannot invest emotionally in the female progeny she produces (*Voile*: 24–25), and Djura herself cannot, in consequence, relate to her genetrix except as a supplicant, endlessly pursuing a maternal affection she is enduringly denied. 'Phase two' coincides with the period of Djura's adulthood during which her artistic career develops and she opts to assume economic responsibility for her mother – now separated from her father – and younger siblings (*Voile*: 103ff.). It is marked by a failure, on Djura's part, to realise an authentic, loving, intersubjective connection either with her mother or, indeed, with the sisters who temporarily join her musical group, only to decry the political, feminist projects subtending its formation. This failure, *Le Voile* intimates, is caused by the revulsion the women of her family (especially her mother) experience in the face of Djura's ('French') conquest of a 'public' status/authority traditionally the preserve of the male subject – or, at the very least, of the established Muslim matriarch. It confirms Irigaray's argument that, when women are patriarchally enclosed within a state of disempowered commonality ('indifference'), they will themselves resent and work against manifestations of female subjective individualism/independence (1993: 103–4). It is emblematised in the fact that Djura's mother rejects the 'maison du bonheur' (house of happiness) her daughter purchases in order to create a realm of harmonious mother–daughter and familial relatedness, preferring to live mainly in Algeria, in the home her eldest son provides (*Voile*: 163–64). 'Phase three' follows Djura's decision to privilege her own life and relationships over her family ties. This final stage of the mother–daughter dynamic chronicled in *Le Voile* is one in which maternal violence prevails. Enraged by her daughter's refusal to go on performing the substitute paternal/marital function she has profited from (even as she has found it unpalatable), the mother becomes a prime mover in the violent settling of scores on which Djura's family embarks, and which almost results in the loss of Djura's baby.

Clearly, none of the above 'phases' reveal the mother–daughter connection depicted in Djura's autobiographical narrative to be an enabling one. What, though, does the way in which it is represented tell us about *Le Voile du silence*'s relationship to the mother–daughter discursive paradigm outlined in the first section of this chapter? On the one hand, *Le Voile* consistently connects the absence of maternal love which its author was exposed to with the brutalisation suffered not only by her mother, but also, collectively, by the women of the mid-century Franco-Maghrebian immigrant community. That it does so suggests that Djura's autobiography represents a reconciliatory, exculpatory, 'contextualising' opus of the kind emblematised by Cardinal's *Mots*. Yet, in contrast to *Les Mots*, *Le Voile* also conveys its creator's final inability to forgive the particular kind of maternity her mother incarnated – a maternity whose shortcomings are not only illuminated/criticised from the very beginning of Djura's story, but are also magnified by virtue of the nexus of instances of 'bad' motherhood that Djura's account locates outside of, as well as within, the confines of her family environment (*Voile*: 25, 44, 53, 84, 85). Manifestly, in terms of the positions it adopts with regard to the act of maternal inscription, *Le Voile du silence* attests to a significant degree of discursive 'inconsistency'. Consequently, it must be recognised as a narrative production which, if it confirms the binary paradigm addressed extensively in this chapter, does so by exploiting both its conciliatory and its 'matricidal' aspects without opting to privilege either one of them.

Beyond Binarism?

A primary facet of the critique of patriarchy elaborated in the 1970s by radical French feminists was the denunciation of the binary aspect of patriarchal thought. Binarism, signalled essays such as Cixous's *La Jeune Née* (1975, *The Newly Born Woman*, 1986), is a cornerstone of the patriarchal value system, symbolising its hierarchical inequalities, and must be undone in (revolutionary, 'feminine') forms of discourse that seek to subvert patriarchal language and ideology. In view of this, it is surprising, and ironic, that a binaristic mode of 'writing the mother' should find support in the five, key female-authored mother–daughter narratives dissected above. More unexpected still, perhaps, is the fact that the binary paradigm is mirrored in *Les Mots*, *L'Amant*, and *Le Voile* – texts published after the birth of the contemporary French women's movement, by politically committed authors whose post-1968 work generally bears the imprint of the influence of French neofeminism.

It is certainly not the case that every single one of the modern and contemporary French women writers who have addressed the mother–daughter relationship has neglected to transcend the personalised parameters of the denunciation/reconciliation binary. In *Une femme* (1987, *A Woman's Story*, 1991), a memoir produced in the months following her mother's death and presented as combining biography, literature, ethnography, and history, Annie

Ernaux (born 1940) writes in order to situate her mother as a social, historical subject, possessed of sociological as well as individual significance. Partly (and this recalls the 'recuperative' dimension of *Ravages*) this socially mobile author inscribes her maternal parent as a product of her class so that she can understand the factors that alienated her from her proletarian mother, mourn their divisive effects, and 'reaccess', albeit incompletely, the woman who brought her into the world, as well as the social universe for which her mother stood (a universe Ernaux casts herself as 'dislocated' from). Ernaux writes, in other words, from a standpoint generated by her experience of, and guilt about, social displacement and class betrayal, and with 'reparative', reconnective intent (see Miller 1995: 156–59). Partly also, in placing her mother, and the mother's maternal antecedents, into a social and ethnographic context of which she makes herself the 'archivist', Ernaux seeks to textually chart the mother–daughter bond as a socially valid genealogical relation with its own particular history and mode of evolution, and its own right to cultural and literary recognition. In so doing, she moves away from a daughterly discursive practice circumscribed by a self-regarding, solipsistic, emotive condemnation/recuperation dynamic. It is by no means true to say that *Une femme* is an 'unemotional', or indeed binary-free, narrative entity. As Nancy K. Miller contends, Ernaux's accounts of the repressions her mother inflicted on her adolescent self in order to keep her on the road to social and educational success (*Story*: 50–51; *femme*: 61) and, conversely, her 'matrophilial' recollections of the mother's luminosity and strength, work quite passionately with the Kleinian psychoanalytic categories of the 'good' and the 'bad' mother, and with a manifestly binarised thematic of rage and reparation (Miller 1995: 154, 159). Equally, Ernaux's class-focused opus strives explicitly to move beyond a mode of mother-narrative entrenched uniquely in the personal/affective and in issues of condemnation and conciliation, in order to pursue a model of 'neutral' (*Story*: 50; *femme*: 62) discourse that records mother–daughter relationality as part of the social landscape, associates the personal with the general, and works to accord female–female connectivity an audible voice and visible space in the literary and sociocultural spheres. Significantly, the latter model is not a dominant feature of *Je ne suis pas sortie de ma nuit* (I Have Not Emerged from My Darkness), a text which Ernaux published in 1997, but which is composed in the main of material written during her mother's descent into dementia and final agony. *Je ne suis pas sortie de ma nuit* is not concerned, primarily, with mapping the mother–daughter bond as a socially inflected or genealogical phenomenon. Neither is it concerned with experimenting with and combining ethnographical, biographical, historical, and literary modes of writing. Rather, it is a diaristic, visceral narrative – a 'residue of pain' (*Je ne suis*: 13) – in which Ernaux repeatedly articulates profoundly intimate, violent feelings of grief, desolation, and overidentification with a mother she is soon to lose.

In *Rose Mélie Rose* (1987) – unusual amongst French-language mother–daughter narratives for its departure from the autobiographical and its use of a 'fairy-tale' style of storytelling – Marie Redonnet (born 1948) adopts a strategy not entirely unlike that employed by Ernaux in *Une femme*. She works, in other words, to imagine the lineaments of a functional mother–daughter genealogy. By evoking a world in which women's names and identities are disconcertingly interchangeable, Redonnet's fable pinpoints the fusional 'indifference' that Irigaray locates as women's collective lot. At the same time, as it charts the loving, altruistic relations that obtain between Mélie, its youthful heroine, her adoptive mother Rose, and Mélie's baby daughter Rose, Redonnet's novel utopically envisions a fantastic realm in which mother figures willingly aid their female children to emerge from mother–daughter symbiosis, achieve filial separation and maturation, and position themselves as individuated beings within a mother–daughter lineage they need not either struggle against or leave behind. The positive dimension of this working lineage is made apparent by the role played in its formation by the act of maternal giving – emblematised in the 'book of legends' that the older Rose offers Mélie just before her death, and in the photographs and jewelry Mélie leaves for her own daughter to inherit. More pessimistically, however, *Rose Mélie Rose* implies that it can only come into being if its maternal participants are ready to die in the service of daughterly independence.[22]

Manifestly, then, some recently published works by contemporary French female authors escape enclosure within the sphere of influence of the binarised discursive model. So, too, do individual francophone novels by women writers from France's Caribbean overseas departements; novels such as Simone Schwarz-Bart's *Pluie et vent sur Télumée Miracle* (1972, Rain and Wind on Télumée Miracle) which, like *Rose Mélie Rose*, chronicles the enabling effects of (grand)maternal inheritance. That said, the binary model is globally shored up by, and evidenced in, 1940s–1960s and post-1968 French-authored mother–daughter writings alike. That this is the case is confirmed by Santos's *Malcastrée* (1973) and Chawaf's *Retable* (1974), autobiographically marked narratives that are clearly inflected by their denunciatory, matricidal aspect. Each of these texts, for all that they constitute exemplars of the radical, polysemic, 'feminine' writing (*écriture féminine*) associated with the revolutionary discourse/gender-politics of the post-1968 moment, incorporates a critical, matrophobic vision of a destructive, unbalanced mother. My case for the dominant role played by the condemnation/reconciliation paradigm is further supported by Leduc's *L'Asphyxie* (1946) and *La Bâtarde* (1964), Beauvoir's *Une mort très douce* (1964, *A Very Easy Death*, 1969), which records Françoise de Beauvoir's last illness, and

---

22. As Elizabeth Fallaize notes, good mothers always die in Redonnet's fiction (1993: 163).

Duras's *L'Amant de la Chine du Nord* (1991, *The North China Lover* 1992), which reprises elements of *L'Amant*. The first of these narratives, which predates *Ravages* by nine years, foregrounds maternal deficiency, eschews any attempt to imagine the phenomenon of mother–daughter reconnection, and has been qualified as a production that 'crucifies' an uncaring mother (Hall 1988: 233). The second, conversely, details the trying circumstances in which Leduc's mother's maternity evolved, conveys daughterly understanding and forgiveness, and signals its author's nostalgia for lost maternal/filial intimacy. The latter two are characterised, in their evocations of the mother figures inscribed within them, by a warmness of tone and a conciliatory stance absent from the 'matricidal' *Mémoires* and *L'Amant*.[23] Read with/against *Ravages*, the *Mémoires*, and *L'Amant*, all four texts suggest that while their creators were ready to shift between the constrastive poles of the denunciation/recuperation binary, they were loath to move outside of it.

Conclusion

I want, now, to return to the texts scrutinised in the first three sections of this chapter, and to make a further, final point about the manner in which the maternal is represented within them. None of these narratives, whether they transcribe the mother in a reconciliatory or a condemnatory fashion, casts maternity as a condition conducive either to enduring maternal satisfaction or to daughterly growth.[24] In other words, none of them presents the reader with a mother who is (wholly) happy or (wholly) beneficent. This phenomenon is not in fact surprising, given that, as elements of my discussion have already indicated, the motherhood incarnated by each of the mother figures evoked in these five key works (avatars, all, albeit to varying degrees, of their creators' flesh-and-blood mothers) may broadly be construed as 'imposed'. Its 'compelled' dimension can be connected, moreover, to a sociosexual phenomenon that was particular to the France of the late nineteenth and the early to mid-twentieth century: namely, its overwhelmingly pronatalist demographic ethos.[25]

---

23. It is worth noting that Alice Jardine reads Beauvoir's *Une mort* as a 'matricidal' tomb book, in which the mother's body is 'exorcised' so that she may continue to write (Jardine 1985: 94).
24. We should note that Djura and Cardinal are positive about their own experiences of motherhood. Further, and not unproblematically/unpredictably, Djura, Cardinal, and Duras signal that the mother figures of their narratives do derive satisfaction from giving birth to sons.
25. Four of the texts considered here intimate fairly explicitly that the maternity of the mothers portrayed within them was not the product of free choice. The fifth, *L'Amant*, does not dwell openly on the 'obligatory' character of its mother figure's motherhood. According, however, to Lia van de Biezenbos (1995: 113–14), Duras's writing does, generally, signal an awareness of the compelled nature of maternity and of France's 'politique culturelle du maternage' (cultural politics of maternity).

During the years dividing the early 1920s and the late 1960s to the early 1970s – years in the course of which the protagonists of Cardinal's *Mots* and Djura's *Voile* were born – contraception, abortion, and the dissemination of anticonceptional information were outlawed in France and its dependent territories by punitive legislation brought into force between 1920 and 1923 (see Knibiehler and Fouquet 1980). For much of this mid-century era, a powerfully pronatalist climate prevailed, epitomised in postwar welfare reforms passed by the French state in order to encourage mothers to produce large families. Even French women who were not exposed to the ideological restrictions to which the maternal personae of *Les Mots* and *Le Voile* were subjected faced obstacles, therefore, if they wished to opt out of the maternal function.[26] As Djura and Cardinal make plain, for women who were prevented from controlling their fertility, not only by legal statutes but also by powerful cultural pressures – women of the Catholic bourgeoisie, or women of immigrant, Muslim status – the production of children would have represented an inevitability. In the pre-1920 period, which witnessed the births of the narrator-protagonists of Beauvoir's *Mémoires*, Duras's *Amant*, and Leduc's *Ravages*,[27] compulsory maternity will probably have been more easily avoidable. Abortion was not legal, but neither was it subject to the kind of repression introduced after World War I, and, according to the pronatalist constituency formed by France's medical profession, was practised widely (Knibiehler and Fouquet 1980: 282–83). That said, French women were at this time being urged by France's demographers not to shirk their civic role as producers of their motherland's future defence forces. Further, motherhood was a destiny that bourgeois women in particular – who did not generally receive the parental financial support for further study accorded to their brothers, and were expected to marry – were culturally encouraged to embrace unquestioningly (Daumard 1987: 155), even if it could entail a domestic restriction denounced by the mother figure of *Ravages* as a 'calvary' (*Ravages*: 49). That this was the case is confirmed by Beauvoir's *Mémoires*, whose narrator states that 'my mother's whole education and upbringing had convinced her that for a woman the greatest thing was to become the mother of a family' (*Memoirs*: 106; *Mémoires*: 147).

None of the texts comprising my central corpus foregrounds pronatalism as a factor contributing to the evolution of the (negative) maternity that each

---

26. That said, French women did manage to control their fertility. In the 1930s, the decade at whose start Cardinal's narrator-protagonist was born, France's birth-rate reached its nadir.
27. Unlike *L'Amant* and *Mémoires*, *Ravages* is not so manifestly autobiographical as to invite the reader to assume automatically that, in terms, for example, of birth dates, its narrator-protagonist's life history parallels its author's. Yet, sufficient 'likeness' exists between Violette Leduc and her narrative creation Thérèse for us to suspect that this is nonetheless probable. Leduc was born in 1907.

of them, however differently, depicts. Its influence is, however, alluded to in Leduc's *Ravages*, Cardinal's *Mots*, and Djura's *Voile*, all of which signal how difficult it was for France's women to manage their fertility or terminate their pregnancies, and flag the fact that abortion was not a legalised practice in mid-twentieth century France. An awareness of France's pronatalist climate certainly helps us to comprehend the particular kind of motherhood represented in all of the narratives dissected in the main body of my discussion, even if that climate is not explicitly/extensively highlighted within them. Equally, it seems likely that the understanding of maternal inadequacy conveyed by the writings of all of these authors, regardless of whether they opt, in their mother–daughter histories, to privilege a condemnatory or a conciliatory narrative stance, can be attributed, to a degree, to their recognition of the ideological pressures under which women of their mothers' generation were interpellated into the maternal state.

Bibliography

Baisnée, Valérie (1997) *Gendered Resistance: The Autobiographies of Simone de Beauvoir, Maya Angelou, Janet Frame and Marguerite Duras*. Amsterdam: Rodopi.

Cardinal, Marie (1975) *Les Mots pour le dire*. Paris: Livre de Poche. *The Words To Say It*, trans. Pat Goodheart. London: The Women's Press, 1993.

Chawaf, Chantal (1974) *Retable/La Rêverie*. Paris: des femmes.

Chester, Suzanne (1992) 'Writing the Subject: Exoticism/Eroticism in Marguerite Duras's *The Lover* and *The Sea Wall*' in Sidonie Smith and Julia Watson (eds) *De/Colonizing the Subject: The Politics of Gender in Women's Autobiography*. Minneapolis: University of Minnesota Press, 436–57.

Cixous, Hélène (1983) *Le Livre de Promethea*. Paris: Gallimard. *The Book of Promethea*, trans. Betsy Wing. Lincoln: University of Nebraska Press, 1991.

Cixous, Hélène and Catherine Clément (1975) *La Jeune Née*. Paris: 10/18. *The Newly Born Woman*, trans. Betsy Wing. Manchester: Manchester University Press, 1986.

Clancy-Smith, Julia (1992) 'The "Passionate Nomad" Reconsidered: A European Woman in L'Algérie Française' in Nupur Chaudhuri and Margaret Strobel (eds) *Western Women and Imperialism: Complicity and Resistance*. Bloomington and Indianapolis: Indiana University Press, 61–78.

Corbin, Laurie (1996) *The Mother Mirror: Self-Representation and the Mother–Daughter Relation*. New York: Peter Lang.

Daumard, Adeline (1987) *Les Bourgeois et la bourgeoisie en France*. Paris: Aubier Montaigne.

de Beauvoir, Simone (1949) *Le Deuxième sexe*. Paris: Gallimard. *The Second Sex*, trans. H.M. Parshley. New York: Bantam, 1952.

—— (1958) *Mémoires d'une jeune fille rangée*. Paris: Gallimard. *Memoirs of a Dutiful Daughter*, trans. James Kirkup. Harmondsworth: Penguin, 1963.

―――― (1964) *Une mort très douce*. Paris: Gallimard. *A Very Easy Death*, trans. Patrick O'Brian. Harmondsworth: Penguin, 1969.

―――― (1967) *La Femme rompue*. Paris: Gallimard. *The Woman Destroyed*, trans. Patrick O'Brian. London: Collins, 1969.

Djura (1990) *Le Voile du silence*. Paris: Livre de Poche.

Duras, Marguerite (1950) *Un Barrage contre le pacifique*. Paris: Gallimard. *A Sea of Trouble*, trans. Antonia White. London: Methuen, 1953. *The Sea Wall*, trans. Herma Briffault. New York: Perennial Library, 1986.

―――― (1950) (1984) *L'Amant*. Paris: Minuit. *The Lover*, trans. Barbara Bray. London: Flamingo, 1986.

―――― (1991) *L'Amant de la Chine du Nord*. Paris: Gallimard. *The North China Lover*, trans. Leigh Hafrey. New York: New Press, 1992.

Ernaux, Annie (1987) *Une femme*. Paris: Gallimard. *A Woman's Story*, trans. Tanya Leslie. New York: Four Walls Eight Windows, 1991 (orig. 1990).

―――― (1997) *Je ne suis pas sortie de ma nuit*. Paris: Gallimard.

Fallaize, Elizabeth (1993) *French Women's Writing: Recent Fiction*. Basingstoke and London: Macmillan.

Ferrières-Pestureau, Suzanne (1997) *Une Etude psychanalytique de la figure du ravissement dans l'oeuvre de M. Duras*. Paris: L'Harmattan.

Grosz, Elizabeth (1989) *Sexual Subversions*. St Leonards: Allen and Unwin.

Haigh, Samantha (1994) 'Between Irigaray and Cardinal: Reinventing Maternal Genealogies' in *Modern Language Review*, vol. 89, 1994, 61–70.

Hall, Colette (1988) '*L'Ecriture féminine* and the Search for the Mother' in Michael Guggenheim (ed.) *Women in French Literature*. Saratoga, Calif.: Anma Libri, 231–38.

Hargreaves, Alec (1991) *Voices from the North African Community in France*. Oxford: Berg.

Hirsch, Marianne (1989) *The Mother/Daughter Plot: Narrative, Psychoanalysis, Feminism*. Bloomington and Indianapolis: Indiana University Press.

Hughes, Alex (1994a) *Violette Leduc: Mothers, Lovers and Language*. London: MHRA.

―――― (1994b) 'Murdering the Mother: Simone de Beauvoir's *Mémoires d'une jeune fille rangée*' in *French Studies*, vol. 48, no. 2, 1994, 174–83.

―――― (1996) 'The City and the Female Autograph' in Michael Sheringham (ed.) *Parisian Fields*. London: Reaktion books, 115–32.

Hyvrard, Jeanne (1976) *Mère la mort*. Paris: Minuit. *Mother Death*, trans. Laurie Edson. Lincoln: University of Nebraska Press, 1988.

Irigaray, Luce (1974) *Speculum, de l'autre femme*. Paris: Minuit.

―――― (1985a) *Speculum of the Other Woman*, trans. Gillian Gill. Ithaca and London: Cornell University Press.

―――― (1977) *Ce Sexe qui n'en est pas un*. Paris: Minuit.

―――― (1985b) *This Sex Which Is Not One*, trans. Catherine Porter with Carolyn Burke. Ithaca and London: Cornell University Press.

―――― (1979) *Et l'une ne bouge pas sans l'autre*. Paris: Minuit.

—— (1981a) 'And the One Doesn't Stir Without the Other', trans. Hélène Wenzel, in *Signs*, vol. 7, no. 1, 1981, 60–67.
—— (1981b) *Le Corps-à-corps avec la mère*. Montreal: Éditions de la pleine lune (reprinted in Irigaray, *Sexes et parentés*. Paris: Minuit, 1987). 'The Bodily Encounter with the Mother', trans. extract David Macey, in Whitford (ed.) 1991, 34–46.
—— (1984) *Ethique de la différence sexuelle*. Paris: Minuit.
—— (1993) *An Ethics of Sexual Difference*, trans. Carolyn Burke and Gillian Gill. Ithaca and London: Cornell University Press.
Jardine, Alice (1985) 'Death Sentences: Writing Couples and Ideology' in Susan Suleiman (ed.) *The Female Body in Western Culture*. Cambridge Mass. and London: Harvard University Press, 84–96.
Knibiehler, Yvonne and Catherine Fouquet (1980) *L'Histoire des mères*. Paris: Editions Montalba.
Knibiehler, Yvonne and Régine Goutalier (1985) *Le Femme au temps des colonies*. Paris: Stock.
Kristeva, Julia (1983) *Histoires d'amour*. Paris: Denoël. *Tales of Love*, trans. Léon S. Roudiez. New York: Columbia University Press, 1986.
—— (1987) *Soleil Noir: Dépression et mélancolie*, Paris: Gallimard. *Black Sun: Depression and Melancholia*, trans. Léon S. Roudiez. New York: Columbia University Press, 1989.
Krieger-Krynicki, Annie (1985) *Les Musulmans en France*. Paris: Editions Maisonneuve et Larose.
Laronde, Marc (1995) 'Stratégies rhétoriques du discours décentré' in *Etudes littéraires maghrébines*, vol. 7, 1995, 29–39.
Le Clézio, Marguerite (1981) 'Mother and Motherland: The Daughter's Quest for Origins' in *Stanford French Review*, vol. 5, 1981, 381–89.
Leduc, Violette (1946) *L'Asphyxie*. Paris: Gallimard. *In the Prison of Her Skin*, trans. Derek Coltman. London: Hart-Davis, 1970.
—— (1955) *Ravages*. Paris: Gallimard. *Ravages*, trans. Derek Coltman. London: Barker, 1968.
—— (1964) *La Bâtarde*. Paris: Gallimard. *La Bâtarde: An Autobiography*, trans. Derek Coltman. London: Peter Owen, 1965; London: Virago, 1985.
Lionnet, Françoise (1989) *Autobiographical Voices: Race, Gender, Self-Portraiture*. Ithaca and London: Cornell University Press.
McClintock, Anne (1995) *Imperial Leather: Race, Gender and Sexuality in the Colonial Contest*. New York and London: Routledge.
Miller, Nancy K. (1995) 'Our Classes, Ourselves: Maternal Legacies and Cultural Criticism' in Mae Henderson (ed.) *Borders, Boundaries, and Frames: Essays in Cultural Criticism and Cultural Studies*. London and New York: Routledge, 145–70.
Mills, Sara (1994) 'Knowledge, Gender, and Empire' in Alison Blunt and Gillian Rose (eds) *Writing Women and Space: Colonial and Postcolonial Geographies*. London: Guilford Press, 29–50.

Portuges, Catherine (1986) 'Attachment and Separation in *Memoirs of a Dutiful Daughter*' in *Yale French Studies*, no. 72, 1986, 107–18.
Redonnet, Marie (1987) *Rose Mélie Rose*. Paris: Minuit.
Ruscio, Alain (1995) *Le Credo de l'homme blanc*. Brussels: Editions Complexe.
Santos, Emma (1987) *La Malcastrée*. Paris: des femmes.
Schwarz-Bart, Simone (1972) *Pluie et vent sur Télumée Miracle*. Paris: Seuil.
Van de Biezenbos, Lia (1995) *Fantasmes maternels dans l'oeuvre de Marguerite Duras*. Amsterdam: Rodopi.
Whitford, Margaret (1989) 'Rereading Irigaray' in Teresa Brennan (ed.) *Between Feminism and Psychoanalysis*. London and New York: Routledge, 106–26.
Whitford, Margaret (ed.) (1991) *The Irigaray Reader*, intro. Whitford. Oxford and Cambridge, Mass.: Blackwell.
Wittig, Monique (1973) *Le Corps lesbien*. Paris: Minuit. *The Lesbian Body*, trans. David Le Vay. London: Owen, 1975.

CHAPTER SIX

BAD DAUGHTERS AND UNMOTHERLY MOTHERS

THE NEW FAMILY PLOT IN THE CONTEMPORARY ENGLISH NOVEL

Paola Splendore

Introduction: A New Family Plot?

Women's narratives, in the form of the domestic or family novel, generally tend to focus on the web of relationships and emotional bonds between the women of a family: mothers, daughters, sisters, grandmothers, with the male figures relegated to the shadows. Metaphoric expression of these ties and affections has often been a house; a space with marked feminine connotations and a close association with the maternal. From Jane Austen to George Eliot, from Elizabeth Bowen to Doris Lessing, many fictional houses have been inhabited by happy or, more often, tormented families, yet it has rarely been possible to find a dominant plot in these novels based on mother–daughter relationships, especially in past centuries. When this does exist it remains submerged, or on the fringe, because the emphasis of the novel is almost invariably laid on the young heroine, the daughter. Only in the twentieth century has this relationship become an independent narrative theme, the centre of the plot rather than its corollary.

Even in the twentieth century, however, the development of the mother–daughter plot and the figuration of motherhood remained linked for a long time to literary stereotypes reflecting patriarchal roles and values, in novels which basically rewrite what Marianne Hirsch has defined as 'the heterosexual family romance' (Hirsch 1989: 44). May Sinclair's autobiographical novel, *Mary Olivier: A Life* (1919), can be taken as the paradigmatic text of early twentieth-century mother–daughter relations. Written entirely from the daughter's point of view, the plot shows Mary's painful transition from an ecstatically adoring child into a thwarted and rebellious adolescent because of her mother's overt preference for her sons and her repression of Mary's intellectual curiosity. When she grows into an attractive young woman, Mary's sexuality becomes especially threatening to her egotistic mother who, after failing to make Mary a replica of herself, persuades her to reject a marriage proposal from the man she loves, who admires her also for her intellect. Although Mary is aware of the sacrifice her mother requires of her, being the product of her upbringing, she is unable to forsake her, thus implicitly accepting the 'gendered split between the intellectual and the domestic' (Phillips 1996: 134). Subsequent generations of female authors rarely offer an equally poignant analysis of the mother–daughter bond which probes beyond predictably hierarchical relationships and stereotyped roles. Daughters tend to be modelled on the subdued type or the rebel type, while mothers are generally cast as absent, conformist, and incompetent. The theme disappears almost completely from the plots of the major female authors of the first half of the twentieth century who, while continuing the pattern of 'maternal repression', prefer to dramatise a conflict between roles, or a woman's dilemma over having to choose, for instance, between motherhood and self-fulfilment as an artist, as in Virginia Woolf (1882–1941), May Sinclair (1863–1946), and Rebecca West (1892–1983).[1] Later authors appear to concentrate instead on the daughter's dilemma: whether to be a good daughter, complying with her mother's expectations and, in so doing, thwarting her own desires, or to break the bond, turning wicked, and setting herself free. Daughters emotionally crippled by their mothers' egotism appear in *The House in Paris* (1935) by Elizabeth Bowen (1899–1973) and in *The Ballad and the Source* (1944) by Rosamond Lehmann (1901–1990).

It is only in the second half of the century that mother–daughter relations have been more consistently explored in a new kind of ethos, mainly from the standpoint of a woman's right to live her own life regardless of social conventions or family constraints. This is especially true of Doris Lessing (born 1919) who, drawing on her own experience, has made this one of the main themes of her vast narrative output. Although her novels of the 1950s and

---

1. See Woolf's *Mrs Dalloway* (1925) and *To the Lighthouse* (1927); Sinclair's *The Creators* (1910) and *The Tree of Heaven* (1917); West's *The Return of the Soldier* (1918). On this issue, see Humm 1991, especially Chapter 1. See also Ingman 1998 for an analysis of mothers and daughters in the context of the latter's artistic vocation, in the work of Rose Macaulay, Elizabeth Bowen, Ivy Compton-Burnett, Jean Rhys, Virgina Woolf, and Dorothy Richardson.

1960s are in keeping with a dominant ideology of devaluation of the mother–daughter relationship, displaying a prevailing matrophobic focus as in *Martha Quest* (1952) and *A Proper Marriage* (1954), her later, postfeminist works offer a more articulate representation of mother–daughter dynamics, sometimes including the mother's perspective, as in *The Four-Gated City* (1969), *The Summer Before the Dark* (1973), and *Memoirs of a Survivor* (1974). Nevertheless, the dominant perspective remains the daughter's and in particular that of the 'bad' daughter, as in *The Good Terrorist* (1985) whose protagonist, Alice Mellings, is unable to cut the umbilical cord which still ties her to her mother, and enacts a self-destructive strategy of separation from everything her mother represents. Thus, even Alice's participation in a serious terrorist attack is above all a way of disobeying her mother and showing her autonomy as inferred by Alice's thoughts, 'what would Dorothy say if she knew her daughter had been at the bombing?' (*Good Terrorist*: 366). Gayle Greene offers a similar reading of the novel when she writes:

> The novel builds to Alice's confrontation with her mother, Dorothy Mellings, working back to this relationship as though to a point of origin or explanation. Her mother has been on Alice's mind throughout. Alice carries her around like an aching conscience, a gnawing awareness of something she needs to remember but would rather forget: in some sense this story is a quest for the mother. (Greene 1994: 216)

Filial atonement is at the heart of *Diary of a Good Neighbour* (1983), a novel originally published under a pseudonym, in which Lessing moves beyond matrophobia to accept the maternal and is finally able to confront what Julia Kristeva has called 'maternal abjection' (Kristeva 1980). In *Diary*, the unfulfilled relationship between mother and daughter, recognised too late as an absence, becomes the mainspring of Janna's existence and finds a form of compensation in her relationship with old Maude. Although Janna ends up mothering the latter, she can also project upon her the ugly experiences of life which she has never known and is incapable of accepting, such as old age, poverty, and illness, as well as the maternal part of herself which she has denied twice: once through not becoming a mother and once through not having known how to take care of her dying mother. Lessing's recent autobiography, *Under My Skin* (1994), is largely devoted to exploring her relationship with her mother, and confirms the author's need to confront the maternal figure and retrieve her female genealogy while coming to terms with her own self. It is worth noting that, although *Diary* can be read as an atonement for the author's guilt at having been unjust towards her mother, the speaking voice in *Under My Skin* is very much that of a daughter who still resents her mother for not having wanted her, for not having fed or loved her enough, for neglecting her for her younger brother and later for oppressing her and pushing her into rebellion for survival (see Sprague 1987 and Splendore 1998).

In the late 1960s, with the emergence of a new generation of novelists such as Margaret Drabble (born 1939), Nell Dunn (born 1936), and Fay Weldon (born 1932), a shift occurs. Novels like Drabble's *The Millstone* (1965) and *The Waterfall* (1969), Dunn's *Poor Cow* (1967), Weldon's *Down Among the Women* (1971), *Female Friends* (1975), and *Puffball* (1980) lay a new and different emphasis on the experience of motherhood, by looking at it above all with a demystifying and unsentimental attitude. Maggie Humm argues that by 'relocating' motherhood outside the bounds of conventional marriage Drabble, Dunn, and Weldon made, each in her different way, 'one major and transgressive dissent from postwar conservatism' (Humm 1991: 44). Taking advantage of a new publishing space, their fresh outlook, based at times on clear feminist tenets, prepared the way for a new kind of family plot which emerged in the next two decades.

In novels written over the past twenty years both in England and other anglophone countries the 'resurgence' of the mother–daughter theme clearly expresses the wish to go beyond the usual iconography, not only by reversing certain literary stereotypes like the Oedipal plot but also by questioning the new feminist reappraisal of the maternal.[2] While highlighting the relationship between plot and gender, the new novelists' representation of family life and in particular of the mother–daughter relationship reveals highly innovative traits, particularly in the skill and depth of analysis, sharpened by the tools of psychoanalytic, cultural, and feminist criticism. Even when the authors do not choose to identify with defined theoretical and/or ideological positions, these can be considered to have been assimilated by them. Their works, whatever their style, show an unprecedented degree of frankness and sensitivity in the representation of a relationship which is often problematic if only because it involves a confrontation between generations and roles which are, by definition, antagonistic. It is as if many taboos concerning the representation of maternal feeling and filial attachment had fallen away. This enables the authors to go beyond the rhetoric of sentiments and attain a greater expressive freedom and lucidity, thus untying even the most entangled emotional knots. On the formal and stylistic level this freedom is manifest in the great variety of rhetorical and narrative strategies, and in the combination, within each novel, of various languages and registers, from the loftiest to the most colloquial.

2. Many feminist studies, published from the end of the 1970s onwards, question some fundamental Freudian paradigms about parental dynamics and mother–daughter relationality. In particular, Chodorow 1978 maintains that the basis of female identity is located in the pre-Oedipal phase, when the mother–daughter dyad, free of the father's interference, enjoys fusion and solidarity. Rich 1977 recuperates the 'good' mother helping orienting woman's quest for identity in her female genealogy. She advocates the end of matrophobia, the fear of becoming one's own mother.

My study focuses on a number of works published in the last twenty years which I have selected and grouped according to their thematic and formal aspects. Three main narrative models have been identified on the basis of their prevailing registers – confessional/memorialistic, melodramatic, and comic-grotesque – each of which is dealt with in a separate section. The first section concentrates on autobiographical narratives in which a daughter reconstructs her mother's life and, in the process, comes to term with her own identity. These works lay a definite stress on gender and set the idea of motherhood in a sociocultural perspective. They can be usefully read as a response, critical at times, to the psychoanalytic and feminist studies of the late 1960s and 1970s on the family and the reappraisal of the maternal. The texts I have selected are *Landscape for a Good Woman* (1986) by Carolyn Steedman (born 1947), *Poppy* (1990) by Drusilla Modjeska (born 1946), and *Skating to Antarctica* (1997) by Jenny Diski (born 1947). The second section looks at novels presenting highly dramatic plots with a cross-generational focus and a multiperspective narrative strategy in which mothers, daughters, and grandmothers confront one another, each telling in turn their version of the story, often climaxing in a sensationalistic crescendo. The texts I analyse more closely are Jenny Diski's *Like Mother* (1988), Lisa St Aubin de Terân's *Joanna* (1990), and Emma Tennant's *Faustine* (1992). The third group includes novels written entirely from the daughter's point of view in a comic-grotesque register, in which the mother figure, constructed as a mirror of negative identification, is used as a debunking maternal icon. The texts analysed – Jeanette Winterson's *Oranges Are Not the Only Fruit* (1985) and Kate Atkinson's *Behind the Scenes at the Museum* (1995) – display a combination of narrative styles and modes ranging from fairy tale to social realism, sitcom humour, and black humour. A fourth section, devoted to the analysis of *You Can't Get Lost in Capetown* (1987) by the South African author Zoë Wicomb (born 1948), provides an example of the mother–daughter theme enriched by ethnic and linguistic issues.

The Quest for the Lost Mother

Just as the death of the father has been a recurrent literary topos in the Western novel and an important rite of passage for the fictional hero, so the mother's death has become a topos in women's literature,[3] an opportunity

---

3. According to Gardiner the maternal deathbed trope can almost be considered as the female counterpart to the Oedipus myth: 'In the Oedipus myth, the son murders his father in order to replace him. Contrastingly, in the new woman's myth, the daughter "kills" her mother in order *not* to have to take her place' (1978: 146).

– in Elaine Showalter's words – to reappropriate a denied plot: 'now the death of the mother as witnessed and transcended by the daughter has become one of the most profound occasions of female literature' (Showalter 1986: 135). Many narratives of the 1980s and 1990s take their cue from the event of the mother's death and the acute awareness of a failed relationship. The three works I have selected for analysis do not so much focus on the loss, as on the attempt to understand the maternal figure as an individual set in the context of the social and ideological pressures of her generation, and of her personal experience. The mother emerges in these narratives as a person with the desires, expectations, and frustrations typical of her time and her social situation, and inevitably conditioned by patriarchal culture as well as by her own personal failures and responsibilities towards her daughter. The daughter's narrative – a sort of virtual dialogue with her dead mother in which the itineraries of two lives interweave – is presented as personal memory. It reconstructs, however, a social and cultural fabric which extends the private terms of the reflection to the portrait of a generation, and of a period and its ideologies.[4] This dual motive is reflected in the composite style of these narratives, in which the essay form, though never impersonal, alternates with memoirs and confession, two modes which allow the most intimate aspects of the relationships to be explored and the most painful memories to surface. The three texts under consideration are also constructed as journeys, both literal and symbolic, to distant and unexplored territories.

Steedman's *Landscape for a Good Woman*, written in a hybrid form between essay and fiction, autobiography and social history, combines psychoanalytic insight and cultural analysis. The daughter's discourse is an attempt to retrieve the sense of her mother's marginal life and enter her perspective in order to reveal her dreams, her forbidden desires, and her frustrated ambitions. Modjeska's *Poppy* follows a similar pattern. Like Steedman's text, it deals with unfulfilled relationships and the recovery of an individual story which would otherwise be lost. Unlike Steedman, however, Modjeska gives her characters fictitious names and, in her attempt to fill in the gaps in her mother's story, she combines facts, fantasies, and myth. The author appears to believe in the possibility of retrieving her pre-Oedipal mother, through the recovery of letters, diaries, and testimonies of her mother both in England and in Australia, where the daughter had moved to get away from her. Diski's *Skating to Antarctica* also tells of a difficult quest, but it does so obliquely. It is the author's daughter, Chloe, who wants to find out

---

4. I should mention here the family memoir *Hidden Lives* (1995) by Margaret Forster (born 1938), a text constructed along similar lines which also reflects on the changes in women's lives across three generations, and *The Lost Father* (1988) by Marina Warner (born 1946), a moving portrayal of her mother's and grandmother's youth in a Southern Italian village at the beginning of the century.

whether her grandmother – whom her mother has not seen for thirty years – is still alive. Thus, the mother–daughter theme emerges almost as secondary to the apparent travelogue of a sea journey towards Antarctica, which turns into a painful story of affective deprivation and perversion.

'She lived alone, she died alone: a working-class life, a working-class death'. It is with this statement, formulated in opposition to Simone de Beauvoir's description of her mother's death as a very gentle 'upper-class' death in *A Very Easy Death* (1964), that Steedman begins her account of two lives, her own and her mother's. She intends, on the one hand, to rescue her mother's life from the nothingness to which it is condemned by her marginalised condition and to show the singularity of her individual experience. On the other hand, she wishes to show how her mother's feelings conditioned her own self, shaping her own desires and expectations: 'My mother's longing shaped my childhood. From a Lancashire mill town and a working-class twenties childhood she came away wanting: fine clothes, glamour, money; to be what she wasn't' (*Landscape*: 6). Thus, the two stories overlap, and the mother's youth merges into the author's childhood in an inextricable tangle of unhappiness, poverty, and frustration. Although Kay (as Steedman was called as a child) and her little sister did not discover until much later that their parents were not married, their illegitimacy entirely conditioned their family life, which in retrospect seems to her to be a collection of lies, subterfuge, and resentment.

Day after day the mother transmitted to her children a lesson of hatred towards their father, making the very fact of their existence weigh on them too, like an unwanted burden. The family seemed to keep going on the mother's wages rather than the father's. Because of this he was exiled to the attic and generally treated by the mother as an object of contempt and animosity until he left to go and live with another woman. In fact the mother used her daughters to hold on to their father: 'We were an insurance, a roof over her head, a minimum income. We were her way of both having him and repudiating him. We were the cake that she both had and ate, before he left ... and after' (*Landscape*: 57). Steedman's attitude is polemic, not only towards sociological studies of the proletarian family, with their gender stereotypes and sentimentalised portrayals of working-class life (Hoggart 1959, Young and Willmott 1962, Seabrook 1982), but also towards Freudian psychoanalysis and its feminist revisions, of which she questions, for example, the notion of female dependence.

Steedman challenges Nancy Chodorow's notion that motherhood is an instinct passed on from mother to daughter almost like a natural legacy. She explains her own refusal to be a mother on the basis of the difficult relationship she had with her mother. Steedman's mother was often incapable of playing with her own children or of showing them affection and was sometimes violent, almost as if the very existence of the little girls was the cause and proof of the failure of her naive dreams. In a recent essay Nancy K. Miller sides with Steedman in her criticism of Chodorow, in view of her own 'choice' not to be a mother: '*Landscape for a Good Woman* is powerful for me ... because of the ways in which it renders the maternal legacy that makes the daughter *not a mother* ... I meet Steedman autobiographically in a gesture of *counteridentification*' (Miller 1995: 148, Miller's emphasis). However, when the young Steedman is forced to choose between father and mother she does not act as traditional psychoanalysis 'prescribes'. She does not take her father's side, even though she loves him very much, but gives him up, perhaps also because she cannot have him, thus reinforcing her relationship with her mother to the point of completely identifying with her and appearing, in Raphael Samuel's words, 'a palimpsest of her mother's will'. (Samuel 1986: 22) It is with a sense of unquenched resentment that Steedman admits having identified as a child with her mother's dreams, desires, and fears: 'She made me believe that I understood everything about her, she made me believe that I was her ... She made me good because I was a spell, a piece of possible good fortune' (*Landscape*: 141).

Steedman's account of her feeling of rejection of her mother's body as a 'recognition of the problem that my own physical presence represented to her' (*Landscape*: 95) is strikingly lucid. So is the record of her inner struggle against becoming as her mother wanted her to be: the refusal to be manipulated, to be made good, 'to *be* my mother' (*Landscape*: 106, Steedman's emphasis). We are also struck by the force of her resentment towards her mother for having given her so little affection and solidarity while instilling in her the notion that she was such a lucky little girl to have such a good mother. It is not surprising that, as an adult, Steedman grows away from her mother, does not see her for many years, and only after her death feels that she must recognise the fact that after all she had been a good mother, careful about a 'brown bread diet' for her children. Nevertheless, she does not sentimentalise over their unfulfilled relationship, or try to disguise her story as a new incarnation of a myth so dear to feminism: 'we were certainly not Demeter and Persephone to each other, nor ever could be, but two women caught by a web of sexual and psychological relationships in the front room of a council house' (*Landscape*: 19). Rather than as a monument to her mother, the text can be read as a rationalisation, and as self-compensation for the author's unhappy childhood. The case-study format of the book helps her create a distance from a painful material without renouncing a considerable emotional density.

Lalage, the narrator of *Poppy* and the author's alter ego, speaks, on the other hand, from a clearly feminist standpoint: 'I'm interested in the representation of the maternal bond' (*Poppy*: 152). Weaving together scraps of fact and imagination, Modjeska constructs her mother's imaginary biography, trying to bring her back to life in an almost ideal inversion of the myth of

Demeter and Persephone: 'My mother had died and it was true what I'd said, I did not know her, and ... I knew that by not knowing her, I could not know myself' (*Poppy*: 5). In the process, she acknowledges the extent to which their two lives are interwoven, 'Did I think I could investigate Poppy's life without investigating my own?' (*Poppy*: 102). As in Steedman's text, the two quests, the two stories, end by overlapping: 'She is delivered in a ream of paper but when I take her out and breathe life into her, I find a woman who is close to myself' (*Poppy*: 171).

Modjeska's emphasis on her mother's voice echoes Hélène Cixous who maintains, in *The Newly Born Woman* (1987), that feminine writing is an extension of the mother's voice which precedes the symbolic language: 'In feminine speech, as in writing, there never stops reverberating something that, having once passed through us, having imperceptibly and deeply touched us, still has the power to affect us – song, the first music of the voice of love, which every woman keeps alive' (Cixous and Clément: 93). Modjeska yearns for a form of pre-Oedipal fusion with her mother, 'a dim region, an ancient possibility that has long been surpassed, and yet lives on, shadowy and grey with age, and yearning to be revivified' (*Poppy*: 116). This fusion might be accomplished through the daughter's journey to Crete in her mother's footsteps, which she identifies as an important stage of her mother's awakening. Later, Poppy, looking for a more psychic, more feminine reality, goes further East on a sort of spiritual pilgrimage, 'There is something about India – Poppy writes in a letter – which seems to unlock places in people that have been hidden for years' (*Poppy*: 272). What she finds there is not so much the answer to her unfinished quest but a way of defining herself in the most basic way as a daughter and as a mother:

> Who am I?
> Who am I?...
> I am the mother of three daughters.
> I am the wife of two men.
> I am the daughter of China.
> I am the daughter of Jack...
> I am a friend.
> I am a mother...
> I am many, not one.
> I am none of these things. (*Poppy*: 277)

It is on a note of uncertainty about the possibility of really knowing oneself or the other that Modjeska concludes that 'mothers are hard to make peace with' (*Poppy*: 226). Lessing expresses this same difficulty in 'Impertinent Daughters' (1984), a portrait of her mother which she wrote in her late sixties, pursuing it further in *Under My Skin*: 'Writing about my mother is difficult. I keep coming up against barriers, and they are not much different now from what they were then. She paralysed me as a child by the anger and pity I felt. Now only pity is left, but it still makes it hard to write about her. What an awful life she had, my poor mother!' ('Impertinent Daughters': 68).

If the works mentioned above are journeys towards the mother, *Skating to Antarctica* follows a different textual strategy. Diski conceals the quest pattern within the plot of a journey through the polar region of Antarctica to satisfy her passion for *whiteness*, the principal metaphor of the book representing the uncontaminated purity to which she aspires. Hers is a story of violence and forced separation from her parents; a manipulative and alcoholic mother, and a father who was often in prison, both of them with several failed suicide attempts behind them. Diski speaks of herself as a 'survivor', something she feels ashamed of at times, but nevertheless something to hang on to, 'to put against the flaky genes and the training in hopelessness' (*Skating*: 216). She is above all the survivor of a child called Jennifer of whom there are no photos and who, she feels, has almost become a fictitious character like Jane Eyre: 'There are no pictures, no written words, no other person who, remembering her, has spoken to me of her. She has existed exclusively inside my head... I might have made her up – I did make her up from time to time' (*Skating*: 86). Here too we have a dual quest, but it is to herself, to finding out what happened to little Jennifer, that the author seems most drawn.

In her early years, Jennifer is suffocated by the attentions of her well-to-do parents, spoiled with expensive clothes and toys and subjected to daily ice-skating practice so that she can become a champion. The father and mother involve the child in erotic games which she does not understand but which frighten her, giving her a tremendous sense of insecurity. When the money runs out the skating lessons also come to an end and the father becomes less and less present. Instead of a champion, Diski says, the mother is left with 'an ice maiden' (*Skating*: 20), an image which connects with the metaphor of ice and whiteness running through the book. We are also reminded of Steedman's analogy between herself as a child and the hero of Hans Christian Andersen's *The Snow Queen*, a boy called Kay – bearing both her name and 'a lump of ice' in his heart. The sense of class diversity perceived by Diski as a source of anxiety and humiliation is another element in common with Steedman's experience. Steedman, as the daughter of parents who had emigrated from the north of England to London (probably to hide their illegitimate position) lived in isolation, without relatives or friends. Diski, as the daughter of Jewish parents without a clear social position, also felt excluded: 'We weren't middle class, not exactly working class; it was *different*. Much easier now to see that we were the children of immigrants' (*Skating*: 105, Diski's emphasis).

When Jenny/Jennifer is fourteen, she attempts suicide for the first time with an overdose (*Skating*: 24) and is taken to a psychiatric institution; neither of her parents, who are separated by this time, can look after her and she is entrusted to a foster family. As she grows older, she experiments with various types of drugs and is repeatedly hospitalised. The girl is looking for oblivion, for a condition of suspension from being, 'a release from the feeling of helplessness' (*Skating*: 189). In time, however, she has to surrender to memory, as the very existence of this book shows, and to the need to confront the maternal ghost. Set off by the rolling of the ship taking her to Antarctica, the memory of a more distant, prenatal time stirs within her, the memory of her blissful floating in amniotic waters: 'I've tried to avoid the unavoidable conclusion all my life: always happier to imagine I was a foundling, an alien even, than to suppose that I spent nine warm contented months in my mother's uterus. That my first comfort was from within her body: Her body nurturing me... I didn't know my mother then... Both of us were innocent and ignorant' (*Skating*: 81–82).

The text contains neither an attempt at emotional redress nor the desire for rehabilitation; it is not an excuse for elaborating a foundling fantasy, it merely tries to look unflinchingly at what has been. Whereas Steedman and Modjeska tell their mothers' stories in order to uncover the truth about their lives, in spite of the emotional interference which prejudiced their relationship, Diski's quest excludes such a possibility. When she questions the women who lived next door to the London apartment she lived in as a child, they express many truths, which she has to place beside those given to her by her father and her mother when she was young: 'All this was *truth*. Truth, I learned, was up for grabs, entirely dependent on who was doing the telling' (*Skating*: 100). Her mother remains an indecipherable enigma for whom she has no hard words, only the image of an emotionally disturbed and very unhappy woman:

> She was sad, rather than bad, and, I think, genuinely baffled by the way life was out of her control. She did not, for reasons of her own emotionally deprived upbringing, have enough insight to be considered responsible for the results of her behaviour. It leaves me little room for anger towards her personally. Living with her, day by day, was like skating on newly formed ice. It constantly shattered, every day, but there was no alternative, no other place to go. No room for anger, but no room for affection either. You might as well be enraged at the ice for being too fragile to hold your weight. (*Skating*: 107–8)

Nevertheless Diski wonders how it has been possible for her to elude primary attachment to her mother: 'How could this primary maternal connection have passed me by?' (*Skating*: 30). Was she irremediably bad, then, as her mother deemed her? 'If anywhere, this badness was where my attachment to my mother existed. It was an area of agreement, with different implications for each of us, that we held separately but in common' (*Skating*: 30). In the end, Diski concludes, as Steedman does, that in spite of everything, her mother,

> hadn't been a neglectful mother, erratic, demanding, alarming but not neglectful. She was devoted to me, to how I looked, to what I ate, to my progress at school... And perhaps she loved me. I don't know. I know that she thought that having a child guaranteed that she would be loved... Sometimes she said, 'I have to love you, you are my daughter'. Love was obligation, and in saying that she was reminding me of my obligation to her. (*Skating*: 205)

One possible explanation for her emotional tangle lies in the sense of having been loved out of duty, as in Steedman's case, and the sense that the loss of her father had been her mother's responsibility.

Although the three texts may have originated in the authors' sense of guilt towards their mothers, they succeed in dealing with the mother–daughter relationship without sentimentalism and without ever taking it for granted, thus implicitly devaluing abstract notions such as maternal instinct and filial love. They present instead situations in which it was difficult for the mother to offer love and protection to the daughter, because of poverty, illegitimacy, mental illness, or alcoholism. Much is forgiven in the end and one has the feeling that the confrontation with the maternal ghost was necessary for the daughters' acceptance of their own identity. The mother, in conclusion, appears rehabilitated, in spite of the severe shortcomings and failures towards their daughters.

The Mother–Daughter Melodrama

The novels grouped together in this section use a number of elements from popular narrative such as melodrama and the Gothic to intensify their sentimental and sensationalistic aspects and thus induce strong emotional reactions in the reader.[5] The texts are often constructed dialogically, through three generations of women of the same family. In some of them the narrators alternate, creating a prismatic effect, almost a mirror game, which dramatically highlights both the perpetuation of certain family situations and the relativity of truth when feelings and blood ties are involved. While they overthrow the nineteenth-century theme of maternal sacrifice, they dramatise abusive and violent relationships between mothers and daughters which prevent the daughter from attaining a satisfactory adult life, both in connection with a partner and as mothers. This is all the more devastating because of the absence of significant male parental figures. Strong emotional topoi abound in this type of novel. Physical and psychological illness – cancer, madness, depression, alcoholism – not only devastate the lives of the char-

---

5. In this section I draw on Ann Kaplan's analysis of the representation of the maternal figure in popular culture and melodrama (Kaplan 1992).

acters but are used as emblematic reinforcements of the destructiveness of the mother–daughter relationship. The corollary of child abuse, sexual assaults, persecution of the innocent, and/or orphanhood serves to emphasise the melodramatic nature of the plots, sometimes assuming symbolic and metaphorical connotations. Another recurrent topos is that of growing up an orphan in a children's home, like in Margaret Forster's *Private Papers* (1986) and in *The Birds of the Innocent Wood* (1988) by Deirdre Madden (born 1960), where mothers' and daughters' contrasting ways of telling a family story are juxtaposed. Parental neglect or maternal inadequacy is the cause of the estranged relationship between a mother and a daughter both in *Moon Tiger* (1987) by Penelope Lively (born 1933) and in the painful and bitter autobiographical exposé *Deceived With Kindness* (1984) by Angelica Garnett (1918–1995). In *Sacred Country* (1992) by Rose Tremain (born 1943), Mary Ward, whose parents had hoped for a boy, decides at the age of six to become one, thus also avoiding her mother's fate of depression and solitude.

The authors' choices of setting for the bleak plots of the three novels under consideration are significant: Jenny Diski's *Like Mother* and St Aubin de Terán's *Joanna* evoke war with bombed houses, a general precariousness of living conditions and instability of feelings, while Tennant's *Faustine* is set at the time of the economic boom of the 1960s, a period of transformation of attitudes and values, especially within the family, which sanctioned the dissolution of the traditional patriarchal codes. The houses in which the dramas are played out emphasise the oppressiveness and narrowness of family life: a secret place in a bomb site in Diski, a crumbling isolated villa in St Aubin de Terán, a flamboyant and sinister mansion in Tennant.

Like Mother is, in a way, a paradoxical text, not so much for the story it tells as for the way it is told: the narrator is Nony, the protagonist's daughter, a child born without a brain, who cannot feel, see, or think, but who, having the 'genetic' knowledge of her mother's story, is the only one who can tell it, 'Blind, dumb, know-nothing kid I may be, but I have the whole story of my mother, all the knowledge I need to make the story, floating about in the watery spaces inside my skull' (*Like Mother*: 16). Nony's story is interspersed with a series of brief dialogues between herself and the virtual reader, dialogues which, while framing and commenting on the facts narrated, highlight the self-referential nature of the novel and invite the reader to reflect on the symbolic value of Nony. So, while the narrating voice is Nony's throughout, it becomes incorporeal and impersonal as if it were the voice of the text itself.

The story focuses on Nony's mother Frances and, in the first part, on the destructive relationship Frances had with her own mother Ivy, an immature and alcoholic woman who spoilt her as a child, treating her without any respect, as if she were a doll. The impressive description of the luxurious pram in whose cavernous interior the tiny baby is almost lost, is a case in point: 'The glassy black-lacquered coachwork with its sleek swirls of silver chrome decoration bounced gently on the big-wheeled silvered chassis... Ivy loved to walk around London with Frances in the pram and receive congratulations from the passers-by' (*Like Mother.* 41). Thus Ivy sees Frances as an extension of herself existing merely for her own gratification, and when her husband leaves her it is to her daughter that she turns for sexual satisfaction. At the age of twelve Frances discovers that she too can be bad and secretly makes her choice to be so, as a triumph of independence from her mother: 'Badness became Frances' secret. For safety and disguise she continued to be the outwardly good girl she had been taught to be. But for each virtuous act she performed the bad girl inside her deep inside her lit a dark candle, until a strange illumination glowed in the place that now came to seem the real centre of herself' (*Like Mother.* 50).

Embarking on a career of wickedness, Frances performs a series of transgressive acts, stealing phials of ether from the school science laboratory to do 'experiments' which she uses to dominate time and space, and building a secret house in a bomb site she passes every day on her way to and from school, and which attracts her with its disembowelled houses, 'Rubble and weeds and crumbling monuments to family life' (*Like Mother.* 57). There Frances creates an alternative home for the wicked double in herself, a home 'for the bad girl to live in' (*Like Mother.* 58), and it is here that she meets Stuart, two years older than she, with whom she forms a deep and secret association.

In spite of her close relationship with Stuart, Frances grows up unable either to give or receive love; dancing is her only passion and she devotes herself to it tenaciously, attaining a disconcerting form of 'immaculate control' (*Like Mother.* 150). Eventually, she accepts marrying Stuart even though she does not love him, on condition that she need not give up dancing. The news of her mother's death, run over by a car as she was walking drunk along the street, does, however, produce in her a sense of unrestrained sorrow which she refuses to recognise as such: 'She felt a stubborn refusal rise from her even as the grief swelled in her throat and threatened tears... What was she grieving for? Even now she couldn't think of a single reason. The lump in her throat was physical, there was nothing that matched it deeper in herself' (*Like Mother.* 139). When she discovers that the child she is bearing has a serious malformation she decides, against the advice of her doctor and Stuart – who leaves her because of this – to continue with her pregnancy. Her child will never be able to betray her as all the people she has loved had done, and this is the only reason why Frances can love her. Nony is almost a prefiguration of the cancer her mother is harbouring inside and which she refuses to have removed, describing it as a new life within her: 'She would let the cancer grow and bloom inside her like a flower, filling the space that Nony had evacuated. Time was running out for all of them; they would reach their conclusion' (*Like Mother.* 187).

Thus, on the one hand the novel appears to brutally debunk the rhetoric of maternal love, offering an anatomy of family life as something which hides a reality of estrangement, oppression, and violence. On the other hand, by allowing her daughter to be born, Frances appears to want to redeem the creative function of motherhood, which becomes even more resonant if one attributes a symbolic and metaphorical meaning to Nony: 'She had nothing to fear from the future, no anxiety that too much, too little, or the inappropriate would alter the blank page she held in her arms. There was nothing that could be written on it. Nony wasn't going to become; no person would struggle through, weighed down by the burden of memory and experience' (*Like Mother.* 184). Thus blank-page-Nony is not only the voice which mediates the text, she is possibly the story itself, the allegory of the book-as-a-child. At the end of the novel, Frances, who has started writing stories during her pregnancy, signs a contract with a publisher while cradling her little girl: 'She didn't feel empty any more. She never had been ... It had all been there, waiting, right from the very beginning, from before the beginning. Nothing *did* go on for ever ... There was a continuity, a complete circle' (*Like Mother.* 187, Diski's emphasis).[6] *Like Mother*, although autobiographically based (as the publication of *Skating to Antarctica* ten years later has confirmed), succeeds in transforming a story of antagonism and abuse into a metaphor of creativity.

Tennant's *Faustine* exploits an intertextual gimmick – the myth of Faust transposed to a female context – in order to illustrate a kind of postfeminist parable on the life cycles and the various ages of woman. Set in the 1960s, at the time of the consumer boom, the text offers the reader an immediate frame of reference in the form of a series of cultural elements and stereotypes of the period, such as the birth of youth subculture, the spread of transgressive attitudes, permissiveness, and 'sympathy' for the devil. The story, filtered through a dream-like/Gothic atmosphere, unfolds through four tales told by the nurse, the grandmother, the mother, and the devil himself, all of them uncannily subject to metamorphoses.

Ella, a young woman recently arrived from Australia where she grew up with foster parents, comes to a luxurious villa looked after by two repulsive caretakers, in search of her adored grandmother who had mothered her in her early years. The patchy stories told by the people she meets lead her to uncover a terrible secret which she will have to piece together with her own confused memories. Her feminist mother, too engrossed in herself and her work to be able to take care of her daughter, had neglected her, although

---

6. Nordius offers an interesting reading of Nony in the same key: 'This idea of seeing Nony as the secret version of Frances, the wicked little girl of the inner cave finally set free, sheds light on how the creative energy in the novel feeds on negativity and on the deconstitution of opposites' (1991: 449).

Ella does not condemn her for this: 'I learnt not to blame my mother. If it took me a long time – twenty years, maybe, it's more a sign of my own immaturity than of Anna's cruelty and selfishness' (*Faustine*: 14). However, it is her grandmother Muriel whom she misses most and she cannot understand why she could not have gone on living with her. While looking after her granddaughter, Muriel, who is adjusting with difficulty to middle age and social and sexual 'invisibility', develops a strong antagonism towards her daughter, envying her comparative youth and her sexual freedom. One day she meets the devil who offers her power, beauty, and youth for twenty-four years in exchange for her soul. Overnight she becomes Lisa Crane, 'Queen of the Air'. Lisa-Muriel-Faustine steals her daughter's lover Harry (who, of course, turns out to be the devil) and embarks on a public and scandalous life as a media star. In a room of the villa dominated by a giant video screen, Ella is finally allowed to watch the images of this incredible story flow by.

Anna, Ella's mother, tells the story in a different way: referring to the myth of Demeter and Persephone, she explains how, in the present-day world, woman is no longer ready to accept such natural processes as growing old and the ensuing social invisibility, and is prepared to do anything to improve her look and the quality of her life:

> Just as the myth of Demeter and Persephone represented the ancient cycles of the year, and the climate and the seasons and the fruits and crops have now been thrown into chaos by the greed of man, so the huge numbers of human beings on earth, and the invention of artificial methods of preventing their future conception, have stopped the natural progression of generations and thrown up hybrids and freaks – such as Lisa Crane, who returned to youth and then found herself unable to relinquish it. (*Faustine*: 115–16)

This is a plea against consumerism, pollution, and the reification of woman, but although its intention may be progressive, emancipating women from the myth of youth and beauty, it sounds artificial, reflecting facile ideologisms and in no way helping to untie the knots of the complex relationship between mothers and daughters. Seen in a feminist light, Muriel and Anna's parable might be read, as Barbara Hardy suggests, almost as a revision of the Oedipus myth, exposing for once women's need to kill their mothers (Hardy 1992). However, the novel offers little substance for such an interpretation for it fails to look into the mother's politics and role.

St Aubin de Terán's *Joanna* is another prismatic and cross-generational construction staging a mother's hatred for her daughter in a kind of horror show, with no limit as to the representation of physical and psychological maternal abuse, for which no plausible explanation is offered. Through the retrospective accounts of the three main female characters the novel reconstructs the story of Joan/Joanna, the unloved daughter, who lives with her mother and grandmother on the island of Jersey. The girl is waiting to grow up to be able to get away from her unbalanced mother's hatred, which predates her very birth: 'My unborn self became the focus of her malaise. Then my birth came, like the removal of a tumour. I left a wound which was stitched and cauterised, but the cancer had already seeded' (*Joanna*: 14). The violence to the child's body is described in brutal and imaginative language: 'After the first few slaps she would tire and clench her fists tightly, using her right hand as a hammer to pound into my skull... It traced a record of Mother's state of mind on my scalp; a path of blue scars buried under my hair. It was maternal graffiti, subtly coded now, if brutally written at the time. The scars read "Mother was here"' (*Joanna*: 28). In her turn, when Joan is sent to a very strict boarding school run by German nuns, she duplicates the model of violence by venting her own unhappiness on her peers. But Joan/Joanna survives all this, marries, and gives birth to four daughters. She does not see her mother for many years until, at the end of the novel, she finds her again in a mental home. Overwhelmed by guilt, Joanna attempts suicide – 'For once I was doing what Mother wanted' (*Joanna*: 256) – but soon dies of cancer inexplicably hoping to be reunited with her. After the daughter's tale, we are given the other points of view – the mother's: Miss Kitty, and the grandmother's: 'poor Florence' – whose narratives carry the representation of violence and the atmosphere of terror even further, without any irony or metaphoric insight. Kitty's madness, manifested from childhood through evil powers, is given as the explanation for her refusal to have sexual intercourse in marriage, thus provoking her husband's rape. This episode and the ensuing gruesome childbirth are told sparing no detail and never going beyond melodrama and pure sensationalism.

The novels in this group, like those in the previous section, lay a strong emphasis on gender, focusing on all-female families. Whereas in the former group, however, daughters speak for their mothers, in these novels mothers are no longer remembered figures in the background: we hear them speaking in their own words, often arguing with their own mothers. Casting the mother in the dual role of mother and daughter, the authors appear to want to fulfil a reparatory intention towards the often negative mother figure, providing an explanation for her authoritarian and unloving behaviour. At the same time, showing the inescapability of certain attitudes passed on from mother to daughter, they seem to deny the possibility of dialogue between them.

Nothing Sacred: The Daughter's Voice

The last group of novels under consideration derive their amusing and provocative tone from the situations they describe and from their irreverence towards every cliché about motherhood and good feelings. Although they can be classed as novels of growth and development, both *Oranges Are Not the Only Fruit* (1985) by Jeanette Winterson (born 1959) and *Behind the Scenes at the Museum* (1995) by Kate Atkinson (date of birth unknown) present bold mixtures of narrative registers which shatter the realistic illusion usually created by the *Bildungsroman*, and which confers upon them a postmodernist quality. Themes like the formation of the protagonist's subjectivity and the crisis of the patriarchal family are dealt with in a grotesque way alongside other serious issues like religion, death, and betrayal. *Anita and Me* (1996), another novel about growing up in a Midlands provincial town by Meera Syal (born 1963) with humorous scenes between mother and daughter, adds the issue of racism to a generally light treatment of the ironies of Anglo-Asian life.

Oranges Are Not the Only Fruit (1985) consists of eight chapters each bearing the title of one of the first eight books of the Old Testament. This immediately introduces the reader to the novel's breezy tone of biblical pastiche/fairy story, which acts as a parodic framework for the events recounted. 'I cannot recall a time when I did not know I was special' (*Oranges*: 3), says the protagonist, not unexpectedly named Jeanette, introducing herself as the heroine of an unusual experience, since she had been adopted to be consecrated to the Lord. In the first chapter, aptly entitled 'Genesis', the girl describes her 'birth' as if it were Christ's birth recast in new circumstances: the mother, a member of a Pentecostal community in a small Lancashire town, who shares a wild visionary tendency with William Blake, one day 'dreamed a dream and sustained it in daylight. She would get a child, train it, build it, dedicate it to the Lord: a missionary child, a servant of God, a blessing' (*Oranges*: 10). A shooting star shows her the way to an orphanage where she finds a child with a great deal of hair in a crib: 'She said, "This child is mine from the Lord"... Her flesh now, sprung from her head. Her vision' (*Oranges*: 10). Thus, the sexphobic mother succeeds, rivalling the Madonna, in having a child without conceiving it: 'She was very bitter about the Virgin Mary getting there first' (*Oranges*: 3).

For many years mother and daughter share an indissoluble bond of affection and common aspirations. Her mother is Jeanette's only teacher, a task which she carries out with zeal and imagination: 'She taught me to read from the Book of Deuteronomy, and she told me all about the lives of the saints, how they were really wicked, and given to nameless desires' (*Oranges*: 15). She also teaches her to believe in a world in which women are the only beings of any importance, thus creating a world of values for her which excludes the father. But the law steps in forcing the mother to send the child to school and, in the chapter entitled 'Exodus', Jeanette's diversity, in comparison with her peers and with more conventional teaching methods, makes her an outsider, while her mother consoles her with the words 'We are called to be apart' (*Oranges*: 43). The mother – 'a missionary on the home front' (*Oranges*: 55), as she likes to define herself – is cast in a grotesque mold: engaged at every moment of her existence in fighting crusades against sin which she perceives as always lying in ambush, she has to fight her most relentless battle against her own daughter who has been possessed by the devil. Unfortunately, repeated exorcisms are unable to save the girl from the abyss into which she has fallen.

What is Jeanette's sin? Interpreting the title in the light of Bible symbology, one can cull the allusion to another fruit, the fruit of knowledge, and to its implied sexual sin. The title undercuts the superiority of oranges – the favourite fruit of the mother, whose frequent stock phrase 'have an orange' serves to cut short potential embarrassing situations – in order to express the daughter's achieved autonomy and her acquisition of the knowledge of other fruits, in this specific case the discovery and acceptance of her own lesbian identity. The mother's inability to accept her daughter's lesbianism determines not only Jeanette's marginalisation from the religious community, but also deprives her of her faith in her mother's loyalty to her against male power. Rejected by her mother and later by the girl she loves, Jeanette earns her living by driving an ice-cream van and by making up corpses in a funeral parlour, while at the same time living her own loves and disappointments. In the last chapter she returns home for Christmas and realises that the bond with her mother involves something more powerful and lasting: 'My mother was treating me like she always had; had she noticed my absence? Did she even remember why I'd left?' (*Oranges*: 169); 'Families, real ones, are chairs and tables and the right number of cups, but I had no means of joining one, and no means of dismissing my own; she had tied a thread around my button, to tug when she pleased' (*Oranges*: 176). Thus the alliance between mother and daughter creates a strong emotional bulwark and appears to be the basis for the daughter's identity and confidence in her own convictions, however opposed they may be to her mother's.

In her introduction to the 1991 edition of *Oranges*, Winterson declares it a 'threatening' novel, because it 'exposes the sanctity of family life as something of a sham; it illustrates by example that what the church calls love is actually psychosis and it dares to suggest that what makes life difficult for homosexuals is not their perversity but other people's' (Winterson 1991: xiii). The fact that she deals with the theme of lesbianism within a novel addressed to a wider public than that usually reached by openly gay literature, and succeeds in doing so with a light touch and a sense of humour, is not the least of the book's merits and explains the popularity of the TV serial based on it. Pauline Palmer also admires the novel for its subtle combination of political radicalism grafted on a comic tradition of lesbian humour (Palmer 1993).

Conversely, *A Piece of the Night* (1978) by Michèle Roberts (born 1949), another novel on mother–daughter relations and lesbianism, is weighed down by the dogmas of 1970s radical feminism and by the crusader spirit in favour of lesbianism that runs through it, with involuntarily comic or improbable dialogues. Although these two novels are very different, the presence in both of them of the protagonists' religious vocation alongside their lesbianism is a curious coincidence. However, while the protagonist of *Oranges* deserts religious militancy when she discovers her lesbian identity, Robert's protagonist, Julia, sublimates her sense of guilt in the decision to become a nun after she is punished for her 'amitié particulière' with another girl in the convent school she attends: 'I would become Mother Superior in time, able to punish as I had been punished, to make others do as I wanted. I lusted for power which girls and women do not have in this world; I would have it, by going beyond womanhood into sanctity, and reaching a kingdom far beyond the earth' (*Piece*: 53).

Julia does not join the convent after all; she grows up, marries, has a daughter, separates, and goes to live in a lesbian communal household where the care of the children is shared by the mothers. Returning to the village in Normandy where she was born and where her mother is seriously ill, Julia discovers that her mother has not included the photos she had sent her of the commune and her child in the family album. This makes her long-repressed anger towards her mother explode in violent accusations, totally inappropriate considering they are directed at a dying woman: 'My house... Full of lovely dirty women having a good time, and with a room each all for themselves, and not feeling they have to clean up all the time, and sharing the housework and cooking, and having time to themselves, and a good time in bed. You'd like that too, wouldn't you? I got something you haven't got, and you hate it, it really frightens you' (*Piece*: 90). When her mother reacts by blaming herself for not having loved her daughter enough – 'I suppose I didn't love you enough, that's why you go in for these ideas. I failed you' (*Piece*: 91) – Julia, switching from aggression to forgiveness, explains what feminism is all about: 'Feminism's about mothers ... it's about backing them up' (*Piece*: 90–91).[7] With her subsequent works, Roberts overcomes her didacticism and writes fine interesting stories about mothers and daughters both in *During Mother's Absence* (1993) and in *Flesh and Blood* (1994).

Kate Atkinson's *Behind the Scenes at the Museum* (1995) is, like Winterson's, a first novel and a prize-winning best-seller. The narrating voice, deftly moving between different tones and periods of time, belongs to Ruby Lennox, telling the story of several generations of an ordinary family from the north of England. In contrast with the contents – the humdrum events of everyday life, the misfortunes and joys common to every family – the novel opens in a grand way with echoes which go from Laurence Sterne to Salman Rushdie. It begins in fact with Ruby's conception to the chimes of

---

7. Palmer 1989 offers a very appreciative reading of this novel.

midnight, by her unhappily matched parents, George and Bunty. The mother's name, short for Berenice, is the occasion for the narrator to qualify her as unmotherly and generally inadequate, 'Would I be better off with a mother with a different name?' (*Behind the Scenes*: 9), and to fantasise about being some other mother's daughter:

> I do not believe that Bunty is my real mother. My real mother is roaming in a parallel universe somewhere, ladling out mother's milk the colour of Devon cream. She's padding the hospital corridors searching for me, her fierce, hot, lion-breath steaming up the cold windows. My real mother is Queen of the Night, a huge, galactic figure, treading the Milky Way in search of her lost infant. (*Behind the Scenes*: 42–43)[8]

The chronicle of the daily life of the Lennoxes above the family-run pet-shop, is linked, through mentions of worthless objects like a button or a spare saucer, to a series of 'footnotes' which go back in time, reconstructing the life of Ruby's female ancestors and widening the perspective and scope of the novel. Presenting first the married life of Ruby's great-grandmother and then of her grandmother through various wars, the novel shows women as the true 'survivors' of a patriarchal culture which has tried to crush them for centuries. Bunty appears at the end of a line of disillusioned but never entirely defeated women, uncertain of her future and her identity, 'The Second World War for Bunty was not so much a matter of getting a husband as a personality' (*Behind the Scenes*: 92). Without enthusiasm she marries George who gives her no sexual satisfaction and who soon entrusts the care of the house and their three little girls, as well as the pet-shop, almost entirely to her. He is a low-key parody of patriarchal authority, being completely devoid of authority, a liar, and stupidly 'macho'. Belittled as a woman, Bunty feels inadequate as a mother too, and believes she is not fond of children: 'Well I don't like children' (*Behind the Scenes*: 15). She takes care of them out of a sense of duty, almost as an extension of housework, in a way that Ruby later defines as 'autistic mothering' (*Behind the Scenes*: 375).

Despite this, in two of the most exhilarating episodes in the book Bunty emerges as a rebel and a heroine to domestic oppression: first, when she abandons her husband and children on the eve of a holiday trip, leaving him to cope, even though she later returns and picks up the threads of her usual life as if nothing had happened; second, when she involuntarily burns down the house and the hateful pet-shop, as if she were acting out a wishful subliminal fantasy. The most liberating event, though, is not her own doing but

---

8. The reference to the 'foundling fantasy', ironic in this context, is an explicit allusion to Freud's theory of 'Family Romances' (1909), expressing the narrator's subliminal wish of adapting it to a female context and of reevaluating the figure of the mother. On the feminist revisions of Freud's family romance, see Hirsch 1989: 54–58.

her husband's grotesque death while having sex with a waitress during a family wedding, as widowhood grants her freedom and the possibility of a more gratifying future. Commenting on Atkinson's comic genius, Hilary Mantel compares her to Dickens: 'Her novel delivers to the populace its jokes and its tragedies as efficiently as Dickens once delivered his, though Atkinson has a game-plan more sophisticated than Dickens's, and her handling of a child's death scene forestalls any Wildean scorn' (Mantel 1996: 23).

All the dramatic moments in the life of the family are told without emotionalism or sensationalism, but with the liberating effect of black humour. For instance, one of the girls is run over by a car on Christmas Eve during a rare family outing to a pantomime show, thus 'ruining' Christmas for them all. In the last chapter, entitled 'Redemption', an adult Ruby returns to York to look after her mother who has Alzheimer's disease and this is the ironic occasion for establishing an affective bond between mother and daughter: 'Bunty's replacement personality is a much nicer model than the old one... I've waited forty years to play with my mother and now at last we spend long sunny afternoons in an endless state of make-believe on planet Alzheimer' (*Behind the Scenes*: 368).

Both *Oranges* and *Behind the Scenes* characterise the mother figure as a parody of the conventional maternal icon one finds in classic realist texts, succeeding in creating an almost new mythography of the mother. Winterson develops the paradigm of the 'all church and family' mother, making her a kind of religious freak, obsessed with sin and neglectful of everything else, while Atkinson presents her as a pathetic and grotesque figure, a parody of maternal abnegation. Both women lack maternal 'instinct', even though they remain first and foremost 'mothers', subordinating everything else in their life to this function. This typology is adopted in a much more striking fashion in 'Absolutely Fabulous', the 1990s BBC sitcom series written and performed by Jennifer Saunders: although the serial achieves comic effects through a reversal of roles – the mother is as transgressive and irresponsible as the daughter is sensible and conformist – it does, however, present a series of situations which highlight the problematic relationship between a daughter and her mother. The latter is a divorced career woman who has lived through the various cultural and sexual revolutions from the 1960s onward, superficially adopting their most liberating slogans while remaining profoundly insecure, as her addiction to various forms of dependence shows – free sex, drugs, alcohol, and above all 'sisterhood' with her mother-substitute friend, glamorous Joanna Lumley. Yet, paradoxically, it is the mother who is the heroine of the successful television series, just like Winterson's and Atkinson's mothers are, not only because their diversity keeps them from falling into patriarchal paradigms, but also because they represent, in their own understated way, models of resistance and rebellion to conventional family patterns. Palmer comments on Winterson's mother figure as displaying 'a contradictory though convincing amalgam of courage and bigotry, imagination and callousness' (Palmer 1993: 103). Bonded with their mothers rather than their fathers, the daughters finally succeed in escaping maternal imprint, choosing for themselves a different identity to the one both their mothers and the conventional morality of a lower-middle-class family expects of them. In this way they show an autonomy strengthened precisely by the bond with their mothers. In conclusion, though both novels construct oppressive family environments, they present stories of liberation in which mothers as well as daughters succeed in making their escape.

Mother – Motherland – Mother Tongue

Novels about the mother–daughter relationship written by authors who have emigrated to England from the ex-colonies highlight even more forcefully than the novels considered in the previous sections the importance of the female members of the family and of the matrilineal transmission of values. The bond or the rift between mothers and daughters is incorporated in many novels and explored as the terrain on which two opposing linguistic and cultural models clash. Thus, the mother figure takes on a metaphoric content which turns her into an extension of the idea of motherland and mother tongue.[9]

This shows up clearly in the cycle of stories *You Can't Get Lost in Capetown* (1987), by the South African author Zoë Wicomb (born 1948) now living in Great Britain, which find a unifying centre in the perspective and consciousness of the protagonist, a coloured girl who first studies at the 'white girl's school' in Cape Town and then moves to England to attend university. Returning to her own country after a ten-year absence, Frieda feels doubly foreign because the small community she belonged to has, in the meantime, been swept away and relocated in the urban townships on the outskirts of Cape Town. She feels linguistically and culturally alienated from the new reality and wants to go back to England, where she has discovered a new sense of herself which paradoxically reconciles her with her African identity. However, it is in the relationship with her mother that Frieda will have to come to terms with her confused feelings and perceptions about herself and her country.

On her arrival, Frieda is met at the airport by a crowd of relatives. Everyone is there except her mother, who never forgave her for going to England. However, during an excursion to the Gifberge, the mountain on which wild proteas (the national flower of South Africa) grow, mother and daughter are thrown together in the majestic setting of the veld for a confrontation which

---

9. For an in-depth exploration of these themes see Nasta 1991, a collection of essays covering a wide range of African, Caribbean, and Asian novels by women.

can no longer be avoided. The mother blames herself for making her daughter learn English and so contributing to alienating the girl from herself and her surroundings. She remembers that her own mother had warned her:

> 'My mother said it was a mistake when I brought you up to speak English. Said people spoke English just to be disrespectful to their elders, to You and Your them about. And that is precisely what you do. Now you use the very language against me that I've stubbed my tongue on trying to teach you it. No respect! Use your English as a catapult!'. (*You Can't*: 171)

When the daughter proudly tells her about the imminent publication of her stories, the mother comments: 'Stories ... you call them stories? ... Dreary little things in which nothing happens ... A disgrace ... What do you know about things, about people, this place where you were born? About your ancestors who roamed these hills? You left. Remember?' (*You Can't*: 171), and again: 'To write from under your mother's skirts, to shout at the world that it's all right to kill God's unborn child! You've killed me over and over so it was quite unnecessary to invent my death. Do people ever do anything decent with their education?' (*You Can't*: 172).

In England Frieda has discovered for the first time in her life 'African pride'; she has stopped straightening her hair, which she now wears in the afro style – something her mother teases her about: 'What do you do with that bush?' (*You Can't*: 178) – even if she provocatively declares that she hates her own country – 'I don't care about this country; I hate it' (*You Can't*: 174). Nevertheless, when she teases her mother for wanting to take a protea plant home, because she only sees it as the Boer nationalist symbol, her mother explains that they are not the same thing: 'Proteas belong to the veld ... a bush is a bush; it doesn't become what people think they inject into it. We know who lived in these mountains when the Europeans were still shivering in their own country. What they think of the veld and its flowers is of no interest to me' (*You Can't*: 181). The confrontation between the two women primarily expresses the conflict between those who remain and those who leave, the mother's feeling of betrayal and the daughter's still confused sense of identity, torn between the call of her native culture and that of her country of adoption. However, the mother's words underline the intrinsic bond between herself and the linguistic and cultural patrimony she represents.

Conclusion

In the novels examined in this chapter, mothers are often cast in a negative light. While previous representations were modelled on a binary opposition of either conservative, authoritarian, manipulative or all-caring, sacrificing, self-denying mothers, later generations of authors have shown mothers as socially harassed, incompetent, and uncaring human beings. This in itself is the sign of a deeply changed attitude towards a role and an institution both of which have been the object of serious historical and psychoanalytical investigation in the course of the last decades. The novels selected for this chapter scrutinise not so much a role as an individual, the most important person in the formation of female subjectivity, as Adrienne Rich was among the first to stress in her pioneering *Of Woman Born* (1977). The work of French feminist philosophers and psychoanalysts like Julia Kristeva and Luce Irigaray has also proved very influential in the formation of a new ethos. Revising Freudian assumptions, they have tried to understand the relationship between mothers and daughters, reevaluating it in the generally matrophobic tradition of Western culture.

Seen in a psychoanalytic perspective, rivalry between mothers and daughters – endemic under patriarchy – still exists in the present situation of erosion of the patriarchal family. When we look at the younger novelists, all this need not necessarily be considered in a negative light. They write from the vantage point of the increased capacity for analysis and self-analysis available nowadays, the greater awareness acquired through the enormous corpus of feminist theoretical studies, and the sense of freedom – from religious prohibitions and ideological taboos – with which certain problems can now be approached, especially family problems, however intricate, intimate, and painful. This leads to deeper analysis which does away with any form of protective shield or false shame and uncovers feelings and experiences repressed until now. The daughter, in other words, tries, and is in a position, to understand her mother better, and to feel love and pity for her as a woman who has lived through the experience of two world wars, at a time when personal fulfilment and finding a husband were difficult, and family situations were generally troubled because of the losses suffered. The lack of 'maternal instinct' in most cases can be explained simply with the fact that not all women choose to be mothers, but become so under the pressure of circumstances.

The expression 'children of violence' – which Doris Lessing used as a collective title for her well-known cycle of novels – can perhaps help us explain the involuntary violence of parents of the generation of her own parents towards their children, since they themselves had suffered the violence of war and its consequences. This is true not only of older writers but also of the younger authors discussed in this study who often, as we have seen, use the war as the setting and specific background for the construction of their mother figures. Introducing a collection of personal memoirs by women about growing up in the 1950s and 1960s, at a time of great industrial development and social mobility, Liz Heron points out the enormous, widening gap between their mothers' generation and their own – in lifestyle, values, and opportunities – and the increased difficulty of dealing with one's mother:

> Mothers are people and motherhood is a condition not likely to bring out the best in people if it is undergone with reluctance (however unacknowledged), with material hardships or with bitterness. Women today, with more room to choose what they want, and with more room to know there is a choice, also have the possibility of being more fulfilled as mothers. But if we reproach our mothers, or feel that they failed us, it is also because of what motherhood had to be – often a relationship that stifled in its enforced bonding of mother and child and was jealous of its very tyranny over both.
> (Heron 1985: 8–9)

Displacing the still powerful negative image of the mother handed on from patriarchy and looking at mothers beyond their role, as individuals, is certainly what younger authors are doing with increasing openness and freedom, a freedom which is also expressed and emphasised in the great variety of narrative and linguistic codes which these writers deploy.

It is only within genre narratives, and especially feminist science fiction, that ideas of reproduction and motherhood abandon their conventional and 'natural' definitions, projecting new and alternative images of mothers. During the 1960s and 1970s, influenced by feminism and radical politics, science fiction by women, especially in the USA, challenged the prevalent masculine concerns of the previous decades by experimenting with issues of gender roles, sexuality, and the new reproductive technologies. This trend caught on in England in the 1980s, in coincidence with the big public debates on motherhood following the development of *in vitro* fertilisation. In 1985 the Women's Press launched a science fiction series with the aim of presenting 'exciting and provocative feminist images of the future' and of challenging the patriarchal values which dominated science fiction. *Despatches from the Frontiers of the Female Mind* (1985), a collection of short stories by English and American authors, reflects this new perspective, focusing on the experience and the dilemmas of contemporary women, in particular reproduction and child rearing. As the editors Jen Green and Sarah Lefanu state in their introduction, 'years of seeing women presented in science fiction as baby machines and full-time nurturers has made many women writers fight shy of depicting women as mothers in their stories at all... Feminism allows us to reclaim the importance of bearing children on our own terms ... and expose its radical meaning and potential' (1985: 5–6).[10] Motherhood and gender roles are a concern also of science fiction by mainstream novelists such as Doris Lessing, Angela Carter, and Fay Weldon, who, however, give little space to personal relationships. Weldon's *The Cloning of Joanna May* (1989), for instance, suggests doing away with the mystique of motherhood and, consequently, with

---

10. Lefanu was the editor of the Women's Press science fiction series and is the author of *In the Chinks of the World Machine* (1988), the first book-length critical assessment of contemporary science fiction by women.

the tyranny of repetition: 'The thing is, I'm not my mother's daughter. I thought I had to be like her, but I don't. I'm free to be me. Now everything can change' (*Cloning*: 285). This is the response of one of Joanna May's four daughters/clones to Joanna who, having discovered their existence and being horrified to see herself falling almost automatically into the nagging and screaming maternal stereotype, has just disclaimed her maternal role. Another interesting comment on motherhood is to be found in an earlier novel, *Memoirs of a Spacewoman* (1962), by Naomi Mitchison (1897–1999), which was reissued in 1985 by the Women's Press in their new science fiction series, together with many American novels. Mitchison's protagonist, an expert in communications with beings from other worlds and fascinated by the processes of reproduction, has given birth to several offspring through grafting, ovular activation, parthenogenesis, and genital stimulation, all of whom she fondly loves and cares for like 'a twentieth-century mum'. It is ironical that intrepid and promiscuous Mary who never hints at a family life of the conventional kind should feel like an old-style mum: 'It must have been just like that in the old days, being a Mum. Only I could get away, that was the difference' (*Memoirs*: 71). Being able to leave her children, the awareness that being a mother does not entail renouncing one's life, is the new element capable of interrupting the spiral of dependence, guilt, and responsibility between mothers and daughters, yet without severing the bond of love. The recent advances in reproductive technologies and genetic engineering are narrowing the gap between science fiction and reality. Before long new stories will be written which present the point of view of children who have been conceived by alternative means of reproduction or have been raised by parents of the same sex. Only then will we probably know if the fear of repetition and the power relationship between mother and daughter, the ghosts still haunting contemporary women's narrative, have vanished.

Bibliography

Atkinson, Kate (1995) *Behind the Scenes at the Museum*. London: Black Swan.
Beauvoir, Simone de (1969) *A Very Easy Death*, trans. Patrick O'Brian. Harmondsworth: Penguin (orig. *Une mort très douce*. Paris: Gallimard, 1964).
Bowen, Elizabeth (1935) *The House in Paris*. London: Gollancz.
Chodorow, Nancy (1978) *The Reproduction of Mothering: Psychoanalysis and the Sociology of Gender*. Berkeley: University of California Press.
Cixous, Hélène and Catherine Clément (1987) *The Newly Born Woman*, trans. Betsy Wing. Manchester: Manchester University Press (orig. *La Jeune Née*. Paris: Union Génerale d'Éditions, 1975).
Diski, Jenny (1990) *Like Mother*. London: Vintage (orig. 1988).
—— (1997) *Skating to Antarctica*. London: Granta.

Drabble, Margaret (1965) *The Millstone*. London: Weidenfeld and Nicolson.
—— (1969) *The Waterfall*. London: Weidenfeld and Nicolson.
Dunn, Nell (1967) *Poor Cow*. London: McGibbon and Kee.
Forster, Margaret (1986) *Private Papers*. London: Chatto and Windus.
—— (1995) *Hidden Lives: A Family Memoir*. London: Viking.
Freud, Sigmund (1909) 'Family Romances' in *The Standard Edition of the Complete Psychological Works of Sigmund Freud*, ed. and trans. James Strachey, vol. 9. London: The Hogarth Press, 1959, 235–41.
Gardiner, Judith Kegan (1978) 'A Wake for the Mother: The Maternal Deathbed in Women's Fiction' in *Feminist Studies*, vol. 4, 2, June 1978, 146–65.
Garnett, Angelica (1984) *Deceived with Kindness: A Bloomsbury Childhood*. London: Chatto and Windus.
Green, Jen and Sarah Lefanu (eds) (1985) *Despatches from the Frontiers of the Female Mind*. London: The Women's Press.
Greene, Gayle (1994) *Doris Lessing: The Poetics of Change*. Ann Arbor: University of Michigan Press.
Hardy, Barbara (1992) 'Dabbling with the Devil' in *Times Literary Supplement*, 6 March 1992.
Heron, Liz (ed.) (1985) *Truth, Dare or Promise: Girls Growing Up in the Fifties*. London: Virago Press.
Hirsch, Marianne (1989) *The Mother/Daughter Plot: Narrative, Psychoanalysis, Feminism*. Bloomington and Indianapolis: Indiana University Press.
Hoggart, Richard (1959) *The Uses of Literacy*. Harmondsworth: Penguin.
Humm, Maggie (1991) *Border Traffic: Strategies of Contemporary Women Writers*. Manchester and New York: Manchester University Press.
Ingman, Heather (1998) *Women's Fiction between the Wars: Mothers, Daughters and Writing*. Edinburgh: Edinburgh University Press.
Kaplan, E. Ann (1992) *Motherhood and Representation: The Mother in Popular Culture and Melodrama*. London and New York: Routledge.
Kristeva, Julia (1980) *Pouvoirs de l'horreur*. Paris: Seuil. *Powers of Horror: An Essay on Abjection*, trans. Léon S. Roudiez. New York: Columbia University Press, 1982.
Lefanu, Sarah (1988) *In the Chinks of the World Machine: Feminism and Science Fiction*. London: The Women's Press.
Lehmann, Rosamond (1984) *The Ballad and the Source*. London: Virago (orig. 1944).
Lessing, Doris (1952) *Martha Quest*. London: Granada.
—— (1954) *A Proper Marriage*. London: Granada.
—— (1969) *The Four-Gated City*. New York: Bantam.
—— (1973) *The Summer Before the Dark*. London: Cape.
—— (1974) *The Memoirs of a Survivor*. London: Octagon Press.
—— (1983) *Diary of a Good Neighbour* in *The Diaries of Jane Somers*. Harmondsworth: Penguin, 1985.
—— (1984) 'Impertinent Daughters' in *Granta* 14, Winter 1984, 51–68.
—— (1985) *The Good Terrorist*. London: Grafton.

——— (1994) *Under My Skin*. London: Flamingo.
Lively, Penelope (1987) *Moon Tiger*. London: André Deutsch.
Madden, Deirdre (1988) *The Birds of the Innocent Wood*. London: Faber and Faber.
Mantel, Hilary (1996) 'Shop!' in *London Review of Books*, 4 April 1996.
Miller, Nancy K. (1995) 'Our Classes, Ourselves: Maternal Legacies and Cultural Criticism' in Mae Henderson (ed.) (1995) *Borders, Boundaries, and Frames: Essays in Cultural Criticism and Cultural Studies*. London: Routledge, 145–70.
Mitchison, Naomi (1985) *Memoirs of a Spacewoman*. London: The Women's Press (orig. 1962).
Modjeska, Drusilla (1990) *Poppy*. London: Serpent's Tail.
Nasta, Susheila (ed.) (1991) *Motherlands: Black Women's Writing from Africa, the Caribbean and South Asia*. London: The Women's Press.
Nordius, Janina (1991) 'Molds of Telling' in *English Studies*, 5, vol. 72, 442–53.
Palmer, Pauline (1989) *Contemporary Women's Fiction: Narrative Practice and Feminist Theory*. New York: Harvester Wheatsheaf.
——— (1993) *Contemporary Lesbian Writing. Dreams, Desire, Difference*. Buckingham and Philadelphia: Open University Press.
Phillips, Terry (1996) 'Battling with the Angel: May Sinclair's Powerful Mothers' in Sarah Sceats and Gail Cunningham (eds) *Image and Power: Women in Fiction in the Twentieth Century*. London and New York: Longman, 128–38.
Rich, Adrienne (1977) *Of Woman Born: Motherhood as Experience and Institution*. London: Virago (orig. 1976).
Roberts, Michèle (1984) *A Piece of the Night*. London: The Women's Press (orig. 1978).
——— (1993) *During Mother's Absence*. London: Virago.
——— (1994) *Flesh and Blood*. London: Virago.
Samuel, Raphael (1986) 'A Family of Strangers' in *New Society*, 6 June 1986, 22–24.
Seabrook, Jeremy (1982) *Working-Class Childhood*. London: Gollancz.
Showalter, Elaine (1986) 'Toward a Feminist Poetics' in Showalter (ed.) *The New Feminist Criticism: Essays on Women, Literature, and Theory*. London: Virago, 125–43.
Sinclair, May (1910) *The Creators*. London: Hutchinson.
——— (1917) *The Tree of Heaven*. New York: Macmillan.
——— (1980) *Mary Olivier: A Life*. London: Virago (orig. 1919).
Splendore, Paola (1998) 'Le figlie *cattive* di Doris Lessing' in Lidia Curti and Laura Di Michele (eds) *Gli Amici per Nando. Giornata di Studi in onore di Fernando Ferrara*. Naples: Istituto Universitario Orientale, 337–55.
Sprague, Claire (1987) *Rereading Doris Lessing: Narrative Patterns of Doubling and Repetition*. Chapel Hill and London: University of North Carolina Press.
Steedman, Carolyn (1986) *Landscape for a Good Woman: A Story of Two Lives*. London: Virago
Syal, Meera (1996) *Anita and Me*. London: Flamingo.
Tennant, Emma (1992) *Faustine*. London: Faber and Faber.
Terán, Lisa St Aubin de (1991) *Joanna*. London: Virago (orig. 1990).

Tremain, Rose (1992) *Sacred Country*. London: Sinclair-Stevenson.
Warner, Marina (1988) *The Lost Father*. London: Chatto and Windus.
Weldon, Fay (1971) *Down Among the Women*. London: Heinemann.
—— (1975) *Female Friends*. London: Heinemann.
—— (1980) *Puffball*. London: Hodder and Stoughton.
—— (1989) *The Cloning of Joanna May*. London: Fontana.
West, Rebecca (1980) *The Return of the Soldier*. London: Virago (orig. 1918).
Wicomb, Zoë (1988) *You Can't Get Lost in Cape Town*. London: Virago (orig. 1987).
Winterson, Jeanette (1985) *Oranges Are Not the Only Fruit*. London: Pandora.
Woolf, Virginia (1964) *Mrs Dalloway*. Harmondsworth: Penguin (orig. 1925).
—— (1964) *To the Lighthouse*. Harmondsworth: Penguin (orig. 1927).
Young, Michael and Peter Willmott (1962) *Family and Kinship in East London*. Harmondsworth: Penguin.

CHAPTER SEVEN

POWER AND POWERLESSNESS

MOTHERS AND DAUGHTERS IN POSTWAR GERMAN AND AUSTRIAN LITERATURE

Chris Weedon

Introduction: The Ideological Legacy of the Past

Since the birth of second-wave feminism in Germany and Austria in the late 1960s and early 1970s, mothers and daughters have become a significant theme in women's writing. Whereas the family has long been an important subject in novels by women, recent decades have seen a shift of focus to the meaning of motherhood and how patriarchal power affects both mothers and daughters within the family.[1] This can be understood as an effect of a broader move within second-wave feminism to analyse discourses of motherhood in Western culture, to give voice to the experience of motherhood and to revalue its meaning and role within society.

Germany and Austria share a long tradition of thought which defines women in relation to motherhood, declaring them to be intrinsically different from men: complementary but inferior. Since the 1970s the ideas, debates, and practices which make up this history have been the focus of feminist critique. In nineteenth-century Germany and Austria motherhood became the object of a wide range of discourses which attempted to define

---

1. For more general accounts of recent women's writing see Weigel 1989 and Weedon 1997. For accounts of the mother–daughter theme throughout the history of German literature see Kraft and Liebs 1993. This includes four chapters on the postwar period. See also Roebling and Mauser 1996.

and fix gender difference. Religion, philosophy, and science all sought to ground women's nature in their biological capacity to give birth. Motherhood was widely seen as woman's God-given role. For example, the influential German philosopher Artur Schopenhauer (1788–1860), who helped shape Freud's (1856–1939) thinking, argued in *Über die Weiber* (1851, On Women) that women were suited neither to significant physical nor intellectual work. Like children, women were silly and short-sighted and biologically destined for wife and motherhood. They were, he argued, naturally subordinate to men who were the only *truly human* beings. Similar ideas can be found in nineteenth-century science, for example, the work on gender difference by the well-known Leipzig doctor, Paul J. Möbius, who used comparative brain sizes to ground women's inferiority. In his widely read text, *Über den physiologischen Schwachsinn des Weibes* (1900, On the Physiological Weakness of Woman),[2] Möbius argued that the education of girls should be determined by the biological prerequisites for healthy and successful motherhood. This precluded any form of higher education which, he argued, would jeopardise their ability to produce healthy children.

These ideas were fiercely contested by the radical wing of the women's movement in Germany and Austria between 1870 and the First World War. Hedwig Dohm, in particular, wrote a number of pamphlets from the 1870s onwards which took issue with theories of motherhood as the fundamental female bodily process which determined all other physical, mental, and emotional dimensions of women.[3] In their more progressive articulations, turn-of-the-century theories which grounded femininity in motherhood argued that women were equal but different. This was an important feature of much moderate first-wave German feminism. Between 1880 and 1914, the women's movement was very much concerned with the social position and role of mothers. Issues ranged from the rights of single mothers, which were central to the political campaigning of the radical wing of the movement, to the moderate strategy of arguing for women's rights on the basis of their special social and cultural role as mothers. The moderate wing of the bourgeois Women's Movement articulated a position on motherhood, different in emphasis from the ultraconservatism of much male discourse but similar in many of its assumptions:

> We, too, start from the proposition that the woman's whole being is determined by motherhood. But we conceive of it, where psychological questions are concerned, as a quality, as a certain essence of being; not as an impediment to intellectual development... This determining role of motherhood can be seen – irrespective of individ-

---

2. Extracts from this essay are available in Filser 1977: 32–39.
3. See Hedwig Dohm's *Emanzipation* (1982, orig. 1874) in which she takes issue with medical science.

ual deviations from the norm – in the whole genus. It constitutes the specifically feminine; it is the source of psychological altruism, pity and love which, in its spiritual forms, too, bears the traits of woman. It contrasts with the more abstract, speculative disposition of man which is directed towards the systematic and impersonal. (Lange 1977: 49–50, orig. 1899)

Central to this argument is the assertion that motherhood is the essential feature of women determining their special cultural and social role, an idea which resurfaces in second-wave radical feminism. Turn-of-the-century feminists argued that while women do not – as Möbius would have it – possess inferior brains, they draw on different parts of their brain from men. They develop a different range of qualities and characteristics which fit them for motherhood. Furthermore, feminists in this period argued that women needed to take these special feminine qualities out into the wider world of public life and help to transform it.[4]

Long-established, conservative ideas of women's biological difference came to the fore once again in Nazi Germany. National-Socialist ideology, which was explicitly masculinist and asserted women's natural inferiority to men, sought to reduce women to biological mothers and celebrate them as such. The Nazi régime produced a rigid set of ideological norms which confined women to traditionally feminine roles. The reality of women's lives was, of course, very different, given the pressing need for women in the labour force and the demands of a war economy. If anything, the discrepancy between Nazi ideology and women's day-to-day experience, together with the effects of war, added to the attraction for women of traditional family life. Thus after the Second World War many women embraced conservative ideas of the sexual division of labour and women's primary role as wife and mother.

Throughout this history, gender difference – with motherhood at its centre – has been conceived in terms of a fundamental dualism between mind and body in which the former is privileged over the latter. This dualism, which identifies the body and nature with the feminine and the rational mind and culture with the masculine, is a widespread feature of modern Western thought which feminist theorists and philosophers as different as Mary Daly, Adrienne Rich, Julia Kristeva, and Luce Irigaray have recently explored and deconstructed.[5] The association of the feminine with the body and the masculine with the rational mind has remained an important theme in German and Austrian writing about motherhood in the postwar period, as have many of the other traditional ideas about motherhood outlined above.

---

4. For more on turn-of-the-century German feminism see Gerhard 1990.
5. See, for example, Daly 1979, Rich 1976, Kristeva 1986, and Irigaray 1985 and 1991a.

Postwar Mother–Daughter Novels

Mothers and daughters did not become a significant theme in postwar women's writing in Germany and Austria until second-wave feminism created the discursive space and the audience for novels dealing with this largely silenced area of female experience. A widely held consensus that women are naturally predisposed to mothering, together with the reaffirmation of the traditional nuclear family in the immediate postwar decades, deflected attention both from motherhood and mother–daughter relations. Of the writers who took up the theme of mothers and daughters in the new climate of the 1970s and 1980s – Helga Novak (born 1935), Jutta Heinrich (born 1940), Gabriele Wohmann (born 1932), Karin Struck (born 1947), Helma Sanders-Brahms (born 1940), Christa Wolf (born 1929), Ingeborg Drewitz (born 1923), Claudia Erdheim (born 1945), Brigitte Schwaiger (born 1949), Waltraud Anna Mitgutsch (born 1948), and Elfriede Jelinek (born 1946) – many were born under Nazism and experienced its collapse at a relatively early age. The immediate postwar years in both Germany and Austria were marked by social upheaval, hunger, and poverty, followed by reconstruction and the reconsolidation of long-established patriarchal norms and values.

For both mothers and daughters in the novels of the 1970s and 1980s, Nazism and its collapse, war and its aftermath, flight from the East, refugee status, and the more general hardships of the first postwar decade are the contexts in which mother–daughter relationships are played out. Important, too, is the redrawing of national borders and the division of Germany into two mutually hostile German states. This uproots and divides families both physically and ideologically. In these novels representations of mother–daughter relationships are often part of a wider attempt to give an account – from the largely hidden perspective of women – of a particularly traumatic period in German and Austrian history.

The focus on the family in novels of the 1970s and 1980s is not in itself new. In the late 1940s, 1950s, and 1960s many women writers wrote novels which detailed the repressive power relations within the family.[6] As Franziska Meyer argues in her account of women's writing during these years: 'Numerous women writers of the period 1945–1968 take up themes which have become identified with feminist literature of the 1970s. In women's writing from the 1950s onwards, we find lesbian love, women's search for identity in the prison of existing norms of youth and beauty, as well as illusionless depictions of marriage and authoritarian patriarchal family structures' (1997: 28–29). Yet, with the impact of second-wave feminism, attention turned

---

6. See, for example, the work of Gisela Elsner and Renate Rasp. Both are discussed in some detail in Meyer 1997.

explicitly to mothers and daughters and necessarily – given this cross-generational focus – to family history. This focus produced a number of important themes. Among them were what it means to be a mother in a patriarchal society and the internal dynamics of the traditional nuclear family. Novels also look in detail at how childhood experiences affect women's ability to mother and the ways in which mothers pass on modes of relating, values, and character traits to their daughters. Related to this is the question of how women exercise power in the context of the nuclear family.

The largely autobiographical mother–daughter texts published between 1970 and the early 1990s explore a number of different, yet often related, themes. For the purposes of discussion, it is possible to categorise texts according to the different emphases which emerge from them. In this chapter I have organised the relevant texts under four main headings. I begin with texts which use mother–daughter relationships to recover a lost or repressed history. Here I take two examples: Helma Sanders-Brahms's screenplay and film *Deutschland, bleiche Mutter* (1980, Germany, Pale Mother) and Christa Wolf's *Kindheitsmuster* (1976, *A Model Childhood*, 1988). My second category is novels which analyse the destructive power of mothers who abuse their daughters and the ways in which daughters respond to this abuse. This is a recurrent theme in women's writing of the 1970s and 1980s, found, for example, in the work of Helga Novak, Jutta Heinrich, Waltraud Anna Mitgutsch, and Elfriede Jelinek. These writers produce narratives which trace the history of repressive, even brutal mother–daughter relationships from the daughter's perspective, either in absence of men, or with the tacit complicity of fathers. They further analyse how negative maternal power affects and distorts the potential of the daughter to live a healthy independent adult life. I analyse two examples, Novak's *Die Eisheiligen* (1979, The Ice Saints) and Mitgutsch's *Die Züchtigung* (1985, *Punishment* 1987) in detail. My third section looks at the most sustained feminist attempt to investigate the social and cultural significance of motherhood, Karin Struck's *Die Mutter* (1975, The Mother). This novel sets out to unmask the devaluation of motherhood by patriarchy, to revalue it, and, in the process, to analyse, revise, and celebrate mother–daughter relationships. My final section looks at novels which focus on the internal dynamics of the patriarchal nuclear family with particular emphasis on how male power undermines and, in some cases, even destroys positive mother–daughter relationships. At issue is the type of role models that mothers in these families provide for their daughters. The enduring nature of this theme, which can already be found in the prefeminist postwar era, is clear from the texts discussed, which include an example from the late 1970s, Brigitte Schwaiger's *Wie kommt das Salz ins Meer* (1977, *Why Is There Salt in the Sea*, 1988) and a more recent text from the early 1990s, Birgit Vanderbeke's (born 1956) *Das Muschelessen* (1993, A Meal of Mussels). I also look at Ingeborg Drewitz's novel *Eis auf der Elbe* (1982, Ice on the Elbe), which takes as its subject a mother who appears to provide a positive role model for her three daughters.

Mothers, Daughters, and the Recovery of History

In the preface to *Deutschland, bleiche Mutter* (1980), Helma Sanders-Brahms writes of her published screenplay and film as:

> A history constructed from personal experience and from the experience of many women with whom I have spoken and whose tape-recorded interviews and written records etc. I possess.
> This is the positive history of Germany during fascism, the Second World War and afterwards. The history of the women who kept life going while the men were employed to kill. It should have been depicted long since. Now, when this generation of women, that of our mothers, is about sixty-five and will not live for much longer, it is high time to write this history. (*Deutschland*: 25)

Commenting on German women's experience of the Second World War, Sanders-Brahms continues:

> In all my interviews I came across men, again and again, who mourn this period of heroism for everyone as a time of adventure.
> Women experienced it differently, more objectively.
> They were indifferent to heroism; they would have preferred to have their men by their sides.
> And then, when they had been left to their own devices for a long time, had survived in burning towns, had extracted oil from beechnuts, patched shoes, milked cows, they became aware of their strength: not the strength necessary for heroism but in order to survive. (*Deutschland*: 25–26)

Sanders-Brahms suggests that the tragedy of these women was that after the war their new-found independence and strength were no longer required. They were forced back into the oppressive dependency of the patriarchal nuclear family. Nonetheless, the effect on their daughters of their wartime ability to survive is profound:

> But we children of that generation, born during the war, realised their strength. It is not surprising that women like Gesine Strempel, Helke Sander, Margarethe von Trotta, Alice Schwarzer, Grischa Huber are all children of the ruins, children of these mothers. Women who live without men, something that they learned from their mothers in their first years of life. They cannot get their mothers' history out of their minds. Emancipation was their first childhood experience, a much more profound emancipation than ours …
> Never again have I heard my mother sing. At that time she sang a lot. (*Deutschland*: 26)[7]

---

7. The women mentioned here are all involved in feminist politics and/or the production of feminist films and books.

In *Deutschland, bleiche Mutter*, Sanders-Brahms attempts to reconstruct the life of her mother from her courtship and marriage in the immediate prewar years, through her experience of war, which she shares with her young daughter, to her reinsertion into a traditional family structure in the early postwar period.[8] It is a story which depicts the upheaval of war as a form of liberation for women from the oppressive structures of family life. It is an explicitly partial, realist feminist project, comprising the writing of a positive history of women in the war and a documenting of the negative effects on women of reconstruction and the reestablishment of the nuclear family. Nazism is not, in itself, the central issue, although it is the cause of the events depicted. While the focus is on one family, divided by war, the historical context is constantly present in the screen version in the form of documentary extracts from radio broadcasts and documentary footage from the war years. The family – who are not party members – have no strong political views; for them it is a case of getting by, if possible without becoming involved. They do not profit from the régime as do friends and family who join the Nazi party.

Forced to cope alone in extreme conditions, the mother, Lene, finds independence, strength, and a joy in life that she has never known before and will never know again. Effectively a single mother since the drafting of her husband, Hans, at the beginning of the war, she is finally freed from all the normal constraints placed on wives and mothers by the physical destruction of her marital home in a bombing raid. Now she has only to concentrate on survival. In the course of the narrative, she and her daughter overcome poverty, hunger, cold, and rape.

Organised chronologically as a series of events in the life of the mother, which include the birth during an air raid of the daughter who narrates the film, the text offers a dual perspective on events. In the screenplay each scene is set with a few lines of detailed description which form the basis for the *mise-en-scène*. The narrative shows both what the events depicted meant to the mother at the time when they occurred and how they might be read and interpreted from the perspective of the late 1970s. Using an interrogative voice-over, the daughter comments on events as they unfold, stressing the closeness of mother and daughter in the absence of the father, their independence and strength. The war years are characterised by extreme hardship but also a freedom from patriarchal power structures which made her mother whole. The narrative is structured as a series of short scenes which evolve chronologically and juxtapose brutalising elements from Hans's experience at the battle front with Lene's life on the home front. Hans's brief

---

8. The screenplay contains scenes not found in the film. These include incidents that suggest that Hans, the father, is closer to the Nazis than he appears in the film, and scenes which allude to concentration camps. The film version downplays some of the nastier aspects of Nazism which occur in the screenplay.

periods of leave make clear the increasing alienation between the couple which will be the starting point for their postwar relationship. This alienation is contrasted with the increasingly close relationship between mother and daughter.

With the end of the war comes reconstruction and destructive family conflict:

> *My Voice*: Lene, what should we expect of peace? To begin with after the war, clearing up was fun. But the stones that we hammered were made into houses, which were worse than the previous ones. Lene, if only we had known...
> *My Voice*: That was the return of the living room. In there war broke out when there was peace outside. (*Deutschland*: 113)

This domestic war destroys Lene, who, in a powerful image of the effects of patriarchy, loses her teeth as a result of facial paralysis. Locked in the bathroom with the gas tap fully open, the mother only abandons her attempted suicide in response to the desperate cries of her daughter. The effects of this family life on the daughter are lasting: she comments that she has not married because of them.

The alienating effect of the postwar years on daughters who see their mothers lose the independence and strength which they had gained during the war is also alluded to in Gabriele Wohmann's *Ausflug mit der Mutter* (1976, Excursion with Mother). In this novel, the first-person narrator is also an adult daughter who is a successful writer, as well as a wife and mother. The novel examines the relationship between mother and daughter in the context of a society which expects daughters automatically to care for their ageing mothers. Instead of love for her mother, the narrator feels indifference and the text analyses the reasons for this. Raised in a traditional family, the daughter identifies with her father, rejects her mother as a role model, and constructs her as the opposite of herself: nothing more than a self-sacrificing wife and mother. Yet *Ausflug mit der Mutter* also suggests that the mother's experience is in many ways similar to that of Lene in *Deutschland, bleiche Mutter*: wartime emancipation followed by reinsertion within a traditional family structure. Unlike the narrator in Sanders-Brahms's text, however, the daughter in *Ausflug mit der Mutter* effectively imprisons her mother within the restricted image that she has of her, denying the mother any positive agency or respect. As in many mother–daughter novels of the 1970s and 1980s, this has negative consequences for the daughter, whose failure to relate to her mother as a person in her own right and whose feelings of indifference produce guilt. Moreover, the daughter's denial of her mother's value leads to a rejection of the positive caring aspects of traditional femininity.

In contrast to Wohmann, mothers, daughters, and positive feminine experiences and values are a recurrent theme in Christa Wolf's oeuvre. In her autobiographical novel, *Kindheitsmuster* (1976), they serve as the major vehicle for an investigation of Germany's tabooed Nazi past. *Kindheitsmuster* – like *Deutschland, bleiche Mutter* – is a text in which the narrator seeks to depict the Nazi period through her own family history. Unlike in Sanders-Brahms's text, however, the emphasis is not on creating a positive feminist narrative. Rather it is on understanding and coming to terms with this past across generations through a process of remembering and reconstructing past experience. This process of recovery is placed in the context of the narrator's relationship with her own younger daughter Lenka, who has reached the age that she herself was when forced to flee her home in the last months of the war.[9]

Kindheitsmuster touches on the lives, experiences, and perspectives of four generations of mothers and daughters: the narrator, Nelly, as both an adult and a child, the narrator's mother Charlotte, her two grandmothers, and her own younger daughter Lenka.[10] The narrative focuses on a visit to the town in Poland – formally part of Germany – where the narrator was born in 1929, grew up, and lived until the final months of the war when the family fled westwards in the face of the Soviet army. The return to Poland is part of an attempt to recover the experience of the narrator as a child. It also evokes the life and values of the child's mother, Charlotte, and to a lesser extent that of her grandmothers. The text moves frequently between past and present, juxtaposing perspectives in an attempt to understand and come to terms with the Nazi past, its effects on individuals, on family life, and on mothers and daughters.

The different female perspectives in play – those of the child Nelly, of Charlotte Jordan, of the narrator as an adult, and of her own daughter Lenka – mark the differences between the past and the present. These differences encompass ways of life, values, and actions. A key example is the relationship of Nelly and her mother Charlotte to Nazism. Whereas Charlotte silently resists many aspects of Nazism, going against Nazi rules and regulations, Nelly, as she grows up, develops an unquestioning belief in Nazi ideology and an emotional commitment to the Führer. While this inevitably distances mother and daughter, Nelly's motives are depicted as complex:

> Nelly was involved in a compensation deal, and it could almost be assumed that she knew it, because she was crying as she defiantly railroaded her mother into giving her permission [to accept a leadership position in the league of German girls]. Recognition, and comparative security from fear and from overwhelming guilt feelings are guaranteed, and she in turn contributes submission and strict performance of duty. There had been moments when she wasn't able to cope with her doubts. She rids herself of any possibility of doubt; above all self-doubt. (*A Model*: 194; *Kindheitsmuster*: 256)

---

9. For a fuller discussion of the themes of memory and coming to terms with the past see Weedon 1999.
10. It also includes the narrator's recollections of her father and younger brother, Lutz. Lutz accompanies the narrator and her daughter on their trip to Poland.

In addition to drawing out the differences between Nelly and her mother, the text also contrasts Lenka's views and values, formed in the GDR, with those of her mother at the same age. When Lenka secretly borrows her mother's *Tenth-grade Biology*, a textbook from her Nazi childhood which depicts members of inferior races, she returns it silently and her mother has the feeling that her daughter is looking at her with different eyes. Unlike many other texts dealing with mothers and daughters, the emphasis in *Kindheitsmuster* is on how broader social relations and ideologies shape subjectivities making change difficult, painful even, but possible, as in the case of Nelly herself, as she seeks to come to terms with and move beyond her childhood formation under Nazism.

Familial relations across the generations are depicted through a series of short incidents. The narrator recalls, for example, how Nelly puts a pea up her nose 'to scare her own mother to death by inflicting damage to what the mother held most dear: her daughter' (*A Model*: 22; *Kindheitsmuster*: 35). After it is removed by a doctor she recalls her reaction: 'A slap, a harsh word, even a walk home in silence would have been the proper thing at this point, in Nelly's opinion. Instead, Nelly was told that she had been "brave". No complaining. No tears. Nothing, Mother seemed to derive satisfaction from calling her daughter "brave". She had no desire to find out about her daughter's inner self' (*A Model*: 23; *Kindheitsmuster*: 36). It is this aversion to probing differences which allows the mother–daughter relationship to survive Nazism intact. The narrator notes similarities between her mother Charlotte, herself, and her own daughter. These include things as different as inherited pessimism, a tendency to fear for their mothers' safety and to reject incidents that their mothers remember, as well as everyday things like shared childhood games. Unlike many other novels dealing with mothers and daughters, there is no suggestion in *Kindheitsmuster* that men and boys are preferable or better than women and girls, an idea officially contested in the GDR throughout its forty-year history. Indeed, when faced with the birth of a younger brother, Nelly is reassured by her mother that she has enough love for both of them. There are also moments of shared amusement, lacking in the other novels discussed in this chapter. On one occasion Nelly is upset at a classmate's house by a game of 'The Jew has slaughtered a pig, which part of it d'you want!'. She makes up excuses in order to go home, refusing such treats as pudding and whipped cream and a drive home in a car:

> Her mother, having been informed by telephone, looks at her critically, even puts her hand on her forehead. Do you think you have a fever? No, Nelly says. I'm not going to go there again.
> Her mother makes her a liverwurst sandwich. Suddenly their eyes meet and they have to laugh, at first with a giggle, then openly; finally they scream with laughter, slap their thighs, wipe the tears of laughter off their faces with the back of their hands. Oh, you fibber, Charlotte Jordan says. Just you wait! (*A Model*: 132; *Kindheitsmuster*: 176)

Kindheitsmuster explores the assumption – widespread in mother–daughter narratives – that it is the past which makes us what we are. The formation and transformation of subjectivity is central to the text, yet unlike many other mother–daughter narratives, the emphasis is not on the immediate emotional and psychological effects of dysfunctional families. In contrast the focus is social and historical. Differences are grounded in the immediate historical and cultural contexts in which mothers and daughters find themselves: pre-Nazi Germany, Nazism, and the GDR and it is these factors which shape subjectivity, gender relations, and experiences for the different generations.

Destructive Mothers

The turn to the theme of mother–daughter relationships in women's writing of the 1970s and 1980s brought with it a number of novels which analyse in detail the long-tabooed subject of destructive mothers. Going directly against conventional assumptions about mothers, these novels focus on how mothers abuse their daughters, both psychologically and physically, and the ways in which such treatment affects the daughters' ability to live happy and fulfilled lives as adults. Where reasons are given for maternal abuse, they are most often to be found in the mother's own childhood and upbringing in families where they are neither loved nor valued, but are themselves abused. This is often seen as part of a wider undervaluing of female children. The long-term effects of childhood abuse are shown to produce women who are often masochistic in their adult relationships and who themselves become abusers of their daughters. These novels opened up areas of family life hidden from view and attempted to throw light on what is at issue in child abuse.

Among the most powerful depictions of destructive mother–daughter relations is Helga Novak's autobiographical novel *Die Eisheiligen* (1979). The novel is set in the same period as the texts by Sanders-Brahms and Wolf discussed above. It spans the pre- to the postwar period, covering life in Nazi Germany, the war, and the immediate postwar years in the Soviet Occupied Zone. Yet if both Sanders-Brahms and Wolf portray positive mother–daughter relationships, Novak focuses on the microdynamics of a particularly brutal, abusive mother–daughter relationship. While history plays an important part as the stage on which the relationship is played out, it is the relationship itself which is the main focus of the narrative. The novel traces the unnamed, adopted daughter's experience of family life up to the age of sixteen.

Die Eisheiligen is told from the perspective of the child, but incorporates the mother's voice and occasionally the voices of relatives directly within the child's narrative as she evokes scenes from her childhood. This technique enables the reader to gain a critical distance on the child's first-person narrative and to see the relationship from the perspective of the mother. The daughter calls her mother 'Coldsophie' ('Kaltesophie'), a name which signifies both the mother's coldness towards her daughter and her date of birth, 14 May, which is the last of the three saints' days known as the 'ice saints'. The daughter's voice gives graphic accounts of an everyday normality, interspersed with episodes of physical and mental abuse. Such warmth as the child finds comes from other relatives and neighbours. Only towards the end of the book, as the daughter gains in age and maturity does she come to understand her mother, as she learns of her unhappy childhood and adult life.

The novel is best understood in the context of the traditional assumptions about women and motherhood outlined in the introduction to this chapter which reached a high point under National Socialism. For all her desire to conform, Sophie defies any definition of maternal instincts as natural. Rendered infertile at an early age by an illegal abortion, she is at no time a willing adoptive mother. Living under Nazism, in a society in which motherhood was officially proclaimed the patriotic duty of all German women, she agrees under pressure from her husband Karl first to foster and later to adopt a child. Her first attempt is a disaster when, at the age of thirty, she fosters a small girl, Christa, but is driven to physical abuse by her lack of patience at the child's inability to eat properly. While the child has a throat disease, Sophie interprets her behaviour as obstinacy. This inability to see the real causes of children's behaviour also shapes her relationship with the daughter whom she adopts when she is forty, the minimum age for adoption under Nazi law. The novel traces Sophie's inability to mother back to her early life. Forced to work in her parents' shop from the age of ten, she was regularly beaten by her father and did badly at school since she was not allowed to read at home. Anxious to escape from her home environment, Sophie became engaged at the age of eighteen but, once pregnant, was abandoned by her fiancé. Desperate to keep any knowledge of her pregnancy from her violent father, she had an abortion from which she nearly died.

Sophie's life, the novel suggests, is governed by the desire to conform to middle-class norms of respectability, even when they go against her individual preference. Having adopted a child on the wishes of her husband, she has definite ideas of what she wants her daughter to be like. She makes her practice walking with books on her head. She refuses to speak to her daughter if she uses dialect, or to be seen with her if she looks untidy. She does not like her daughter mixing with neighbours whom she considers inferior. Sophie attempts to enforce these norms by means of physical punishment. As this strategy fails, she turns to psychological abuse and the relationship between mother and daughter gradually deteriorates to the point where both parties can only express hostility and hatred. Nowhere in the novel do we see any verbal or physical expressions of love on the mother's part, though she cares for her daughter's material welfare adequately until the desperate circumstances of the immediate postwar years make even this too difficult.

Whenever her daughter fails to conform to her expectations Sophie resorts to physical violence and psychological humiliation. In the early years of their relationship, the child does not intentionally go against her mother's wishes, indeed the first violent incident in the narrative is the mother's public beating of her young daughter after the latter is pushed into a stream by another child. Here, as in the incidents that follow, Sophie's violent reaction is depicted as quite out of proportion to the misdemeanour, even in a society which endorses physical punishment. In the course of the novel there are a number of descriptions of serious physical and emotional abuse. On one occasion Sophie discovers a cracked plate for which she blames her daughter:

> Blows right and left, making me shake like a monkey at a Christmas fair, and me crying, kissing her fingers individually – 'It wasn't me' – and the back of her hands covered in tears – 'I didn't break the plate' – as if I had small cups full of water in my head – 'I really didn't' – and my eyes were just like eggs.
> Really touching, and you think I believe you? (*Eisheiligen*: 61)

Another time the mother beats her daughter until the child collapses and is left unable to walk. Afterwards Sophie shows guilt and remorse, sitting continuously at her daughter's bedside, meeting her every request.

Sophie's treatment of her daughter produces a range of disturbed behaviour in the child, ranging from bed wetting to nail biting and the development of a lisp. As if to assert her identity the child takes to carving her name on table tops. Yet the mother's response to the child's behaviour is governed not by her concern for her daughter's welfare but by her fear of what the neighbours will think. Indeed, Sophie shows no interest in her daughter's life or experiences beyond appearances. On returning from a school trip, the daughter recounts how her mother destroys her positive experience. She is only interested in the fact that her daughter has lost her hair ribbons and immediately announces a beating:

> I arrive at Lehrter Station in the middle of lots of children and mothers and fathers rush towards us. Kaltesophie is there too. I have lots to tell her. What have you got in your hair? Where are your bows? Just what do you look like? But that's string, mere string, in your plaits.
> She inspects my suitcase while we are still in the station. It has a list of contents carefully stuck to its inside lid.
> I only establish one thing: all the bows have gone.
> But I haven't wet the bed, not once.
> I'm not interested in that now. You just come home with me. Just wait until we are by ourselves. (*Eisheiligen*: 30)

As the daughter grows older, her mother's treatment of her produces various forms of resistance which range from consciously going against her mother's wishes to murder fantasies and suicide attempts. She steals from her mother, she is rude to her and refuses to conform to the neat and tidy image her mother attempts to impose. She goes around barefooted and does not wash her feet before going to bed, has buttons missing, torn clothes, badly groomed hair and spits on the street. Yet, just as her mother's cruel behaviour brings her no satisfaction, the daughter's behaviour is also ultimately self-destructive, leading to severe bouts of depression, self-hatred, and suicide attempts as she internalises her mother's negative view of her, reinforced by the fact that she is adopted and her real mother has already given her away.

Throughout the novel Sophie fails to realise her own responsibility for her daughter's behaviour. She expects love and respect despite her (in her own eyes justified) brutality. She fails to comprehend her daughter's feelings towards her. Thus, for example, when the child has diphtheria, her mother dutifully visits her in hospital:

> If she stood behind – or from her perspective in front of – the window on Wednesdays and Saturdays, I turned on my side in my bed and closed my eyes. Quarantine, that meant, she couldn't get near me.
> At first she got into a rage, then she came less often. Finally she rang up to ask about how I was getting on. (*Eisheiligen*: 64–65)

The text suggests that it is not so much that the mother is without feeling for her daughter, more that her ideas and aspirations are totally inappropriate. This is reflected, for example, in Sophie's Christmas gifts which every year consist of household linen rather than toys. Moreover, the novel repeatedly suggests that Sophie reproduces the way in which she herself was treated as a child. Just as she was beaten, so she beats her daughter. Just as she had to work from a young age, so now she makes her daughter spin cord, crochet, and weave in every spare moment. Yet Sophie gets neither pleasure nor satisfaction from her treatment of her daughter. Like many other aspects of her life, her relationship brings her anger and hurt, leading her to regret both marriage and motherhood.

The deterioration in the mother–daughter relationship as the daughter grows older is reflected in Sophie's shifting attitude to her daughter's adoption. During her early childhood, when they are evacuated to the countryside, Sophie goes so far as to prosecute her landlady for talking about her daughter's adoptive status in front of the child. She genuinely wants to protect her daughter from this disreputable knowledge. The child discovers her adoption papers by chance as she searches through drawers while her mother is out. Yet it is some years before the mother–daughter relationship deteriorates to the point where Sophie tells her that she is adopted, in an attempt to control her behaviour by threatening to send her back to the children's home. Once again, this is not something that brings her any pleasure:

> She reels her head around, throws it back and stands there, trembling, red patches on her face. An extended crying, wailing, howling comes from her mouth, while she moves her hands gently over her hips down to her calves. No one is as desperate, unfortunate, as trapped as I am, punished with a changeling who is nothing but nastiness. I have raised the sheer embodiment of deceitfulness, a viper, a whore's baby. I stand in the doorway, silent, and stiffen. Even though she is talking about me, there is no look, no bridge between us. She is completely alone, concerned only with portraying her misery. (*Eisheiligen*: 219)

If the mother–daughter relationship is a disaster, the child's relationship with her father is unproblematic until the final stages of the narrative when he turns against her for political reasons. Profoundly anti-communist, her parents are unwilling to allow her to stay on at school. Things take a turn for the worse when she joins the Free German Youth, (FDJ, the official communist youth organisation in the GDR), and her father beats her for the first time. Away from home on an FDJ training course, she finds the sense of well being that she has always been denied at home:

> Here I feel good. Here I am needed. Here I receive recognition. Here life has a future. Here I'm not subjugated, here I'm not obsequious. Here we are nice to each other. Here everything isn't in vain. Here there's hope. Here I'm learning for socialism. Here each one of us matters. Here darkness has an end. Here we eat together. Here life begins. Here there is an end to beatings. Here I am not alone. Here there is an end to fear. Here I'm coming to my senses. Here I begin with myself. Here there are no reproaches, threats, blackmail and punishments. Here there is trust. Here I'm in the right place. (*Eisheiligen*: 339)

Her situation is finally resolved by leaving home.

Die Eisheiligen offers no resolution to the destructive mother–daughter relationship that it describes. While the novel emphasises the destructive power of a woman who is incapable of mothering, it is shown to be not only destructive but self-destructive. The daughter is only saved by the knowledge that she is adopted and intervention of the new socialist state which offers her a place at a boarding school. Written after the author settled in West Germany, the novel does not comment on the daughter's future ability to realise herself within the GDR beyond mentioning a trip to the theatre with her Aunt Concordia in later years. The child's break with her family is presented positively with the possible exception of the closing image which, in describing the broken glass cemented on to the top of the walls surrounding the school, can be read as suggesting that the East German state will not offer her the space that she needs for her self-realisation.

If *Die Eisheiligen* ends on an optimistic note for the daughter, novels which suggest that destructive mothers destroy their daughters' future ability to live whole and fulfilled lives are more typical. They depict how patterns of relating are passed on from generation to generation. Among the most powerful and negative depictions of destructive mothers in recent women's writing are those by two significant Austrian writers, Waltraud Anna Mitgutsch and Elfriede Jelinek. Both Mitgutsch's *Die Züchtigung* (1985) and Jelinek's *Die Klavierspielerin* (1983, *The Piano Teacher*, 1988) invite psychoanalytic interpretations which focus on the role of sadism and masochism in mother–daughter relationships and both have been analysed in detail in these terms.[11] The novels depict mother–daughter relationships in which child abuse denies the daughter a positive identity as an adult and lays down patterns of relating which distort the daughter's adult relationships with her own body and sexuality, with men, and with her own daughter.

Mitgutsch's *Die Züchtigung* is set on a farm on the outskirts of a small town in Austria and spans the 1920s to the 1960s. It focuses on the childhood and married life of Marie and her daughter Vera's childhood and youth up to the age of eighteen when Marie dies. The narratives of Marie's life, told in the third person by her daughter, and Vera's own life, told in the first person, are intertwined. They are further interspersed by episodes from later years which depict Vera's adult relationships with men and with her daughter.

The novel focuses on physical and psychological abuse which reproduces itself in mothers and daughters across generations. Drawing on autobiographical experience, it details how the central mother figure, Marie – an unwanted daughter with none of the beauty or charm of her older sister – was systematically abused as a child by her family. Denied love, she learned a self-hatred which renders her incapable of any normal relationship with her own husband, whom she despises, or with her daughter. Both class and Catholicism are important factor in Marie's unhappy life. A farmer's daughter, she marries beneath her, and spends her life trying unsuccessfully to move into the ranks of the middle classes. She sees her brutal methods of child rearing as preparing her daughter for a better future. She abuses her daughter physically and emotionally, creating a child who both fears and loves her, and who internalises a sense of worthlessness that seems to justify the beatings and other forms of abuse. She teaches her daughter to hate her body and to regard sex as impure and evil. She insists on bathing Vera until she is in her mid-teens in order to prevent her from touching herself. Vera is rendered incapable of normal relations with other people and grows up a dowdy, unattractive, and overweight child, ashamed of her body, and a total stranger to any physical affection. Her only arena of success is intellectual. She transcends her social class and her teachers' expectations by winning places at a grammar school and at university. Despite this, however, she

---

11. See Fiddler 1994 and 1997, Kraft and Liebs 1993, and Schmidt 1996.

remains emotionally disturbed, repeatedly looking for sadistic treatment in her adult relationships.

Marie's own self-image is based on her conventional understanding of her role as dedicated housewife and mother. Unlike the mother in *Die Eisheiligen*, she attempts to hide the physical and emotional abuse that she inflicts on her daughter. She complements her brutality with an exaggerated, publicly visible attempt to do the best for her by trying to facilitate her upward mobility into the ranks of the middle classes. She dresses Vera in old-fashioned clothes made from the most expensive cloth and overfeeds her. She pays for private education, including dancing lessons and an expensive skiing holiday. Meanwhile both parents do without food and other necessities in order to pay for Vera's education. The desire to do well at school is beaten into Vera from a young age. Later, once Vera has become totally masochistic and dependent on her mother's approval, academic success becomes a way of securing this approval. Her parents exist side by side in a loveless marriage which explodes periodically in scenes where Marie verbally abuses her husband on account of his class, background, and lowly job as a ticket collector. Marie's ambition for her daughter brings her praise from an outside world which knows little of the extent of abuse within the home and turns away from all evidence of it.

The novel traces how the constant physical and psychological abuse to which Vera is subject takes its toll on her. She learns to empathise with her mother and starts to become like her. After her death, Marie continues to haunt Vera. Even when, years later, she thinks she is free of her mother, she unconsciously reproduces her mother's modes of relating to others:

> Later, when I was a different person and discovered the world, I began to hate her. When I couldn't live without adventures any more, I began to despise her. I became everything that would have outraged her. I slept with every man who wanted me and a lot who didn't. I hitchhiked across two continents and went for three months without bathing. I gave up my career for a man, and gave up that man for another one, just so I could leave him, too. 'You are a gypsy like your grandmother, the old witch,' I heard my mother say, and suddenly I stopped hating her and forgot her; she no longer had a place in my life. But the fate of mothers lives on in their daughters. One day your mother appears and says, 'All right, my daughter, you are old enough; now I'm going to show you my life.' I screamed, 'You don't love me, you bastard,' and saw the bloated face of my mother, saw with horrified eyes how she spat in my father's face; but it was the man I lived with who wiped off the saliva and slapped my face. (*Punishment*: 6; *Züchtigung*: 9–10)

If Vera repeats her mother's treatment of her father, she also ultimately fails in her relationship with her own daughter:

> The one thing I wanted from the beginning was to keep my child from this heritage of self-destruction. I did not want her ever to be forced into anything, to be afraid of punishment, to feel the humiliation of being the weaker one and the inability to fight

against it. 'You are smothering your child with love,' the psychologist said, 'you are unable to let her go; you are blocking her development.'... I remembered my own childhood and knew how I did not want to do it, but not doing it wrong doesn't mean doing it right. (*Punishment*: 133; *Züchtigung*: 153)

Thinking back on her experience with her mother – a peculiar mixture of violence and love – Vera concludes that her mother loved her with desperate masochism and hated her because she was not the spontaneous fulfilment of all her dreams. Yet despite her conscious awareness of the patterns laid down by her childhood and upbringing, Vera is unable to escape repeating them. The effect is an emotionally disturbed daughter and a recognition that she cannot escape her mother's destructive legacy:

> For sixteen years I buried her over and over, but she always rose and followed me. She caught up with me long ago. She looks at me with the eyes of my child; she observes me from the mirror when I think I am unobserved; I meet her in my lovers, and run her off with her own arguments. Then she punishes me with loneliness, and I try to win her back through achievement, brilliant achievement, the epitome of achievement. I never please her. I married her, then divorced her, but she transformed herself and lay in wait for me. Her embrace, granted so hesitantly and only in exchange for perfect behaviour, always turns into a grip in which I suffocate. I push her away and feel pushed away. I am her and say, You are worth nothing, and sink into grief for my loss, my loss of I, my loss of Thou, the loss of all the love in the world... She has transformed herself into me; she created me and slipped inside me; when I died sixteen years ago, when she beat me to death thirty years ago, she took my body, appropriated my ideas, usurped my feelings.
>
> She rules and I serve, and when I gather all my courage and offer resistance she always wins, in the name of obedience, reason and fear. (*Punishment*: 216; *Züchtigung*: 246)

Power, subservience, and the inability of a daughter to free herself from her mother's control are also central to Elfriede Jelinek's *Die Klavierspielerin*. The novel details the relationship between Erika Kohut, a woman approaching forty, and her mother, and how this has affected Erika's sexuality and her relationships with men. The text depicts a family in which men are absent. Erika, the piano player of the title, has been brought up by her mother following the death of her father in a mental asylum. The narrative focuses on Erika's upbringing, home life, and failed masochistic affair with a young male piano student. Frau Kohut dedicates her life to maintaining her power over Erika. Mother and daughter share a flat and, although still treated like a child, Erika is expected to fulfil some of the roles of the absent husband. Not only is she the breadwinner for the family, but she even shares her mother's bedroom. Within the confines of the flat, Frau Kohut controls both the domestic space and their income. Beyond the home she attempts to dictate Erika's appearance, ensuring she is too dowdy to attract men, and she monitors how Erika spends her time, staging jealous scenes if she stays out late.

The third-person narrative voice creates an ironic distance between reader and characters. Whereas the first part of the novel focuses on the mother–daughter relationship, the second part concentrates on Erika's failed masochistic affair with her student Klemmer. In her extensive analysis of sex and sexuality in *Die Klavierspielerin*, Allyson Fiddler argues that Jelinek shows 'interaction between men and women ... to be completely unsatisfactory and based on violence and misunderstanding' (1994: 126). Fiddler details the sexual dimensions of Erika's relationship both with her mother and Klemmer and argues convincingly that the link between sexual pleasure, power, and submission in Jelinek's oeuvre is fundamental to the broader relations of patriarchy which extend even to families where men are absent.

In the course of the narrative, Erika shows small signs of resistance to her mother's domination which increase once she starts her liaison with Klemmer. Unable to sustain any kind of mutual, loving relationship with a man, her relationship with Klemmer is structured through forms of domination and submission and accompanied on Erika's part by extreme masochistic fantasies which she communicates to Klemmer by means of a letter. Frightened off by her demands, Klemmer abandons Erika who in turn makes a sexual revenge attack on her mother. Subsequently she sets out with a knife to find Klemmer but, in keeping with the distorting effects of her upbringing, she uses it to inflict a flesh wound on herself and heads for home, unable to survive outside the power structures within which her mother has imprisoned her.

Of the mother–daughter novels discussed in this chapter, Jelinek's is the one which foregrounds the link between power, control, and sexual desire, suggesting, in a Freudian manner, that desire will out, whatever the circumstances and form of its expression. The degree to which novels about destructive mother–daughter relationships lend themselves to psychoanalytic readings varies from the overtly Freudian references found in Jelinek to the more general analysis that novels offer of familial relations in societies in which women are valued less than men and lack access to creative forms of power, both within and beyond the nuclear family. A widespread theme is how socially induced self-hatred gives rise to mothers who are at the same time both sadistic towards their daughters and masochistic in their exaggerated adherence to their social roles as wives and mothers. Their lack of power and struggle for self-esteem suggest metaphorical readings of Freudian notions of castration and penis envy in which the absence of the penis represents lack of female power within society and an overvaluation of the male. Only the revaluation of women and of the roles of mother and daughters could transform the social and familial relations which give rise to destructive mothers. The revaluation of the maternal found in the feminist psychoanalytic writings of Irigaray (1991b) and Kristeva (1986) and in the work of Adrienne Rich (1976) has yet to be realised in positive depictions of mothers and daughters in German and Austrian women's writing.

Motherhood as 'Experience and Institution'

> The secret of life is the hidden search for maternal warmth: lost or never found.
> (Struck 1975: 13)

Early second-wave feminist thinking on what Adrienne Rich calls 'motherhood as experience and institution' (1976) is brought together in Karin Struck's extensive novel, *Die Mutter* (1975). The text is written in the third person as an investigation into the social, psychological, biological, material, and emotional dimensions of motherhood in contemporary Germany. It presents an overwhelmingly negative picture of women struggling to live up to ideologies of motherhood as natural in a society which radically undervalues the role of mothers. These themes have their roots well back in nineteenth-century theories of female difference. Organised in six long chapters, *Die Mutter* brings together a widely shared feminist concern in the 1970s with the lost history and experience of mother–daughter relationships and a feminist account and critique of the ideologies and lived realities of motherhood. It looks at pregnancy, childbirth, and mother–daughter relations across generations and classes, as well as the links between mothers and *Heimat,* a sense of a place where one belongs and has one's roots. Drawing strongly on elements of social documentary writing, which was very much in vogue in the late 1960s and early 1970s, *Die Mutter* offers multiple descriptions of the physical dimensions of pregnancy, childbirth, breastfeeding, and child rearing.[12] It describes in detail bodily fluids, natural processes, and medical interventions, in an attempt to make visible, dignify, and celebrate tabooed areas of women's experience. It further details the emotional and psychological dimensions of motherhood, with particular emphasis on how mother–daughter relationships are distorted by the patriarchal tendency to value boys over girls and men over women.

Whereas most documentary writing of the 1960s and 1970s was set in the workplace and dealt with a largely male working-class experience, Struck takes as her subject what she calls the 'work' of reproduction and motherhood.[13] The novel implicitly references the feminist debates of the 1970s about the relationship of procreation to Marxist models of productive labour. Feminist campaigns in the period focused on the struggle to have motherhood and domestic labour revalued as socially important and to see them as an integral precondition for productive labour outside the home. One form this took was the wages for housework campaign. The central character of *Die Mutter*, Nora, who is both a writer and a mother, sets out

---

12. Examples of feminist documentary texts include Runge 1970 and Schwarzer 1975.
13. Important here was the work of the Worker Writers' Circles, *Werkkreis Literatur der Arbeitswelt*. This movement supported the work of working-class writers and in 1975 it published a novel by Margot Schroeder about women's emancipation (1975).

to show how motherhood is indeed productive labour: 'Production and origin interest Nora most. She wants to make quite clear to herself the extent to which bearing children is a form of production. She describes the work of midwives. She is ashamed of people because they rank nursery school teachers as less important than mathematicians or atomic physicists' (*Mutter*. 36). Motivated by her own experience of pregnancy and childbirth, Nora combines it with the results of her research and her own critical reflections as she attempts to write 'Hundreds of pages about my birth, birth itself, the birth of my mother' (*Mutter*. 114).

Two connected aspects of motherhood in Western cultures are central to the narrative. The first is its invisibility, which the text attempts to redress with long, vivid descriptions of the physical side of motherhood. The second is the lack of value attributed to being a mother. This in turn is linked to the privileging of mental over manual labour. These themes are investigated through Nora's own family history, which, like those described earlier in this chapter, encompasses Nazism, flight from the East, and *Heimatlosigkeit*, the lack of a place where Nora feels she has her roots and where she belongs.

In the course of the narrative, the novel raises a wide range of issues which the Women's Movement in the early 1970s identified as central to motherhood under patriarchy. These include cultural beliefs about motherhood, the destructive power of mothers, parallels between motherhood and nature, social attitudes towards women's bodies – especially pregnant bodies – mother–daughter relationships, and the medicalisation and technologisation of childbirth. Against the negative images and taboos of patriarchal German society, Struck attempts to revalue motherhood, in particular its physical dimensions.

In the opening pages of *Die Mutter*, Nora suggests that there is no more intensive form of power than the power of the mother. Yet it is a power distorted by a society which values men over women, the masculine over the feminine, and which attempts to limit women to the family: 'Exiled from world history, mothers determine the history of their children, cling to their children like bloodsuckers, have them carry out their secret wishes. Created from man's rib, they are devalued' (*Mutter*. 28). This has profound implications for mothers and daughters. Echoing Freud and feminist theorists such as Rich (1976) and Chodorow (1978), the novel offers repeated examples of how a mother's desire for a son affects her ability to bond with her daughters. Although she does not invoke psychoanalytic language, Struck's analysis, like Freud (1977) and Lacan (1977), suggests that male children function as an indirect mode of access to power for women. As a consequence they neglect their daughters. Nora's relationship with her own mother, Marie, is depicted as ambivalent. Even now as an adult, she feels that she hardly knows her mother, yet has an overwhelming need to discover her mother's secrets.

She asks Marie to write to her about her experiences of pregnancy and childbirth: 'Mother gives me memory' (*Mutter*: 42).

Marie's early rejection of her daughter produces an ambivalence in the narrator towards her mother which surfaces repeatedly in the course of the novel, particularly in her dreams, which she interprets for the reader:

> Nora experiences her mother's concern as a sham. The mother is gigantic as she stands before Nora in the darkened room in front of the taut string. Nora is tiny. The mother is completely naked, the mother is huge, her large heavy breasts and her mossy genitals force their way out of the enormous mother's body towards Nora. Her concern is a mockery. (*Mutter*: 14)

Here, female sexuality is seen as threatening, rather than as the joyful, exuberant, positive force that it represents in the recent French feminist psychoanalytic writings of Irigaray (1985, 1991a, 1991b), Kristeva (1986), and Cixous (1987). Yet despite her ambivalence towards her mother, Nora is committed to communication, however intermittent and unsatisfactory: 'Rare conversations with her mother, letters. Then the conversations peter out. No more letters for weeks and months on end. A terrible alienation. Hatred for her mother' (*Mutter*: 42).

In response to her daughter's request, Marie details her experience of pregnancy, childbirth, and motherhood in three letters. She also tells of her childhood experiences with her own mother, Anna. This testimony reaffirms what the novel suggests are the inescapable links between mothers and daughters, however unable they are to communicate, and the ways in which daughters repeat their own mother's behaviour and modes of relating. Thus, Marie was the fifth consecutive daughter, born only out of her mother's desire for a son. Marie, too, desires a son, rejecting her own daughter. Nora, in her turn, privileges her son Friedrich over her daughter Rosa. Like her mother before her, Nora has problems breastfeeding, and both women experience similar feelings of inadequacy towards their children. Nora's mother writes:

> I struggled with myself. I was so often impatient with the children, then came the scoldings. The children were supposed to be what I wanted them to be. I was at odds with myself, when you were in bed in the evenings. Why aren't you more patient? I said to myself. Dear God, help me to be better to the children, more patient, calmer and kinder. I never managed it. It got worse the older you became. (*Mutter*: 41)

Nora has similar feelings of ambivalence and inadequacy:

> She lives with a terrible conflict. On the one hand she wants to have lots of children and wonderful relationships with them. On the other, she hates children because they seem to her like cannibals with the demands that they make. She isn't able to recognise these demands. She doesn't understand the children's language, talks to them as if to foreigners. 'Mummy will give you something to eat now'... Rosa squeals and screams continuously; her screaming is a language that Nora doesn't understand. (*Mutter*: 15)

When she is away from her children, Nora misses them intensely. Yet within two hours of her return, her joy at their reunion is transformed into emptiness and a longing for the space to work.

Nora describes her relationship with her toddler daughter Rosa as profoundly ambivalent. She recognises 'two forces within her: the one hate, the other love. I must learn mother love. Mother love is the greatest thing' (*Mutter*: 75). Yet in the description of her failure to bond with her daughter, a description which strongly suggests postnatal depression, it is her own nonrelationship with her mother, which Nora sees as the key to her situation: 'Who ever dedicated herself to me? says Nora. I get withdrawal symptoms when I am suddenly left completely alone with two small children, myself and my horrible childhood. I'd like to roll into a ball, start to suck my thumb, I'd like to suckle, sleep and be rocked all the time. I'd like to dive into darkness' (*Mutter*: 93). Nora uses the word 'hatred' to describe her feelings for her daughter, yet, the text explains, it is a hatred derived from her own past experience: 'In Rosa Nora hates herself as a girl. In Rosa Nora hates herself as a mother. She notices how often already she has destroyed Rosa' (*Mutter*: 127).

If the social privileging of the masculine over the feminine lies at the heart of unhappy mother–daughter relationships, this is seen most clearly in attitudes to the female body. Once again echoing Freud, Rich, and Chodorow, *Die Mutter* suggests that it is the female body which links the daughter inextricably with her mother, a body that society does not value. It is the widespread degradation of motherhood, Struck suggests, that leads women to want to escape from it. Their fertile bodies come to be seen as prisons, and women have abortions in order to preserve the small amount of freedom which comes from denying their own bodies. Moreover, pregnancy is widely seen as a source of social embarrassment and negative social attitudes towards pregnant women are often internalised by the women themselves, who seek to hide their bodies. Against these widely held, negative images of pregnancy, *Die Mutter* sets out to present graphic positive images of pregnant bodies:

> Very pregnant Nora is blessed with love. A butter yellow, buttercup yellow liquid runs from her breasts when her breasts become warm during love-making. Like egg yolk, Nora says, or like the asparagus soup with lots of egg yolk that my mother prepared for me with asparagus from the garden...
> Nora's breasts aren't the lust-provoking objects of advertising, strung up, imprisoned in a bodice. They are not the objects of jokes and lecherous looks. Her breasts are areas of her beautiful, free body. (*Mutter*: 98, 117)

The idea of pregnant bodies as beautiful and free echoes radical and ecofeminist views of natural, fertile women. Yet, it is not only pregnant bodies which patriarchal culture denigrates; *Die Mutter* suggests that it is all aspects of women's bodies which do not serve the interests of male titillation. Menstruation is a case in point. *Die Mutter* describes how it is seen as shameful and how this affects women: 'There are women who do not want their bodies, thousands of women. Nora feels her body strongly when the first drops of blood, heavy, dark, thick drops flow from her vagina' (*Mutter*: 202). This textual strategy of documenting and celebrating aspects of the female body which are usually banished to the arena of silence and taboo is taken to extremes in the novel as Nora discovers pleasure in the smell of her son's faeces or beauty in a placenta: 'She sees a placenta in a bowl. At first the sight repels her. Like fresh liver, she says, shocked. Then she sees the beauty' (*Mutter*: 218).

The fourth chapter of *Die Mutter* looks at hospitalised childbirth. The title of the chapter, 'In the Factory', suggests what is at issue: the dehumanising, alienated nature of hospital confinements. Consisting mostly of documentary descriptions of the labour ward and childbirth, the text explores a central theme in radical and ecological feminist thought: the relationship between women and nature. In the hospital, a natural process has been technologised. The work of midwives has been transformed from a creative enabling role in which expectant mothers are treated as whole individuals to that of servants of male controlled machinery. Nora interprets this as part of a wider problem: man's desire to control and even replace nature. Men's treatment of mothers, she suggests, parallels their wider treatment of nature: 'They denigrate nature, because she is mighty. They denigrate the mother because she is mighty' (*Mutter*: 27).

At the opening of 'In the Factory', Nora relates how her experience of a large hospital makes her realise that contempt for nature and contempt for motherhood go hand in hand. Spending weeks observing practice on the labour ward, Nora sees doctors handling women like butchers would meat. She documents in detail 'normal' childbirth, episiotomies, and caesarean sections. As a mechanised process, governed by machinery and drugs, childbirth is no longer a positive experience. In consequence women have problems bonding with their infants and breastfeeding them. The hospital's answer is infant feeding formulas. Moreover, the conveyor-belt-like nature of the labour ward leads to indifference among all who work there.

The lack of respect and value attached to motherhood is presented in *Die Mutter* also as part of a broader problem of social attitudes to large families. This, in turn, is linked to questions of social class and manual labour. In chapter two, Nora visits a working-class family who already have ten children and are expecting their eleventh. The Velte family live on social security in an area of town which has special housing for large families. The father of the family, Karl Velte, resents how he is seen, but has also internalised wider negative social perception of large families. Because bringing up children is not seen as real work, those who dedicate their lives to it are not seen as productive members of society. Moreover, society tends not to respect manual tasks. Thus, the novel suggests, attitudes to mothers are part of a broader problem of attitudes to manual labour: 'Practical work is despised always and everywhere, as if it were a completely unintellectual work. The body is despised always and everywhere' (*Mutter*: 76). The novel rehearses negative popular perception of full-time mothers. For example, Nora overhears a woman in a train comment on how someone she knows has five children and sits around all day, reading novels in the sun. Meanwhile employers see pregnancy and childbirth as disruptions in the normal work process.

The only answer, *Die Mutter* suggests, is radical social change, which would bring about a revaluing of motherhood as a socially productive task. This would require change at a number of levels, ranging from cultural representations (an idea developed by Luce Irigaray in her work on motherhood)[14] and social attitudes to changes in the economic basis which could be secured by wages for motherhood. Ultimately, the text suggests, a new form of matriarchy is the answer: 'The mothers do not rule. But the mothers rule in secret. The time has come for an open rule of the mothers, for a new matriarchy' (*Mutter*: 16). *Die Mutter* does not, however, explore what this positive power might mean.

Mothers, Daughters, and the Dynamics of the Patriarchal Family

As suggested above, the detailed analysis of the repressive internal workings of the family was already an important feature of prefeminist postwar women's writing. Yet during the 1950s and 1960s – in the absence of a political and social movement – it remained difficult to imagine alternatives. The advent of feminism called into question the naturalness and inevitability of the patriarchal nuclear family. Feminist novels of the 1970s and 1980s which analyse the family often suggest that it is better for women to abandon traditional family life. This is the message of the best-selling Austrian novel, Brigitte Schwaiger's *Wie kommt das Salz ins Meer* (1977), which sets out to expose the true nature of traditional family life.

Wie kommt das Salz ins Meer is a first-person, stream-of-consciousness narrative in which a young, middle-class woman tells of her wedding, failed marriage, extra-marital affair, and divorce. While much of the text offers a detailed realistic account of the everyday life and interpersonal dynamics between the young married couple, equally important is the narrator's own family experience. The realist narrative is interspersed with poetic metaphors which evoke the narrator's alienation. Unlike many novels that take moth-

---

14. See Irigaray 1985 and 1991a. See also Braidotti 1991.

ers and daughters as one of their central themes, *Wie kommt das Salz ins Meer* depicts a happy childhood and nonconflictual relationship between mother and daughter. The cross-generational focus on the narrator's mother and grandmother, and the role models that they provide for the daughter, however, throw light on why her marriage fails.

At the centre of the narrative is an unmasking of how power functions within families, and its effects on women. We see the narrator enter into a marriage that she no longer wants in order to fulfil the expectations of her family for whom appearances are everything. Respectability, the text suggests, is the dominant ideology among the Austrian middle classes, and it is deemed to be more important than the individual happiness. The narrator's mother has long since come to terms with her precarious role as a doctor's wife where she is at the mercy of her husband's whims:

> At the lunch table, always the big meal of the day, there was always a certain nervousness noticeable in my mother's voice and gestures after my father had sat down at the table. Mother took the pieces of meat from the pan. I handed her Father's plate. Muttering. Small irritation. Doubts, hesitancy. This piece for Father? No, the lean one for Father. He doesn't like fat. Who says I don't like fat? Why isn't there any soup? Well, says Mother, if I make soup along with meat like this you ask why I made soup. And when I don't then you ask why I didn't make any! A spoonful of soup wouldn't be bad, Father then said diffidently, and Mother would feel guilty. The sword of Damocles was always hovering over her, and that is how it always was at lunch time, and resignation when father didn't finish, helplessness and despair when he pushed back his plate without a word and then declared he wasn't hungry. However, at meals when father was in a good mood we got the same thing laced with witty comments. The glider! First mother defended herself. It wasn't her fault that the goose was too thin. And too old. You just left it in the oven too long and didn't baste it enough. All right then, let's eat. Mother cut up the dry pieces. The word 'glider' came up again and again, and when mother realized that father had forgiven her long ago she joined the laughter and we had wine, and there were other jokes: Is this duck? No, a goose. A glider? When Father felt like it he was magically able to produce a lot of happiness in mother's face. (*Why Is There*: 33–34; *Wie kommt*: 36–37)

The role model that the mother provides for her daughter is one of compliance, weakness, excessive sentimentality, and a tendency to assume that she is always responsible for anything that goes wrong. She finds relief from the constant stress of her familiar role in forms of excessive sentimentality. She cries openly at news stories on the television and during films in the cinema. She collects news cutting about tragedies which she pastes into scrap books. Whenever there is any conflict within the family, she is always quick to assume responsibility. As her daughter – trapped in an unhappy marriage – thinks about suicide, she reflects on how her mother would assume all the guilt for it, since this would be the easiest way out. Yet when her daughter marries, the mother assumes that her daughter's life will be different, since she wrongly supposes that, for the younger generation, relationships have become more equal.

The narrator's sense of being special and her positive identity as a child comes from her father who is respected in the community as the local doctor:

> I was a special child. I wore a green coat with round buttons, we were walking along a green path, Mother and I, to a house with small windows, with people who were unlike us, they were poorer people who recognized immediately that it was an honor, to be allowed to receive mother and me because we were affiliated with Father, and Father was the most important man in town. (*Why Is There*: 27; *Wie kommt*: 30)

When she goes to study in Vienna, she loses this identity. Moreover, she has to withdraw from medicine – the subject that her father has chosen for her – because she cannot cope with dissections. Changing to German, she fails to complete university and looks to marriage with Rolf for a new positive sense of self. In reality she loses all independent identity, but, unlike her mother, cannot come to terms with her new position in which her identity is derived solely from her status as Rolf's wife: 'Occupation: housewife, it says in my new passport. They should have written snail … The greengrocer bows. Madame Diplomingenieur, please, thank you, Frau Doktor, I kiss your hand, Auf Wiedersehen! May I hold the door for Madame? I am not me. I am Rolf's wife' (*Why Is There*: 30–31; *Wie kommt*: 33–34). The young wife comes to realise that this is an exact repetition of how her mother is treated. It is a status that she enjoyed as a child but does not want as an adult, as she learns at first hand the different power relations involved in being a bourgeois wife rather than a bourgeois only child.

In *Wie kommt das Salz ins Meer*, broader social attitudes to married women are compounded by the internal power relations within the family. Echoing a long tradition of German thought on gender difference, Rolf treats his new wife much as she has seen her father treat her mother, that is, like a child rather than an equal. She is unable to confide in Rolf because he distorts everything she says:

> I can't say anything because he squeezes flat whatever I confide to him. He gives me back only the peel: see, this is how empty your contention was. Say something else, I will examine it. See, again it's nothing. There you have it back. And don't always think of your stupid childhood, deal with the present, grow up at last… Rolf, when I was a child, I was looking forward to being an adult… And now I want to go back, I want to return to my mother's womb, when I look at us. (*Why Is There*: 26; *Wie kommt*: 29)

The way Rolf exercises power over her also destroys a previously good sex life, rendering her frigid. She is forced to wonder if she cannot make a success of her marriage because her mother spoilt her as a child. She blames her parents for feeding her myths which did not prepare her for the real world.

Yet in trying to make sense of her marriage, she looks to her mother for advice: 'I ask my mother if it ever happens that a person you picture in a particular way, could suddenly change or if the image was wrong, or if you yourself change. I don't change, she says, your father changed some. I think men change. Only men? Yes, she says' (*Why Is There*: 68; *Wie kommt*: 70). Yet she also realises that her mother, too, puts on a façade which she lets slip if she thinks she is not being watched. Ultimately the mother's support for her daughter remains circumscribed by norms of respectability and traditional family life. When the daughter decides to get divorced, her mother opposes her decision, saying that her daughter cannot do this to the family, that she should think of the gossip, that Rolf is part of the family, and that all marriages have their problems. Blamed by her whole family, the daughter nonetheless goes through with the divorce, moves back to her parents' temporarily, and looks for a job.

Wie kommt das Salz ins Meer suggests that mothers bear a large degree of responsibility for their daughters' future happiness. Echoing feminist critiques of the part that women play in perpetuating patriarchal relations – a theme explored in detail in Mary Daly's work (1979) – the novel shows the dire effects of inadequate role models and the privileging of bourgeois norms of respectability over individual happiness.

A much more radical picture of the distorting effects of the traditional family on mothers and daughters can be found in Jutta Heinrich's novel, *Das Geschlecht der Gedanken* (The Gender of Thoughts), completed in 1972 but first published in 1977.[15] The novel is quite explicit about its feminist project of examining the workings of power, powerlessness, and resistance in mother–daughter relationships, and highlighting the distorting effects of the patriarchal family on women. The first-person narrative examines a family in which an oppressed mother fails to provide a viable long-term role model for her daughter. The mother is depicted as a traditional housewife who is trapped in a marriage where she is abused physically and psychologically by her husband. As such she is despised by her daughter. Yet the effects on the daughter of seeing her mother submit time and time again to an abusive husband are profound. Unlike Brigitte Schwaiger's protagonist, who remains within the bounds of bourgeois respectability, even if she stretches them to the limit by insisting on a divorce, Heinrich's daughter becomes a female avenger: 'She pursues men as perpetrators but also women who, through their meekness, reaffirm and consolidate the power relationship' (Rapisarda 1997: 87). Moreover, Heinrich claims representative status for her protagonist. She writes in her preface to the novel: 'The first-person narrator, representative of my gender, is so deeply and hermetically sealed in an

---

15. For full discussions of this text see Rapisarda 1997 and Kraft and Liebs 1993.

impenetrable normality, in patriarchal earnestness ... that she has to become a distorted mirror of structures of power and powerlessness' (*Geschlecht*: 3).

The investigation of mother–daughter relationships in recent German women's writing can be linked to a broader critique of patriarchy and the family. The theme of the oppressive and distorting nature of the patriarchal family, which predates second-wave feminism, is enduring. It is taken up, for example, in a new, ironic fashion, by Birgit Vanderbeke in *Das Muschelessen* (1993). Published nearly two decades after *Wie kommt das Salz ins Meer*, *Das Muschelessen* depicts family life through the ironic gaze of a teenage daughter. It spans the course of one evening as the mother, son, and daughter await the father's return from a business trip. When he fails to arrive in time for supper at six, the family open the wine and talk increasingly frankly of their experiences of family life. Drinking wine breaks with a family convention according to which only the father would drink alcohol in the evenings. It also radically changes the family's mood and their perception of their lives. The picture created in the course of the evening is of a repressive patriarchal order in which they are all subject to the father's every whim.

Written as a first-person narrative, the text, like *Wie kommt das Salz ins Meer*, shows the interrelation of class and patriarchy. Yet its style is radically different, emphasising ironic distance rather than the subjective working through of experience. The family are originally from the GDR and the father is from particularly humble origins. These factors fuel his desire to be accepted among his middle-class West German colleagues, and to achieve what he believes to be 'proper' family life. He has long been driven by his desire to impress. Thus, for example, when they first come to the West, he gives inordinately large tips, even when the family do not have enough money to last until the end of the month. He does not consider his own wife – who is a school teacher – presentable enough to mix with his colleagues, and never takes her to work socials. Nor does he consider his children's friends good enough for them to be allowed into the home. He is ashamed of his own mother, who still lives in poverty in the GDR. He neither writes to her nor stays with her when they visit her. When she dies, however, he pays for a lavish funeral and headstone, succumbing once again to the need to impress. His behaviour, the novel suggests, has always been governed by his abstract ideals and principles, rather than people's needs or the realities of everyday life. Thus, when his wife becomes pregnant for the third time in the refugee camp in West Germany, the father reproaches her both for her abortion, which he considers immoral, and her subsequent illness, which prevents her from looking after his needs.

On the evening on which the novel is set, the family are expecting the father to return home with a promotion in his pocket. To celebrate the occasion, the mother decides to cook mussels. They are her husband's favourite dish, partly because they were unobtainable in the GDR. The preparation of the mussels, a meal which neither mother nor daughter likes, involves considerable effort, standing bent double over the bath tub scrubbing out the sand under cold running water. Until this evening this preparation had always been undertaken by the wife and husband together. It is the absence of the father, and the uninhibiting effects of the wine, which enable the mother and daughter to reevaluate their family life. As the novel progresses the daughter describes the radical discrepancy between family life when the father is at home and when he is away on business trips. On these latter occasions the family is freed from the pressure to conform to his expectations. The theme of adapting to the father's views and wishes surfaces repeatedly in the novel. It is shown to be the dominant feature of the mother's behaviour as she changes face several times a day. This is something that both daughter and son dislike, and it produces contempt in the children for their mother.

The daughter recounts how, although the mother has a demanding full-time job as a teacher, she is expected to realise her husband's ideas of a proper family. She is a slave to his needs and ideas:

> At home she always had a weary exhausted face, her domestic face. When she came home from school at midday, she said, I'm exhausted today, after six hours of school I don't have much strength left. My father often said, the way you treat your mother, please show her respect. My father tried in vain to fill us with that respect for mother which she herself could not inspire in us. He said, don't you see how she wears herself out for you. She works hard all day long. Of course we saw the hard work and the slaving away, how she carried heavy carriers and bags. In the evening, too, when my father came home, she grafted and slaved away, and when there was no beer in the house, she ran off to get some, cigarettes, too, everything that my father had forgotten to bring home with him, she went out and bought. My father smoked a lot and my mother often had to go for cigarettes. But he couldn't see my mother's exhausted face. She changed to her evening face which she quickly fixed in the bathroom at half-past five before he came home. (*Muschelessen*: 19)

When the father is away on business trips, it is not only the rigorous routine of meals, family walks, opera records, and card games that changes. The three of them get on well, the daughter feels respect for her mother, they share the housework and suit themselves. They do not observe regular meal times and they talk more naturally. There is no longer any adaptation to the father's ideas of what a proper family should be, yet ironically it is only at such times that they achieve anything like a positive sense of family life. Moreover, there is no longer any tale-telling, something the father encourages as he seeks to maintain his absolute power. When the daughter asks her mother why she adapts herself to her husband in this way, the mother says: 'that's what marriage and a profession are like, you'll experience it too' (*Muschelessen*: 20).

Das Muschelessen focuses on a mother who, despite her professional career, fails to provide her daughter with an adequate role model. It shows how all the mother's desires, interests, and preferences are consistently sacrificed to her husband's whims. The mother had wanted to be a violinist, but her husband does not think music a useful thing. The mother hates the furniture chosen by her husband but does not dare tell him since he thinks he has the best of taste. The father insists that they go to Southern Europe every year when the mother would prefer the Alps. Once there, he insists that they stay out in the sun, using every minute of it, even though, unlike him, their skin burns. The mother enjoys concerts but he cancels the subscription once he sees it as no longer socially advantageous. The way in which he goes about this offers a good example of how power functions in the family:

> My father never forbade anything directly. He never said to my mother, 'you're not going to any more concerts,' even if he didn't want her to go. My father would have calmly explained to her that concerts were only something for high-ranking employees, not for those at the top. If my mother didn't understand straight away, because she liked going to concerts so much on account of the beauty, the harmony and the balance, which were very important to my mother, he would have had a cognac and explained it to her once again. Then he would have added: 'Have we understood one another?' and my mother would have hurriedly answered that she understood now... Basically a misunderstanding is impossible in a proper family. (*Muschelessen*: 103)

Like her counterpart in *Wie kommt das Salz ins Meer*, the mother resorts to forms of resistance which are either imaginary or sentimental. For example, as she drinks, she admits to having poisoning fantasies. During family rows – her husband having slammed out of the house – she consoles herself by sitting at the piano and singing Schubert songs. Sometimes she even sabotages her own work, producing dried-up Sunday lunches, or burning the Christmas goose. She is well aware that the domestic labour which she herself resents is not valued by her husband. He despises what he calls 'lowly work', including tasks connected with being a wife and mother, yet he is incapable of managing on the domestic front even when his wife is away on school trips or at parents' evenings.

Despising her compliant mother, the daughter identifies with the powerful figure of the father, a feature of patriarchal societies taken up in much feminist writing. Her brother – a disappointment to his father – is identified with his mother because he is affectionate, clinging, and musical. Moreover, the father blames the mother for what he considers his son's laziness, beating his son for his low marks at school. It is precisely the power relations of the patriarchal family which encourage the daughter to behave as she does:

> I take after my father, I thought, who was a logical man, and my mother and brother were anything but logical. That's why my father and I always made fun of them, and

they were very hesitant about saying anything to me, for example complaining about father, because they thought I would tell on them so that all could see that I was father's daughter. (*Muschelessen*: 24)

The reality, however, is that they all tell tales on each other, and the father, drinking beer and cognac, interviews each family member individually about any misdemeanour while the others have to wait outside the room. He allocates punishments on the basis of a logic that none of them understands, although the daughter pretends that she does. Yet the daughter does not match up to her father's ideas of a proper daughter either, since she is not 'properly' feminine any more than the son is 'properly' masculine. As the evening progresses, and the family communicate openly with each other for the first time, the realisation of what the father's imposition of ideas of 'proper' family life has done to them leads mother, daughter, and son all to conclude that they would prefer it if he never came back: 'Preferably no proper family than one like this' (*Muschelessen*: 64). In the closing pages, as the telephone eventually rings, they do not answer it; the mother simply gets up to throw away the uneaten mussels.

Not all mothers in recent German women's writing provide obviously negative role models for their daughters. Some, for example the narrator in Ingeborg Drewitz's *Eis auf der Elbe* (1982), would appear to fulfil all the requirements for a positive role model. Born in 1926, the mother, like others discussed above, is able to escape the restrictions of traditional feminine roles as a result of the war and its aftermath. She is a highly successful lawyer with her own practice. She is also socially and politically engaged, while fulfilling her domestic duties. Indeed she resembles the superwoman of the 1980s. Written as a diary begun on the death of her husband, the novel focuses on the question of the mother's responsibility for the fate of her three adult daughters. Despite the apparently excellent role model that she provided, each one has ended up in an exploitative relationship with a man. Her eldest daughter, Christine, has betrayed her own youthful idealism and lives with the unemployed father of her children, who beats her. She now works in the very same chemical factory outside of which she used to demonstrate against environmental pollution. Her second daughter, Leonie, lives with her older husband as a traditional housewife and mother. Her youngest daughter, Almuth, has moved into a squat in order to stay with a man who no longer wants to live alone with her. The diary traces the fate of the daughters back to familial relations governed by a lack of openness. As in *Das Muschelessen*, there has been little or no real communication between family members. The mother did not love her husband nor find him sexually fulfilling and she remained with him for the sake of the children. This compromise finds an echo in the situations of her daughters, who, unlike her, do not have a professional career as compensation. The lack of openness characteristic of the daughters' homelife as children continues to govern their adult relationship with their mother, who concludes that their lives will only change once they acknowledge their problems.

Conclusion

The turn to the theme of mothers and daughters in recent German women's writing cannot be understood without reference to second-wave feminism. Prior to the rebirth of the women's movement there was no identifiable tradition of mother–daughter novels within women's writing. Among the effects of the movement was a new concern in fiction with a range of issues central to second-wave feminism. Among these issues were motherhood and mother–daughter relationships. The cross-generational focus of mother–daughter narratives has served to document a hidden history of women in the family.

The spate of novels which have appeared since the late 1960s are predominantly autobiographical in character, a factor that has important implications for the ways in which they are written. They are concerned first and foremost to give realistic accounts of experiences long hidden from view. Stylistically relatively simple, often written in the first-person and with little use of metaphor, they implicitly claim truth status via their straightforward narrative techniques.

Whereas writers like Wolf and Sanders-Brahms focus on similarities and changes across generations in relation to the immediate social and political contexts in which the mothers and daughters find themselves, other writers privilege the internal dynamics of familial relationships. For the most part, their focus is on the negative dimensions of mother–daughter relations. For writers such as Novak, Mitgutsch, and Jelinek, this focus produces disturbing accounts of destructive mother–daughter relationships which often mark the women concerned for life. These abusive and exploitative relationships are traced to the unsatisfactory position of mothers and daughters within patriarchal societies.

Unlike traditional representations of women, mothering in these novels is not depicted as a natural female attribute. Rather it is a learned process in which daughters draw on their own childhood experience. Moreover, its undervaluing by society, together with widespread negative social attitudes to the female body, create problems for the women concerned. These problems are further compounded by the power structures that make the traditional family a negative environment for both mothers and daughters. Novels such as those by Schwaiger and Vanderbeke, which focus on the traditional patriarchal family, explore this position in some detail. The autobiographical elements in these novels, depicted as they are from a feminist perspective, work against positive images of mother–daughter relations. Moreover, the problems with which mother–daughter novels deal all have their source in the social position of women. This has been the central focus of feminist theory, research, and writing since the late 1960s, and it finds a particularly sharp articulation in fictional depictions of mother–daughter relationships. In some cases – for example, the work of Karin Struck – writers combine theoretical insights and documentary material with an imaginative evocation of motherhood as experience and institution. Yet the picture remains a predominantly negative one. For Struck, as for most feminist writers, the only answer to the problems of mothers and daughters would be a radical shift in social and cultural attitudes to women in general, and mothers in particular. Only then would mother–daughter relations be freed from the oppressive and distorting power of patriarchy.

Bibliography

Braidotti, Rosi (1991) *Patterns of Dissonance*. Oxford: Polity.
Chodorow, Nancy (1978) *The Reproduction of Mothering: Psychoanalysis and the Sociology of Gender*. Berkeley: University of California Press.
Cixous, Hélène and Catherine Clément (1987) *The Newly Born Woman*, trans. Betsy Wing. Manchester: Manchester University Press (orig. *La Jeune Née*, Paris: Union Générale d'Éditions, 1975).
Daly, Mary (1979) *Gyn/Ecology*. London: The Women's Press.
Dohm, Hedwig (1982) *Emanzipation*. Zürich: ala Verlag (orig. 1874).
Drewitz, Ingeborg (1982) *Eis auf der Elbe*. Düsseldorf: Claassen.
Fiddler, Allyson (1994) *Rewriting Reality: An Introduction to Elfriede Jelinek*. Oxford: Berg.
—— (1997) 'Reading Elfriede Jelinek' in Weedon (ed.) 1997, 291–304.
Filser, Franz (ed.) (1977) *Die Frau in der Gesellschaft*. Stuttgart: Reclam.
Freud, Sigmund (1977) *On Sexuality*. Harmondsworth: Penguin.
Gerhard, Ute (1990) *Unerhört. Die Geschichte der deutschen Frauenbewegung*. Reinbek bei Hamburg: Rowohlt.
Heinrich, Jutta (1977) *Das Geschlecht der Gedanken*. Munich: Frauenoffensive.
—— (1984) *The Gender of Thoughts* (extract), trans. Jeanette Clausen, in Edith Hoshino Altbach, Jeanette Clausen, Naomi Stephann, and Dagmar Schultz (eds) *German Feminism. Readings in Politics and Literature*. Albany: State University of New York Press, 276–83.
Irigaray, Luce (1985) *This Sex Which is Not One*, trans. Catherine Porter with Carolyn Burke. New York: Cornell University Press (orig. *Ce Sexe qui n'en est pas un*. Paris: Minuit, 1977).
—— (1991a) *The Irigaray Reader*, ed. and intro. Margaret Whitford. Oxford: Blackwell.

——— (1991b) 'Women-Mothers, the Silent Substratum of the Social Order' in Irigaray 1991a, 47–52 (orig. 1981).
Jelinek, Elfriede (1983) *Die Klavierspielerin*. Reinbek bei Hamburg: Rowohlt. *The Piano Teacher*, trans. Joachim Neugroschel. New York: Weidenfeld and Nicholson, 1988.
Kraft, Helga and Elke Liebs (eds) (1993) *Mütter, Töchter, Frauen. Weiblichkeitsbilder in der Literatur*. Stuttgart und Weimar: Verlag J.B. Metzler.
Kristeva, Julia (1986) 'Stabat Mater' in *The Kristeva Reader*, ed. Toril Moi. Oxford: Blackwell, 160–87 (originally published as 'Hérethique de l'amour' in *Tel Quel*, 74, Winter 1977, 30–49).
Lacan, Jacques (1977) *Écrits. A Selection*, trans. A Sheridan. London: Tavistock.
Lange, Helene (1977) 'Intellektuelle Grenzlinien zwischen Mann und Frau' in Filser (ed.) 1977, 49–50 (orig. 1899).
Meyer, Franziska (1997) 'Women's Writing in Occupied Germany, 1945–1949' in Weedon (ed.) 1997, 25–43.
Mitgutsch, Waltraud Anna (1987) *Die Züchtigung*. Düsseldorf: Claassen (orig. 1985). *Punishment*, trans. Lisel Müller. London: Virago, 1987. First published in the United States under the title *Three Daughters*, New York: Harcourt Brace Jovanovich, 1987.
Möbius, Paul J. (1907) *Über den physiologischen Schwachsinn des Weibes*. Halle a. d. S.: Marhold (orig. 1900).
Novak, Helga M. (1979) *Die Eisheiligen*. Darmstadt und Neuwied: Luchterhand.
Rapisarda, Cettina (1997) 'Women's Writing, 1968–1980' in Weedon (ed.) 1997, 77–100.
Rich, Adrienne (1976) *Of Woman Born: Motherhood as Experience and Institution*. New York: W.W. Norton and Co.
Roebling, Irmgard and Wolfram Mauser (1996) *Mutter und Mütterlichkeit. Wandel und Wirksamkeit einer Phantasie in der deutschen Literatur*. Würzburg: Königshausen und Neumann.
Runge, Erika (1970) *Frauen. Versuche zur Emanzipation*. Frankfurt a. M.: Suhrkamp.
Sanders-Brahms, Helma (1980) *Deutschland, bleiche Mutter*. Reinbek bei Hamburg: Rowohlt.
Schmidt, Ricarda (1996) 'Die böse Mutter. Zur Ästhetik sadomasochistischer Mutter-Töchter-Beziehungen in literarischen Texten aus dem Kontext der Frauenbewegung' in Roebling and Mauser 1996, 347–58.
Schopenhauer, Artur (1977) *Über die Weiber* in Filser (ed.) 1977, 28–31 (orig. 1851).
Schroeder, Margot (1975) *Ich stehe meine Frau*. Published in collaboration with the Hamburger Werkstatt schreibender Arbeiter. Frankfurt a. M.: Fischer.
Schwaiger, Brigitte (1979) *Wie kommt das Salz ins Meer* (orig. 1977). Reinbek bei Hamburg: Rowohlt. *Why Is There Salt in the Sea?*, trans. Sieglinde Lug. Lincoln: University of Nebraska Press, 1988.
Schwarzer, Alice (1975) *Der 'kleine Unterschied' und seine große Folgen. Frauen über sich-Beginn einer Befreiung*. Frankfurt a. M.: Fischer.
Struck, Karen (1975) *Die Mutter*. Frankfurt a. M.: Suhrkamp.

Vanderbeke, Birgit (1993) *Das Muschelessen*. Berlin: Rotbuch Verlag.
Weedon, Chris (1999) 'Confronting the Past: Christa Wolf's *Kindheitsmuster*' in Helmut Peitsch, Charles Burdett, and Claire Gorrara (eds) *European Memories of the Second World War*. Oxford: Berghahn, 238–46.
Weedon, Chris (ed.) (1997) *Postwar Women's Writing in German. Feminist Critical Approaches*. Oxford: Berghahn Books.
Weigel, Sigrid (1989) *Die Stimme der Medusa. Schreibweisen in der Gegenwartsliteratur von Frauen*. Reinbek bei Hamburg: Rowohlt.
Wohmann, Gabriele (1976) *Ausflug mit der Mutter*. Darmstadt und Neuwied: Luchterhand.
Wolf, Christa (1976) *Kindheitsmuster*. Berlin und Weimar: Aufbau Verlag. *A Model Childhood*, trans. Ursule Molinaro and Hedwig Rappolt. London: Virago, 1988.

INDEX

abandonment (of and by mother), 14, 16, 54, 58, 72, 98, 107, 123, 131, 138, 139, 186
Abel, Elizabeth, 22
abjection (maternal), 15, 20, 105–6, 108–9, 187. *See also* Kristeva
abortion, 17, 23, 24, 24n, 27, 58, 138, 161, 226, 237, 243
abortion laws: Britain, 23; France, 180–81; Ireland, 87, 88n. 7, 106; Italy, 149; Spain, 48–50
'Absolutely Fabulous', 206
Accati, Luisa, 18n. 7, 120
Ackelsberg, Mary, 48
adultery, 49, 54, 57, 58, 59. *See also* Family Romance
Aeschylus, *Oresteia*, 13
affidamento (entrustment), 16–18, 66n, 120
aggression (vs. reparation), 20, 26, 31, 57, 120, 204. *See also* Klein
Alborg, Concha, 48n. 3, 52, 65, 70, 72, 73
Alcalde, Carmen, 48, 48n. 2
Aldecoa, Josefina
 Historia de una maestra, 73
 La enredadera, 65–66
 La fuerza del destino, 51, 73–76
 Mujeres de negro, 73
Allen, Isobel, 34n. 21
Alós, Concha, *Os habla Electra*, 72
Altolaguirre, P.U. (and Méndez),
 Memorias habladas, memorias armadas, 71n
Amazons, 62
 rewriting of myth, 37
Andersen, Hans Christian, *The Snow Queen*, 194
Anderson, Benedict, 2n
anger
 daughter's, 33, 95, 107, 112, 130, 177, 194, 195, 204
 mother's, 33, 56, 59, 86, 112, 139, 175, 228
Aniston, Nancy, 34n. 20
anorexia, 139, 146–47, 148

Apter, Terry, 7
Arcana, Judith, 12n. 2, 33n
Arditti, Rita, 37n
Arendt, Hanna, 17, 122
Arkinstall, Christine, 49n. 5, 57, 64n. 17
Arnau, Carme, 57
artificial womb, 39, 39n
Atkinson, Kate, *Behind the Scenes at the Museum*, 189, 202, 204–6
attachment (daughter's to mother), 19, 19n, 21, 121, 122–32, 148, 188. *See also* desire, separation
Austen, Jane, 1, 185
Bachofen, J.J., 62, 120
Baisnée, Valérie, 171, 172
Balaguer, Soledad, 50n. 7
Balakrishnan, Gopal, 2n
Barberá, Carmen, *Adolescente*, 57, 60–61
Bardini, Marco, 125, 125n
Barrachina, María, 49
Bart, Pauline, 22
bastard, myth of, 53, 132–33, 137–38. *See also* illegitimacy, Family Romance
Beaumont, Caitriona, 88n. 8
Beauvoir, Françoise de, 159, 178
Beauvoir, Simone de, 4n, 157, 173
 La Femme rompue, 160
 Le Deuxième sexe, 11, 155, 157
 Mémoires d'une jeune fille rangée, 157, 158–64, 168, 169, 172, 179, 180, 180n. 27
 Une mort très douce, 178, 179n. 23, 191
Beckett, Mary
 'Failing Years', 93n
 'Inheritance', 111n
 'Under Control', 93n
Benjamin, Jessica, 24, 25–27, 29, 30, 100n. 18, 121–22. *See also* intersubjectivity
Benstock, Shari, 60
Bert, Paul, 165n. 12

Bildungsroman, 56, 88, 93, 112, 143, 149n. 22, 202
Bimbi, Franca, 24n
binarism
 gender, 27, 38
 mind/body, 68, 217
 in patriarchal thought, 176, 217
 in writing the mother, 163, 165, 173, 176, 177, 178–79, 181, 208
birth control, 23, 27, 200; France, 180, 180n. 26; Italy, 149; Spain, 50, 50n. 8
birth-rates: France, 180n. 26; Italy, 24, 24n, 149, 149n. 23; Spain, 50
Bjerrum Nielsen, Harriet, 23
Blake, William, 202
Blelloch, Paola, 135n
Boccia, Maria Luisa, 39
body (female/maternal), 27n. 15, 39, 63, 135, 195, 237–38
 and language/writing, 13, 15, 27, 30, 63, 66, 69. *See also écriture féminine*
 lesbian, 61, 63
 vs. mind. *See* binarism
 mother's, as object of daughter's love, 135. *See also* desire
 mother's, rejected by daughter, 192
 pregnant, 235, 237
Boixadós, María Dolores, *Gabriel: Coda final*/'La madre', 72–73
Boland, Eavan, 87n. 3
Bordons, Teresa, 53
Borreguero, Concha, 48n. 2
Bosio, Laura
 Annunciazione, 149
 I dimenticati, 149n. 22
Bourke Dowling, Shirley, 34n. 21
Bowen, Elizabeth, 96, 185, 186n
 The House in Paris, 186
Boylan, Clare
 'A Model Daughter', 110n
 Home Rule, 93n

– 251 –

Index

Braidotti, Rosi, 3n, 69, 239n
Bravo, Anna, 120
Breen, Mary, 99n
Brenkman, John, 18n. 7
Breuilly, John, 2n
Broner, E.M., 4, 4n, 100n. 19
Bruck, Edith, *Lettera alla madre*, 144, 144n
Bulgheroni, Marisa, 'Gli Orti della Regina', 144
bulimia, 145, 147. *See also* anorexia
Butler, Victoria, *Xenogenesis*, 38n
Camaiti-Hostert, Anna, 3
Capel Martínez, Rosa María, 50, 53n
Caplan, Paula J., 12n. 2
Capmany, María Aurèlia, 48n. 2
Carbonell, Neus, 52
Cardinal, Marie, 157, 173, 179n. 24
  Les Mots pour le dire, 164–68, 171, 172, 176, 180, 180n. 26, 181
Carroll, Lewis, 96
Carter, Angela, 210
Castillo, Debra, 71
castration, 75, 233
  women's cultural, 55, 75
Catholicism, 18n. 7, 31, 48, 52, 57, 87, 106, 119–20, 124, 136, 165–67, 180, 230. *See also* religion
Cavarero, Adriana, 18, 30, 121n. 1, 122, 125, 139
Cela, Camilo José, *La familia de Pascual Duarte*, 52
Centro Documentazione Donna di Firenze (Florence Women's Cultural Centre), 18, 121n. 1
Cerati, Carla, *La cattiva figlia*, 143, 148, 148n. 21
Chacel, Rosa, *Memorias de Leticia Valle*, 50–51, 53–56, 57, 58, 68
Chamberlayne, Prue, 24n, 120
Charnas, Suzy McKee, *Motherlines*, 36, 37–38
Chasseguet-Smirgel, Janine, 27n. 14
Chawaf, Chantal, *Retable/La Rêverie*, 158, 178
Chemello, Adriana, 142n
Chester, Suzanne, 171
Chodorow, Nancy, 20–23, 24, 25, 26, 27n. 14, 60, 141, 188n, 191–92, 235, 237
Ciplijauskaité, Birutė, 71
Cixous, Hélène, 15n, 236
  on binarism, 176
  and critical practice, 22, 30n
  on *écriture féminine*, 15, 29, 63
  and female imaginary, 67
  (and Clément), *La Jeune Née* 176, 193, 236
  Le Livre de Promethea, 158
  and realism, 30
Clancy-Smith, Julia, 165
Clear, Caitriona, 87n. 5
Clément, Catherine (and Cixous), *La Jeune Née*, 176, 193, 236
Clytemnestra, 13, 86
Coakley, Anne, 87n. 6

Cohen, Emma, *Toda la casa era una ventana*, 71
Colette, 4n, 158n
colonialism
  colonial tales, 32, 164–73, 207
  decolonisation, 2
  and Ireland, 86
Connolly, Linda, 88n. 8
Constitution of Ireland, 87–88
contextualisation
  of mother, 30, 122, 140, 167–68, 171–72, 176, 177, 190
  of mother–daughter relationships, 2, 4, 6, 29, 31, 158, 164, 166, 171, 177
contraception. *See* birth control
Contratto, Susan, 26
Corbin, Laurie, 158n, 159, 169n. 16, 170n. 18, 172
Cornelio, Valeria (and Violi), *Di madre in peggio*, 149n. 24
Corva, Lisa, 148n. 19
Coulson, Anthony, 3n. 3
Council of Trent/Counter Reformation, 119
Criado, Azucena, 50n. 8
criticism, inspired by: Chodorow/object-relations theory, 21–22; Cixous, 15, 22; Flax, 24; Irigaray, 22; Klein, 20; Kristeva, 15, 22. *See also* contextualisation, Hirsch
Daly, Brenda O., 73
Daly, Ita, 111n
  A Singular Attraction, 93n
  Ellen, 93n
Daly, Mary, 87n. 6, 217, 217n. 5, 242
daughter
  adolescent/teenager, 7, 37, 60, 63, 106, 126, 134, 142, 147, 169, 177, 186, 243
  devouring, 88, 97, 100, 111
  dutiful, 51–52
  good/bad, 31, 148n. 21, 186, 187, 195, 198, 199n
  'good enough', 51, 56–57, 61
  immigrant, 173–76, 207–8
  Jewish, 32, 142–43, 144, 194
  lawless/rebel, 95, 96, 112, 186
  lesbian. *See* lesbianism
  and melancholia/psychosis, 14, 15, 25, 26, 89, 93, 104, 113, 123, 126. *See also* madness
  monstrous/perverted, 96–100
  See also attachment, dereliction, desire, mother–daughter bond, mother–daughter relationship, separation, sexuality, subjectivity
Daumard, Adeline, 180
Davidson, Cathy N., 4, 4n, 100n. 19
Davies, Catherine, 48n. 2, 65, 70, 71n, 72n
death (mother's), 51, 89, 91, 92–93, 95, 100, 101–3, 113, 125, 128–29, 131, 144, 145, 146, 148, 149, 176, 177, 178, 189–90, 191–92, 196, 231

defilement/denigration (of mother), 15, 22, 30–31, 94, 113, 148, 150, 237–38, 244.
  See also abjection, idealisation
Delgado Capeans, R.P., 49n. 5
De Luca, Laura, *Vuota per sempre. Appunti dall'anoressia*, 146–47, 148, 149
Demeter–Persephone myth
  feminist readings of, 59n. 11
  rewriting of, 32, 51, 52, 57, 59, 62, 124, 192–93, 200
dereliction (daughter's), 14, 89, 107, 107n, 123. *See also* Irigaray
desire (sexual, female), 15, 19, 86, 94–95, 101
  daughter's for maternal body, 16, 33, 122, 125, 127, 128, 129–30, 131–32
  daughter's vs. mother's, 169–70
  mother's, 16, 21, 27, 33, 74, 99, 109, 122, 125, 127, 131, 134, 190
Deutsch, Helen, 19
Devlin, Anne, 111n
Díaz-Más, Paloma, 'La niña sin alas', 73
Dickens, Charles, 206
Di Lascia, Mariateresa, *Passaggio in ombra*, 132–34
Dinnerstein, Dorothy, 12n. 2, 21, 27n. 14
Diotima, 17, 27n. 15, 30, 121, 121n. 1
Diski, Jenny
  Like Mother, 189, 197–99
  Skating to Antarctica, 189, 190, 194–96, 199
divorce, 17, 27, 34, 166, 167, 239, 242
divorce laws (Spain), 48–49
Djura, 157, 179n. 24
  Le Voile du silence, 173–76, 180, 181
Doane, Janice, 22
Dohm, Hedwig, 216, 216n. 3
Donnawomanfemme, Aliene Quotidiane, 38n
Donoghue, Emma, 111n
Drabble, Margaret
  The Millstone, 188
  The Waterfall, 188
Duelli Klein, Renate, 37n
Dunn, Nell, *Poor Cow*, 188
Dupláa, Christina, 71
Duranti, Francesca, *La bambina*, 121
Duras, Marguerite, 157, 158n, 173, 179nn. 24, 25
  L'Amant, 164, 168–72, 176, 179, 179n. 25, 180, 180n. 27
  L'Amant de la Chine du Nord, 178–79
  Un Barrage contre le pacifique, 171–72
écriture féminine. *See* Cixous
Eichenbaum, Luise, 7
Electra, rewriting of myth, 13, 72
Eliot, George, 185

– 252 –

Index

Elsner, Gisela, 218n
Erdheim, Claudia, 218
Ernaux, Anne
   Je ne suis pas sortie de ma nuit, 177
   Une femme, 158, 176–77, 178
ethnicity, 1, 2n, 3, 4, 22, 29, 32, 164, 172, 189, 207–8. *See also* identity, contextualisation
European Union, 2–4, 5
   and Spain, 50
exile, 3, 73, 95
   in literature, 3n. 3
   mother–daughter e. in patriarchy, 63, 128, 156, 161, 163, 166, 166n, 168
experimentalism
   vs. realism, 15, 30n
   in writing mother–daughter relationships, 29–30, 63, 67–68, 143, 177
fairy tale, 69, 113, 178, 189, 202
Falcón, Lidia, 50
Fallaci, Oriana, 121, 121n. 2
Fallaize, Elizabeth, 178n
Family Romance/*familienroman*, 53, 80, 94, 125, 125n, 205n
   feminist, 103, 109–113, 163n. 8, 205n
   heterosexual, 186
   rewriting of, by women writers, 29, 53, 58, 94–95, 101, 107, 109, 114, 136
   See also foundling fantasy, Hirsch
father
   daughter's desire for, 53, 33, 86n. 2, 95, 95n, 161
   daughter's rejection of, in Spanish narrative, 53–58
   discredited, in Irish narrative, 86n. 1
   in Italian culture, 32, 119, 126, 134
   murder of, 13, 189n
   paternal symbolic/Law-of-the-Father, 12, 13, 14, 17, 27n. 15, 95, 132
   as third term, 20, 21, 27, 27n. 14, 188n
   See also Lacan, Family Romance
Faust, 199–200
feminism/feminist movements, 5, 14, 17, 21, 23–24, 27–28, 29
   Britain, 23
   France, 157–58, 176
   Germany, 215, 216–17, 218, 234–35, 239, 243, 247
   Ireland, 88, 88n. 8
   Italy, 16–18, 120–21, 142–43
   postcolonial, 164n. 9
   Spain, 48, 48n. 2, 50, 70
Ferguson, Ann, 68
Ferrante, Elena, *L'amore molesto*, 122, 126, 128–31
Ferraro, Fausta, 146n
Ferrières-Pestureau, Suzanne, 169n. 17
Fiddler, Allyson, 230n, 233
Figuera, Ángela, 49n. 5
Filser, Franz, 216n. 2

Firestone, Shulamith, 36, 37n, 39n
Flaubert, Gustave, 59
Flax, Jane, 7, 24–25, 27n. 14, 58, 74, 75
Folguera, Pilar, 48n. 2
Formica, Mercedes, 49
   A instancia de parte, 49
   'Bodoque', 48n. 3
   La hija de Don Juan de Austria, 70
   La infancia, 48n. 3
   María de Mendoza. Solución a un enigma amoroso, 70
Forster, Margaret
   Hidden Lives, 190n
   Private Papers, 197
foundling fantasy/plot, 53, 195, 205n
Fouquet, Catherine, 180
Franco dictatorship, 47–50, 51, 52, 56, 64, 70, 73, 74
Freixas, Laura, *Madres e hijas*, 76
Freud, Anna, 19
Freud, Sigmund, 1, 13, 18, 18n. 7, 19, 19n, 20, 29, 53–54, 58, 94, 95n, 107, 125n, 126, 129, 129n. 7, 147, 157, 161n. 6, 188n, 191, 205n, 209, 216, 233, 235, 237. *See also* Family Romance, Oedipus complex
Friday, Nancy, *My Mother/Myself*, 12
Gaglianone, Paola, 141
Gallego Méndez, María Teresa, 49
Gallop, Jane, 95n
Galvarriato, Eulalia, *Cinco sombras*, 52
Gardiner, Judith K., 189n
Garner, Shirley Nelson, 4, 4n, 22, 56
Garnett, Angelica, *Deceived with Kindness*, 197
Gascón Vera, Elena, 72
Gearhart, Sally Miller, *The Wanderground*, 36
Gellner, Ernest, 2n
genealogy (female/maternal), 13, 17, 51, 62, 70–71, 75, 93, 134, 138, 142–43, 155–56, 177, 178, 187, 188n. *See also* Irigaray, maternal legacy
Gerhard, Ute, 217n. 4
Gilligan, Carol, 7
Gilmore, Leigh, 63
Giorgio, Adalgisa, 18n. 6, 66n, 121n. 1, 128n, 144, 144n
Glenn, Kathleen, 53, 72n
Glover, Jonathan, 37n
Goddard, Victoria, 5, 129n. 9
Gómez Ojea, Carmen, *Otras mujeres y Fabia*, 71
Gorrara, Claire, 3n. 3
Gothic plot, 31, 96, 101–3, 104, 196, 199
Gould Levine, Linda, 64
Goutalier, Régine, 164n. 10, 172
Graham, Helen, 48, 50
Grandes, Almudena
   'Amor de madre', 57

'La buena hija', 57
Graves, Robert, 62
Great (Mediterranean) Mother, 71, 72, 120
Green, Jen (and Lefanu), *Despatches from the Frontiers of the Female Mind*, 210
Green, Miranda, 89n
Greene, Gayle, 187
Groen, Martine, 7
Grosz, Elizabeth, 59n. 11, 63, 167
Guacci, Rosaria, 128n
Guild, Elizabeth, 63
Guzmán, Eduardo de, 49n. 6
Hagar, 136–37
Haigh, Samantha, 167n, 168
Hall, Colette, 179, 152
Hall, Nor, 32n
Hall, Stuart, 2n
Hammer, Signe, 12n. 2
Hansen, Elaine Tuttle, 110
Harding, Esther, 32n
Hardy, Barbara, 200
Hargreaves, Alec, 173
Hegel, G.W.E., 26n. 12
Heinrich, Jutta, 218, 219
   Das Geschlecht der Gedanken, 242–43
Herbert, Máire, 89n
Herman, Nini, 12n. 2, 32n
hero, myth of, 132, 132n, 136–38. *See also* bastard
Heron, Liz, 209–10
heterosexuality, 21, 22, 27, 33, 62, 98–99, 186
   compulsory, 61
   in science fiction, 36
   See also lesbianism, sexuality
Higonnet, Margaret, 129
Hildegart, 49, 49n. 6
Hirsch, Marianne, 1–2, 4, 13, 21n, 33, 53, 58, 59n. 11, 60, 74n, 86, 89, 94, 163n. 8, 169n. 16, 170n. 18, 172, 186, 205n
Hobsbawm, Eric J., 2n
Hodges, Devon, 22
Hoggart, Richard, 191
Holocaust narratives, 101n. 20, 144, 221n
Homans, Margaret, 22
homosexuality, 27, 33, 34, 64n. 16, 98–99, 203. *See also* heterosexuality, lesbianism
Horney, Karen, 19
Huber, Grischa, 220
Hughes, Alex, 158, 159, 160
Humm, Maggie, 186n, 188
Hyvrard, Jeanne, *Mère la mort*, 158
Ibárruri, Dolores, *El único camino*, 49n. 5
idealisation (of mother)
   by daughters, 22, 30–32, 143, 148, 150
   by Freud, 19
   See also defilement
identity
   'core', 24
   crisis/dissolution of, 3–4
   cultural, 2n, 143

– 253 –

Index

female, 7, 16, 21, 22, 24, 75, 86, 88, 89, 90, 100, 106, 140, 156, 157, 188, 241
gender, 7, 21, 24, 25, 27, 38
and language, 67
lesbian, 62, 64, 203, 204
matrilinear, 70, 72
national/regional, 2–3
women's social/political, 87
See also ethnicity
illegitimacy, 22, 57, 86, 132, 132n, 136–37, 191, 194, 196. *See also* adultery, bastard, Family Romance
imaginary
creation of a new female/maternal, 14, 18, 34, 67, 69, 119, 121
current maternal, 31, 120, 149
Greek, 124
Judaeo-Christian, 124
Irish, 87–89
Italian, 120, 149
See also symbolic order
incest, 33, 95, 101, 132, 133. *See also* sexual abuse
infertility, 23, 34–35, 110n, 226. *See also* birth-rates, reproductive technologies
Ingman, Heather, 4n, 186n
intersubjectivity/recognition
vs. domination/submission, 26, 26nn. 12, 13, 97, 124, 159, 233
female-to-female, 14, 156–57, 162, 163n. 8, 164, 166
mother–child, 24, 25–27
mother–daughter, 29, 31, 32, 34, 121–22, 124–25, 143–44, 149, 155, 158, 163n. 8, 174–75
See also Benjamin
Ireland as Mother, 87
Irigaray, Luce, 13–16, 155–57, 209, 233, 236
critique of psychoanalysis/philosophy, 13, 14n, 119, 217, 217n. 5
on daughter's dereliction, 14, 107, 107n, 123
on debt to mother, 13, 70
eurocentrism/universalism of I.'s work, 164, 164n. 9, 174
on female body/desire and language/creativity, 15, 16, 66, 86, 128, 156
on female genealogies, 119, 155
on female imaginary, 14
on female symbolic, 14, 51, 66, 156, 168, 239, 239n
on female-to-female relations, 14, 86, 155, 162, 166, 168, 174
influence of, on Italian feminism, 16, 17, 18
on inscription of femininity in culture, 15
on matricide, 13, 51, 86
on mother–daughter relationships, 14, 16, 51, 63,

86, 97, 107, 119, 155–57, 162, 168–69, 175
on sexual difference, 156
on women/mothers in patriarchy, 16, 68, 93, 156, 167, 168, 178
on women's reproductive capacities, 163n. 7
Islam, 165, 165n. 11, 173
IVF (*in vitro* fertilisation), 23, 34–35, 36. *See also* reproductive technologies
Jackson, Pauline Conroy, 34n. 21
Janeczek, Helena, *Lezioni di tenebra*, 144
Jardine, Alice, 160n. 3, 179n. 23
Jelinek, Elfriede, 218, 219, 247
Die Klavierspielerin, 230, 232–33
Jewishness, 32, 141–43, 144, 194, 224
Jiménez, Vicente, 49n. 5
Jocasta, 86
Jones, Margaret, 51
Josefowitz Siegel, Rachel, 73
jouissance (female), 14n, 92, 122, 169, 170
in pregnancy, 23
Joyce, James, 86n. 2, 108
Jung, Carl G., 91n. 12
Kahn, Coppélia, 22
Kahane, Claire, 22, 57
Kaplan, Caren, 3n. 3
Kaplan, E. Ann, 53, 196n
Kaufman, Franz-Xaver, 28n
Keane, Molly, 99n, 113
Good Behaviour, 93, 96–100
Loving and Giving, 96n
Loving Without Tears, 96n
Keane, Patrick, 87n. 3
Kearney, Richard, 87n. 3
Kelly, A.A., 90n. 11
Kelly, Maeve, 'Orange Horses', 109, 111–12, 113
'Kerry Babies' tribunal, 88n. 7
Kiberd, Declan, 86n. 1
Kirkpatrick, Susan, 53
Klein, Melanie, 19–20, 26n. 13, 27n. 14, 177
and art/criticism, 20
Knering, Amanda, xi
Mia madre era una donna, 138–41, 142
Knibiehler, Yvonne, 164n. 10, 172, 180
Koch, Francesca, 120
Kraft, Helga, 215n, 230n, 242n
Krieger-Krynicki, Annie, 174n. 20
Krips, Madelien, 7
Kristeva, Julia, 15n, 209, 217, 217n. 5, 236
and critical practice/experimental writing, 15, 22, 30n
on cult of the Virgin, 23–24, 31
on daughter's linguistic/psychic disorder, 15. *See also* daughter, madness
on father, 27n. 14
on maternal abjection, 15, 20, 105–6, 108, 187

on motherhood/pregnancy, 15, 23–24, 33n, 90, 155, 233
on semiotic, 15, 103
Lacan, Jacques, 1, 13–14, 18n. 7, 22, 157, 235
Laforet, Carmen, *Nada*, 52
Lagorio, Gina, 121, 121n. 2
Lampl-de Groot, Jeanne, 19n
Lange, Helene, 217
Laronde, Marc, 174n. 21
Larraburu, Carmen, 50n. 7
Lavin, Mary, 89–90, 91–93, 113
'A Family Likeness', 92, 93
'Happiness', 92–93
'Lilacs', 91n. 13
Mary O'Grady, 90–91, 93
'The Nun's Mother', 91n. 13
Lázaro, Reyes, 53, 56
Le Clézio, Marguerite, 166n
Leduc, Violette, 4n, 160, 173, 180n. 27
La Bâtarde, 160, 178
L'Asphyxie, 160, 178–79
Ravages, 157, 158, 160–62, 163–64, 172, 179, 180, 180n. 27, 181
Lee-Bonanno, Lucy, 61, 72
Lefanu, Sarah, 36, 210n
(and Green) *Despatches from the Frontiers of the Female Mind*, 210
Leggott, Sarah J., 70
Le Guin, Ursula, *The Left Hand of Darkness*, 38n
Lehmann, Rosamond, *The Ballad and the Source*, 186
Leira, Halldis, 7
Lentin, Ronit, *Songs on the Death of Children*, 101n. 20
lesbianism, 27, 33, 98–99
in French narrative, 160–61
in English narrative, 203–4
in German narrative, 218
in Irish narrative, 99n
in Italian narrative, 144–45
in Spanish narrative, 61–64
See also heterosexuality, homosexuality, identity
Lessing, Doris, 185, 186–87, 209, 210
A Proper Marriage, 187
Diary of a Good Neighbour, 187
'Impertinent Daughters', 193–94
Martha Quest, 187
Memoirs of a Survivor, 187
The Four-Gated City, 187
The Good Terrorist, 187
The Summer Before the Dark, 187
Under My Skin, 187, 193
Levi della Torre, Stefano, 143
Lewis, Jane, 28n
Libreria delle donne di Milano (Milan Women's Bookshop Collective), 16, 18n. 6, 120–21
Lidoff, Joan, 22
Liebs, Elke, 215n, 230n, 242n
Lionnet, Françoise, 165n. 13, 168
Lively, Penelope, *Moon Tiger*, 197

– 254 –

Index

Llobera, Josep R., 5
London Women's Therapy Centre, 7
Longley, Edna, 87n. 3
Lonzi, Carla, 17
Lovenduski, Joni, 28n
Loy, Rosetta, *La porta dell'acqua*, 121
Lugnani, Lucio, 126
Lumley, Joanna, 206
Lynch, Rachel Jane, 106n
Macaulay, Rose, 186n
Maclean, Marie, 132, 132n, 136, 137, 138
Madden, Deirdre, 101n. 21, 111, 113, 114
  The Birds of the Innocent Wood, 101–4, 197
madness
  daughter's, 86, 103, 132, 134
  mother's, 32, 167–68, 170–72, 196, 201
  women's, 167n
Madonna
  and child icon, 31, 119–20, 124
  as ideal of motherhood, 31, 56, 120, 149, 202
  in maternal trinity, 136
  See also Virgin Mary
Mangini, Shirley, 48, 53
Mantel, Hilary, 206
Maraini, Dacia, 121, 121n. 2
Marchi, Ena, 133n
Martin, Augustine, 90n. 11
Martín Gaite, Carmen, 49, 49nn. 5, 6, 55, 59
  Lo raro es vivir, 74n
  Nubosidad variable, 51, 63, 64, 66–70
  Retahílas, 64–65
Martone, Mario, 147n
mater dolorosa, 49n. 5, 90
maternal apotheosis, and bastardy 132–38
maternal archetypes, 72, 90, 91n. 12, 112, 120, 136. *See also* Great Mother, Madonna, Virgin Mary
maternal effacement (vs. daughter's development), 12, 16, 89, 178
maternal function/role, 16, 24, 33, 35, 47, 54, 55–56, 58, 63, 66, 68, 86, 87, 91, 121, 122, 139–40, 142, 146, 156, 167, 168, 180, 200, 206, 209–10, 211, 215–17, 231, 233, 234. *See also* motherhood
maternal instinct, 21, 140, 191, 196, 206, 209, 226. *See also* mothering
maternal legacy (or heritage or inheritance)
  as a burden, 87, 90, 91, 95, 101, 103, 104, 105, 109, 144, 170, 170n. 18, 191–92, 231–32
  ambivalence of, 87n. 3, 105, 126
  positive, 5, 12, 34, 70–71, 72, 100, 100n. 19, 113, 126–27, 141, 142, 178, 207
  See also genealogy

maternal neglect (of daughters), 32, 96, 99, 111, 125, 139, 146, 148, 187, 196, 197, 199, 235. *See also* mother
maternal perspective/point of view, 73, 86, 90, 110, 121, 146, 147, 149, 150, 187, 189, 190, 226. *See also* maternal voice
maternal politics: France, 179–81; Germany, 215–17; Ireland, 31, 87–89; Italy, 24, 24n, 119–21; Spain, 31, 47–51
maternal power
  ambivalence of, 16, 87, 89, 106, 120, 159, 235, 239
  destructive, 31, 89, 91, 91n. 12, 92, 100n. 18, 106, 108, 109, 113, 120, 132, 148–49, 159, 219, 229, 232–33, 235
  generative, 128
  recovery of, 72
  symbolic, 17–18, 66n
maternal silence. *See* maternal voice
maternal violence, 31, 175, 191–92, 196, 198, 200–201, 225, 226–28, 231
maternal voice (vs. silence), 22, 24, 33, 56, 57–58, 71, 73, 86–87, 107–8, 122, 125, 135, 136–37, 143–48, 150, 172, 177, 193, 201, 225, 240
maternity. *See* motherhood
matriarchy, 62, 72, 239
matricide
  actual, 52, 72, 96, 100, 144
  at origin of patriarchy, 13, 51, 86
  textual/symbolic, 5, 12, 15, 130, 156, 159–63, 164, 168, 172–73, 176, 178, 179, 179n, 189n. 23, 200, 208
matrophobia, 5, 32, 54, 74, 74n, 89, 93, 100, 101, 109, 111, 112, 113, 167, 178, 187, 188, 209
Matute, Ana María, *Primera memoria*, 52
Mauser, Wolfram, 215n
Mayans Natal, María Jesús, 52, 60, 61
Mayoral, Marina, *La única libertad*, 71
McCafferty, Nell, 88n. 7
McClintock, Anne, 164, 165, 166, 172
Meaney, Gerardine, 87n. 3
Medea, rewriting of myth, 59, 59n. 12
mediation (female/maternal), 12, 17, 121, 134. *See also affidamento*, genealogy
Melandri, Lea, 18
melodrama, 90, 96, 126, 196, 196n, 201
Méndez, Concha (and Altolaguirre), *Memorias habladas, memorias armadas*, 71n
Menniti, Adele, 149n. 23
Merlin, Tina, *La casa sulla Marteniga*, 143–44

Merril, Judith, 36
Meyer, Franziska, 3n. 3, 218, 218n
Micheo, J. Luis de, 50
Miller, Nancy K., 177, 192
Mills, Lia, 114
  Another Alice, 109, 112–13
Mills, Sara, 165
Minden, Shirley, 37n
Minetti, Maria Grazia, 120
Minotaur, 63
Mitchell, Juliet, 18, 27n. 14
Mitchison, Naomi, *Memoirs of a Spacewoman*, 36, 211
Mitgutsch, Waltraud Anna, 218, 247
  Die Züchtigung, 219, 230–32
Möbius, Paul J., 216, 217
Modjeska, Drusilla, *Poppy*, 189, 190, 192–93, 195
Molfino, Francesca, 120
Montero, Rosa, *Temblor*, 72, 72n
Morales, María Pilar, 61
Morante, Elsa, *Menzogna e sortilegio*, 123–26, 132, 133n
Moratti, Francesca (and Sotis), *Mamma com'è difficile. Quando tra madre e figlia è meglio scriversi*, 148n. 19
Mori, Anna Maria, *Nel segno della madre*, 148n. 19
Morrison, Toni, 12
Morrissy, Mary, *Mother of Pearl*, 109, 110–11, 113, 114
mother
  ageing/dying/old, 73–75, 94, 127–28, 135, 141, 143, 148n. 20, 187, 200, 204, 206, 222. *See also* somatophobia
  as angel in the home, 49, 56, 72–73
  as asexual, 87, 90, 200. *See also* sexuality, desire
  as autonomous individual, 92, 122, 125, 139, 177, 190, 209–10, 238
  bloodmother vs. heartmother vs. sharemothers (in science fiction), 36–37
  castrated/powerless/lacking in value, 14, 16, 25, 27, 31, 57, 91–92, 120, 233, 235
  castrating/phallic/omnipotent, 16, 30, 52, 60, 88, 89, 91, 97, 100, 111. *See also* maternal power
  childless, 110. *See also* infertility, motherhood
  in colonial patriarchy, 165–66, 171–72
  destructive, 178, 219, 225–33. *See also* maternal power, maternal violence
  excluded from discourse, 12–13, 30. *See also* maternal voice
  exiled from history, 235
  fantasy of perfect m., 26, 26n. 13
  in feminism/feminist discourse, 5, 7, 11–12, 120–21
  good/bad, 20, 25, 31, 97, 147, 167, 177, 178n, 188n, 192

– 255 –

Index

'good enough', 21, 51, 56–57, 61–62
hindering daughter's autonomy, 5, 25, 34, 56, 88, 120, 162, 175, 187, 203, 219
immigrant, 174, 174n. 20
indifferent/uncaring, 58, 96–97, 121, 122, 135, 138, 139, 148. *See also* maternal neglect
as metaphor of origin, 32, 129, 207–8, 234
as monster, 15, 20, 96n, 97, 112
mythification/demythification of, 51, 70, 93, 188, 189
post-Freudian, 147
reappraisal/recuperation of, 5, 11–12, 28, 32, 51, 188–89
as regulator of daughter's sexuality, 33. *See also* sexuality
as vehicle of patriarchy, 5, 12, 22, 32, 52, 56, 112, 143, 164–66, 174, 242–43
See also defilement, idealisation, motherhood
mother-blaming, 12, 12n. 2
mother–daughter bond
current relevance of, 6–8, 34, 39, 76
and female identity, 7, 19, 19n, 22, 102, 121, 158, 188n, 193, 203, 209
psychodynamics of, in feminist accounts, 19–29
mother–daughter conflict (repairing/negotiating), 4n, 12n. 2, 24, 26, 111–13, 121, 163, 168, 173, 177
mother–daughter confusion/ indifferentiation, 14, 15–16, 27, 32, 60, 91, 92, 93–94, 104, 105, 107, 130, 135, 138, 149, 156, 158–63, 168, 169n. 17, 170n. 19, 171, 178, 192, 210, 232. *See also* intersubjectivity
mother–daughter fusion/symbiosis, 22, 24–25, 104, 105, 111, 127, 148n. 20, 178, 188n, 193
desire to return to, 128, 129–30, 179, 193, 195, 234, 241
See also pre-Oedipal
mother–daughter relationality (vs. separation/autonomy), 21, 24–25, 27,155, 156–57, 162, 163, 171, 177, 188n. *See also* intersubjectivity, separation
mother–daughter relationship
absence in literature/criticism, 1–2, 4–6, 29, 34, 51–52, 85–86, 89, 122–25, 185–87, 218, 247. *See also* criticism
abusive/sadistic, 97, 136, 196, 199, 200–201, 219, 225–28, 230–32, 233, 241, 247. *See also* maternal power, maternal violence, sexual abuse
and class, 22, 32, 56–57, 127–28, 159, 165–68, 173, 177, 191, 194, 207, 226, 230–31, 234

erasure/inscription in culture, 11–18, 29, 34, 37, 124, 155, 218. *See also* affidamento, Irigaray
in immigrant communities, 6–7, 32, 173–76, 202
and language/representation, 12–14, 29–32, 51, 66–69, 85, 108, 169n. 17, 188. *See also* representation
pathological, 25, 32, 100, 157
in science fiction, 37–38
and writing, 64, 66–70, 166, 168, 169–70, 179n. 23. *See also* binarism, writing
See also contextualisation, mother–daughter bond
mother–daughter rivalry, 92, 101, 142, 156, 163, 200, 209
mother–daughter rupture (in patriarchy), 52, 58, 60, 91
motherhood
as a devalued institution, 11, 50, 57, 113, 140, 219, 234–39, 247
as biological destiny, 11, 36, 39n
biological/gestational/social, 23, 35–36. *See also* maternal function, reproductive technologies
compulsory vs. free choice, 22–24, 36, 64–65, 148, 179–80, 191–92, 209–11, 226
and creativity/writing, 12, 12n. 3, 33, 33n, 64–65, 68, 186, 199
debunking rhetoric of, 100, 189, 199, 210
difficult/thwarted, 110, 149n. 24
discourses of. *See* maternal politics
ideal vs. reality of, 57, 234, 236
ideologies of, 19, 65, 140, 147, 234
imagined, 110–11
and nationalism: Germany, 217; Ireland, 31, 87, 87n. 3; Italy, 120; Spain, 31, 48–49
need for new representations of, 23–24
vs. personhood, 64, 65
as productive labour, 234–35, 238–39
reclaiming/valorising the experience, 11, 24, 65, 215, 219, 234–39
rejected by feminists, 11–12, 23–24, 65
sacrificial, 21, 61, 87, 90, 105, 120, 146, 196, 208–9, 222
as site of resistance, 15
teenage. *See* pregnancy
women's desire/quest for, 21, 23–24, 36, 110, 149n. 24
See also maternal politics, mother, mothering
mothering
adequate, 25
as a natural predisposition, 218, 247. *See also* maternal instinct

'autistic', 205
bad/poor, 139
'good enough', 21
models/practices/standards of, 7, 19, 21, 28, 147, 149n. 24, 150
mothering daughters, 21, 25, 33n, 219
reproduction of, 21, 23, 89, 141, 191
shared, 204. *See also* parenting
shared in science fiction, 36–38, 211
See also mother, motherhood
motherland, 32, 48, 51, 166n, 174, 180, 207–8
mother-love, 16, 52, 54, 57, 62, 73, 98, 99, 105, 112, 124, 133, 146, 161, 166–67, 176, 193, 196, 204, 211, 224, 227, 232, 237
debunking rhetoric of, 91, 199
mother-quest, 2, 5, 52, 54–55, 61, 63, 187, 188, 189–95
mother–son bond, 19, 31, 33, 33n, 48, 52, 64, 65, 119–20, 122, 123–24, 137, 144, 171, 174, 179, 186, 187, 235, 236
mother tongue, 140, 207
Muraro, Luisa, 16, 17, 18n. 6, 27n. 15, 119, 121n. 1
myths, recovery/rewriting of female, 18, 32n, 70. *See also* names of mythological characters
Nabokov, Vladimir, *Lolita*, 53
Nash, Mary, 48, 49, 50, 53n. 7, 70
Nasta, Susheila, 207n
nationalism, 2n, 3
and motherhood. *See* motherhood
Neumann, Erich, 120
Nice, Vivien E., 12n. 2
Ní Dhuibhne, Eilís, 111n
Niola, Marino, 129n. 8
nomadism, 3, 69
Nordius, Janina, 199n
Novak, Helga, 218, 247
Die Eisheiligen, 219, 225–29, 231
Nunziante Cesaro, Adele, 146n
object-relations theory, 19–20, 22, 24
O'Brien, Edna, 101, 106n, 111, 113, 114
'A Rose in the Heart of New York', 109n
Down By The River, 101, 104, 106–9
The Country Girls Trilogy, 104–6, 109
O'Crualaoich, Gearóid, 89n
O'Donnell, Mary, 'Breath of the Living', 110n
Oedipal plot, 26–27, 86, 95, 103, 121, 133, 141, 161, 161nn. 5, 6, 163, 188
Oedipus complex, 18–19, 26, 27n. 15, 54, 95, 95n, 124, 156, 161, 161nn. 5, 6, 163. *See also* pre-Oedipal

– 256 –

Index

Oedipus myth, 13, 18, 86, 122, 189n, 200
O'Faoláin, Julia, 113
  The Irish Signorina, 93–96
O'Hara, Kiera, 106n
Olivier, Christiane, 91–92
Oppo, Anna, 120
Orbach, Susie, 7
Ordóñez, Elizabeth, 47n, 52, 61, 64, 72
Ortega y Gasset, José, 53
Palmer, Pauline, 203, 204n, 206–7
Parenti, Francesco, 120
parenting
  and IVF, 35
  shared, 21, 23
  and teenage motherhood, 35n. 21
Parra, Isabel, 49, 50
Pateman, Carole, 58, 60
Pearlman, Mickey, 4
Peri Rossi, Cristina, 'Primer amor', 64n. 16
Petracci, Franca, *Lo sai che non moriremo più*, 148n. 20
Phillips, Shelley, 4n
Phillips, Terry, 186
Piercy, Marge
  He, She and It/Body of Glass, 38n
  Woman on the Edge of Time, 36, 39n
plot
  daughter's, 92, 96
  family, 59, 185, 188
  female/feminine, 21, 102
  maternal vs. Oedipal, 121, 141
  mother–daughter, 1, 7, 88–89, 100, 101, 104, 110, 112, 113–14, 133, 185
  romance, 88, 126
  See also Bildungsroman, Family Romance, foundling fantasy, Gothic plot, Oedipal plot
Portuges, Catherine, 159
pregnancy/childbirth, 15, 35, 49, 68, 72, 89, 90, 108, 110, 134n, 138, 143, 145, 146n, 147, 149n. 24, 161, 166, 167, 168, 173, 197, 198, 199, 200–201, 226, 234, 235, 236, 237, 238–39
  teenage pregnancy, 34–35, 87, 88n. 7, 106
  pre-Oedipal, 14, 15, 19, 20, 21–22, 24, 26, 27n. 15, 163n. 8, 188n, 190, 193, 195
Prieto, Enrique, 64n. 16
Primo de Rivera, Pilar, 49
psychoanalysis. *See* Freud, Lacan
  feminist critiques of. *See* psychoanalytic theory
  in Cardinal, 165–68
  in Italian writing, 148n.19
  in Martín Gaite, 66
  in Mills, 112
  'mothering' psychoanalysis, 19–20. *See also* Klein
psychoanalytic theory (feminist), 13–15, 18–27, 112, 188,

188n, 189, 191. *See also* Benjamin, Chodorow, Flax, Irigaray, Kristeva
and literary criticism. *See* criticism, Hirsch
Puértolas, Soledad, 'La hija predilecta', 74n
Quiroga, Elena, *Escribo tu nombre*, 52
Rabuzzi, Kathryn Allen, 32n
Ramondino, Fabrizia, xi, 150
  Althénopis, 122, 123n, 126–28
  Terremoto con madre e figlia, 147–48
Rapisarda, Cettina, 242, 242n
Rasp, Renate, 218n
Ravasi Bellocchio, Lella, *Di madre in figlia*, 148n. 19
Ravera, Lidia, 121, 121n. 2
realism
  in English narrative, 189, 202, 206
  vs. experimentalism, 30, 31
  in German narrative, 221, 239, 247
  in Irish narrative, 88, 93, 96, 104, 106, 112, 113, 114
  in Italian narrative, 126, 143
  nineteenth-century, 163n. 8, 206
  See also experimentalism
recognition. *See* Benjamin, intersubjectivity
Reddy, Maureen T., 73
Redonnet, Marie, 178n
  Rose Mélie Rose, 158, 178
religion, 3, 4, 11, 23, 29, 49, 50, 65, 87, 106, 120, 123, 131, 137, 140, 165, 166, 202, 203–4, 206, 209, 216
  religious images of mother/motherhood, 31–32, 100, 119, 132
  religious parody in narrative, 202
  See also Catholicism, Islam
representation (of mothers/motherhood)
  comic/grotesque, 31, 32, 96, 97, 100, 145, 189, 201–6
  irreverent, 100, 201
  parodic, 206
  tragi-comic, 148, 149
  See also mother–daughter relationship, plot
reproduction/procreation, 23, 36, 37n, 39n, 147, 156, 162, 163n. 7, 174, 234
  as a form of production, 234–35, 238–39
  vs. artistic/intellectual production, 16, 64n. 17, 128
  in science fiction, 37, 210–11
reproductive technologies, 23, 34–37, 39n, 149, 210, 211
  and parenting, 35
Révesz, Andrés, 49n. 5
Rhys, Jean, 186n
Rich, Adrienne, 5, 11–12, 18, 33, 33n, 59n. 11, 61, 62, 63, 75,

85, 140, 188n, 209, 217, 217n. 5, 233, 234, 235, 237
Richardson, Dorothy, 186n
Riddel, María del Carmen, 56
Robert, Marthe, 53
Roberts, Michèle
  A Piece of the Night, 203–4
  During Mother's Absence, 204
  Flesh and Blood, 204
Roche, Anthony, 86n. 1
Rodoreda, Mercè
  Isabel i Maria, 50, 51, 57–60
  La Plaça del Diamant, 49, 52, 60n
Rodríguez Carballeira, Aurora, 49, 49n. 6
Roebling, Irmgard, 215n
Rogers, Anne, 7
Roig, Montserrat, 70
  L'hora violeta, 71n
  Molta roba i poc sabó, 71n
  Ramona, adéu, 70–71
Rooks-Hughes, Lorna, 106n
Rudberg, Monica, 23
Ruddick, Sara, 73
Runge, Erika, 234n. 12
Ruscio, Alain, 165n. 11
Rusconi, Gian Enrico, 2
Rushdie, Salman, 204
Russ, Joanna, *The Female Man*, 36
Rutherford, Jonathan, 2n
Samuel, Raphael, 192
Sánchez López, Rosario, 49
Sand, George, 4n
Sander, Helke, 220
Sanders-Brahms, Helma, 218, 247
  Deutschland, bleiche Mutter, 219, 220–22, 223, 225
Santacroce, Isabella, *Luminal*, 131–32, 149
Santos, Emma, *La Malcastrée*, 158, 178
Sanvitale, Francesca, xi
  Madre e figlia, 132, 134–38, 143, 148
Saraceno, Chiara, 147, 148, 150
Sargent, Pamela, *The Shore of Women*, 36
Saunders, Jennifer, 206
Sayers, Janet, 7, 19
Scanlon, Geraldine, 48, 48n. 2, 58n
Scarano, Emanuela, 125
Scarlett, Elizabeth, 53
Scattigno, Anna, 120
Schmidt, Ricarda, 230n
Schopenhauer, Artur, 216
Schroeder, Margot, 234n. 13
Schwaiger, Brigitte, 218
  Wie kommt das Salz ins Meer, 219, 239–42, 243, 245, 247
Schwarz-Bart, Simone, *Pluie et vent sur Télumée Miracle*, 178
Schwarzer, Alice, 220, 234n. 12
science fiction (women's), 36–38, 210–11
  in Italy, 38n
Seabrook, Jeremy, 191
Segal, Naomi, 33n

– 257 –

Index

separation (daughter's from mother vs. attachment) 21, 24–25, 169, 170, 187, 195. *See also* attachment
Sereni, Clara
  'La figlia buona', 148n. 21
  Il gioco dei regni, 138, 141–43
  Manicomio primavera, 149n. 24
Sereni, Marina, *I giorni della nostra vita*, 142
Servodidio, Mirella, 61
sexual abuse (of daughter): by father, 106–7, 109, 112; by mother, 197, 198; by parents, 194. *See also* incest
sexual difference (female), 5, 16, 27n. 15, 156
  and biology, 11, 21, 216–17, 234
  in colonial contexts, 171
  erasure in Western culture, 13, 30
  and female symbolic, 14
  inscription in culture, 17–18, 30
  Italian theory and practice of, 16–18, 120
  See also Irigaray
sexuality
  alternative sexualities, 27, 38
  child abuse and daughter's s., 230, 232–33
  female, 16, 51, 55, 57, 60, 126, 128, 129n. 9, 169n. 17, 236
  lesbian. *See* lesbianism
  mother's, 33, 57, 74, 120, 130–32
  mother's influence on daughter's s., 5, 7, 33, 186
  vs. motherhood, 51, 61, 74
  in science fiction, 38, 210
  and social policy, 28, 87–88
Shannon, Catherine B., 88n. 8
Shore, Chris, 5
Showalter, Elaine, 190
Shumaker, Jeanette Roberts, 106n
Silverman, Kaja, 27n. 15
Sinclair, May
  Mary Olivier, 186
  The Creators, 186n
  The Tree of Heaven, 186n
sisterhood, 12, 75, 206
Slonczewski, Joan, *A Door into Ocean*, 36
Smith, Anthony, 2n
Smith, Paul Julian, 63
Smyth, Ailbhe, 88n. 8
Soliño, María Elena, 73
somatophobia, 74, 74n
Sophocles, *Antigone*, 13
Soriano, Elena
  Caza menor, 52
  'Medea', 59n. 12
  Testimonio materno, 64n
Sotis, Lina (and Moratti), *Mamma com'è difficile. Quando tra madre e figlia è meglio scriversi*, 148n. 19
sovereignty goddess (Celtic), 89, 89n

Spanish Civil War, 48–49, 52, 56, 73
Sphinx, 86
Splendore, Paola, 187
Sprague, Claire, 187
Sprengnether, Madelon, 19, 22, 27n. 15
Stancanelli, Elena, *Benzina*, 144–46, 147, 149
Steedman, Carolyn, *Landscape for a Good Woman*, 22, 23, 189–92, 193, 194, 195, 196
Sterne, Laurence, 204
Stone Centre (USA), 7
Strempel, Gesine, 220
Struck, Karin, 218
  Die Mutter, 219, 234–39, 248
Stuart, Mary, 71
subjectivity
  daughter's and repudiation of mother, 13–14, 15, 102
  maternal, 2, 13, 21, 25–27, 33, 90, 92–93, 95, 159
  mothers and daughters as subjects in history, 51, 70–76, 177, 220–25
Suleiman, Susan, 12n. 3, 26, 64
Surrey, Janet, 7
Syal, Meera, *Anita and Me*, 202
symbolic order
  Lacanian, 13–14, 156
  female/maternal, 14, 16–18, 27, 66, 66n, 72, 120–21, 156, 163
  hom(m)osexual, 156, 163
  See also Diotima, Irigaray, Muraro
Tanner, Tony, 58
Telo, María, 49, 50
Tennant, Emma, *Faustine*, 189, 197, 199–200
Tepper, Sheri, *The Gate to Women's Country*, 36
Terán, Lisa St Aubin de, *Joanna*, 189, 197, 200–201
Thelma and Louise, 146
Tremain, Rose, *Sacred Country*, 197
Treviño, J.G., 49n
Triple Moon-goddess, 62
Trotta, Margarethe von, 220
Truxa, Sylvia, 51
Tsuchiya, Akiko, 63
Tucker, Martin, 3n. 3
Tusquets, Esther
  'Carta a la madre', 62
  El mismo mar de todos los veranos, 51, 57, 61–64, 68, 71
Valente, Joseph, 86n. 2
Vallejo, María Dolores, 50
Van de Biezenbos, Lia, 179n. 25
Vanderbeke, Birgit, *Das Muschelessen*, 219, 243–47
Vannocci, Claudia, 124
Vegetti Finzi, Silvia, 23–24
Ventimiglia, Carmine, 34n. 21
Villa, Luisa, 30

Villena, Luis Antonio de, 53
Violi, Tonci (and Cornelio), *Di madre in peggio*, 149n. 24
Virgin Mary, 23, 24, 31, 90, 120, 131, 202. *See also* Madonna
Waal, Mieke de, 7
Walker, Alice, 11–13
Warner, Marina, 57
  Alone of All Her Sex, 31, 90
  The Lost Father, 190n
Weedon, Chris, 215n, 223n. 9
Weekes, Ann Owens, 90n. 11
Weigel, Sigrid, 215n
Weil, Simone, 17
Weldon, Fay
  Down Among the Women, 188
  Female Friends, 188
  Puffball, 188
  The Cloning of Joanna May, 210–11
Werkkreis Literatur der Arbeitswelt (Worker Writers' Circles), 234n. 13
West, Rebecca, *The Return of the Soldier*, 186n
Whitford, Margaret, 14n, 66, 66n, 107n, 156
Wicomb, Zoë, *You Can't Get Lost in Capetown*, 189, 207–8
Williams, Anne, 102n
Willmott, Peter, 191
Winnicott, Donald W., 19, 20–21, 25, 56–57
Winterson, Jeanette, *Oranges Are Not the Only Fruit*, 189, 202–3, 204, 206
Wittig, Monique, *Le Corps lesbien*, 157
Wohmann, Gabriele, 218
  Ausflug mit der Mutter, 222
Wolf, Christa, 218, 222, 247
  Kindheitsmuster, 219, 223–25
Wolmark, Jenny, 38
Women's Press, 36, 210, 210n, 211
Woolf, Virginia, 186, 186n
  Mrs Dalloway, 186n
  To the Lighthouse, 186n
Wright, Simona, 135n
writing
  as an erotic process, 68–69
  the mother, 12n. 2, 13, 30–34, 193–94
  See also binarism, Cixous, contextualisation, criticism, écriture féminine, experimentalism, Irigaray, Kristeva, maternal voice, matricide, mother–daughter relationship, motherhood, realism, representation
Young, Michael, 191
Zatlin, Phyllis, 61, 71, 72n
Zimmerman, Bonnie, 62
Žižek, Slavoj, 14n
Zuffa, Grazia, 39

www.ingramcontent.com/pod-product-compliance
Lightning Source LLC
Chambersburg PA
CBHW071153070526
44584CB00019B/2767